THE POPULAR NOVEL
IN ENGLAND
1770–1800

THE POPULAR NOVEL
IN ENGLAND
1770-1800

J. M. S. TOMPKINS

"Books are *atrocious*. . . . They are in
general so much *above* or *below* life,
that either way one can expect no truth"
(COURTNEY MELMOTH, *Shenstone-Green*,
1799.)

University of Nebraska Press, Lincoln

1961

First published in 1932 by
Constable & Company, Ltd.
London

Reprinted by arrangement with the author
MANUFACTURED IN THE UNITED STATES OF AMERICA

Second Bison Book printing April, 1967

PREFACE

A BOOK devoted to the display of tenth-rate fiction stands in need of justification. This one has been written in answer to the question : What sort of novels were read between 1770 and 1800 ? What interests, tastes and principles do they reflect ? What types do they exhibit ? The novel has been approached rather as a popular amusement than a literary form, though I have made notes of formal developments and literary relationships, when these presented themselves. Between the work of the four great novelists of the mid-eighteenth century and that of Jane Austen and Scott there are no names which posterity has consented to call great, but there is a large body of fiction which fed the appetite of the reading public, reflected and shaped their imaginations, and sometimes broke out into experiment and creative adventure. In this tract a generation of readers took their pleasure, and it is the conditions of this pleasure that I have tried to make out.

In such an inquiry strictness of definition would be out of place. " Novel " was a comprehensive word in 1770, and I have used it in its widest sense. Nor is it so important for the inquirer to classify his specimens according to their literary qualities as to keep fresh his sympathy with imperfect expressions of imaginative life. Dead books can provide little information when exposed on the gibbet of scorn. Therefore I have treated this inferior fiction with perhaps over-scrupulous gentleness and consigned its most ludicrous manifestations to notes ; for these are not good books, whose vitality springs from

an inner source, but poor books, on which the colour of
life was reflected from their readers, and must now be
renewed by imaginative sympathy. In the following
pages, even such a moderate talent as Fanny Burney's
makes few appearances, whereas Samuel Jackson Pratt,
whose wares have proved entirely perishable, makes
many. There is little said of Beckford and much of
pedestrian melodrama and crude romance, little of Jane
Austen (who wrote, though she did not publish, within
the period) and much of her forgotten predecessors, the
leaf-mould in which that exquisite and thriving plant
was rooted. These spirits would have been too strong
for my book, if I had suffered them to intrude with all
their immortality about them. Such appearances as
their books make are resumptions of the humbler part
they once played, indiscriminately mingled on a reviewer's
table with the productions of the Minerva Press.

I have read nearly all the novels to which I refer;
where I have relied on the accounts of contemporary
reviewers I have tried to make this clear. I have also
preserved in extracts the original punctuation. During
the 'seventies and 'eighties there survived in the novel a
dramatic punctuation, unconnected with grammatical
structure; it directs the movement of the voice, and,
while it is certainly not consistently carried out and
sometimes falls into chaos, it seemed a pity to obliterate
it. Attributions of anonymous books are made from the
usual sources, including the British Museum Catalogue;
where I have added fresh ones (as in the case of Elizabeth
Blower, Elizabeth Sophia Tomlins, and the identification
of Mrs. Cox, later Mrs. Johnson, with Anna Maria
Mackenzie) it has been on the authority of signed prefaces, title-pages and the comments of reviewers. To
deal adequately with the subject of this study—popular
taste at the end of the eighteenth century—would require
parallel research in contemporary drama and art and in

foreign popular fiction. This I am not able to undertake, but I have noticed these analogues where I could.

This book, which has long lain in my mind, would not
have been so soon finished but for the award to me of
the Amy Lady Tate scholarship by the Council of Bedford College. This has meant liberty to read and write,
and for this I wish to express my thanks. I have also
great pleasure in acknowledging the grants in aid of
publication which I have received from the Special
Research and Publication Fund of the same College and
from the Publication Fund of the University of London.

CONTENTS

CHAPTER I

THE NOVEL MARKET

Why not engage with *Noble* or with *Bell*,
To weave thin novels that are sure to sell ?—
Thrice happy authors, who, with little skill,
In two short weeks can two short volumes fill.
                    CHARLES JENNER, *Town Eclogues*, 1772.

DURING the years that follow the death of Smollett, last of
the four great novelists of the mid-eighteenth century, the
two chief facts about the novel are its popularity as a form
of entertainment and its inferiority as a form of art.
Evidence of popularity are those circulating libraries,
abominated by Sir Anthony Absolute and other moralists,[1]
whose yellowing labels are to be found inside so many
old books. London, the headquarters of the book trade,
was full of them ; for besides solid businesses like Hookham's famous shop in New Bond Street, or, at a lower
level, the two libraries of the brothers Noble near Middle
Row, Holborn, and at St. Martin's Court, Leicester Square,
there were numerous small firms, combining bookselling,
stationery, a little printing and a lending library. The
provinces were less well provided, and James Lackington,
the cheap bookseller and future proprietor of the Temple
of the Muses in Finsbury Circus, who toured the north
and west of England in the late 'eighties, found the book-
shops ill-stocked.[2] Yet Humphry's Circulating Library

---

[1] *E.g.* Clara Reeve, who, in *The Progress of Romance* (1785), calls
them " one source of the vices and follies of our present times."
[2] *Memoirs of the First Forty-five Years of the Life of James Lackington. Written by Himself.* Originally published in 1791. I quote from
the 13th, much enlarged, edition of 1810.

in Chichester had over nine hundred volumes in 1771,[1] and Lackington admitted that in farmhouses and country cottages one could see *Tom Jones*, *Roderick Random* and other entertaining books stuck up on the bacon-racks. Solid literature might be poorly represented in the country, but the novel went everywhere. The winter evening pastime of story-telling by the fire had gone out of use, and the older generation listened while their sons and daughters read romances. In town the milliner's apprentice, who turns up in contemporary satire with the regularity of Macaulay's schoolboy, spared twopence at the library for a volume of *The Fatal Compliance* or *Anecdotes of a Convent*.[2] The reading public grew rapidly, especially, says Lackington, after the American War, and he enumerates among the contributory causes Sunday schools, book-clubs and the use of fiction in schools. The booksellers, who had been shy of the libraries at first, soon found their account in them,[3] for the increasing wealth, leisure and refinement of the middle classes had turned the women into readers, and it soon became " no less necessary for a lady to unbend her mind than to unlace her stays."[4] The subscription was usually half a guinea a year, or three shillings a quarter, though where a reading-room was provided the charges ran higher. Hookham had a graduated scale of subscriptions, ranging in 1788 from sixteen shillings to two guineas a year, and rising by 1791 to three guineas, while at Bath Lydia Melford   paid a crown a quarter

[1] *v.* label inside the British Museum copy of the *Genuine Memoirs of Miss Faulkner* (1771).

[2] Cf. the reading-list of Mrs. Lewston, a waiting-woman, in the *Amicable Quixote*, I, p. 107 (1788): " I subscribed a month to a circulating library; and I read a volume of *Mr. Shandy's Travels*—and I read the *Adventures of a Pump*—and the *Memoirs of an Old Hat*, and the *Life of Peter the Postman*, and half a volume of the *Fortunate Fool*, and a chapter in the *Civility of Sentiment*."

[3] Cf. William Lane's offer to stock and instruct any person desirous of commencing a circulating library, advertised in *Anthony Varnish* (1786) and elsewhere.

[4] *v. Critical Review*, June 1771, p. 479.

and, considering the accommodation, found it cheap.[1]
Single volumes could be hired for twopence, but novels
were never less than two volumes in length and towards
the end of the century ran out into four or five, so that
the pastime was not a cheap one.

It was largely the means taken to keep the shelves of
the circulating library stocked that brought the novel
into disrepute. As a new and rather shapeless literary
kind, with little discipline and no classical tradition, its
foothold in critical esteem had always been precarious,
though Richardson, with his moral earnestness, and
Fielding, with his magnificent craftsmanship and half-
playful provision of a respectable lineage, had vindicated
its dignity, and something of a critical canon was beginning to take form. But with the death of Smollett the
line of great writers ends, and the novelists of the second
class—Jenner and Graves and Mrs. Brooke and Mrs.
Griffith—for all their pleasant qualities, lacked strength
to maintain the novel where Fielding had established it.
The good work that was published bore no proportion
to the bad, and the bad was very bad indeed and infected
the reputation of the good. Writers of standing dissoci-
ated themselves ostentatiously from the libraries, " those
slop-shops in literature," as Mrs. Griffith called them,[2]
and critics tried to cleanse the Augean stables with a
torrent of scorn ; but the name of the novel was tainted,
and its popularity so shamefaced that, as Jane Austen
was to protest with some indignation, the very heroines
join in the cry and apologize for spending their time on
what is " only a novel." [3] In general, heroines do not

---

[1] Alex. Todd, at his Circulating Library at 2, St. Patrick's Square,
Edinburgh, charged £1 1s. a year, or 3s. 6d. a month. Non-sub-
scribers paid 4d. a day for new volumes, 1d. a day for old. *v.* label
in B.M. copy of *A Tour to the Isle of Love* (1788).

[2] *v.* Preface to *Lady Barton* (1771) ; and cf. John Potter's *Arthur
O'Bradley*, I, p. 16 (1769) : " I do not design this History for the use
of *Circulating Libraries.*"

[3] *v. Northanger Abbey*, ch. 5.

read novels except as a prelude to seduction, while a scene in a circulating library, with its personnel of ignorant bookseller, driven hack, avid girl readers and empty-witted fine ladies, is a commonplace of satire.[1]

The critics found the circulating library novel flimsy, immoral and tedious. It was formless, too, but that troubled them less. All kinds of bastard products, whose home would now be the columns of the sensational press, appeared on the library shelves. Contemporary scandals and *causes célèbres*, lightly dished up in " two curious *open-worked* volumes " ;[2] fictitious or semi-fictitious biographies of statesmen, actresses and prostitutes ; secret histories ; travels and memoirs of uncertain value ; these and other obscure blends of fact and fiction counted as " novels " in the book lists of the day. No doubt the fact that authors of real novels still liked to pose as editors of authentic documents, though the trick was stale, pointed to such a classification ; but explanations are hardly necessary, for " novel " in common speech meant little more than " entertaining narrative." " Pernicious " and " trifling " are the epithets that run most readily from a critical pen ; only less frequent is " threadbare." The complaint over the " threadbare patterns of modern novels " is more than the irritation of a critic in face of the sameness of mass-production. There was, in

---

[1] *E.g.* S. J. Pratt (Courtney Melmoth), *Pupil of Pleasure*, I, p. 27 (1776); *Family Secrets*, I, ch. 48 (1797).

[2] v. *Monthly Review*, May 1770, p. 489, on *The Unhappy Wife*, which, like de Vergy's *Lovers*, was based on Lady Sarah Bunbury's affair ; cf. also *Harriet ; or, the Innocent Adultress* (1771), alluding to the intrigue of the Duke of Cumberland and Lady Grosvenor; Sir Herbert Croft's *Love and Madness* (1780) to the murder of Martha Ray by Rev. J. Hackman ; *The Memoirs of Miss Arabella Bolton* (1770), aimed at Colonel Luttrell, and *The Life, Adventures, Intrigues and Amours of the celebrated Jemmy Twitcher* (1770) at the Earl of Sandwich; *Memoirs of an unfortunate Lady of Quality* (1774) founded, according to the *Monthly Review*, on the story of Lady Jane Douglas, and *Fatal Follies* (1788) on the abduction and imprisonment of Lady Strathmore ; also *The Correspondents* (1775), the supposed letters of Lord Lyttelton and Mrs. Peach ; and the various " true histories " connected with Mrs. Rudd and the Perreau case.

the period that followed the masterpieces of the four great novelists, a real conviction that the novel was played out. The works of Fielding and Richardson were seen as the culmination of a development, not the starting-point. Authors lamented that all types had been displayed and all themes used up,[1] and as late as 1790 the *Monthly Review*, splenetically blind to the signs of new life, grumbled : " The manufacture of novels has been so long established, that in general they have arrived at mediocrity. . . . We are indeed so sickened with this worn-out species of composition, that we have lost all relish for it." [2] Matter for this melancholy to work on was provided by the barefaced trickery of the libraries. Old books were re-issued with new title-pages, and new books that had failed to attract were summarily re-baptized and launched again upon the reading public within a few weeks. Thus in September 1771 the *Critical Review* detected under the disguise of *Cupid turned Spy upon Hymen, or Matrimonial Intrigues in High Life*, the very *Cuckoldom Triumphant, or Matrimonial Incontinence Vindicated* noticed and condemned the month before, and in January and February 1772 the *Monthly Review* exposed three examples of " the shameless plunder of superannuated and worthless novels," one of them from a forty-year-old publication of Curll's.[3] Editions were faked, and an edition of five hundred might have five different title-pages, " so that the third edition of a book shall be advertised and selling before a sufficient number are sold to pay even paper or print," [4] while old magazine stories were strung together and offered as a

---

[1] Cf. Preface to *Maria ; or, the Vicarage* (1796).
[2] v. *Monthly Review*, Aug. 1790, p. 463.
[3] *Love in a Nunnery*, from the French, already translated as *The Fortunate Country Maid ; The Oxonian*, originally entitled *The Adventures of Charles Careless*, and *The Reclaimed Prostitute*, once *Spanish Amusements*.
[4] John Trusler, *Modern Times*, III, p. 103 (1785).

new book.[1] Authors and reviewers drew attention to
these practices, but their reproofs hardly affected the
needy booksellers, whose discreditable shifts to fill their
shelves without paying author's fees had obtained as
much success as could be expected weeks before the
reviews came out; for critics were dilatory when it came
to their *tristes Calendæ*, as they dubbed the season of
novels.[2] " Books of this class," declares Bage in his
Preface to *Mount Henneth* (1781), " are printed, published, bought, read, and deposited in the lumber garret,
three months before the reviewers say a syllable of the
matter." The rage for novelty was extreme, and it was
to circumvent it and ensure another season's life for their
ephemeral wares that the booksellers in the 'eighties
extended the practice of post-dating books, and thus gave
the critics another abuse to detect.[3]

We get satiric glimpses of the organization of the
novel trade in the prefaces of many books, and more
reliable information from memoirs and private letters.
A year or two before our period begins, Mrs. Griffith,
having embarked on her first novel, writes to her husband :
" I find the Booksellers will give nothing worth taking
for it. Mr. J—— has tried them. They say that they
do not dispute the Merit of it, but that while the Public
continue equally to buy a bad thing as a good one, they
do not think an Author can reasonably expect that they
will make a Difference in the Price. They print a
Thousand of either Kind—the Circulating Libraries,
they say, take off Four Hundred, and the Remainder
seldom lies on Hand, the only Difference is, that the
Sale of the good one is somewhat brisker than the

---

[1] *v.* Mrs. Susanna Rowson, *The Inquisitor ; or, Invisible Rambler*,
I, p. 101 (1788).
[2] v. *Monthly Review*, Dec. 1785, p. 418.
[3] v. *Critical Review* on *The Minor :* " In the middle of the year
1786 we reprehended a publisher for dating his work 1787.   On this
day the first of April, 1787, we peruse a book of 1788."

other."[1] Bookseller-baiting is a sort of inaugural game in which novelists indulge before getting to work. In appearance, of course, it is the author who is baited. The bookseller discards his book without reading a line of it; indeed, he boasts that he has not read a book since he left school; but he knows his trade; he has a flair for a title, and a book with a good title will have a clear run of three weeks before the reviews get at it. In the case of " slight summer readings," publications that " are to be devoured immediately—like a morning paper, or a hot roll," it is not necessary for the title to agree with the contents; it is better to challenge attention with " some quaint but insignificant phrase," as for instance *Something New, Did you ever see such damned Stuff?*, *Agreeable Ugliness* or *Beauty put to its Shifts*. Alliteration " succeeds incomparably well . . . and saves an author's wit for the *inside* of his book. As for example: *Adultery Anatomized, Country Cousins, Female Falsehood, Fortunate Foundling*, etc., etc." " Where all these methods fail," concludes the bookseller shamelessly, " . . . what think you, sir, of reprinting the first page of a book, that has not been asked for a dozen times, and boldly calling it the *Second Edition, corrected and improved?* "[2] In *The Egg, or the Memoirs of Gregory Giddy, Esq.* (1772), an odd miscellany of stories, parodies and satirical sketches, young Giddy is persuaded by his friend Flimsy to try his luck as a novel-spinner. Flimsy has turned out seventeen two-volume novels in two years, and " there is pretty picking to be got by dis-

[1] v. *Genuine Letters of Henry and Francis* (*i.e.* Richard and Elizabeth Griffith), V, p. 15 (1770). The first edition of *Cecilia* (1782) was 2000, and Lowndes told Charlotte Burney that 500 was the common number for a novel; *v.* her journal, *Early Diary of Frances Burney*, II, p. 307, ed. A. R. Ellis (1889); and cf. Trusler, *ante*, p. 5, *n.* 4. Lowndes printed 500 of the first edition of *Evelina* (1778), v. *Diary of Mme. d'Arblay*, ed. Dobson, II, p. 481.

[2] *v.* Dr. T. Cogan, *John Buncle, Junior, Gentleman* (1776), Samuel Paterson, *Joineriana* (1772) and *The Younger Brother* (1772).

figuring the passions and burlesquing human nature."
But he strongly discourages Giddy from taking any
pains. "The booksellers pay mechanically at the rate
of so much per sheet. . . . A flowing style is half the
battle. . . . Sit down and write as fast as you can.
Nine sheets make a volume, and eighteen sheets two
volumes. It's very easily calculated; never trouble
yourself about meaning, it can't be too bad to be admired,
when you have finished it. If it happens to be nonsense,
you may be sure it will meet with a kind reception from
the two *Noble Brothers ;* but if it has not the merit of
nonsense, but should happen to be stupidity itself,
L-(owndes) is your man, he'll gulph it down with rapture,
and fancy it the purest milk of erudition."

The wares purchased with such apparent recklessness
were advertised with some ingenuity. G. Allen, proprietor of a circulating library at 19, Duke's Court, St.
Martin's Lane, brought out in 1788 a new edition of
Lord Winworth ; or, the Memoirs of an Heir, and caused
reminders to be inserted not only at the end but in the
body of his other ventures. Thus the heroine of *Edward
and Harriet ; or, the Happy Recovery* (1788) adds a
postscript to a letter to her friend, promising to send
her by the next post the famous novel of *Lord Winworth*,
while *Belinda ; or, the Fair Fugitive* (by Mrs. C——,
1789) is on one occasion revealed " sitting in the drawing-
room with her father ; he was reading a newspaper, she
Lord Winworth, or the Memoirs of an Heir." G. Allen
had apparently no connection with any particular newspaper. After this it is without surprise that we find the
hero of *Frederic and Caroline*, which issued from the
Minerva Press in 1800, strolling at Margate into a circulating library, " furnished from the Minerva."

Prices were low, but climbed slowly towards the end
of the century. Lackington says that he has been told
of booksellers who frequently offered as little as half a

guinea per volume for novels in manuscript—" a shocking price to be sure," though authors often have immoderate expectations. The usual payment for a library novel seems to have been between five and ten guineas, and the profit could be doubled by a judicious dedication. Sometimes the bookseller gave as much as twenty guineas, and in 1781 Bage sold *Mount Henneth*, a first novel, to Lowndes for £30. The good novel, a rare article, still commanded its price; it is true that no publisher was tempted to risk anything like the £1000 that Millar paid Fielding for *Amelia*, but Fanny Burney got £250 from Payne and Cadell for *Cecilia* (1782) and Hayley £200 for his worthy but tedious *Young Widow ; or, The History of Cornelia Sedley* (1789), though it is hard to believe that the latter was really marketed anonymously, as the author declares. The first big prices were Mrs. Radcliffe's, to whom Robinson is said to have given £900 for *The Italian* (1797), while Mrs. Inchbald, by careful marketing, made between £1000 and £1500 out of her two novels.[1] During the earlier part of our period the uncertain state of copyright helped to keep down prices,[2] and then and later the most lucrative way of publication for an author was by subscription, if he could fill his subscription list. It did not do, however, to rely on the bookseller to push the sale, where his profits were so small; indeed, he was commonly supposed to obstruct it, in order to get the remainder cheap, " for it is incon-

---

[1] *v.* epitomes of literary contracts in the *Gentleman's Magazine*, Feb. 1824, p. 136; Susanna Rowson's *Invisible Rambler*, III, p. 57 (1788); Jean Marishall's *Series of Letters*, II, p. 156 (2nd edition, 1788); C. Kegan Paul's *Life of Godwin*, I, p. 20; Hayley's *Memoirs*, I, p. 377, etc. The hack in Bage's *Man as he is* (1792) gets £6 for two small volumes in the novel way, and Wilmot in Holcroft's *Hugh Trevor* (1794) is paid £10 for his first novel. *Caleb Williams* brought Godwin £84 (*v.* Meyer's *William Godwins Romane*, 1906). Boaden in his Memoir of Mrs. Inchbald says that she sold her *Simple Story* (1791) for £200 and *Nature and Art* (1796) for £150; later, Robinson gave £600 for the extended copyright of both, and in 1810 it was resold to Longman for an unspecified sum.

[2] *v.* Mrs. Griffith, Preface to *Lady Barton* (1771).

ceivable," writes Lackington, "what mischief booksellers *can* and often *will* do to authors," and Samuel
Paterson, himself a bookseller, repeats the charge in his
Joineriana (1772), where he exhibits a fellow-tradesman
putting off purchasers with the story that the books are
not bound and the ratcatchers are in the warehouse. It
was by subscription that the two Miss Minifies (to use
the contemporary plural) began their career as novelists ;
" Perdita " Robinson's first books were subscribed, and
Fanny Burney's *Camilla* (1796), published on this plan,
was said to have made something in the neighbourhood
of three thousand guineas. But where there was neither
social position, notoriety nor acknowledged merit to
swell the list the author could not emancipate himself
this way without difficulty and painful rebuffs. John
Trusler, whose Literary Society, founded in 1765, was
intended to lead to the abolition of publishers and to
procure for authors the full fruits of their industry, was
able to bring out his own novels unaided,[1] but I have met
no instance of any other novelist benefiting by his reform.
Nevertheless, in spite of all disadvantages, by the end of
the century an adroit novelist could make money without much difficulty, and Lamb, writing to Coleridge,[2]
tells him rather ruefully of a young man in the office
who has just cleared fifty or sixty pounds by a bad
translation from the French, less than a week's work, first
publishing it by subscription and afterwards selling the
copyright.

Novels were dear to buy. In the 'seventies they are
invariably advertised in three forms, bound at 3*s.* a
volume, sewed—that is with a stout paper cover—at
2*s.* 6*d.*, and in sheets, for sale to the country libraries,
at 2*s.* ; during the 'eighties this custom is gradually dis-

---

[1] *Modern Times, or the Adventures of Gabriel Outcast.* Printed for
the author, by the Literary Society, at the Logographic Press (1785).
[2] June 14, 1796.

used [1] and by the 'nineties it has died out. We read of
the paper cover [2] in Jean Marishall's charming account
of her first acquaintance with booksellers, in *A Series of
Letters*. The young Scotswoman had come south on a
visit in the late 'sixties, and, infected by the air of a
country where literary women, though rare, were not
monstrosities, conceived the ambition of making her
fortune by literature. *Clarinda Cathcart* was written
with high hopes, which were dashed when the best price
obtainable was found to be Noble's five pounds. Miss
Marishall rallied, however, accepted the offer, and resolved to dedicate her book to the Queen, hoping for
what Miss Burney afterwards attained, a place in her
household. Means were found to have the book presented, but the author learned that no ordinary copy,
" stitched in blue paper," could be allowed to meet the
royal gaze; etiquette demanded an elegant binding.
Clarinda Cathcart was bound and presented; and then
fell the heaviest blow; for the young foreign Queen
knew not the Marishalls and with undiscrimating bounty
sent their daughter ten guineas. At this point Miss
Marishall's mother burst into tears, convinced that her
child was mad, but Miss Marishall, though horror-struck,
sensibly pocketed the ten guineas, and two years later
made use of her experience to publish *Olivia Montague*
by subscription and clear ten times that sum.

During the 'nineties the price of novels went up, as
costs increased, but books on the whole became more
substantial. The little duodecimo or small octavo
volumes are packed closer, and broad margins and wide
spacing disappear, together with the devices that had

---

[1] *v.* F. Noble's list of publications in Mrs. P. Gibbes's *The Niece*
(1788): " Every Article in the above Catalogue is marked as it is sold,
bound, unless otherwise stated."

[2] Examples of this cover, now faded to grey, are the B.M. copies of
G. L. Way's *Learning at a Loss*, C. H. Wilson's *Wandering Islander*,
and Claris de Florian's *New Tales*.

caused the *Gentleman's Magazine* ironically to compliment Cadell, the publisher of Mrs. Brooke's *Excursion* (1777), on his art " in spinning out this small work into 492 pages, by means of the divisions and subdivisions of viii books, 102 chapters, and paragraphs frequently of one or two lines only." The purchaser who gave 3s. 6d. a volume for Mrs. Smith's *Old Manor House* (1794) or Godwin's *Caleb Williams* (1794), sewed, or 5s. a volume for Mrs. Radcliffe's *Mysteries of Udolpho* (1794) or S. J. Pratt's *Family Secrets* (1797), in boards, was getting value for money as far as length went, although, seeing that *Family Secrets* is five volumes long, *Caleb Williams* three, and the other two books four each, the disbursement was heavy enough. One-volume tales, however, are growing in popularity ; at the beginning of the period only a rare pastoral or legendary tale appeared in this form, but by 1800 the *Anti-Jacobin Review*, noticing *Ormond ; or, The Secret Witness*,[1] remarks that its one volume, from smallness and closeness of typography, contains nearly as much matter as the usual three volumes, and should appeal to those who are fond of a cheap pennyworth. But while Lane, publisher of *Ormond* and proprietor of the Minerva Press, was trying to suit the shallow pocket with his wares, other firms were experimenting with a more dignified format, and in 1789 Strahan and Cadell published Dr. John Moore's *Zeluco* in 2 vols. 8vo. at 12s., to be followed by Dilly in 1792 with Miss Knight's *Marcus Flaminius* in 2 vols. 8vo. at 10s. 6d. Both books were something a little different from the ordinary novel, Miss Knight's an historical survey of the most conscientious type, and Dr. Moore's weighted (though far from heavy) with psychology and ethics ; and no doubt they were felt to become their bulk.[2]

---

[1] By Charles Brockden Brown.

[2] Harrison's reprints of Fielding, Smollett, etc., in the 'seventies and 'eighties were in 8vo. with double columns and small print. The sixth edition of *Pamela* (1772) was in 8vo. But *Zeluco* is the first novel of the late eighteenth century to make its first appearance in the larger form.

Illustrations are very rare, except in reprints of well-established books, and this at once differentiates the English novel from the contemporary French product. Casual amateur novelists sometimes arranged for a frontis-piece or a vignette on the title-page, but the library novel did without such additional graces, and the subject is never broached in those frank self-revelations of the bookseller which the novelist loved to record. Gothic Romances are occasionally frontispieced, especially by the Minerva Press during the last few years of the century; but they form the only substantial exception.[1]

The output of novels, which moralists found so sinister and so formidable, slackens unaccountably in the half-dozen years at the end of the 'seventies and the beginning of the 'eighties. In 1771, designated by the *Critical* " this prolific, scribblerian year," the *Monthly* and *Critical* dealt between them with some sixty novels, though some of these were reprints and a few translations, while one or two may have escaped the critical net. After 1775 the numbers drop rapidly; 1776 can muster but sixteen in all, and in 1780 the *Monthly Review* writes, *à propos* of *The Relapse :* " There has been of late such an uncommon dearth of this kind of food, that, at this time, no doubt, many thousand eager appetites are craving for *something new*, to whom a dish prepared by the author of *Indiana Danby* will be a delicious morsel." There was, then, a real shortage, which first made itself felt soon after the outbreak of war in America, and continued until within a few years of the French Revolution. The *Monthly* reviewer does not attempt to account

---

[1] De Vergy's *Lovers*, Part I (1769), was illustrated ; the author had recently left France and was probably influenced by French customs. Also *The Spectre* (Stockdale, 1789), *The Solitary Castle* (Lane, 1789), and Mrs. Parsons' *Voluntary Exile* (Minerva Press, 1795). In 1793 Hookham advertises, in *The Minstrel, Emma; or, the Unfortunate Attachment,* " a new Edition, with beautiful Engravings."

for it, and in the absence of other evidence one can only guess. Perhaps authors' fees were too low, after all; perhaps the trash was too trashy, so that at length even the milliners' stomachs revolted and upset the novel-market. At all events, when the booksellers' lists begin to fill again in the early 'eighties, there are fresh themes and a slightly higher standard of technique.

The most important organs of literary criticism were the two big reviews, the *Monthly* and *Critical ;* after them came, for the first half of our period, the *London Magazine*, with whose " frontless editor " the brothers Noble kept up a spirited feud for some years, because he had dared to call one of their novels immoral. The feud was probably an adroit advertisement ; the Nobles cannot have been sensitive upon that score.[1] There was no regular distribution of review copies ; the reviewer noticed those novels that came from his own publishing

[1] The feud appears to have been begun when the editor of the Impartial Review in the *London* accused Francis and John Noble of keeping hack-writers in pay. This they disclaimed in an *Advertisement to the Public*, dated Jan. 14th, 1769, and a *Rejoinder*, dated Feb. 2nd, 1769, both prefixed to *The Rational Lovers* (1769). It broke out again when the *London* (Nov. 1772, p. 543) censured two of the Nobles' novels, *The Way to Lose him* and *The Way to Please him*, for immorality, describing the first as " very proper to debauch all young women who are still undebauched," and commenting briefly on the second : " See the last article. The same character will do for both." The Nobles printed an *Appeal to the Public* in Jan. 1773, enlarged it, and afterwards appended it to *The Self-Deceived : or, the History of Lord Byron* (1773), in which they gave their correspondence with Baldwin, publisher of the *London*, and reprinted with comments the Editor's remarks in the December and January numbers. Neither side bated a jot. The Nobles also appended an advertisement to country booksellers, warning them that as they, the Nobles, have refused to let Baldwin have any more of their books, until he has retracted his impudent falsehood, they have reason to believe that orders coming from the country to him will not be complied with ; such orders should be sent direct to them. This suggests that the reviews and magazines acted as retailers. The last echo of the warfare is a prefatory letter by the author of the novels assailed, prefixed to his new book, *'Twas Right to Marry Him* (1774), and dated June 25th, 1773. It is addressed to the Nobles and was doubtless inspired by them, and concludes with the hope that their *Appeals* " will induce every man, who sees a book advertised in his favourite walk of literature, to read that book without consulting any printed opinions on it."

house and sent his collector to procure anything else that he thought worth his attention. Hence it occasionally happens that a popular book is not reviewed at all until it has reached the second edition, because it was sold out before the collector arrived.[1] Average novels were despatched in batches every two or three months, and these reviews, as well as those of better books, were often much belated. The *Gentleman's Magazine* was notably dilatory, reviewing *Evelina* in September 1778 after the book had enjoyed over half a year's popularity. The critics did not disguise their reluctance. " The Reviewer of the modern novel is in the situation of Hercules encountering the Hydra," wrote the *Monthly*. " One head lopped off, two or three immediately spring up in its place." [2] The figure is apt to their murderous reputation. " Arbitrary and decisive," Miss Reeve called them, and she had reason, for they spoilt the sale of her *Argenis* through omitting to read her preface.[3] She found fault, too, with their " pilfering practice " of printing long extracts from books under review. It was the custom to cite liberally ; the *Gentleman's Magazine* gave nine columns to *Humphry Clinker* and the *Monthly Review* twelve pages to the *Spiritual Quixote*, of which space very little was allotted to the business of criticism. No doubt the practice lightened the reviewer's work, especially as in most cases the quotations are drawn from the first fifty pages of the book. The *Younger Brother* (1770) explains that his method as a *Critical* reviewer was to read the preface, close the book, stick a pin between the leaves, open the book and transcribe a few pages. Nor was quotation confined to books of which the reviewer approved ; it was considered a suitable method of

[1] Cf. the *Critical* on Mrs. Robinson's *Vancenza* (1792). The reviewer speaks of the widespread and excessive praise with which the book has been greeted.
[2] v. *Monthly Review*, Jan. 1788, p. 82.
[3] v. *Progress of Romance*, p. 81 (1785).

bringing home their faults to the faulty, and reminded
Isaac d'Israeli of the treatment meted out to Cicero ;
fragments of the author's corse are hung up, he said,
after massacre and mutilation.[1]   Inferior books are dealt
with summarily ; if harmless, a brief note indicates their
moral trend ; if dubious, one line blots them.   The collection of these critical finger-prints has its charms.
" Invention, judgment, and taste are all wanting to rescue
these volumes from oblivion," remarks the *Critical* on
Miss Dorinda Catsby (1772), while the *London* dismisses
Woodbury (1773) even more simply : " We think this
volume will not bear to be twice read."   *False Gratitude*
(1771) apparently would not bear to be read at all.   " The
first volume is extremely bad," said the reviewer.   " We
had not patience to read the second volume."   As for
poor Charlotte Palmer, who rashly christened her book
It is and it is not, a Novel (1796), she can hardly have
hoped to get off scot-free.   " No, my dear," said the
Critical, " it is *not* a novel ; but be a good girl ; do so
no more ; and we will say nothing about it this time " ;
and that is the whole review.   The reviewers were much
abused for their high-handedness,[2] and it is incontestable
that they did not give themselves the trouble to distinguish between different shades of incompetence ; nor,
when " candour compelled them to observe——" did they

---

[1] v. *Vaurien*, II, p. 300, *n.* (1797).
[2] The *London* was a great field for reviewer-baiting.   Readers sent
in parallel and contradictory passages from the *Monthly* and *Critical*.
Richard Griffith in *The Koran* (1770) compared critics to hangmen
who " are obliged to *execute* for bread."   Jenner in *The Placid Man*
(1770) accused them of judging the whole of an author's design from
his title-page, and Anti-Zoilus, a correspondent of the *Gentleman's
Magazine* (1782, p. 58) of praising the books of those booksellers who
had property in the review, and running down those of the others.
This gentleman would confine a reviewer's duties to listing and epi-
tomizing books.   " It is very immaterial to the reader what judgment
of the merit or demerit of any work may be formed by the doer of a
monthly pamphlet."   John Trusler in *Modern Times*, III, p. 94 (1785),
says that some reviewers take tips to let authors contribute their own
reviews.   Dr. Johnson, on the other hand, found them impartial, and
so did Herbert Lawrence, *v.* his *Contemplative Man* (1771).

spare the susceptibilities of their authors. But they were glad to get anything tolerably good, forgave any fault in favour of simple pathos, and on the whole dealt out rough justice. Little jets of warm approval rise up in the desert of their scorn ; the *Monthly* calls *The Trial ; or, the History of Charles Horton, Esq.* (1771), " indeed a beautiful display of the judgment and sensibility of its author," and deals gently with *George Bateman* (1782) because, " though it will not bear the severity of criticism, yet it sometimes affects the heart without offending the judgment." Their pay was not high ; two to two and a half guineas a sheet was the usual rate,[1] and on this scale it would take a goodly batch of novels to fetch a crown. To remember this is to tolerate a little more readily the heavy sarcasm and hectoring jocosity with which the critics, especially the *Monthly* critics, fill their pages. In criticism, as in all forms of literature at this time, streaks of exaggerated sensibility lie beside streaks of grossness, and the critic, who declares his intention of cherishing the tender bud of one young lady's genius, will crack bawdy jokes on another and, referring to the latest of Mrs. Cowley's frequent publications as " another bantling," extend the metaphor forwards and backwards.[2] Some novelists kiss the rod—young ladies in particular use what may be called a curtseying preface ; others allow themselves a jaunty and uneasy defiance, the rather if they have published by subscription and have already received the money. A third class protest, but do not pass scatheless, for the least invasion of his right raised the critic's bile, and the poor lady who ventured to use the editorial plural had to submit to the jeer : " We

---

[1] William Renwick, *Misplaced Confidence*, I, p. 65 (1777), says that the *Critical* paid two and a half guineas shortly before 1771. Trusler in *Modern Times*, III, p. 94 (1785), gives two guineas as the rate, and Godwin got two guineas from the *English Review*, v. Elbridge Colby's *Life of Thomas Holcroft*, xxiii.

[2] Cf. *Critical* on *Belinda, or, the Fair Fugitive*, by Mrs. C——, (1789).

suppose the lady is pregnant and the unborn child shares her emotions."

It is not surprising that novelists sometimes supplemented the activity of the reviews by introducing critical dissertations into the body of their novels. *Humphry Clinker* is discussed in Lawrence's *Contemplative Man ; or, the History of Christopher Crab, Esq. of North Wales* (1771), and Mrs. Smith's *Emmeline* in *The Spectre* (1789), while Mrs. Robinson in *Walsingham ; or, the Pupil of Nature* (1798) finds occasion to debate the merits of several novels.[1] Nevertheless, the critics, in spite of abuse and distaste, were groping towards the criteria of novel-writing. It was a difficult task, complicated further by the vagueness of the object for which they were to legislate,[2] and by the uncertainty, which some of them at least felt, as to how fiction could be reviewed. What were they to say about narratives ? An epitome, if it p..cuded curiosity, was injurious, extracts were misleading, and a mere critical pronouncement " an arbitrary prejudgment of the writer." [3] It is a similar dilemma to that of the reviewers of detective novels and crook plays to-day, with this additional difficulty, that the eighteenth-century novelist gave the critic no opportunity to talk about technique. But if craftsmanship was neglected, and if a definition of the novel is far to seek, there is, on the other hand, complete unanimity among

---

[1] *v.* also *Orlando and Lavinia* (1792), which contains a conversation on *The Recess, Monmouth* and other romances.

[2] The use of the term " novel " in the sense of " novella " still survived ; witness the various books of *Select Novels* that appeared. The book-lists of the various reviews are quite inconsistent in their classification. The *Gentleman's Magazine* admits Haller's *Usong* and Barclay's *Argenis* as novels, but groups *The Hermitage, The Spiritual Quixote* and *The History of Rhedi* (Oriental) as *Miscellaneous*. The *Correspondents*, a sequence of letters of no narrative interest, is called an original novel on the title-page, and the *Critical* refers to the *Letters from the Duchess de Crui*, which avowedly consists of seventy-four letters on the character of the female sex, as a novel ; in this case, however, there were inset narratives.

[3] *v. Gentleman's Magazine*, 1772, p. 329.

the critics as to some of the qualities that should distinguish this mode of writing. It should be instructive,
though preferably not blatantly so ; it should have " invention,"—a variety of interesting incidents and well-
supported characters ; it should above all be probable,
for probability distinguishes a novel from a romance,
and its appeal to the reader's sympathies, and the consequent efficacy of its moral lesson, depend on probability.
" We cannot sympathise with what is extravagant, and
out of the order of nature," wrote the *Monthly* reviewer
in 1772, reasonably enough, but erroneously, as the next
thirty years were once more to prove. Natural dialogue,
ease and purity of style, and a warm emotional colour
were much admired, and a novel that, by its pathos,
betrayed " an enlarged acquaintance with the human
heart," and was " calculated to touch the springs of tender
sympathy," was sure of a welcome. As time goes on,
moreover, and it becomes clear that the art of prose
fiction did not expire with Smollett, we find the critics
insisting on the difficulty of the novelist's task [1] and the
high degree of talent that it requires. But in the 'seventies
these notes, at once monitory and optimistic, are seldom
struck. If a novel is decent, clear of affectation and
improbability, it is all that the reviewer expects.

Novelists were recruited from every rank of society,
for the novel was held to be an unexacting form of
literature, easy to approach and possibly remunerative.
It was a bow from which literary amateurs liked to loose
one shaft, and which ladies and gentlemen in financial
straits twanged continually. Working dramatists turned
aside to try their hands at it, and antiquarians sought in
it a relaxation from their toil. Many of them are novelists

---

[1] Cf. *Critical*, Sept. 1796, on Miss Burney's *Camilla*, and Feb. 1797
on J. Arnold Jun.'s *Creole*. Arnold had remarked that it is not
necessary to bestow any great labour or attention on the composition
of a novel ; the critic demurs, and calls the novelist's task " perhaps
one of the most arduous and difficult of literary labours."

in right of one book only; of these are Thomas Hull, actor and playwright, whose *History of Sir William Harrington*, published in 1771 but written years before, had, he declared, received the corrections of Richardson himself; Thomas Bridges, the ruined wine-merchant, whose crude and vigorous picaresque *The Adventures of a Bank-Note* (1770–1) was successful enough to induce him to add two more volumes to it, but not to make him forsake parody and drama for the novel; Helenus Scott, M.D., who was in the employ of the East India Company at Bombay, and wrote *The Adventures of a Rupee* (1782); Thomas Vaughan, lawyer and dramatist, who published *Fashionable Follies* in 1781 and added a third volume in 1810, thus providing an interesting example of the changes of taste in a generation;[1] and Edward Bancroft, who polished off his *History of Charles Wentworth* (1770) after a visit to Guiana and before settling down to business as a calico-dyer in England. Bancroft published his novel anonymously, and so did many a respectable man who did not care to be seen openly amusing himself with such a trifling production. In C. H. Wilson's odd miscellany *The Wandering Islander ; or, the History of Mr. Charles North* (1792), the author's friend says : "I find you do not intend to prefix your name to it ; " and the author replies : " Do you not know that there is more pleasure in begetting than in fathering children ? " The practice gradually declined as the standing of the novel became more assured, and by the end of the century the learned professions were cheerfully acknowledging their indiscretions.

Meanwhile pseudonyms suggest how the tide of self-expression was rising. In turn An Unbeneficed Clergyman, A Farmer's Daughter of Gloucestershire, A Warrant

---

[1] The third volume is ascribed to William Combe in *D.N.B.*, article on Combe, but to Vaughan in the article on Vaughan. Vaughan signed the dedication of the whole book to Colman in 1810.

Officer belonging to the Navy (" It is fortunate for this gentleman," wrote the *Monthly*, " that he does not place his point of honour in the management of his quill "), A Young Libertine Reformed and A Gentleman of the Middle Temple essayed the market, and to these we must add countless Ladies and Young Ladies, postulants sometimes for fame, but more often and pitifully for a little hard cash. Youth was no bar, for in 1779 Dodsley issued *The Indiscreet Marriage* by Miss Nugent and Miss Taylor of Twickenham, " whose ages together do not exceed thirty years," while the school-boy novelist was already evolved if, as the *Monthly* reviewer believed, *The Fortunate Blue-Coat Boy* (1769) by Orphanotrophian was really the product of Christ's Hospital.[1] Curious evidence of the appeal of the novel to the lower middle classes is afforded by an autobiographical narrative, *The Scotch Parents ; or, the Remarkable Case of John Ramble, written by himself (in the month of February, 1773)*. A note in the British Museum copy glosses John Ramble as " Mr. Carter, son of a Statuary in Piccadilly." Some young draughtsman it was, at any rate, who found his case remarkable enough to merit print, and relieved his wounded feelings in what his contemporaries would have called a " novel," using the word in the same way as our newspapers use " romance." The Scotch Parents of the title were the parents of Nell Macpherson, the milliner's apprentice, whom Ramble, her fellow-lodger, wooed with a sullen and jealous fervour, seduced under promise of marriage, and finally took to his new home, where she kept house and posed for his studies in the nude (he reproduced one of these efforts in his book),

---

[1] I have not been able to find this book. It was an accepted classic of the lower school in Lamb's day : v. *Christ's Hospital Five and Thirty Years Ago*. Its appearance rather shook the *Monthly* reviewer, who feared that the example might spread, and foretold the announcement : " Six-and-thirty novels this month, by the Blue-coat Boys of Christ's Hospital, each 2 vols. 5s. sewed, Noble, Lowndes, Wilkie, Cooke, Bell, Roson, etc. etc."

until she was forcibly removed by her family.   Ramble,
who was ready with his pen, a versifier and theatre-goer
and, on internal evidence, a patron of circulating libraries,
published his discreditable story, partly to spite the
Macphersons, and partly to divert the pain of his own
undisciplined emotions.   He told it in two keys.   The
main body of the narrative proceeds with an admirable
and unconscious realism, setting before us not only the
habits of speech and thought of people in a " middling
state of life," but the character of Ramble himself, with
its obstinacy, its passion, its streak of meanness and its
typical capacity for perverted reasoning.   Fielding could
have conceived such a character, but he would have
embalmed it in irony, of which there is here no spice ;
the display is meant to be justificatory.   At the crisis of
his history, however, Ramble passes abruptly into another
key and superimposes upon the homely scene all the
tawdry eloquence of the play-house.   He sees Nelly and
himself as romantic figures, labouring under heroic passions and worthy of as much rhetoric as he can muster
up.   This combination of unconscious realism and voluntary illusion gives the book an odd flavour ; but its real
importance does not lie in any of its special qualities ; it
lies in its mere existence.   Ramble's class are reading
themselves into articulateness.   Only the popularity of
the novel could have given that young man his chance
of self-expression, for only the novel could accept his
material in its crude state.   It was a continuous narrative
and it dealt with love, and that was enough.

Ramble was not the only novelist of his class, nor the
lowest, if we are to credit the allusions of embittered
writers to the " worn-out Chambermaids and indigent
Valet-de-Chambres (sic) " whose " memoirs " found a
place on the shelves of the libraries.[1]   Critics sometimes
condescend to point out the faults of breeding in these

[1] v. Preface to Anecdotes of a Convent (1771).

books, and the *Critical* told the author of *The Contrast ;
or, the History of Miss Weldon and Miss Moseley* (1771)
that cold ham, pickled oysters and arrack punch were not
among the refreshments offered at a rout. Except in
satire, however, where they abound,[1] it is not easy to
come to close quarters with these inhabitants of the
cellars of literature ; few people cared to acknowledge
that they were hacks or that they employed them. The
brothers Francis and John Noble, who were commonly
supposed to conduct a novel-factory on a large scale,
indignantly denied " so injurious and malicious a charge " ;
on the contrary, their novels were " many of them written
by persons of rank, property and fortune, above accepting
any other return for their labours than a few printed
copies for themselves and friends." [2] This was very
convenient for the Nobles. As for the hacks, they were
not candidates for fame. They betrayed their names at
their peril ; witness Mrs. Fogerty, author of *The Fatal
Connexion, Colonel Digby and Miss Stanley,* and other
delights, of whom the *Monthly* wrote : " Surely Mrs.
Fogerty was begotten, born, nursed and educated in a
circulating library, and sucked in the spirit of romance
with her mother's milk." [3] Satirists afford us a glimpse
of pale young men in attics, blowing together the flimsy
pages of a novel for Lowndes or Bell, and signing the
title-pages " By a Young Lady." Their labours, it was
asserted, were often rather manual than intellectual, and
the hero of *The Younger Brother* (1770), who spends
some time as a literary hack, employed on all subjects
from history to cooking, defines his method as " cutting
and pasting." [4] From this obscurity, nevertheless, one

---

[1] *E.g.* Johnstone's *Chrysal, or the Adventures of a Guinea,* I, ch. xx.
(1760–5).　　[2] v. *ante,* p. 14, *n.* 1.　　[3] v. August 1773, p. 150.
[4] v. II, p. 168 : " I have often stolen the plot, the incidents, the
characters, and the catastrophe of a Novel, from some old obsolete
Play ; and the impression has been as frequently swallowed up by
the numerous proprietors of our circulating libraries and others, in the
course of a fortnight."

audacious figure detaches itself, whose brief residence in Grub Street can be traced now chiefly in the startled comments of the reviewers.

In December 1770, the *Critical Review* devoted a whole page and a liberal display of capitals to warning the FATHERS, MOTHERS and GUARDIANS of Great Britain against the works of a " profligate foreigner," who is writing " as no one ever dared, with impunity, to write before," and moreover " has impudently declared that the favourable reception which he meets from his fair readers, is in proportion to the degree of immorality displayed in his writings." This is that Pierre Henri Treyssac de Vergy, known to students of the career of the Chevalier d'Éon, but not hitherto, I think, as a novelist. He was then a young man of about thirty, who had come over to England in 1764, during the bitter quarrel between the French Ambassador, de Guerchy, and his secretary, the Chevalier d'Éon de Beaumont. He came over as de Guerchy's man, but after a few months threw in his lot with d'Éon, helped him to discredit his chief and received in return a promise of assistance.[1] This was in September 1764, and for the next five years there is no trace of de Vergy; he may have hung upon the generosity of d'Éon until it frayed; he certainly improved his English and his acquaintance with the scandals of English society; and when he next appears it is as a novelist. His residence in Grub Street seems to have lasted for about three years, from the beginning of 1769 to the beginning of 1772, during which time he dedicated books to pleasure and virtue in a ratio of two to one. His output was large; seven signed

---

[1] *v.* J. Buchan Telfer, *The Strange Career of the Chevalier d'Éon de Beaumont* (1885). Telfer honours de Vergy with a slight gloss of loyalty to d'Éon. The friendship, however, if it can be called such, was not unbroken. On p. 159 of *The Lovers*, Vol. I, d'Éon is jostled by the hero, and in 1772 the *Monthly Review*, ascribing *Memoirs of an Hermaphrodite* to de Vergy, remarks that the two men have quarrelled.

novels belong to this period; three more were ascribed
to him by scandalized critics, and there are indications
that others existed.[1] He could not be ignored, for,
libellous and inflammatory trash as most of his work was,
there was a French adroitness and rapidity about it,
which marked it off from the plodding English product.
There is a grace in his gracelessness; the dialogue flies
along; scenes of coquetry and passion in park and
drawing-room are sketched with a deft hand; we hear
the rustling of a silk gown, see the turn of a head and
listen to the seductive exposition of the philosophy of
pleasure. The critics raged in pursuit. " Another heap
of rubbish swept out of M. de Vergy's garret," wrote the
Monthly of the *Authentic Memoirs of the Countess de
Barré (sic)*, while the *Gentleman's Magazine* labelled the
second part of *The Lovers*—with justification—" too indelicate for the eye or ear of a modest woman." It was,
however, impossible to deny his gifts, and when, every
now and again, he made a bid for a wider audience with
a book which " Virtue had written," they could only
salute him with grudging praise. " How much fair
fame does he lose," groaned the *Critical*, " whenever he
sends a volume to the press unfit for the perusal of the

---

[1] *The Lovers ; or the Memoirs of Lady Sarah B—— and the
Countess P——*. Published by Mr. Treyssac de Vergy, Counsellor
of the Parliament of Paris (1769). *The Mistakes of the Heart ; or the
Memoirs of Lady Caroline Pelham, and Lady Victoria Nevil* (1769).
Henrietta, Countess Osenvor ; a sentimental novel in a series of letters.
By Mr. Treyssac de Vergy, etc. (1770). *The Scotchman ; or the
World as it goes* (1770). *The Palinode : or, the Triumph of Virtue over
Love. A sentimental novel, in which are painted to the life the characters
of some of the most celebrated Beauties in England.* By Mr. Treyssac
de Vergy (1771). *The Lovers ; or the Memoirs of Lady Mary Sc——
and the Hon. Amelia B——* (1772). *The Mistakes of the Heart*, II
(1772). Reviewers also ascribe to him with great likelihood, *Authentic
Memoirs of the Countess de Barré*, by Sir Francis N—— (1770); *The
Nun, or the Adventures of the Marchioness de Beauville* (1771); *Memoirs
of an Hermaphrodite* (1772). A third instalment of *The Lovers* was
announced in 1772, and *Nature : or the School for Demi-Repts*,
advertised in *The Lovers*, II, was probably his. In France he published *Les Usages* (1762) and a *Lettre contre la Raison* (v. *Lovers*, I, p.
189).

fair sex; " while the optimistic *London* hailed in the *Palinode* " his dawn of reformation," and the *Critical,* nearly melted, would " almost venture to recommend it to our fair countrywomen." Nothing, however, could be more insecure than de Vergy's reformation, unless it were his foothold in literature. After 1772 he seems to have lost his market, and we do not know by what needy shifts he lived for the next two years. On October 1st, 1774, he lay dying in lodgings at Blackheath. " Peace to de Vergy," wrote the *Monthly* fifteen months later, " he has followed his works." [1]

It is against the background of this ephemeral, often disreputable work that the better books of the time must be seen. The good cannot be considered apart from the bad ; and if this is the case with all popular forms of art and literature, it is specially so with the novel in the late eighteenth century. The better writers are continually aware of the bad ones and often embarrassed by them. They are on the defensive about the form they have chosen to use, or they are unnecessarily humble about it ; [2] they try to redeem it, like Miss Seward in *Louisa* (1784), by discarding prose in favour of verse,[3] while retaining all the other characteristics of a novel, or like

---

[1] *v.* Feb. 1776, p. 162.

[2] Cf. their sensitiveness about the term " novel." John Potter, in *Arthur O'Bradley* (1769), reluctantly submits to be called novelist. Graves rejects both " novel " and " romance," and calls *Columella* (1779) a Colloquial Tale, as the main part of the narrative is true. C. Melmoth distinguishes between " novel " and " narrative," and applies the latter to his *Liberal Opinions* (1777). The curate in Bage's *Hermsprong* (1796) debates whether he ought to write a novel, as they " are now pretty generally considered as the lowest of all human productions."

[3] A previous experiment in the verse-novel was *Julia, a Poetical Romance,* by the Editor of the *Essay on the Characters of Women (i.e.* Mrs. Russel) (1774), based on *Le Nouvelle Héloïse ;* there was also an adaptation into blank verse of *Télémaque,* Book I, by John Canton in 1788. The critics liked these efforts. *The Sentimental Magazine* (Feb. 1774) calls *Julia* " a bold attempt to retrieve the dignity of Modern Fable," and cf. *Critical* Jan. 1774. Shelley's *Rosalind and Helen* should not be forgotten in this connection.

Courtney Melmoth in *Family Secrets* (1797), by interpolating reflective and critical dissertations. Indeed, the necessity of redeeming the novel was strongly felt, and critics congratulated their readers when an author of standing, like Henry Brooke, " condescended to adopt the same vehicle " as the de Vergys and Fogertys of the day.[1] The champions of the novel—though the name suggests a far more aggressive and confident attitude than was theirs—took up for the most part the old *utile dulci* line of defence that had served Sidney to vindicate " delightful feigning." Either the novel teaches directly, by way of moral doctrine and general information, or it educates the emotions and, by displaying various types of human nature, acquaints the reader vicariously with the world. A few independents were content to call themselves purveyors of amusement; such was Fielding's disciple, Charles Jenner, who, without wholly renouncing the hope of being useful to the reader, wisely limits his expectation to amusing him, and enters on a spirited defence of the pastime commonly called castle-building, " for which species of amusement, nothing affords so good materials as a novel. It is a castle ready built to your hands; and furnished with every accommodation necessary for the bestowing an hour of that happiness which the pliability of man's spirits fits him to enjoy."[2] The word beauty is never used in these apologias, and the word imagination sparingly.

More important than theoretical defence at this stage was practical illustration. The novel was to be redeemed only by being well written; it would then have defenders enough. As Holcroft says, concluding a lament for the decline of the novel on a more cheerful note : " *Tom Jones* shall never want admirers." [3] There was no new

---

[1] v. *Gentleman's Magazine*, Dec. 1773, p. 607.
[2] v. *Placid Man*, Bk. IV, ch. i. (1770).
[3] v. *Alwyn*, Preface (1780).

Tom Jones in 1780 to claim admiration, but there was a
growing body of respectable work, published by respectable firms. A novel might not be a safe passport to
fame, but it was an admirable form of entertainment,
especially for the writer, and the country clergymen of
England, accustomed to fill in their leisure with botany
and archæology, now turned novelists. Graves near
Bath and Jenner in the Midlands constructed at their
ease unpretentious castles for the fancy to roam in,
furnished with odds and ends of reflection and observation, learning and memory. Of the same class, though
not in orders, were Joseph Cradock, Esq., author of the
popular *Village Memoirs* (1774), Dr. Thomas Cogan,
philosopher, economist and physician, who beguiled his
leisure with *John Buncle, Junior, Gentleman* (1776),
William Hutchinson, the Durham solicitor, who occupied himself with romance and topography, and perhaps
we may add the Man of Feeling himself, Henry Mackenzie, though in him the quality of amateur is less
marked. All these books are essentially self-pleasing
reveries; the author has found a form in which he can
do as he likes, and, while indulging the universal taste
for story-telling to an extent that tales in verse do not
easily allow, turns aside at his pleasure to essay, satire,
criticism or topical comment. Indeed, one of the chief
attractions of the novel, to the amateur of letters as distinct from the professional, was the freedom that it
permitted; and this chapter may well end with an
account of the two best-reviewed novelists of 1770,
Edward Bancroft and Henry Brooke, both admirable
exponents of the easy ungirt movement, the leisurely
stroll by highway and byway, which is the typical gait of
the novelist of the late eighteenth century.

In their eyes, the novel was a capacious vessel, into
which anything could be cast, and in any order. It
could even be used to accommodate the overflow from

a work of more serious standing. To this economical purpose it was put by the young doctor, Edward Bancroft, who had come back from Dutch Guiana with his head and his note-book full of information. His *Essay on the Natural History of Guiana* (1769) had been well received, but the note-books were not yet exhausted. The material, however, was miscellaneous—grim details of the recent insurrection of negroes in Berbice, the story of Mr. Gordon, who had gone native among the Arrowauk Indians, reflections on the life of a medical student, on education and on the proper relationship between the sexes. The obvious solution was to write a novel; and so we have *The History of Charles Wentworth, Esq., in a Series of Letters* (1770).[1] In the first volume the erring Charles, a medical student in London, details his gallantries to an unsympathetic brother at Oxford, who replies with punctual rebukes; then sets his heart on an honourable match, only to have it broken by the discovery of his past; and finally breaks his indentures, forges a cheque, and runs away to the West Indies. With the second volume the novel ceases to be a novel and becomes a guide-book—a point that none of the applauding critics thought worthy of note. The apparent theme—the moral education of Charles—is shelved; we are to assume that he repented adequately on the voyage out, for he now takes his place as a mere spectator, while Bancroft's botanical, geographical and historical notes are emptied into the novel. A few pages are spared for Charles to make his fortune in, and at the end, when the botanist has closed his note-book, the novelist hastily cooks up a little fictional interest by

---

[1] Anonymous. The obvious attribution was made by the *Monthly Review*, July 1770. The books are based on the same information, reflect the same point of view, and show verbal resemblances. Watts, *Bibliotheca Britannica*, followed by modern books of reference, assigns the novel to A. B. (*i.e.* A. Bancroft). I can find no evidence to support this.

means of a shipwreck, before uniting both brothers to the objects of their affection. The *Monthly Review* approved the book, finding in it " more good sense and nature . . . than we have seen in fifty such productions "; but Bancroft turned his attention to calico-dyeing and wrote no more novels. He had used up his stores, and was content.

In the same year appeared the fifth and last volume of Henry Brooke's *Fool of Quality* (1766–70), to be followed in 1774 by *Juliet Grenville ; or, the History of the Human Heart*. He, too, after a lifetime of activity in drama, verse and pamphlet, turned to the novel as one seeking elbow-room and exemption from all those more strenuous conditions of craftsmanship that had ceased to interest him. The pride of artistry had died out in his mind, and he had now but two aims—to bear witness in rhapsody and parable to the faith that was in him, and to console himself in the sombre close of his life with a rich and fantastic winter's tale. To Henry Brooke, who had been the companion of Lord Lyttelton and the Prince of Wales, and was now an old, impoverished and bereaved man, the most precious thing on earth was a broken spirit. The substance of his *Fool of Quality* is contrition, the life of the soul that is " melted and minted again." It is in consequence a joyous book. The main thread of story is a happy dream of a boy, fitted by nature and education to be a Christian hero ; and on this thread is strung episode after episode, narration after narration, differing in detail but essentially the same. The proud, the perverse or the merely heedless soul is struck down, like Magnificence in Skelton's play, and in prison, beggary or utmost desolation of spirit draws near to God. " But how long, I say, do you propose to make your story ? " asks the friend whose comments enliven the earlier chapters. " My friend," replies the Author, " the reader may make it as short as he pleases "; but for him, we feel, no length could be wearisome that enabled him to add soul to soul to form an earthly rosary of the blest. Brooke is a mighty hunter before the Lord. The book which began as a tale, improvised during a ride with a much-loved nephew, developed into five volumes, and through these five volumes Brooke ranges, tracking his quarry. Not a worldling who is not first humbled and thereafter reconciled; not a sinner who is not smitten to the dust in order that he may be raised to the embrace of love. There is, I think, only one exception; for, as the villain of each episode automatically becomes the hero of the next, it follows that at the end there is one villain over; and he dies impenitent and is buried in the highway.

The book is discursive, as its author well knew; it has many extravagances of feeling and expression, as he partly guessed. The amazing coincidences, the providential deliverances are part of his creed; they are premisses, which his readers must accept; but the drenched handkerchiefs, the embracings and prostrations that accompany almost every conversation are less easily stomached. Brooke was a man of great natural sensibility, at a time when sensibility was fashionable; he was also a religious enthusiast, using the language of enthusiasm; and these things do not make for restraint, especially in a fluid medium like the novel. Nevertheless, nothing can obscure the nobility of this devout fairy-tale. It sprang from a mind which, in old age, was like an overgrown garden, a fragrant wilderness, still visited at rare and burning moments by the angels of God. Nothing in eighteenth-century literature is finer in feeling—execution is another matter—than the scene where Clement, believing that his wife has been violated, summons her to share the meal he has prepared, or than that other scene where she speaks to him of his soul and the quality

of her love for him.[1] As in the somewhat similar case
of Sir Philip Sidney's *Arcadia*, the ethical seriousness of
these scenes is surrounded by brilliant arabesques of
fantastic colour. The book is not quite in touch with
life at any time, and in the fifth volume it passes wholly
into the land of fable, and we see that spiritual Grandison, the young Earl of Morland, set forth on his marriage
morning in a chariot of burning gold, drawn by six
spotted Arabians, by the side of his bride, the African
princess, having previously in his exultation cleared five
feet " with a standing hop." " Never will any sight so
glorious be exhibited," adds Brooke, " till the heavenly
Jerusalem shall descend upon earth."

The London critics were surprisingly kind to the
eccentric genius who led his life " remote from the
fountain-head of English literature," and the book,
according to Henry Mackenzie,[2] was much read and
admired. Brooke, now living in complete seclusion,
wrote on, caring something, perhaps, for Wesley's praise,
but more, one believes, for the solace he administered to
himself by writing. Sin and sorrow he could never
forget, but he could still, in his fiction, shed over them
the light of heavenly mercy. *Juliet Grenville* is even
more full than *The Fool of Quality* of benign extravagances, for Brooke's vein of playful humour, authentic
enough though never very robust, is now quite dried up.
Of the thirty concubines in white muslin, whom Mr.
Grenville leads from the moated residence of the old
libertine who has just expired in " hopeful horrors,"
only three elope from the hostel where he establishes

---

[1] The speech is omitted in the edition of 1796, which was based
on Brooke's last and not very happy revision. The episodes are con-
siderably retrenched, at the cost of continuity and beauty, while the
repressed extravagance breaks out more violently in the " fairy-tale "
accessories. One does not understand the mentality of the critic
(*Gentleman's Magazine*, Dec. 1773, p. 607) who referred to the book
as " a fund of useful instruction."

[2] v. *Anecdotes and Egotisms*, ed. H. W. Thompson (1927).

them; in twenty-seven cases the seed falls on good
ground. Indeed, nothing is easier than to make fun
of *Juliet Grenville*, with its amazing *accouchement* scene,
its hero who carries twenty guineas in his pocket for
months without suspecting it, and its heroine whose
" features were a group of sentiments "; and it is very
much to the credit of contemporary critics that they met
Brooke on his own ground and discounted his peculiarities
in favour of his strength. He offered them a " history
of the heart "; all else, he felt, was " a dead letter, a
foreign inventory, a mere catalogue of unconcerning
events." His theme was the education in love and grief
of young Lord Thomas and Juliet Grenville. As children
they feel for each other the most passionate affection, for
Brooke loves to trace in the innocence of childhood the
principles on which, for him, life turned—love, humility
and self-abnegation. Later, separated by their parents'
quarrel, they receive that impress of sorrow of which
Harry Clinton had so wistfully boasted, until at last
Thomas, glorified by suffering, returns to Juliet, at first
in disguise to trouble her with vague fears of her own
disloyalty, but afterwards in his own form, " an angel
of salutation, excepting only the wings," and with his
hair " bound behind in a knot of amethysts." It is the
strangest mixture and should be kept from all but sympathetic readers, for the old hand, groping vaguely about
the strings of its extraordinary instrument, can still, at
times, strike out phrases of piercing sweetness. Such
is that dying fall with which, hurt even here by thoughts
of change and mortality, he brings to a conclusion his
account of the felicity of Juliet and her husband : " Close,
close the blissful scene !—lest some casual cloud should
come to overcast it."

CHAPTER II

OLD PATTERNS IN THE NOVEL

Let not therefore a moderate genius be too much ashamed of a guide.—CHARLES JENNER, *The Placid Man*, 1770.

OF the splendid inheritance which fell to the novelists of the late eighteenth century from their predecessors, they were able to avail themselves only of the least splendid parts. This initial failure to occupy effectively ground that the novel had already conquered is apparent in the imitations of all four of the great masters, but is especially marked in the school of Richardson. From him they took the epistolary way of story-telling,— incomparably the most popular up to about 1785,—some notion of the possible uses of detail,—though their round-eared caps and round-table conversations are too often irrelevant,—and the piled-up pathos of Clarissa's end. From him also they learned how to dress up the old themes of Cinderella, Virtue Persecuted, and the Good Young Man in new scenes and characters. The abduction of Miss Byron from the masquerade, Mr. B.'s disguised attempt on Pamela, Clarissa's home-coming to the stony-hearted Harlowe family, these are the patterns from which are drawn the chief incidents of scores of books, with remarkably little variation, and sometimes with a literal closeness.[1] Lovelaces abound, and Lady G——s

---

[1] *E.g.* the masquerade in Mrs. Skinn's *Old Maid* (1771) and in *Anecdotes of a Convent* (1771) by the author of the *Memoirs of Mrs. Williams* ; Mr. B.'s attempt in Miss Padstow's narration in *The Younger Sister* (1770) by Anne Dawe and in *The Modern Fine Gentleman* (1774); the Harlowe-place scenes in *Emma ; or, the Child of Sorrow* (1776); Lovelace's search of the tradesman's house in *Sir William Harrington* (1771) by T. Hull.

burden these narratives with their inflexible vivacity. Richardson's characters even provided categories under which novelists could briefly classify their own personages. " You have, Harriet, read *Sir Charles Grandison*, and must remember Mr. Orme. Mr. Granville was certainly his brother," writes a young lady in the *Genuine Memoirs of Miss Harriet Melvin* (1772),[1] sure that her correspondent will know exactly what she means to convey. Richardson's finest qualities, however, the masterly direction and cumulative force of *Clarissa*, the slow concretion of innumerable particles of fact and feeling into a personality, were unique and did not stimulate imitation, except to some extent in Miss Burney's *Cecilia* (1782). There is nothing of them in Thomas Hull's *History of Sir William Harrington* (1771).[2] The book glows with reverential loyalty for the great author of *Clarissa*. Almost every character has, as it were, a patron among those of Richardson ; there is a Belford, an Emily Jervoise and a Lady G——, and when Sir William takes one of his sisters to a masquerade, the other can only write : " Ah, brother ! would *Sir Charles Grandison*, think you, have carried *his sister* into such company, and to such a place, as *you* did *yours ?* " A virtuous death-bed, elegant mourning designed by the young ladies, teasing and snatching of letters, settlements and wedding-gowns, form the substance of the book, and at the end Sir William " (while Love, Respect, and Confusion swam in his fine eyes)," apologizes to the girl he

---

[1] *Genuine Memoirs of Miss Harriet Melvin and Miss Leonora Stanway. In a series of letters.* By a young lady of Gloucester (1772).

[2] *The History of Sir William Harrington. Written some years since, and revised, corrected, and improved, by the late Mr. Samuel Richardson,* 4 vols. The Richardson family denied the claim, and the author of *Jessy; or the Bridal Day* (1771), pointedly describes her book as written " after the *Manner* of the late Mr. *Richardson* . . . but *not revised* by that celebrated writer." Thomas Hull (1728–1808) was an actor, dramatist and friend of Shenstone. This, his only novel, was reprinted in 1797, and put into German (1771) and French (1773). v. *D.N.B.*

has tried to seduce, and poetic justice is exactly distributed and fully annotated by the author. In the *History of Pamela Howard* (1773), by the Author of *Indiana Danby*, the Grandisons are introduced in their proper persons, still keeping up their " *etiquette* of primitive good breeding . . . and . . . handing about Grandmothers, Uncles, Aunts, and Cousins from one room to another." The book is by no means a parody, however ; the author admires, but not blindly.

Setting aside the insipidities of Hull, and, at the other end of the Richardsonian scale, the sensationalism of *Jessy ; or, the Bridal Day* (1771),[1] we may pause for a minute over the *The Fruitless Repentance ; or, the History of Miss Kitty Le Fever* (1769), a very fair specimen of the Richardsonian school. The book, which is quite short, obeys the tradition that the heroine should be " *great* throughout." Kitty is first seen by Lord Clerage, the Lovelace of the piece, at prayers in Westminster Abbey, and forthwith exposed to an elaborate and unscrupulous pursuit, which culminates in the imprisonment of her betrothed, Leceister, and Kitty's voluntary offer of her hand to Clerage in return for his freedom. Here we meet with the best of those touches which set the book an inch nearer literature than most of its contemporaries. Clerage, confronted by her fierce misery, unexpectedly realizes that his prime need is not to possess but to comfort her. The situation is repeated after Kitty's marriage with Leceister, when Clerage, relapsing from virtue, comes in disguise to make his prey, only to find that he can plot against her in absence, but in her presence

---

[1] Written by a Lady. The plot is as follows :—Sir George Stanley pursues his tutor's daughter, Jessy, and, after the death of her father and the loss of her fortune, overcomes her by means of forgery, abduction and drugs. She behaves like Clarissa. He withdraws and arranges a marriage with another woman. Jessy dies, and a faithful and disappointed lover arranges her funeral to synchronize with Stanley's wedding ; a duel is fought in the church, and Stanley dies embracing the coffin, and saying : " May my death atone."

can only strive to contribute to her peace. His efforts are vain, for Leceister's mind, irretrievably hurt by his imprisonment, has turned to jealousy, and it is an exhausted Kitty who, after his death, gives her hand to Clerage for the sake of her children, dying of deep decline four days after the ceremony. One prefers this fruitless repentance, with its respect for consequences, to the unbridled optimism of the majority of those writers who deal in salutary pangs.

The school of Fielding was far smaller than that of Richardson, but its work was on a higher level. Setting aside the mechanical imitations—one almost writes transcriptions—of such incidents as the encounter between the coach-load of respectability and the naked man, and of such characters as Parson Adams and Squire Western, to be found shamelessly inserted in many a thievish book,[1] the mere fact that a man took Fielding for his model generally implied in him a certain critical appreciation of the problems he had to tackle. Fielding's elaborate structure in *Tom Jones* was not imitated, though it was observed and admired, and his scholars were quicker to take up his facetious metaphor of the ordinary than to learn from him how such a feast should be marshalled ; but, although they disclaimed any attempt to rival the comic epic in prose, and some of them even

---

[1] Intelligent imitations of Fielding's characters and incidents will be found, *e.g.*, in the following books : Squire Western in Squire Howard, *History of Pamela Howard* (1773) and in the Cambrian Sir John Bangham, *Contemplative Man* (1771) by Herbert Lawrence ; the starched uncharitable gentlewoman in the stage-coach in *The Motto ; or, the History of Bill Woodcock* (1795) by George Brewer, and Jane Timbury's *Philanthropic Rambler* (1790) ; the effect of Garrick's Hamlet on Partridge in the *Contemplative Man*, where a simple servant attends a performance of King Lear by strollers ; Mrs. Slipslop and Parson Adams in Cumberland's Jemima Caudle and Ezekiel Daw in *Henry* (1795). Stage-coach scenes were very popular (*v.* John Potter's *Arthur O'Bradley*, I, p. 34, 1769), and had the authority of Addison as well as Fielding ; so were scenes displaying the characteristics of hero and villain in childhood (*v.* Moore's *Edward*, 1796). These last were rendered doubly popular by the interest of the time in systems of education.

doubted whether so careful an art were not wasted on a novel, they did maintain something more of coherence and proportion than we are accustomed to find in the work of their contemporaries, and were prepared to enter modestly on the defence of a form subject to continual abuse.[1] The division into books, which was not, however, generally adopted, the author's prefatory chapters or more informal addresses to the reader on his principles and intentions are the outward signs of a growing critical spirit, ready to occupy itself with questions of method, though not yet ready to be solemn about them ; and this critical spirit, of which the novel had so urgent a need, is hardly found outside the school of Fielding.

There is much pleasant reading in Jenner's *Placid Man* (1770), in the four narratives of Graves, in Chater's *Tom Rigby* (1773), Lawrence's *Contemplative Man* (1771), and the anonymous *Prudential Lovers* (1773), and *Younger Brother* (1770). The authors stand in Fielding's company modestly but with self-possession, for they are not there as plagiarists but out of honest sympathy. They share his gust for country scenes and types, for the young squire, leaning over his pew and accompanying the vicar through both lessons with the Latin Bible he has brought from the University, for the gossiping knot of villagers under the old elm at the cobbler's gate, the " shrewd young carter with a silk handkerchief about his neck " at Captain Dover's games, and the old justice of the peace, hurrying out to do justice in his summer-

---

[1] Graves called *The Spiritual Quixote* (1772) an Epopœa, but he must not be taken too seriously; at other times he, like his fellow-authors, uses the words history and historian. Jenner (*Placid Man*, Bk. IV, Ch. I) defending novels both as pleasing amusements and " natural vehicles of the *utile dulci*," notes with some exaggeration that " numerous as the authors in it are, [he does] not recollect that any of them have ever taken upon them to bestow even a chapter upon the defence of that branch of authorship, to which they owe all their reputation, if they have any to boast of, and, it may be, all their bread, if they have any to eat." Cf. also Cumberland's views on the novel in the prefatory chapters to *Henry* (1795).

house " with the napkin tucked in his button-hole "; [1]
and these things are described, especially by Graves,
with the light assurance of familiarity, and not without
such particular touches as suggest that, in the freedom
of the novel, local peculiarities were soon to diversify
general truth. Their heroes move, like *Tom Jones*,
through a varied social scene, which their adventures
help to display; the plot may be slight, but there is a
brisk succession of incident, and in the portraiture of
types we recognize something of that veracity which we
call Chaucerian, a combined zest and sobriety of line,
admitting heightening but stopping short of burlesque.[2]
No doubt they took to heart Fielding's distinction between
comic painting and caricature, and, while retaining at
will the harsh vigour of eighteenth-century ridicule, had
subtlety enough to enjoy quieter work. The author of
the *Younger Brother*, for instance, is capable of both
notes. His best scenes take place at Oxford, where he
makes play with the humours of the common room, such
as the pigeon-fancying don who keeps birds in his room,
or Dr. Ruby who gives himself away by reading prayers
one dark morning with an orthodox black stocking on
one leg and one of Betty's red ones the other. In
the account of Mr. Cant, the Methodist Fellow, he sinks
to caricature; indeed, few novelists at that time could
resist such a temptation; but he is on higher ground
with Mr. Racket, the undergraduate, and his unpre-
meditated breakfast invitation to the freshman. " Mr.
Racket, having only one teaspoon, he very politely offered
it to me; stirring his own cup with a small key that he
took out of his pocket." Nothing could be more accurate

---

[1] *v.* Graves, *Spiritual Quixote.*
[2] *E.g.* the landlady in *The Prudential Lovers ; or, the History of
Harry Harper*, I, p. 30; and Graves's kindly and ostentatious retired
tradesman, Mr. Nonsuch, in *Columella*, who passes his time " smoking
his pipe upon his terrace, which overlooks a public road, and gaping
about for every wagon or dung-cart that passes by, merely to supply
the place of reflection."

or less pretentious.[1] Something also of Fielding's
ironical phrasing, which it is not impossible to copy
superficially, was transmitted to his followers,[2] together
with that scholar's jest, the burlesque simile ; while the
best of them shared deeply in that attitude of benignant
irony, based on an equal sense of man's frailty and his
worth, which was, indeed, natural to the age, though
Fielding gave it its most perfect expression. Thus
Herbert Lawrence [3] takes young Crab, the hero of his
*Contemplative Man ; or, the History of Christopher Crab,
Esq. of North Wales* (1771), to Chelsea Hospital, where
he talks to an old soldier, who served at Culloden, but
substitutes Blenheim to make a better figure in his story ;
and young Crab defends the substitution, saying gently :
" If he thinks his Story is credited, it pleases his Vanity
by making him of some Importance ; which is a comfortable Cordial to old Age, in indigent Circumstances."

There are plenty of these admirable touches scattered
through the books of Fielding's pupils, oddly blended at
times with other strains from Richardson, Smollett, or
even the religious sensationalism of Brooke.[4] Fielding's

---

[1] University scenes are rare in the novel ; few authors, the reviewers
suggested, had the necessary knowledge. There is a high-wrought
scene of the wilder spirits at Oxford in G. L. Way's *Learning at a Loss*
(1778), and a denunciatory sketch, not written from personal knowledge, in Holcroft's *Hugh Trevor* (1794-7).

[2] v. *Prudential Lovers*, I.d'Israeli's *Vaurien* (1797) and, for a
sustained ironical treatment of vice, modelled on *Jonathan Wild*,
Charles Johnstone's *History of John Juniper, Esq. alias Juniper Jack*
(1781). It is in Fielding's spirit that Chater in *Tom Rigby* describes
the honest farmer's wife, after roughly rejecting her landlord's advances,
" looking through the window at the disappointed Squire trudging
homewards." Cf. also *The Younger Brother :* " The Doctor sat down
again, filled another pipe, and observed, as he held the glass of wine to
his lip, ' sic transit gloria mundi,' and then drank it off with great
philosophy and composure."

[3] Author of *The Life and Adventures of Common Sense* (1769), an
historical allegory, inclining in the direction of the novel of manners.

[4] v. Chater's *Tom Rigby*. For a thorough-going blend of strains v.
The History of Pamela Howard. The basis is *Clarissa* and *Sir Charles
Grandison*, but it is varied with Squire Western scenes, including
hunting songs on the harpsichord, and with a picture of an old
soldier, taking snuff to hide his tears, altogether in Sterne's vein.

sons felt themselves smaller men than their father, and endeavoured to make up by eclecticism what they lacked in force. Richard Graves, whose *Spiritual Quixote ; or, the Summer's Ramble of Mr. Geoffry Wildgoose. A Comic Romance* (1772), has recently enjoyed a revival of interest, comes nearest to Fielding in his blend of seriousness and humour, though his leisurely, generous habit of mind, sweeping moral dissertation, topical character-sketch and rural scene all into the loose mesh of his narrative, was never at all strictly disciplined, and declined with time towards a relaxed garrulity, of which he made a disarming avowal when he put on the title-page of *Senilities* (1801) the picture of a venerable hermit blowing bubbles. A sketchy plot, too weak to focus and control their abundance of natural detail, was a common failing with Fielding's imitators ; the *Spiritual Quixote* does not suffer from it, but in *Columella ; or, the Distressed Anchoret* (1779), *Eugenius ; or, Anecdotes of the Golden Vale* (1785) and *Plexippus ; or, the Aspiring Plebeian* (1790), Graves happened on less fertile ideas and had to supplement more and more with extraneous matter. *Columella* is interesting, partly because of its connection with Shenstone, Graves's old friend, who sat for the distressed anchoret, but it is a good deal of a patchwork. *Eugenius*, which bears no trace at all of Fielding's influence, is an unemphatic narrative of philanthropy and domestic happiness in a Welsh vale, too low-toned and invarious to escape dullness ; but in *Plexippus*, Graves, already seventy-five, takes fresh breath, regains his pace and vivacity, and turns his pen to those light-handed marginal sketches of types in which he excels.

A less-known writer is Charles Jenner, whose *Placid Man ; or, Memoirs of Sir Charles Beville* (1770), provides us with that rather infrequent thing in the eighteenth century, a pleasant book about pleasant people. Jenner, who held two livings in the Midlands and was a keen musical amateur, wrote poetry, drama, essays and sketches, but only one full-sized novel.[1] In this novel, however, he contrived to find a place for all his interests and admirations, and one follows him with pleased recognition, as he tries one after another the themes and modes of his three masters, Fielding, Richardson and Sterne. The education of the hero by his father, the musical baronet, and his uncle, the retired West Indian governor, is after Sterne ; the placid man himself, with his benevolence and his sentiments, would have been a welcome guest at Sir Charles Grandison's table ; while in the introductory chapters, and the reflective and kindly irony of the narrative, we have the disciple of Fielding. Fielding's is certainly the sovereign influence, but the reader who turns to the quiet love-stories of Sir Charles Beville and his tutor, expecting to find anything like Fielding's richness of incident and depth of characterization, will be disappointed. Jenner cannot handle weight or complexity, and he was too modest a man, too conscious of the difficulties of the novelist's craft and the dangers of rivalry, to essay it. In him all is temperate and calm ; even his humorous interest in absurdities is quite outweighed by his interest in the normal human habit of mind, and his best passages are unobtrusive. Thus Sir Charles Beville at a concert falls into conversation with his neighbour and learns that, though a regular concert-goer, he is quite unmusical ; the pleasure that he seeks is the sight of so many human creatures innocently enjoying themselves. This quietness of Jenner's allows us to overhear one note that is peculiarly his. Mr. Norris is telling how, as a boy of nineteen, he travelled and drowsed all night in a dark stage-coach, and at length opened the wooden shutter to see if it was

[1] There is a small amount of narrative in *Letters from Altamont* (1767), the views of an unspoilt young man, brought up in seclusion in North Wales, on London life and society. This Percival settles down to a place in the post-office.

light. " I had better have left it alone; it was light; and by that light I saw over against me a face, which several years' experience of its deceit has hardly been able to reconcile me to consigning to oblivion." We have here a sense of something in the bud, a faint but unmistakable poetic thrill, which recurs when Sir Charles at Bath is surprised into recognition of his first love, by finding the lady's name scribbled on a window in the empty Pump-room. It is the note that is missing in all four of the great novelists, the lyric quickening of prose, no more than a hint as yet, but pregnant with promise.

It is necessary to mention Richard Cumberland,[1] whose *Henry* (1795) is the most diligent of all these imitations. It was carefully and deliberately written, as the author tells us, over some years, and the result, though certainly not void of merit, is heavy-handed. Henry, the hero, is a Joseph who preserves his virtue and his command of English in the most trying situations and is able to say to the most forward of his fair assailants : " Flattered as I am by your attachment, chastity is a virtue indispensable in the female character." More attractive than this counterblast to Tom Jones is Ezekiel Daw, the Methodist preacher, of close kin to Parson Adams, whose enthusiastic language is well kept up, and who is the best example of Cumberland's aim of " endearing man to man, by bringing characters under review, which prejudice has kept at a distance from the mass of society." [2] Further than Cumberland we need not track Fielding's influence. It is strong and pervasive, but it works obliquely rather than directly, proposing a standard to the novelist, or at times suggesting a mood, rather than providing him with a set of patterns for ready-made incidents and characters. Even in the interests of symmetry, it is not possible to

[1] Cumberland (1732–1811) had already published *Arundel* (1789), an epistolary novel about a young scholar placed as dependant in the house of a politician. He also wrote *John de Lancaster* (1809).
[2] *Henry*, Bk. XII, Ch. I.

discover a school of Smollett. The lively miscellanists who repeated his effects, borrowed his characters and mixed them with Fielding's, were not in need of any banner to march under, nor could Smollett, who had no critical or didactic crotchets, have supplied one. Their books can all be classified, when classification is desirable, under his phrase, " a large, diffused picture of life," and the term picaresque, with its gathered implications of roguery, travel, satiric realism and episodic structure, can be made to fit most of them. The authors shared Smollett's journalistic and experimenting temper, relished what Peregrine Pickle called " practical humour," had a strong penchant for low life, and stuffed out their disconnected narratives with the most multifarious materials, real or fictitious. They are often exceedingly coarse in a good-humoured, heavy-handed way, and they are full of lively touches, of real things seen and heard, dresses and street-cries and smoking puddings and the talk of the servants' hall. They are muddy enough, but mud is more fertile than the etherealized substance of the sentimental novel, and it is the merit of these books that they are, in the full sense of the word, vulgar, that they nourished the democratic, realistic and humorous elements in the basement of English fiction, while the majority of respectable novelists were taking tea with the ladies in the drawing-room above.

Professor Saintsbury speaks somewhere of the liberating qualities inherent in the picaresque, and these were at this time signally displayed. It was totally free from pretensions, and its easy episodic structure could accommodate every sort of material, since no plot was to be sustained and no harmony of atmosphere preserved. Moreover, its central figures were very mobile. Smollett had experimented with foreign settings in *Ferdinand Count Fathom*, and the dupes and adventurers, the players and footmen, whose Odysseys the picaresque writer so

casually records, play their see-saw game in a refreshing
variety of circumstances. France and Spain, ancient
territory of the *picaro*, are revisited, and the hero pushes
his explorations to America, Java and India.[1] Meanwhile
the home-keeping rogue, though London is the great
scene of his exploits, is by no means confined to the
bills of mortality, but lays the country under contribution.[2] A crowd of types, boldly drawn and highly
coloured, jostle each other in these rough-and-ready
books ; the reader is thrust into close and often unsavoury
proximity with them, made to note the characteristic
details of their speech and apparel, shown hurriedly round
their shops or dwelling-houses, and hustled away. For
the reader who is prepared to pick his way these are
entertaining picture books. Here are quakers, nabobs
and cheating tradesmen, Scotch and Irish surgeons, testy
Welsh squires, henpecked country parsons, thief-catchers,
turnkeys and the whole rout of mercenary justice. Here
are actors, dressed as to the head and legs only, and
delaying their performance until enough gate-money has
been taken to get the rest of their clothes out of pawn ;
here are French fops in a paroxysm of the mode, mount-
ing the box like coachmen and driving their own servants ;
here is a lady antiquarian, perpetually deceived in her
purchases, saying to her servant-maid : " As often,
Rachel, as I make use of what has been consecrated to
the antients, I feel a certain inexpressible philosophic
composure ; " and here is a poor lad at Portsmouth,
shown by a landlady with a seafaring tongue into a bug-
ridden bedroom.[3] Smollett's seamen, with their rough

---

[1] v. *The Adventures of Jonathan Corncob, Loyal American Refugee*
(1787) ; *Memoirs of Charles Townly* (1789) ; *The Adventures of a Rupee*
(1782) (by Helenus Scott, M.D.).
[2] Cf. *The Sentimental Spy* (1773). The running title is *The Adventures of a Footman*.
[3] v. J. Trusler's *Modern Times* (1785) ; T. Vaughan's *Fashionable
Follies* (1781) ; the *Sentimental Spy* (1773) and the *Prudential Lovers*
(1773).

honour and their metaphorical speech, were not allowed
to die with their creator.   The first part of *The Prudential
Lovers ; or, the History of Harry Harper* (1773) displays
a number of Portsmouth types ; but these uncouth
animals may be found far inland, riding on the tops of
stage-coaches or brawling in stable-yards.   Sensibility
marked them down, and their honest tears began to
trickle ;   the benevolent guardians in domestic novels are
sometimes retired sea-officers, carrying over some of
Smollett's idiosyncrasies into a politer age than his ;
while a further and most natural development, during
the French wars at the end of the century, idealized ship,
officers and crew.[1]   The prevailing tone of the picaresque
is humorous, often savagely so, but melodramatic inter-
ludes are frequent, and the hero's destiny sometimes
takes a romantic twist ; [2] the infusion had been tried with
success by Smollett in *Ferdinand Count Fathom*, and
was repeated upon a larger scale, so that towards the end
of the century we come upon books, constructed on the
pattern of a picaresque, from which the harshness and
crude joviality, commonly associated with the type, have
quite melted.   One of these softened picaresques is the
Memoirs of Maître Jacques of Savoy (1776), which traces
the rise of an honest chairman on the Mt. Cenis pass to
prosperity, his ruin at the hands of gamblers in Paris,

---

[1] For seamen of various types v. *inter alia* Lieut. Finmore in the
Prudential Lovers, Captain Hawser and Lieut. O'Driscoll in *Anthony
Varnish* (1786), the lieutenant and the captain in Bridges' *Adventures
of a Bank-Note*, vols. 2 and 4 (1770-1). Ferguson in the *Gamesters*
(1786) by Mrs. A. M. Johnson is an example of the generous sailor put
to sentimental uses, while the scenes on the frigate in Cumberland's
Henry (1795)—not, of course, a picaresque—show him idealized by
patriotism on the defensive. Cumberland shows us the deserter who
takes service with the French, but will not turn his gun on his country-
men and is stabbed by a French officer.

[2] v. *e.g.* T. Vaughan's *Fashionable Follies* (1781) and the *Adventures
of a Jesuit* (1771). The latter is a book that does not know its own
mind ; with its foreign scene, its birth mysteries, settlement in England
and conversion, it might have become another *Ferdinand Count Fathom*,
but it lacks energy.

his recovery and retreat to the simple life on a small farm in Savoy. More remarkable is the *Memoirs of a Scots Heiress*, by the author of *Constance* (1791).[1] This is a woman's book, unusual in many respects, notably in its easy, rapid style and in the manly tone of the hero's love-letters; it conforms to type, however, in having a moral theme, the education by adversity of Amabel Macgilroy, the Scots heiress. It is the nature of this adversity that ranks the book among picaresque novels; for Lady Amabel, left destitute on her wedding day by a husband who has married her for her fortune and decamps when he finds it illusory, follows the British army to Saratoga, is taken by an American privateer, marooned on the coast of Canada, aided by savages, and picked up from a drifting canoe by a Brazilian ship bound for the Azores. Her behaviour when she returns to England is no less remarkable; when impoverished she tries to get work, when insulted she walks out of the room, and when prevented by her former marriage from accepting Mr. Cyril, she explains her situation to him and does not refer vaguely to an " insurmountable obstacle." So much sense and so little fainting is unusual in a woman's book at this date, and may most probably be referred to the heroine's nationality.

Satiric indignation was the pretext advanced for many of these picaresque miscellanies; it also covered, as Charles Johnstone pointed out, the avidity of the readers.[2] It need seldom be taken seriously. Their real aim was betrayed by John Trusler, when he advertised his own *Modern Times* as " a useful family book . . . [which] will teach more knowledge of life in one reading than

[1] She also wrote *Argus, the House-dog at Eadlip* (1789), *Arnold Zulig, a Swiss story* (1790) and the *Count of Hoensdern* (1792).
[2] Cf. Preface to *History of John Juniper* (1781): " There cannot be a stronger argument against the charge of degeneracy in moral virtue and religion brought against the present age, than the avidity with which all works exposing the breaches of them by the unerring proof of facts, are read by all people."

twenty years' experience." [1]   It was to crowd the canvas
with variety, to touch the Newgate Calendar on one hand
and the jest-books on the other, to faggot oddities and
compile a satiric sketch-book of social types and personalities. The picaresque favoured a dashing rapidity of
stroke at a time when the pulse of sentimental fiction was
at its slowest. *The Adventures of Anthony Varnish* [2]
(1786) begin in Ireland, where the hero's apprenticeship
to a brutal physician gives rise to the usual violence and
horse-play. After spending a few boisterous days with a
travelling show, and tramping the road with a cheating
soldier and his trull, Anthony passes into the service of a
sea-lieutenant, crosses to Liverpool, witnessing picturesque
excesses of sea-sickness on the way, is overset on the
road to London, sees, in a Coventry stable, a performance
of *Hamlet* which ends in fisticuffs, and is presently turned
loose in town, to be bubbled by tricksters in cellar
ordinaries, helped by a poor author, and to pass into the
service of a young lady of fortune, whose husband he
becomes. This is a bare outline of a story that moves
forward through a wealth of detail, which is yet never
suffered to clog its speed. In Ireland there are the
sketches of naked children and piglings eating from one
large wooden dish, and of the mean hostelry where
Anthony passes the night ; in London there is the sixpenny
dip from which the poor author buys his wig, the tallow-
chandler's marriage (a Dickensian scene, though not treated
in the mood of Dickens) and the preaching major, who
has all the air of a real person, as he goes about distributing
good books and rebuking chimney-sweeps for blasphemy.

[1] *v.* advertisement in *Life ; or, the Adventures of William Ramble,
Esq.* (1793).
[2] *The Adventures of Anthony Varnish ; or, a Peep at the Manners
of Society.* By an Adept.   Ascribed to Johnstone by B.M. Catalogue,
and Halkett and Laing ; ignored by other books of reference.   He
sailed to Calcutta in 1782, but that does not prohibit an ascription
which the Irish scenes, quotations from Fielding and satire on the
drunken Methodist parson make likely.

An even more rapid panorama of scenes and types could be achieved when the hero of the adventures was inanimate, or at least non-human. Coventry's *Lap-dog* and Johnstone's *Guinea* had been followed by Thomas Bridges' learned *Bank-Note*, which quotes Lucretius, and by other miscellanies on the same model. " This mode of making up a book," wrote the *Critical* in 1781, " and styling it the *Adventures* of a Cat, a Dog, a Monkey, a Hackney-Coach, a Louse, a Shilling, a Rupee, or—anything else, is grown so fashionable, that few months pass which do not bring one of them under our inspection. It is indeed a convenient method to writers of the inferior class, of emptying their commonplace books, and throwing together all the farrago of public transactions, private characters, old and new stories, everything, in short, which they can pick up, to afford a little temporary amusement to an idle reader." [1] Helenus Scott's *Rupee* (1782) is a good specimen of this unexacting sort of narrative. Beginning with the current anecdote of Hyder Ali and the beguiled fakirs, it passes to England, where the rupee, displayed in a pawnshop, hears an Italian describe the state of political prisoners in Venice and a chimney-sweep that of the poor children whose teeth were sold to be transplanted into the gums of the rich. His little sister, the boy says, " has had nothing but her naked jaws since she was nine years of age. It is but a poor comfort to her, that her teeth are at court, while she lives at home on slops, without any hopes of a husband." His own front teeth are gone, but they fell down the throat of the ancient purchaser in the night and choked her, to his consolation. Then the author, who was a medical man, devotes a few pages to the drinking of vinegar by young women to reduce their figures, and its bad effect on their health and that of their offspring ; a few more, in which he draws on his experiences in India,

[1] *Critical*, Dec. 1781, on *The Adventures of a Rupee* (dated 1782).

on the necessity of a qualifying examination for military officers ; and so concludes with a word on behalf of Jews.

There are very few personalities in the *Rupee*, either avowed or concealed, but the sort of interest that the identification of satiric portraits gives rise to is amply provided by William Combe [1] in his *Devil upon Two Sticks in England : being a continuation of Le Diable Boiteux of Le Sage* (1790), while the very popular *Adventures of a Hackney-Coach* (1781) is a notable example of topical quality of a less cryptic kind. The *Hackney-Coach*, which seems to have been very popular,—the British Museum copy is a Dublin reprint of the seventh edition,—carries in turn Goldsmith, Ned Shuter and Wesley, a gentleman who discusses Garrick, visitors to Shuter's funeral and to Dr. Dodd's execution, as well as resurrection thieves, a country girl, a benevolent lady, and other nameless passengers. With this book, moreover, we part company with the term " picaresque." Nothing but its episodic structure links it with that genre. It betrays no relish for roguery ; rather, its tone is sentimental and lachrymose. " Chance," says the author, dedicating his work to Lady Craven, " put into my hand an old worn-out pen of Yorick's."

Worn-out, indeed ; worn to a stump. To the traveller in these marsh-lands of the novel there is no more ominous sign than a page strewn with asterisks and dashes, for these betoken the calculated abruptions, the dripping tears,—all that insupportably tedious vulgarization of Sterne's technique by which his imitators hoped to capture something of his unique and inimitable spirit.

---

[1] William Combe (1741–1823), after wasting his substance splendidly, took up authorship, *c.* 1771. He began with drama and verse-satire, and proceeded to all kinds of literary work, the majority of it written from within the Rules of the King's Bench. His most popular work was the *Tours of Dr. Syntax.* He invariably published anonymously ; v. *D.N.B.*

" Prithee come hither, honest grave-digger," cries the exasperated *Monthly* over this same *Hackney-Coach*, " and cover up *Yorick's skull.* The flies have blown on it.—Cover it up !—*Maggots* and all." It is, indeed, almost impossible to escape Sterne at this stage of the history of the novel. His track is marked by the loud disclaimers of those who felt his magnetic power, but liked to pretend that they had been going that way before.[1] Everywhere we meet the spectacle of common-place minds lashing themselves through Shandean gambols, cultivating " surprise " and relapsing into sobriety, plodding through the whimsical divagations, the disorderly and poignant sallies of Yorick as through a drill. How often does their style break into those curt sentences that simulate an utterance interrupted by emotion ; how many uncomplaining old soldiers, generous young sailors (or negroes, or footmen) and distracted beauties parade in their pages ; nor is it unknown for Yorick himself, complete with clerical black and shattered constitution, to posture his way through them. As for the ass, a small thesis could be written about him.[2]

Books were constructed on the perambulatory model of the *Sentimental Journey*, such as Mrs. Bonhote's *Rambles of Mr. Frankly, published by his sister* [3] (1773–6),

[1] *E.g.* Graves in *Columella*, which ends with a Preface, says : " I should despise myself for adopting Sterne's oddities," while the author of *The Trifler: or, a Ramble among the Wilds of Fancy, the Works of Nature, and the Manners of Men* (1775), while denying imitation, writes : " Sterne has ruined us all in this way of writing."

[2] The old soldier occurs in *Sentimental Lucubrations* (1770) by Peter Pennyless, *Pamela Howard* (1773), Combe's *Philosopher in Bristol* (1775), the *Man of Feeling* (1771), and elsewhere ; Yorick in Keate's *Sketches from Nature* (1779). The Franciscan and the scene in the glove shop were frequently imitated, and Maria herself reappears in the *Letters of Maria* (1790). To the books already mentioned may be added Mary Latter of Reading's *Pro and Con; or, the Opinionists* (1771), in which, according to the *Monthly*, the author " mistakes for wit the ravings of a deranged imagination " ; James Thistlethwaite's *Man of Experience* (1778), Susanna Rowson's *Inquisitor* (1778) and Jane Timbury's *Philanthropic Rambler* (1790).

[3] Elizabeth Bonhote, 1744–1818, wife of a solicitor of Bungay. She also wrote the *Parental Monitor* (1788), *Olivia ; or Deserted Bride*

William Combe's *Philosopher in Bristol* (1775) and Courtney Melmoth's [1] *Travels for the Heart* (1777). Among the most successful was *Sketches from Nature ; taken, and coloured, in a Journey to Margate. Published from the original designs by George Keate, Esq.* (1779). Keate,[2] whom the reviewers greeted as Sterne's " legitimate offspring," to be distinguished from his " byeblows," was a man of talent and sensibility, who, not content with reflecting his model's mannerisms, could follow him in his oblique chase for his subtle quarry, the moment. For Sterne's great revelation to his age was the significance of the small and of the fleeting, and he excels in capturing the evanescent colour of a momentarily perfect but unconfirmed intimacy, a fellowship built on a breath and dissolved with a breath, but nevertheless, as he felt and persuaded his age to feel, of infinite value. With eyes sharpened by his quest he reads the meaning of that hieroglyphic of a lifetime, the habitual gesture, and applies in the interest of pathos the detail which had been the satirist's preserve. Lastly, he turns his analytic delicacy upon himself, and traces those conflicts of the benevolent impulse with a continually-rising midge-like swarm of mean ideas, which are so whimsically minute in their expression and so deep in their implications. These things were more permanent than his grimace, and played a master-part in that general quickening of the nerves which was taking place in English literature at the end of the eighteenth century, affecting

---

(1789), *Darnley Vale* (1789), *Ellen Woodley* (1790), *Bungay Castle* (1797), and *Feeling*, a poem (1810).

[1] Courtney Melmoth, otherwise Samuel Jackson Pratt (1749–1814), forsook the Church for the stage in his twenties, was for a time a public reader and a bookseller, and became one of the most prolific writers of novels, plays, poetry and miscellanies of his day. His novels are *Liberal Opinions* (1775–7), *The Pupil of Pleasure* (1776), *Travels for the Heart* (1777), *The Tutor of Truth* (1779), *Shenstone-Green* (1779), *Emma Corbett* (1780) and *Family Secrets* (1797).

[2] George Keate, Esq. (1729–1797), a man of birth and means, poet, naturalist, antiquary and artist; v. *D.N.B.*

writers whose general bias was towards one of the other schools of fiction.   His influence is very widely diffused, and to it we must ascribe not only such direct imitations as Courtney Melmoth's Franciscan, but also such odd compounds of reading, fantasy and reflection as *The Wandering Islander, or the History of Mr. Charles North*,[1] lawless displays of the individual mind of the author, which could hardly have existed as they are but for Sterne's reckless emphasis on the personal note in fiction. In sentiment, in technique, he sets models that everyone was anxious to copy.

It is impossible to omit here the name of Henry Mackenzie,[2] that most famous of Sterne's disciples, though many of the aspects of his work must be dealt with in later chapters.   His *Man of Feeling* (1771), which was enormously popular, was conceived during a brief visit to London, at a time when the healthy-minded, practical young lawyer, with sixty years of zest and hard work before him, was still boy enough to dream of an early death, and prone to a cherished " drunkenness of the imagination." Some of the incidents had their basis in experience, and no doubt some of the feelings too, but the sovereign spirit of the book is the spirit of Sterne, and its affinity is to the *Sentimental Journey*. The plot is no more than a light framework for the episodes, though Mackenzie, in common with most of Sterne's followers, has raised the narrative interest to a pitch beyond what his master thought necessary.   Harley, a poor country gentleman, goes up to London to make interest for a lease of some Crown lands ; he meets beggars, tricksters and madmen ; is charitable ; is duped ;

---

[1] Ascribed by Cushing to Charles Henry Wilson of the Inner Temple, editor of *Brookiana, Swiftiana* and *Beauties of Burke*.

[2] Henry Mackenzie (1745–1831), attorney for the Crown, comptroller of the taxes for Scotland, and miscellaneous writer. His novels are *The Man of Feeling* (1771), *The Man of the World* (1773) and *Julia de Roubigné* (1777). All were published anonymously.

restores a wretched woman to her father; fails of his
lease and returns home; falls into love and into decline;
proposes, is accepted, and dies of joy. The disjointed
movement of the book is emphasized in every way
possible. The novel was to be " different from most
others "; [1] it was to concern itself with sensibilities, not
with events, or even characters; and it is entirely in
keeping that the manuscript account of Harley's life
should begin at Chapter XI and suffer under the depre-
dations of a sporting curate in search of wadding. It is
the moment that matters, the throb of the pitiful heart,
the gleam of humour, the sudden gushing of the sense
of brotherhood between men; Mackenzie records these
instants of heightened sensibility and deliberately sinks
all that lies between. " I could never find the author
in one strain for two chapters together," says the sporting
curate, and his friend on examination describes the
manuscript as " a bundle of little episodes . . . put
together without art." This deprecation has a com-
placent air about it; Mackenzie's omissions and excursions are about as artless as Sterne's, and, like many of
his generation, he enjoyed sacrificing a few rules of composition on the tasteful, rustic altar of Nature and the
Heart.

The *Man of Feeling* is always deft and sometimes moving; it is various and brief, and the " cordial drops "
that begin to fall on the third page are, in the first place,
really cordial,—there is no doubt about the pathos of the
old dog who, as his ruined master leaves his farm, stretches
himself under his wonted gooseberry-bush and dies,—
and, in the second place, are relieved by touches of irony
and demure satire. It is the most perfect and most
conscious expression, after Sterne, of that type of novel
which relies for interest on a delicate variety of emotional

[1] v. *Anecdotes and Egotisms of Henry Mackenzie*, p. 186. *My Own
Works*; ed. H. W. Thompson (1927).

hue. What could be done by honest incompetence along these lines may be seen in the work of Jane Timbury,[1] whose *Philanthropic Rambler* (1790) is a series of incidents grouped round the figure of Benevolus, who goes about London doing good. His activities are very meritorious but very dull.

It is a proof of the comparative stagnation of the novel, as a whole, in the 'seventies, however lively its fragments, that this fourfold classification under the names of the four great masters is so satisfactory, and that such a thin fringe of books remains outside it. The reader, looking for variety, will find that Oriental apologues were still written on the old theme of submission to Providence, and enlivened, now that they were spread out to fill a volume, with political allegories and romantic incident;[2] that a slight and tangled thread of so-called historical fiction persisted,[3] and that one or two Lucianic satires appeared;[4] that clergymen were beginning to

[1] Jane Timbury was perhaps a bookseller; her *Philanthropic Rambler* (1790) is " Printed for and sold by the Author, Petty France, Westminster." She published a novel, *The Male-Coquette*, anonymously in 1770, and with her name in 1788 ; a so-called poem, *The History of Tobit*, a versification of the *Story of Le Fevre* in 1787, and *The Philanthropic Rambler* in 1790, with a sequel in 1791. The title-page of the last book refers to a work called *The Triumph of Friendship*.

[2] E.g. *The History of Rhedi, the Hermit of Mount Ararat* (1773), published anonymously by the Rev. William Duff (1732–1815), a minister of Aberdeenshire ; *The Viziers ; or, the Enchanted Labyrinth*, by Madame Fauques de Vaucluse (1774), (this book was written in English by the French authoress) ; *The History of Arsaces, Prince of Betlis*, by the Editor of *Chrysal* (*i.e.* Charles Johnstone) ; *The School for Majesty ; or, the Sufferings of Zomelli* (1784); *The Hermit of Caucasus* (1796), by Joseph Moser. Orientalism is continually renewed by translations from the Arabic, Persian and Turkish, of more or less authenticity ; the East of *Rasselas* grows gradually into the East of Byron. [3] *v.* Ch. VI.

[4] E.g. *A Trip to Melasge ; or, Concise Instructions to a Young Gentleman entering into Life ; with his Observations on the Genius, Manners, Ton, Opinions, Philosophy, and Morals of the Melasgeans* (1778); *The Travels of Hildebrand Bowman, Esq. into Carnovirria, Taupiniera, Olfactaria, and Auditante, in New Zealand ; in the island of Bonhommica, and in the powerful Kingdom of Luxo-Voluptas, on the great Southern Continent* (1778); and *The Man of the Moon ; or Travels into the Lunar Regions, by the Man of the People* (1783), published anonymously by W. Thomson, Lit.D. (1746–1817).

use the novel to supplement the pulpit, in which case
we may prepare for an intolerable deal of good counsel
to one halfpennyworth of story ; [1] and that one or two
obscure writers were experimenting along the line that
divides prose from verse, and producing stories that were
in effect only relaxed poems.[2]   He will also find that the
heroic romances, though out of favour, had not been
quite forgotten ; [3] he will pick up the tracks of Goldsmith's *Vicar* [4] often, and once at least those of that odd
creature, *John Buncle*, for Dr. Cogan's [5] *John Buncle,
Junior, Gentleman* (1776) anticipates the trend of modern
imagination by providing that mountaineering dialec-
tician with a son and giving an amusing account of their
relationship, in which the younger man, a whimsical
sentimentalist of the newer mode, describes his father as
" such a Bigot for *enlarged sentiments*, and so furious for
moderation, that he would be often tempted to *damn* a
man for want of *charity*."   But in spite of such small
gratifications he will probably conclude that the critics'
complaints of the exhaustion of the novel were, if not
justified by the event, thoroughly understandable.   The
novel was failing to improve its ground.   The only new
type that the critics recognized was that of Fanny Burney,
which, however delightful, might be held to betray
decadence, since the " polish of fashionable life " in it,
though it smoothed away the exaggerations which we
find in Smollett, likewise diminished the comic energy

---

[1] *E.g.* Rev. James Penn, vicar of Clavering-cum-Langley in Essex,
and Lecturer at St. Ann and Agnes, Aldersgate, wrote *The Farmer's
Daughter of Essex* (1767) and the *Surry Cottage* (1779) ; and Rev.
James Thomson *The Denial, or the Happy Retreat* (1790).

[2] *v.* Ch. IX.   [3] *v.* Ch. VI.

[4] E.g. *The Vicar of Lansdowne ; or Country Quarters* (1789), by
Maria Regina Dalton, later Roche.

[5] Thomas Cogan (1736–1818), " the free-thinking man-midwife,"
passed from the nonconformist ministry to the study of medicine in
Holland, specialized in obstretrics in London, helped to found the
Royal Humane Society, settled eventually in Bath, where he took up
farming, and wrote on ethics and theology. *John Buncle, Junior,
Gentleman,* is his only novel.

and variety, while the scenes were more loosely connected than in the " laboured and intricate plots of Fielding." [1]

Meanwhile, as is always the case with work that is primarily imitative, the accepted themes were repeated in a shallower tone and overlaid with all the romantic incidents of disguise, abduction, lost heirs and mistaken identity, which had been for hundreds of years the story-teller's stock in trade. In spite of critical admonitions,[2] the average novelist paid, on the whole, very little attention to the probable, and the novel in consequence slipped farther away from reality, as though a window on to the outer world had been changed to a magic lantern. " The incidents which fall under every one's inspection," wrote Jenner, " like a rural landscape, will please universally, from the mere force of nature." [3] But the pleasures of recognition to the general reader are less great than the pleasures of surprise, and where there was one Jenner there were ten or twenty Miss Clarinthia Ludfords. That young lady's criterion of excellence in novels is recorded by Mrs. Charlotte Smith in *Ethelinde* (1789). " The only fault I find with some of the latest is, that they are too probable," she remarks, " and I fancy myself reading what is true. Now the thing I like is to be carried out of myself by a fiction quite out of common life, and to get among scenes and people of another world." Unfortunately these fictions quite out of common life were as stereotyped as the hero's compliments [4] or the heroine's wedding-dress (which is invariably a white lutestring negligee with silver spots, until the

---

[1] v. *Critical Review*, June 1788, on *Henry and Isabella* (by Mrs. Anne Hughes).

[2] E.g. *Critical Review* on the *Embarrassed Attachment*, by Miss Charlotte Elizabeth Saunders. " To recover a lover, supposed to have been drowned, and a father cast on the coast of Guinea, are too much for one work."

[3] v. *Placid Man*, Bk. VI, Ch. I.

[4] Or his name. On a moderate estimate, eighty per cent. of the

French Revolution ruined the silk trade and put her into book muslin and fine white calico). The author of *Argal ; or the Silver Devil* (1793), warning his readers that certain attractions are not to be looked for in his pages, epitomizes some of these plots. There will be found, he writes, " no cross papa with his Phenix of a daughter, so beautiful, mild, benevolent, dutiful, in spite of persecution, who, when she is distressed, prefers starving in a garret on the miserable pittance she earns by painting fan-mounts, to affluence with a man, who does not, in her opinion equal another, that has treated her with contempt. No heroine who most heroically revenges herself upon herself, for the supposed infidelity of her lover, and forgoing the pleasures suitable to her age, mortifies in the country by a constant round of visits, among the dirty inhabitants of a dirty village, immersed in medicines, beggary and salves. No sprained ankles, convenient hospitable cottages, neat old women, with their wonderful daughters, harpsichords, books," . . . etc., etc. We need not follow him farther. From this common stock of foolish incident the circulating library novels were compounded, but it would be a mistake to think that the grosser improbabilities were confined to them. To take only two points ; the extraordinary taste for dramatic effect that causes humane people to leave their friends in the most painful mistakes and even to torture them with ambiguous speeches, while the grand discovery that is to assure their happiness is being stage-managed, is found in books of all shades of merit ; while we are asked by writers of standing to believe that small-pox can so alter, even without disfiguring, a face, that a lover will not recognize his mistress or a son his

---

heroes are called Henry. William, on the other hand, is a name of dubious, often villainous, complexion. In the matter of surnames, the authors seldom step outside the Richardsonian nomenclature of Danby, Danvers, Selby, Wilmot, etc.

father, and that a man can thereby be enabled to woo his beloved twice over without detection, but at the cost of conceiving a strange jealousy of his former self.[1]

The taste for strong scenes was universal. We may connect it in part with the rudimentary state of characterization in all but a few writers, which left the author to get his interest out of his situations. But it is not necessary to explain the appearance of sensationalism in a form of popular entertainment. It goes without saying that it will be there. The desire to shock and be shocked is endemic in human nature, and only the sophisticated feel that it needs apology. The novel-readers at the end of the eighteenth century relished an emotional orgy. They did not require that the situation should be carefully elaborated, and they were quite content that mental states should be suggested by a conventional phrase or gesture,—a faint shriek or a clutched brow; but they demanded and enjoyed scenes in which strong and varied passions exploded one after another like gaudy fireworks.[2] Incredible disturbances take place beside death-beds (real or presumed); misguided husbands extend themselves in agony on the floor, rush out to fight duels in the shrubbery with unrecognized sons and brothers, and rush back dripping with blood into the sick-room; false friends are unmasked and villains threaten vengeance across the counterpane;

---

[1] Cf. Lady Mary Walker's *Munster Village* (1778), Mrs. Gunning's *Anecdotes of the Dellborough Family* (1792) and Richard Griffith's *Gordian Knot* (1769).

[2] For examples *v.* the last scenes of *The Castles of Athlin and Dunbayne* (1789) by Mrs. Radcliffe, and of Mrs. Robinson's *Angelina* (1796). The anonymous *Precipitate Choice* (1772) tells how Lord Ossory marries the beautiful and deplorable Isabella and becomes aware afterwards that her cousin Harriet really commands his affections. Both struggle for self-control, but the revengeful Isabella drugs Harriet, and Ossory cannot forbear taking advantage of her situation. After this, death and murder are liberally spread. This is by no means an exceptionally lurid plot.

mysteries hang on the tantalizing edge of solution, while the physician vainly pleads that repose is the patient's one chance of life; forgiving friends hide behind the curtains of the repentant wrongdoer's deathbed, and erupt at the right moment of the conversation to assure him of pardon and receive his expiring breath or arrest his decay; lastly, if death supervenes, the nearest relatives " madden " with grief, cling to the corpse and have to be forcibly removed. Love scenes take their tremendous way through jealousy, accusation, suffering, regret, abasement and forgiveness to fresh alienation. Fortune's wheel is wrenched round at a giddy rate, and the entire cast are jerked from posture to posture, with barely time to gasp out the appropriate comments. The reasonable plots of Mrs. Brooke and Miss Burney, though the future lay with them, are insignificant in number beside the unreasonable ones; their example penetrated but slowly; and during the whole of our period the critics complain of the abuse of the marvellous in motive and incident. Thus in 1775 the *Monthly Review* gave a synopsis of a novel published by the brothers Noble, *The Morning Ramble ; or History of Miss Evelyn.*

" A young lady in love with her supposed uncle.— An old dotard in love with this same young lady, his supposed granddaughter. These amours made honest by the help of a gypsy, whose child the loved and loving fair one is said to be.—Her virgin chastity attempted by the ancient lover, and rescued by the younger.—Her virgin chastity again attempted by the friend of her beloved *Adonis*, and again rescued by a mad adventurer.—The rescued fair conducted by her new inamorato to the mouth of a dismal cave (in which he threatens instantly to end his life before her eyes, unless she consents to repay his services with those charms which he had preserved) and there terrified into a promise of marriage.—A *third ravishment*, and a murder, introduced for the sake of *variety* and *entertainment*, into the husband's story of himself.—The wife, unmindful of her holy vow, on a sudden suffering her first passion to kindle.—Her husband in a fit of jealousy, encountering his innocent rival.—The helpless fair rushing between their swords.—Wounded.—Expiring.—Lamented.

"This is a true bill of fare of the Morning's Ramble. A very pretty, *romantic, sentimental* morning's entertainment for *Miss in her Teens.*"

It must have been the opulence of the menu that gave the *Monthly* qualms, for there was nothing unusual in the separate dishes. Rape, jealous frenzy and murder are staple ingredients of these novels, and the general method is cumulative. "Honorius and his friend Raymond, accompanied by the author, for the purpose of writing these two volumes," remarked the *Critical* of Thistlethwaite's *Man of Experience* (1778), "in the course of less than a week are witnesses to more scenes of villany than almost any man is unfortunate enough to see in his life." Among professional novelists sensationalism became such a habit of mind,—or perhaps one had better say of the pen,—that they powdered their compositions with irrelevant calamities, and we find the *Monthly* (Nov. 1797, p. 341) complaining that "the sad catastrophe of Lord Trecastle, who kills his son by mistake, is one of those events which inspire horror without answering any purpose, except that of enriching the heroine, who wanted no addition of fortune." Some of the incidents which occur most frequently, notably duels and abductions, can be paralleled again and again in contemporary newspapers and magazines; but too much weight need not be given to this consideration. The novelists were not painting nature, but outdoing her. It is significant that they make little of the sensational possibilities of slavery, a subject much in the public mind; [1] it is also significant that the iniquitous use of private madhouses as places of confinement for the sane, of which several cases came up for judgment in the 'seventies, was so seldom reflected in the novel.[2] Here was a theme richly sensational and vouched for in fact, and it was practically passed over. Sensationalism and propaganda had not yet joined hands, as they did in the " revolutionary " novelists. Moreover, so slight had the contact of the novel with life become, that even sensationalism was out of date. Plenty of material, amassed by the strong nerves of eighteenth-century travellers and historians, lay at hand, but at present it was merely " curious " not " terrific." The novelists had not learnt to use it, although they would occasionally drop a raw lump of horror into the middle of a jauntily-scribbled picaresque by way of variety.

Two points have some interest in connection with the sensationalism of the eighteenth century. In the first place there is, on the whole, little insistence on physical pain, until the excitement of the French Revolution had taught the nerves of polite readers to thrill half-pleasurably to this violent stimulus. Descriptions of torments can be found, though there are fewer in the novels than in the magazines,—they were " curious " to the obtuse and " painfully interesting " to the friend of humanity,— but they are not dwelt on. Secondly, one notes the extraordinary pervasiveness through all grades of the novel of the theme of incest. The notorious *Morning Ramble* began with a double suggestion of incest, averted,

[1] Plantation scenes are introduced into Mackenzie's *Julia de Roubigné* (1777), Johnstone's *Juniper Jack* (1781), Moore's *Zeluco* (1789) and Mrs. Smith's *Wanderings of Warwick* (1794), and later they become more frequent ; but they are introduced rather for their philanthropic than their sensational value.

[2] v. *Gentleman's Magazine*, 1772, pp. 195, 340, 590, and *Annual Register* for Feb. 1771. I have found imprisonment in a private madhouse introduced into only two novels before Holcroft's *Anna St. Ives* (1792), i.e. *The Fruitless Repentance* (1769) and *The Egg, or Memoirs of Gregory Giddy, Esq.* (1772).

as is so often the case, by the discovery that some jugglery has been practised with babes in cradles. This was the way of Fletcher in *A King and No King*, and a disingenuous way it is. Careless nurses, gypsies, unacknowledged marriages, changes of name,—all these devices are used to introduce the theme of incestuous love, and used again to avert the tragedy and unite the lovers. The novelists perpetually hover round the subject; they refer to it by suggestion to enrich the heroine's distress, even if it forms no part of the plot proper, and the persecuting lover, who is most distasteful to her, frequently turns out to be her near relative.[1] Even if the tragedy is not averted, which is sometimes the case, especially when it forms part of the history of some elderly penitent, the eighteenth century preferred that the protagonists should be the victims of a mistake rather than rebels.[2] Some hints of sophistry there are, but very few; and there are no Giovannis or Annabellas. " Incest," says Shelley, " is, like many other incorrect things, a very poetical circumstance. It may be the excess of love or hate. It may be the defiance of everything for the sake of another, which clothes itself in the glory of the highest heroism ; it may be that cynical rage which, confounding the good and the bad in existing opinions, breaks through them for the purpose of rioting in selfish antipathy." [3] But in the eighteenth-century novel it is none of these things ; it is an exciting accident.

The nearest approach to a serious handling of the theme is in *The History of Tom Rigby* (1773), a " religious novel " by John Chater, an ex-minister of the Independent Church, turned bookseller and library-keeper.[4]

[1] Cf. *The Romance of the Forest* (1791) by Mrs. Radcliffe, and Mrs. Anne Hughes' *Henry and Isabella*.

[2] v. *Reuben, or the Suicide* (1787) and *Death's a Friend* (1788) by the Author of *The Bastard*.

[3] v. Letter to Maria Gisborne, Nov. 16th, 1819.

[4] v. Walter Wilson's *History and Antiquities of Dissenting Churches*, III, p. 112.

This odd and interesting book, which is full of clues for the literary historian and defies neat classification, begins with a pleasant but, as it turns out, rather irrelevant prologue in the style of Fielding, and then, shedding its irony, heels over suddenly towards a high-pitched religious romance, recalling *The Fool of Quality*, though still interspersed with natural scenes and dialogue. Tom Rigby meets a dark, morose young man called Hillaston, with the reputation of a madman and a mania for spending his time in enormous walking-tours, punctuated by visits to inns where he has deposited stores of clean shirts. Tom watches this man of mystery perform benevolences, chastise seducers and rescue innocence with an unmoved countenance and a few bitter words. At last, fearing madness, he confesses to Tom his secret guilt, after practising the avowal in the midst of barren heaths and pathless mountains to the accompaniment of the howling tempest, until at last he can bear to hear his own words. He loves his sister; he has fled from his passion as far as the East Indies, but without avail; he is still fighting his delusion, but on the verge of defeat, and Tom hears presently of his suicide. Then the pattern is repeated with variations, for Tom, who is illegitimate, finds that his beloved Maria Leeson is his half-sister. Chater has sincerity enough to carry him through the strange rencounter of the mother with her acknowledged and unacknowledged child, and the rhetoric of her death-bed, though elaborate, is not distasteful. Tom submits to his fate and masters his mind, for Chater has something of Brooke's luxuriating sense of the stern lessons of adversity. From this point the prospect gradually clears and the ways are made smooth towards the novelist's happy ending. Hillaston returns, cured of his passion by a frustrated suicide, and the two young men solve their problem by a happy transference of their affections. One smiles without resentment at the artifice

of the ending and at Chater's astute combination of a
daring thrill with a sound and cheerful morality, for at
least it is not chance that brings about the solution, and
the possibility of contending with one's passions is
stoutly maintained.

"Daring," however, is perhaps not the right word to
apply to the theme of incest, since not a critic protested
against it. Perhaps the large part played by chance in
these stories made them appear innocuous ; perhaps the
artificiality of these permutations and combinations of
consanguinity was so apparent that the mind never
seized on the theme as real at all. At any rate there
were precedents in Fielding and parallels in foreign
novels ;[1] and the theme, to a certain extent, lived on the
stage.[2] Henry Mackenzie in his *Man of the World* (1773)
employs a barely avoided crime of this kind as a motive
of repentance, as did Fielding in *Tom Jones*, and the
effect was crudely imitated in the anonymous *Solitary
Castle* (1789). Henry Brooke introduces it at the end
of *Juliet Grenville* (1774) to intensify the emotion by
severing Juliet and Lord Thomas at the height of their
felicity, and to teach them yet a deeper submission and
renunciation. It is casually inserted, without the excuse
of Brooke's fervour, at the end of a great many books, to
provide the last check, the unexpected obstacle suddenly
thrown in the course of a plighted pair to the altar, for
this last-minute suspense was a regular feature of novels,
and it was by no means necessary for it to arise out of
the foregoing events. Lastly, and most discreditably,
incest supplies the *haut goût* of picaresques and tales of
travel. In *The Adventures of Jonathan Corncob, Loyal*

---

[1] *E.g.* Dubois Fontenelle's *Effects of the Passions*, translated in
1788 and Gellert's *Swedish Countess of G——*, translated first in
1757 and twice in 1776, by A Lady and by the Rev. Mr. N ...
[2] *E.g.* Hoole's *Timanthes* (1770) based on the *Demophoon* of
Metastasio, and Cumberland's *Mysterious Husband* (1783). Walpole's
Mysterious Mother was unacted, and was only released for sale by the
author in 1796.

American Refugee, Written by Himself (1787), the hero, visiting Barbadoes, is introduced to a planter, who, by means of connections with his own daughter by a negro woman, his granddaughter and great-granddaughter, has succeeded in " washing himself white " by the age of sixty, for his great-great-grandchild is fair.   The point, of course, is not the possibility of such an atrocity, but that the writer could offer such an anecdote as a *bonne bouche*.[1]

The theme has been so closely associated with romantic and revolutionary poets that its wide dispersion in the 'seventies and 'eighties, a generation before the master utterances of romantic poetry, is worthy of note.   It was perhaps one of the many signs of that blind craving for the passionate and extraordinary, which the calm façade of eighteenth-century literature had never wholly con-cealed, and which now became from year to year more conspicuous.   The romantic poets did not re-introduce the theme ; they found it, in the first place, in the novels that they devoured as boys.   What they did was to make it painfully real ;[2] and after that it was not long before public taste turned against it.

The stagnation of the novel in the 'seventies and early 'eighties was not broken by any salutary shocks from abroad.   Plenty of French fiction was imported and translated ;[3] Voltaire was read and condemned and Madame Riccoboni read and praised, but the English novel was not greatly affected by either.   Something of

[1] Incest avoided or suspected appears in the following novels : *Indiana Danby* (1765), *The Adventures of a Jesuit* (1771), *The Modern Fine Gentleman* (1774), *The Recess* (1783–5) by Sophia Lee, *Helena* (1788) by a Lady of Distinction, *Argus, the House-dog at Eadlip* (1789), *Zeluco* (1789) by Dr. John Moore, *Gabrielle de Vergy* (1790), Mrs. Smith's *Celestina* (1791), Mrs. Robinson's *Vancenza* (1792).

[2] A turning point in the popular attitude to this theme is suggested by the *Critical Review* (Jan. 1799).   Benjamin Thompson, Junior, translator of Kotzebue's *Adelaide of Wolfingen*, a play in which un-witting incest ends in murder and death, suggests that the situation might have been resolved by the usual expedient of a change of babes at birth.   The *Critical*, however, disdains the evasion.

[3] *v.* Appendix I.

the French delicacy of touch and economy of material was reflected in Mrs. Brooke, who translated Madame Riccoboni's *Milady Catesby*, and John Sealy can flourish a sentiment and counter it with a piece of elegant cynicism quite in the style of " our ingenious neighbours " ;[1] but, while it is not difficult to pick out points of contact between individual writers, or to find themes, like that of parental tyranny or imprisonment in a convent, which were bandied to and fro across the Channel and thus re-emphasized, nevertheless France did not at this time exercise any determining influence over English fiction, and even the *conte philosophique* had to wait for Bage before its seed became fertile in English ground. German books at this time impinged seldom on the literary world in England, and though Wieland was known, and young *Werter* at the end of the 'seventies made his sorrows felt, the only type of English work that shows unmistakable marks of German origin is the Scriptural romance. These highly-ornamented versions of Biblical stories, imitated from the " loose poetry " of Gessner's *Death of Abel*[2] and from Klopstock, were all that the average reader knew of German literature, and Clara Reeve calls them *tout court* " the German stories." The Reverend John Macgowan, Baptist minister in Bishopsgate, perpetrated a *Life of Joseph, Son of Israel*, in eight books (1771). Of the style it is sufficient to say that the author liked decoration, so that Joseph, before he dreamed a dream, " was seized by the lulling charms of balmy rest, and sunk beneath the superiority of the angel of

---

[1] John Sealy, Master of the Academy in Bridgewater Square, London, published educational works, *The Loves of Calisto and Emira ; or, the Fatal Legacy* (1776) and *Moral Tales after the Eastern Manner* (1773). The former suggests a French original, though none is acknowledged ; the latter is Oriental, with Biblical and Ossianic reminiscences.

[2] Translated by Mary Collyer (1761) ; cf. also *The Death of Cain* (1789) by a Lady, published as a continuation of Gessner's *Death of Abel*.

drowsiness "; of the substance, that the old story is modishly equipped with romantic incident, and that it is in saving Potiphar's wife from a lion that Joseph first " made a criminal impression on the mind of the lady." " Shall we not slay our brother," asks Reuben, " for the licentious rovings of unbridled imagination ? " Macgowan, however, lived to see several reprints of his work and a translation into Gaelic.

This stream of influence, definite as it was, affected only a very small number of books, and those were novels only in the most liberal contemporary sense of the word. The new life that was presently to vitalize the novel was not of foreign origin, nor was it so much a matter of new themes as of greater honesty and a higher standard of technique. The new themes occur, however, and are important, because they help to dispel the illusion of exhaustion. One notices with what relief the critics welcome the smallest departure from the beaten track of love and roguery. " A composition of small politics and love," wrote the *Monthly* reviewer, describing *The General Election* (1775), " which, if it is not an improvement, is at least a variation on the ingredients of a modern novel." The measure of his boredom can be gauged, at some cost, if we turn to the book itself, in which the fairly promising theme of a family divided against itself by political bigotry is shelved in favour of discursive comment on Wilkes and liberty, with a composing draught of sensibility at the end.

It is indeed singular how slowly the prevailing interests of the day, as they are reflected in the magazines, make their way into the novel. Education, religious toleration and the crusade in favour of the humane treatment of animals appear frequently, for they blend easily with the sensibility and didacticism that were the dominant notes in fiction ; but such important aspects of society as trade, medicine, and the administration of justice are hardly to be found, except as they serve the comic purposes of the picaresque. Even the scenes on Execution Day, so fully reported by the Press, are not found in novels. Warfare exists to provide sensibility with the figure of the maimed veteran. Travel and exploration, which fill page after page of contemporary magazines and suggested themes to poets, do not enlarge the outlook of the novelist until well on in the 'eighties. There is no English *Paul et Virginie ;* and though Mrs. Brooke's Canadian scenes in *Emily Montague* (1769) have real merit and were much praised, Indian affairs, on the other hand, yielded chiefly the figures of the English nabob, who could be studied at Bath and Cheltenham, and of the enlightened Brahmin, who had not, perhaps, been studied at all. Considering the number of picturesque tours, accounts of and letters from foreign countries that poured from the Press, the tardiness of the novelist in appropriating this rich material is remarkable. Even the American War, with its possibilities of dramatic tension and its mixture of the strange and the familiar in manners and setting, did not immediately attract the novelist, and it was ten years before it was at all freely handled.[1]

One fact must never be lost from view. The novel, with all its insipidity and all its follies, was a widely popular form of entertainment; that is, it nourished the imaginations of a great many people with food which they found pleasant. Here lies the chief, perhaps the only justifiable interest of this obsolete, tenth-rate work, and research moves gladly away from questions of lineage and classification to inquire what attractions these novels offered, and to what emotions they appealed.

[1] The obvious parallel with the Great War is perhaps not very significant, in view of the differences of scale and the immaturity of the novel at this time, as a vehicle of serious conviction. Moreover, the influence of the French Revolution works more quickly; cf. Charlotte Smith's *Celestina* (1791), *Desmond* (1792) and *The Banished Man* (1794).

CHAPTER III

DIDACTICISM AND SENSIBILITY

I

Novels that merely entertain, merit no encouragement, because they divert the mind from more useful objects.—C. BANCROFT, *History of Charles Wentworth*, 1770.

WHEN the *Critical* reviewer said of the author of *Constantia* (1770) that "his intentions as a man sufficiently apologize for his irregularities as a writer," he was merely reaffirming the official creed of authors, critics and public, that the function of the novel was explicitly educational and that its main business was to inculcate morality by example. Eighteen years later he, or his successor, still occupied the same position. "A common tale," runs the notice of *The Penitent Prostitute* (1788), "we fear too common, eked out with trite hackneyed reflections, newspaper essays, and trifling episodes. But the author enlists on the side of virtue; and we respect the meanest pioneer of that camp." That vast and tidy camp of virtue, with its grand and simple plan, is one of the spectacles of the eighteenth century. The great writers move about its streets and harangue in its prætorium, while the humbler brethren toil, or pretend to toil, at its ramparts. Some pay it lip-service, many a deeper allegiance; few cared or dared to stand out. Conduct, the definition and application of the general moral laws that should govern the behaviour of man in society, was the prevailing intellectual interest of the age, and naturally enough this interest was reflected in the novel. It was as conduct-books that Richardson recommended his *Pamela*, his *Clarissa* and his *Sir Charles Grandison*. The church-going, sermon-reading middle classes liked a good plain moral at the end of a book, as they liked a farce after a tragedy, feeling that the performance was incomplete without it, and not over-fastidious as to its connection with what went before. Critics and novelists of the sterner breed scouted mere " amusement " as waste of time : the business of the novel was to teach those who by nature and upbringing were unqualified for serious study.[1] To this end, not only must the novel always show life subservient to moral law, but in addition a little solid information, on whatever pretence inserted, was always favourably received—at least by the critics, for there are not wanting hints of rebellion on the part of the younger readers. No reviewer ever complains of irrelevance in face of the interpolated sermons, dissertations on slavery, Greek music, the penal laws, and the like, which so often impede the progress of a love-tale.[2] The digressions might not be strictly germane to the story, but they were welcome superfluities, and would, it might be hoped, instil a little information, willy-nilly, into the class, already formid-able in size, that read nothing but novels. Authors themselves agreed that the didactic function of the novel would bear enlargement, for, as the author of *Wanley Penson, or the Melancholy Man* (1791), writes, " history

[1] Cf. *Critical*, May 1793, p. 44 ; also *Female Friendship* (1770) : " A large majority, especially of the fair sex, have not time nor talents for the investigation of abstract principles in moral and social life; wherefore a lighter kind of study is essential."

[2] v. e.g. *The Independent* (1784) and *Laura* (1790), by Andrew Macdonald ; also the letter on poverty among the lower classes in Normandy in *Juliana* (1786), by the Author of *Francis the Philanthro-pist*. The novelist's ethical functions are fully catalogued by John Potter in his *Virtuous Villagers* (1784) : " The author's aim has been solely to correct the mistakes of the heart, to enlarge the boundaries of human understanding, to point out the social obligations, to display the beauties of domestic felicity, and to give ardor and confidence to virtue." Solely !

and geography, nay even philosophy and divinity, would readily slide into their compositions . . . and I should not think a dissemination of the rudiments of some of the polite arts impracticable by their means." Nevertheless, it is to be noticed that this didactic prepossession is always strongest with mediocre novelists and with critics who are reviewing mediocre novels; these they often acquit or condemn wholly on moral grounds, whereas before a good book they do not indeed forget their function as public watchdogs, but they remember that they have other functions as well, now that there is a chance to exercise them. Other signs of a surfeit may be detected, which increase in number as the century draws to its close. Even in 1770 the *Critical* found itself unable to follow Bancroft in his logical contention that, since the main business of a novel is to teach, it had better not be too interesting, while in 1772 the *Monthly* remarked dryly of the *Test of Filial Duty* : " The excellent lessons of morality which this work inculcates will not be able to save it from oblivion." On the part of the authors we have the mild scepticism, the moderate hopes of Graves and Jenner, and, after 1790, an increasing taste for passion to which, rather than to any widespread enlightenment about the processes of imaginative art, we must ascribe the recession of the didactic spirit. In the 'seventies and 'eighties, however, the tradition was so strong that it took a very self-sufficient, indeed a very brazen man to defy it.

Theoretically, then, the business of fable was to illustrate moral truth ; it was an *exemplum* anchored to a text, and like all *exempla* exhibited in its perfection that system of punishments and rewards that we call poetic justice, acknowledging in the term that such justice has never been displayed except in the golden world of the poet. The authors, distributing and annotating their symmetrical awards, were perfectly aware of this, but it was their business not to imitate reality but to redress it, or rather, as the more serious of them would have contended, to pierce through the veils of circumstance and draw to light a deeper reality. Such justice, they held, was done, if not here then hereafter, if not in things worldly then in things spiritual. At any rate, as Clara Reeve remarked, shelving the question, young minds should be shown the truth " through the medium of cheerfulness," lest melancholy should chill their generous efforts. Critics praise the tendency of books in which poetic justice is nicely considered and deplore the tragedies of the innocent.[1] Truth to life was no plea with them, for the painter of fictitious life is not bound by past events and " should take care how he mixes his shades." Did the author assert that his novel was founded on fact, they replied without bating a jot : " It may be so ; but we are sorry that the story has been publicly told." [2] Young minds, they held, are prone to imitate what they read of, and nothing can be more dashing to virtuous emulation than the sight of undeserved misfortunes.

It was practical virtue, not metaphysical truth, that was the goal of effort in the eighteenth century ; and if it had been possible to take the coaches and establishments of the good, and the chains and deathbeds of the bad, as adequate symbols of the " complacency " of virtue and the self-destruction of vice, poetic justice would have been less open to attack than it actually was. But they were not adequate symbols, and the best novelists of the time said as much. There is no poetic justice in Mackenzie's *Julia de Roubigné* (1777), while the principle

---

[1] For the former, v. *Critical*, Dec. 1770, on Mrs. Brooke's translation of Framéry's *Memoirs of the Marquis of St. Forlaix*, and Feb. 1771 on Hull's *Sir William Harrington ;* for the latter, v. *Monthly*, Aug. 1775, on *Julia Benson ; or, The Sufferings of Innocence.*

[2] v. *Monthly*, Jan. 1782, on *A Lesson for Lovers*, and *Critical*, June 1791, on *Gertrude ; or, the Orphan of Llanfruist.*

is angrily attacked by Melmoth through the mouth of
Sir Robert Raymond, the rejected lover of *Emma Corbett*
(1780). Raymond has seen Emma's valiant struggles
with her fate, her long misery and her short happiness;
he has yielded her to another man and learned to regard
her only as one placed in the path of his life " to fix and
concentrate the best of passions " without requiting it;
he has sustained her in death and now, thinking of her
and himself, he cries out indignantly on the justice of
novels : " Hath virtue no joys of her *own* ?—joys, which
generous sorrow only can produce ? Is the sacred
struggle of the good man *altogether afflictive* ? "[1]   This,
however, was a flight above the average reviewer, who
grumbled because Miss Burney had not managed to
assure Cecilia's fortune, and scolded Mackenzie for saving his *Man of the World* (1773) *per una lagrimetta*, since
that Baronet " should either have been sent to the devil,
or his reformation should have been in consequence of a
long and bitter repentance."   The reviewers, as will be
seen, weigh out guilt and expiation with a rhadamanthine
scrupulosity.   Briefly, poetic justice can be suspended
on only one consideration, and that is not the irresponsibility of the picaresque, which is intermittent and apt to
give way in the last ten pages, but that product of
sensibility, the cult of distress.

On another point of method these ardent moralists
were not unanimous.   Is virtue better stimulated by the
contemplation of " mixed " or " exemplary " characters ?
Is Tom Jones or Sir Charles Grandison the better pre-
ceptor ?   Would one more enjoy (though the debaters

---

[1] *Emma Corbett* was described by the author as " founded on some
recent circumstances which happened in America "; he seems to
have had in mind the story of Mrs. Ross, who followed her lover in
man's clothes to America, sucked poison from his wound, nursed him
in the woods for six weeks, revealed herself and married him, to die
four years after of poison imbibed from the wound; v. *Scots Mag.*,
1779.   Contact with fact may have helped to guard Melmoth against
poetic justice.

seldom refer openly to enjoyment) identifying oneself in imagination with a faulty or a faultless hero? Opinions differed. On the whole, in spite of frequent protests that the improbably good, like the improbably bad character was out of nature and shocking to reason, the Grandisonians carried the day, if we judge by bulk of testimony. Most of the women were Grandisonians, and the majority of periodical critics. As Clara Reeve pointed out in her *Progress of Romance*, mixed characters in whom virtue is allowed to predominate—Tom Jones, for instance—make dangerous precedents for " young men of warm passions and not strict principles," whereas " no harm can possibly arise from the imitation of a perfect character, though the attempt should fall short of the original." In an age when, as a correspondent to the *Gentleman's Magazine* [1] declared, the estimation of human nature was very much sunk, it was the author's duty to ennoble it, to " raise it to its pitch of primitive grandeur." Exemplary characters were really exemplary then, " perfected and compleated with all the ornaments and embellishments human nature is capable of receiving,"[2] and their conduct underwent a serious and detailed inquisition. Dissimulation was the grand pitfall, especially if there were elopements and disguises in the plot; but the heroine of *Masquerades* (1781) fell from grace in a rather original way, by defending a Saturday night dance for lasting into Sunday.[3] Then there was the question of bad characters. Should they be portrayed

---

[1] *v.* Supplement, 1778, p. 624.

[2] *v.* Dedication to *Lady Frances S——* and *Lady Caroline S——*, by the Miss Minifies (1763).

[3] The same requirements were made in drama. A correspondent of the *Gentleman's Magazine*, Feb. 1778, points out the moral deficiencies of the *School for Scandal*, and contrasts with Sheridan, Cumberland, who " has judiciously executed the whole duty of an author, which is, not *only* to paint nature, but to paint such parts of it as every good man would wish to see imitated." Home, publishing *Alfred* (1778), felt obliged to defend his hero's imposture in going disguised into the Danish camp by analogy with Orestes.

at all? Edward Bancroft thought not; there was the danger of familiarizing the mind with vice; if his readers required contrasts to any of his characters, they might find them among their own acquaintances.[1] The *Critical*, reviewing a translation of *Manon Lescaut* (1786), even assumes that it is impossible for a reader to sympathize with any character that does not reach a high standard of virtue. Manon and her lover " deserve little of our concern, and seldom are they followed by our good wishes." They certainly were not good examples for the young, and it was for the young that reviewers and authors were so deeply concerned. The critical pens bristle round these innocents like *chevaux-de-frise*. They must be guarded from romances, which may make them discontented, and from superstition, in which connection even the " chastened supernatural " of the *Old English Baron*, unaccompanied as it was with " the antidote of laughter and self-evident absurdity," must be viewed with suspicion. For them the novelists introduced those Mentor-characters which stand outside the action and comment upon it, making all its moral bearings perfectly clear; and for them they indited those countless stories of education, in which wise parents inculcate all the virtues, or, alternatively, neglected and passionate children come to a bad end.[2]

Naturally the proportions of doctrine and story-telling vary infinitely. *Village Memoirs*[3] by Joseph Cradock, Esq., a very popular book, is almost entirely given over

---

[1] v. *History of Charles Wentworth* (1770), Preface.
[2] E.g. *The Twin Sisters, or the Effects of Education* (1789), by A Lady, comparing the results of public and private schools; *The Errors of Education*, by Mrs. Eliza Parsons (1791); *The Advantages of Education* (1793), by Prudentia Homespun (*i.e.* Mrs. Jane West), and many others.
[3] The first edition is dated 1765 by mistake for 1775. J. B. Nichols, in his Brief Memoir in Cradock's *Literary and Miscellaneous Essays* (1828), dates the book 1774, and the *Critical* reviewed it in December of that year. 1765 is further disproved by an allusion to the death of Chesterfield, which took place in 1773 (*v.* p. 157).

to instruction. It consists chiefly of letters from a country clergyman to his son in London, who is preparing to take orders, and is full of sound advice on matters human and divine, while, to point the sermons, we follow at the same time the fate of the vicar's daughter, who, neglecting his lessons, falls into fashionable company, is seduced, takes flight and dies repentant. Here the steady pressure of simple moralizing never ceases. On the other hand, in Melmoth's *Family Secrets* (1797) it is often relaxed for chapters, while all the business of an intricate, exciting and tear-stained story is conducted. Appended to the last chapter, however, is a list of fourteen points of morality which the author has endeavoured to enforce in the preceding narrative. The list was omitted from the second edition, a sign of changing fashions and a more sophisticated time.

There was some reality in these didactic themes, for the most frequent bear the stamp of their age and can be illustrated from periodical literature. Its social conscience, for instance, was reflected in the attack on indiscriminating bounty, as distinguished from true charity. Beneficence is incomparably the most popular of the virtues, but the almsgiver has now to consider not only his own salvation but the weal of society; the rain may fall alike on the just and the unjust, but charity must find a deserving object. Goldsmith had recurred often to this line of thought in whimsical self-rebuke, but his humane spendthrifts are spared the worst strokes of fate. Melmoth's Benignus,[1] on the other hand, after six volumes of unflagging benevolence, retires disillusioned to a forest hut, having first sunk the remainder of his

---

[1] v. *Liberal Opinions*. In the first two volumes the meaning is deeper, and the author argues that, since goodness does not ensure happiness, there must be a future state. Later on, however, the point of view alters and the flaw of profusion is found in Benignus' liberality. Melmoth returned to the (second) subject in *Shenstone-Green* (1779).

patrimony on twelve sacks of common biscuit, which do
indeed last this Timon to the end of his pilgrimage.
Then there is the question of duelling, about which the
English conscience was at no time easy. At various points
during our period it was declared to be on the increase,
and gave fresh matter for perturbation and ridicule.[1] It
was no longer confined to the upper classes, in which the
practice might be to some extent justified, for in 1774
two private soldiers in Ireland fought for forty minutes
with the most desperate intention, as if they had been
their betters ; while, at the other end of the social scale,
the Duke of York gave it his sanction when in 1789 he
condescended to meet Colonel Lenox at Wimbledon
and had his curl grazed by his opponent's bullet, whereat
fashionable youth throughout the town incontinently
broke forth into " Wimbledon curls." The women are,
without exception, dead against the duel ; the men
accept it as a deplorable custom to which, at a pinch,
they must conform ; some few even defend it, on the
grounds that the brutish elements in society need to be
kept in awe by the threat of punishment.[2] It was, of

[1] v. *Gentleman's Magazine*. Historical Chronicle, Dec. 16th,
1774, and Domestic Occurrences, May 26th, 1789. Cf. also Dec.
1779, a poem, *The Duellists*, which includes the pertinent question :

> Can the vague pistol's vagrant aim
> Determine aught of right and wrong ?

and calls on men to leave this " Gothic way." The *Sentimental
Magazine*, a short-lived affair, designed to catch the public taste (the
design miscarried), notes the revival of duelling; v. March 1773, I, p. 11.
[2] This is the line of defence in Richard Griffith's *Gordian Knot*
(1769). Cumberland's *Arundel* (1789)—an exception to the rule—
thrashes the question out with a friend, when he expects to be challenged, and gives the decision in favour of fighting. John Fitzorton
in Melmoth's *Family Secrets* (1797), accepts " the imperious compacts
of social men," though conscience speaks against them, and this is
the situation of many men, often solved in practice by a determination
to stand fire without returning it. Such conduct, however, was
sometimes felt to be unfair to the opponent. Dr. John Moore
(*Mordaunt*, Letter XXIV, 1800) admits that duelling serves a purpose,
and proposes to reduce it by instituting a court of honour, with
penalties. Bage goes out of his way to present duelling in a ludicrous
light, but he is not intolerant and recognises the pressure of society

course, a most useful piece of machinery for a novelist, whether for softening hearts or disposing of unwanted characters, and it may be that this usefulness is the reason that the moral issue is seldom squarely met. The rights and wrongs of the question are thrashed out, not in the mind of a young man confronted with the choice between fighting and social disgrace, but in the letters of monitory relatives after the fact.[1] Even Sir Charles Grandison, who, it will be remembered, paid the matter some attention, was in the strong position of being an admirable swordsman who had already proved his courage. The first hero to bear the blow and the stigma for conscience' sake is Holcroft's Frank Henley in *Anna St. Ives* (1792), and he is soon able to re-establish himself by saving his enemy from drowning, though, to do Holcroft justice, it is not his gallant plunge that demands admiration so much as his perseverance in the Royal Humane Society's methods of life-saving.

Duelling, then, though a subject of constant pre-occupation, was in reality baulked by the novelist, but gaming and intrigue, the other scandals of the time, were more manageable. Gaming is one of the women's subjects. The apprehensive wife, raking together the sacred embers of her hearth, sees her infatuated husband scatter them once more, and draws her children to her in the cold wind of misfortune. From the moment when she is told that she is no longer mistress of these splendid apartments, through the arrival of the bailiffs

---

(cf. Capt. O'Donnel in *Barham Downs* (1784)). To Godwin (*Caleb Williams*, I, p. 274, 2nd ed.), " duelling is the vilest of all egotism, treating the public, which has a claim to all my powers, as if it were nothing, and myself, or rather an unintelligible chimera I annex to myself, as if it were entitled to my exclusive attention."

[1] Exceptions are a character in an episode of *Pamela Howard* (1773), who, though a soldier, will not fight a private duel, and is ruined in consequence ; Arundel (v. above, p. 78, *n.* 1) and to some extent the hero of Rev. James Thomson's *Denial ; or, the Happy Retreat* (1790), who debates, fights, suffers, and acknowledges himself wrong.

and the retreat to mean lodgings, to the final disaster
(or alternatively penitence and reform) of her husband,
the novelist's eye is turned on her.[1] It is not gaming
that is studied, but the effects of gaming on the domestic
circle, and this is equally the case when the gamester
is a woman. As for intrigue, the scandals in high places
sharpened the edge of that antithesis between simplicity
on one side and luxury and corruption on the other,
which the late eighteenth century was accustomed to
contemplate. Whether it is the wholesome discipline
of a bygone generation, or the innate rectitude of the
Savoyard or the savage, which serves as foil to the perversions of civilization,[2] whether the laws of restraint
are enforced by authority or merely written in the upright
heart, the lesson is always the same, the danger to
virtue of an artificial form of life. The plot that carries
this lesson usually traces the degeneration of some
country-bred girl or youth, exposed to the temptations
of the town; but other familiar figures, such as the
faithful black and the unscrupulous baronet, decorate
the sermon.

A fresh fillip was given to the theme by the publication
of Lord Chesterfield's *Letters to his Son* (1774). Of all
the counsel given in that rather misunderstood book, it
was the methodized practice of insincerity and the sub-

[1] v. *The Sylph* (1779), by Georgiana, Duchess of Devonshire; this
also contains the story of a woman gamester, a type to which the
heroine of Agnes Maria Bennett's *Ellen, Countess of Castle Howel*
(1794), nearly conforms; v. also *The Gamesters* (1786), by the authoress of *Burton Wood* (i.e. Mrs. Cox, *née* Wight, v. *European Magazine*,
iii. 120). This lady became first Mrs. A. M. Johnson, then Mrs.
Anna Maria Mackenzie. This identification has not been made by
Watts or any book of reference with which I am acquainted. The
evidence is in the title-pages of her books, and in *Orlando and Lavinia*
(1792), where *Monmouth* is ascribed to Mrs. Johnstone. The
fascination of gambling was dissected in Godwin's *St. Leon* (1799)

[2] For the former, v. Clara Reeve's *Sir Roger de Clarendon* (1793);
for the latter, Floresco, the negro boy in Melmoth's *Family Secrets*
(1797). He is all pure sensibility and broken English. "The
seeds of every virtue that ennobles society or endears solitude, were
sown liberally by the hand of nature in the bosom of this sable boy."

stitution of discretion for principle that stamped it in the
eyes of the moralist. An outcry went through Britain
from her pulpits and other high places; letters in the
Press testified to the sense of the British public on the
noble lord's performance, and the stock-in-trade of the
novelist was augmented by the figure of the disciple of
Chesterfield.[1] The new character was seized on by
Courtney Melmoth, otherwise Samuel Jackson Pratt
(1749–1814), a young man of talent, who had made his
mark as a preacher, had become entangled in a love
affair and given up the Church without losing his taste
for preaching, and, after an unsuccessful attempt on the
stage, was now earning his living as public lecturer,
novelist and partner in a library at the corner of Milsom
Street, Bath. There is plenty of ability of a journalistic
kind in Melmoth's voluminous output; he spoke the
fashionable tongue, but his literary existence was not
quite bounded by fashion, and small islands of reality
emerge at times from the lukewarm flood of his eloquence.
In his first book, *Liberal Opinions* (1775–77), we find
such an island in the bailiff's story of how he arrested an
impoverished gentleman in poor lodgings, after a night's
siege, by shouting bawdry through the keyhole to his
wife, and tripping up the tormented husband as he rushed
out; while in his immense *Family Secrets* (1797) he
holds out one hand to Sterne and one to Dickens.
Chesterfield, however, was an easy game, played with his
usual hurried skill. *The Pupil of Pleasure : or, The
New System Illustrated* (1776) was inscribed to Mrs.

---

[1] Chesterfield's *Letters*, lent to Susan Paulet, the Vicar's daughter,
in *Village Memoirs* (1774), helped to undermine her virtue. Lord
Claremont and his son, in Mrs. Brooke's *Excursion* (1777), were
recognized as " formed on the detestable plan of Lord Chesterfield,"
and there were apparently marks of his influence in Mrs. Cartwright's
Generous Sister (1780). In Clara Reeve's *Two Mentors* (1783) Richard
Munden plays the part, giving his ward a copy of the *Letters*, and
sending him to Lady Belmour's ambiguous house to be polished, but
his intentions are shattered on the invincible rectitude of young Savile.

Eugenia Stanhope, the daughter-in-law of the late earl
and the editress of the letters, and it professed to be a
" biographical commentary on the text of Chesterfield."
Philip Sedley, young, rich, well-born and disposed to
pleasure, declares himself a pupil of Lord Chesterfield
and sets out to be the " living comment upon the dead
text." He chooses Buxton for the scene of his operations and singles out as his victims Harriet, the giddy
young wife of the grave and scholarly minister, Horace
Homespun, and Fanny Mortimer, whose heart he had
won and discarded before her marriage, and who is
now in a decline, but " like certain fruits, delicious in
decay." The siege of Harriet is carried on with all
those minutiæ of good breeding which Chesterfield
recommends and in which Homespun, worthy man, is
deficient.

> " Horace's nails are not quite so *accurately clean*
> as they might be ; and, as I observed Mrs. Home-
> spun comparing them with *mine*, I suddenly closed
> my hand, as if out of tenderness, lest the comparison
> should turn to Horace's disadvantage ; yet this *very*
> tenderness, *so managed*, answered the design com-
> pleatly, and I can see plainly, Harriet thinks hardly
> of Horace for neglecting to pick the dirt from under
> his nails : while, on the other hand, when he and I
> are *together*, we laugh at the fopperies of the times,
> and seem mutually to despise all its *delicatesse*."

Harriet is won and wearied of, but retained as a mask
for the excitement roused by the pursuit of Fanny. But
Nemesis waits for Sedley. He has already felt strange
relentings in adjusting the affairs of his valet, also a
humble disciple of Chesterfield, and a bath-maid whom
he has seduced ; these he has interpreted as refined self-
interest and put aside ; but the hour has struck, and his
accomplishment in crime is the sign of the beginning of

vengeance. He sees Fanny, works on her emotions until she faints, and then takes what she would never have given him. Meanwhile Harriet dies in childbed, and Sedley, meeting her coffin and knowing himself responsible for her death, is assailed by conscience in all its horrors. From this point Melmoth, who had no use at any time for a meagre palette, lays on his colours thickly. Sedley entreats for death at Homespun's hand, but it is withheld; he attempts suicide, but is prevented. He then returns to the Mortimers and rushes unannounced into the supper-room, " his shirt spotted with blood at the bosom, his face pale and squallid [sic], and his eyes bearing all the marks of terror and desperation. Without making any apology for his intrusion, he drew a chair from the side of the room, flung himself into it, stampt his foot twice against the floor, smote his breast with an air of inexpressible vengeance, and taking a paper from his pocket, held it at arm's length, and burst into tears." These are the agonies of despair; for even Melmoth, who was to hale Sir Guise Lorrain Stuart heavenward by the hair through a great many gruelling chapters, would not undertake to save the disciple of Chesterfield, and he dies on Mortimer's sword. This book was catalogued by the *Scots Magazine* under the heading *Religion*. Three years later Melmoth completed his design by publishing *The Tutor of Truth* (1779), a calculated counterpiece to the *Pupil of Pleasure*. The book is very dull, however, for Melmoth's flamboyant pen did not lend itself readily to the portraiture of sobriety; and a far more characteristic and amusing counterpiece had been included in the earlier book itself in the person of Sir Henry Delmore, who addresses his children, in his wife's presence, as " pledges of this generous creature's invariable fidelity, and the testimonies of my continent attachment to excellence so distinguished."

Another character that profoundly disturbed the literary world at the end of the century was *Young Werter*,[1] though the disturbance was longer in coming to a head. *Werter* was after all a foreigner, while Lord Chesterfield was a native product, for whom an Englishman might feel responsible. Nevertheless, his melancholy was seductive enough to constitute a real menace, and it was necessary to strip self-murder of the false glamour which he shed on it, and to provide " antidotes " for his " poison." This was accordingly done ; books were published in which the characters of *Werter* reappear and comment on his fate, while elsewhere we find episodes inserted, in which an unhappy youth or girl is brought to the verge of suicide by the influence of *Werter*. These instances increased in number and urgency as it became apparent that the novel was no mere ephemeral, and therefore negligible, product of foreign eccentricity, but a book whose life and influence would endure.[2]

Incomparably the most frequent of all these didactic themes is filial obedience ; and so constant is its recur-

---

[1] First translated through the French in 1779, as *The Sorrows of Werter : a German Story ;* the translation has been ascribed to Richard Graves.

[2] E.g. *Eleonora : from the Sorrows of Werter* (1785) takes up a minor character, slightly mentioned by Goethe. *Letters of Charlotte, during her Connexion with Werter* (1786 ; New York, 1797), were translated into French, together with an extract from *Eleonora*, in 1787. The author of the *Letters*, referring to the bad effect of *Werter*, writes : " It would be painful to be particular ; but in support of what I have said, I cannot avoid taking notice of a single fact, well-known in the metropolis, that a young and amiable lady, who ' rashly ventured on the unknown shore,' had the *Sorrows of Werter* under her pillow when she was found in the sleep of death." The influence of *Werter* is canvassed in *Fashionable Infidelity*, III, p. 27 (1789) ; while in A. M. Bennett's *Juvenile Indiscretions* (1786), Henry Dellmore is brought to contemplate suicide by reading it, and it has the same effect on Jane in *Family Secrets* (1797). Its diffused influence may be felt in the *Curse of Sentiment* (1787), which describes the loves of a married man and a young girl ; they remain " virtuous " and die of decline. The defence of *Werter* is undertaken by Miss Morven in Elizabeth Sophia Tomlin's *Victim of Fancy* (1787) *v.* below, p. 100.

rence, so varied and picturesque its manifestations, that
it is clear we have to do not only with a moral principle,
but with a favourite channel of sensibility. With both,
however. Making all allowances for the heightened
chiaroscuro of most of these stories and the ideal extravagance of some, they were still erected on a groundwork
of honest conviction. Children should be grateful for
their breeding and subservient to their parents' authority.
Parents, of course, should be moderate and kind, but
authority is their function, and they ought not to abdicate
it. Early in the century, Defoe in his *Family Instructor*
(1715–18) had appealed to his readers with stories of
invincibly dutiful sons, and of lax parents who take to
the rod only just in time to avert perdition from their
offspring. By 1770 these strenuous days lay in the past,
and the outer forms of filial duty were falling rapidly
out of use, however the stage might retain them ; [1] moreover, there was a liberal, questioning spirit abroad, soon
to demolish all extreme tenets and to find its way into
fiction in the works of Holcroft and Bage. Under the
cold breath of this spirit the conservatives close their
ranks. Miss R. Roberts writes a sermon to call attention
to the neglected virtue of filial duty, and Clara Reeve
avowedly excludes from her survey of fiction in *The
Progress of Romance* all books that tend to undermine
this piety. The writers in the more dignified periodicals
support paternal authority where they can, and when in
1786 the Prince of Wales, failing to get a larger grant
from Parliament and to persuade the King to back his

[1] Mrs. Berkeley in her *Memoir* of her son George Monck Berkeley
(1797), speaks of the old fashion of asking a parent's blessing as now
obsolete, though it had been retained in her family. Graves, when his
Spiritual Quixote bent one knee to receive his mother's blessing (Bk.
XII, ch. 14), remarks that the action was agreeable to a custom now
obsolete ; the book plays in the 'forties. The gesture is retained in
Anne Dawe's *Younger Sister*, I, p. 156 (1770), but this is probably
convention. Cumberland's Arundel (1780) kisses the hands of his
uncle and his father-in-law, but here we may see the influence of the
stage.

request, was forced to cut down his household expenses, the economy was announced by the *Gentleman's Magazine*, breathless with admiration, in terms of the purest filial duty.[1] Here, however, we are obviously already half-way from conviction to fantasy. The fact remains that no fantasies have a wide popular appeal unless they are fairly closely linked with popular aspiration and even, though less closely, with fact. We may compare the cult of filial duty that penetrates the eighteenth-century novel to the cult of friendship that penetrates the mediæval *Amis and Amile*. Many a man, who would not have dreamed of killing his children to heal his friend's leprosy, heard of this sublime extravagance of Amile's with a glowing mind; and many a tolerably independent young man and woman, whose voice was heard by no means uncertainly in family councils, continued to get imaginative sustenance out of the deferential monosyllables of sons, imprisoned in dungeons by heavy fathers, out of the submissions of prodigals and the measured relentings of offended parents.[2] It was fantasy, but it had some relation to virtues that were admired; and children then read of the obedient child who saw and acknowledged his faults, as children now read of self-reliant young empire-builders and scientists.

This cult of filial obedience in imaginative literature is only part, though the most important part, of a wider cult. The late eighteenth century loved a fine gesture;

[1] Cf. also the correspondence during 1786 on the degree of John Howard's parental severity. The *Monthly Review*, Sept. 1799, p. 97, comments on " a time more remarkable than any former period for relaxation of parental authority," and finds even Clara Reeve's *Destination* (1799) too liberal in this respect.

[2] A typical heavy father's letter is found in *Emma ; or, the Unfortunate Attachment* (1773). His son has married against his will. " You have joined perfidy to disrespect; you have betrayed your own honour and your family's expectations; ruined the wife you have chosen, and can never be forgiven by your offended father, Marmaduke Wentworth." One can only comment, with sprightly Kitty Hartley in G. L. Way's *Learning at a Loss* (1778): " I hold Undutifulness in a Parent to be the worst of all possible Offences."

to them it was both beautiful and conclusive, whether they saw in it a condensed and implicit argument, or the evidence of a force strong enough to set argument aside ; and of all these fine gestures the most significant, the most charged with emotion, was that of generous sub-mission. It is impossible to exaggerate the frequency with which this attitude occurs. Son to father, wife to husband, servant to master,[1] even friend to friend, fulfil with disciplined humility and considerable self-approba-tion a traditional ritual of subjection. The popular hero is as often on his knees to his parents as to his beloved. The wife, if she does not kneel,—and often she does,—makes a daily oblation of her will to her lord and master. Between friends the situation is naturally rarer, and, even where repentance is an ingredient, more artificial, yet even here we notice a remarkable readiness on the part of the faulty to accept, even to request, reproof. There are several interesting points in connection with this theme. In the first place, the situation is almost always domestic ; these filial prostrations have no political or ecclesiastical parallels, though theoretically the submission of subject to king or penitent to confessor is not less pregnant with emotion or less capable of idealization.[2] But the Englishman, whose ears were tickled when foreigners praised the unruly love of freedom in the London mob, did not idealize autocracy in wider spheres than the household or—at most—the manor, while, as

[1] The combination of staunch humility and self-respect in servants is exemplified by True George in Melmoth's *Family Secrets* (1797). He says : " An order is an order. It an't his business to stop, and if he is sent on a fool's errand, that is nothing to him, he is not the fool."

[2] The final submission of the criminal to the law is found in George Walker's *Theodore Cyphon* (1796). Theodore not only pleads guilty, but entreats the jury to hang him. Verdict and sentence are pro-nounced in a court choked with grief, and Theodore is allowed to expiate his crime. The situation is found more frequently in French novels ; *e.g.* Marmontel's *Les Incas* (1773) and Mercier's *Mémoires de l'an 2440* (1770), *v.* Chapter V.

the Protestant heir of the Revolution of 1688, he preserved his self-control with some care among the picturesque attractions of Roman Catholicism. Even the
Gothic Romances, which are full of unattached hermits
in a state of contrition, make little more than a romantic
background out of the organized Church, except where,
to fill the rôle of villain, it becomes a tyranny.

A second point of interest is that the gesture of submission, though common enough in the books of men,—
Clarissa performs it elaborately and it was among Smollett's effects,—is especially characteristic of the books of
women. As a sex, whatever their individual fates were,
they needed to idealize submission to preserve their
self-respect.

This brings us to the third and most important point.
The submission is generous. It was not the collapse of
the weak that the reading public wanted to contemplate,
but the abnegation of the strong, which at once suggests
why the surrender of the son was the most moving form
that the situation could take. Such submission was not
a degradation, but a spiritual grace.[1] The harsh groundwork of dependence, where this exists, is overlaid with a
pattern of fantastic—often fanatic—beauty. Thus the
sons of the Honourable and Reverend Armine Fitz-
Orton, three very emotional and sententious young men,
give back upon their knees the deeds by which their
father has made them financially independent, in order
that his paternal authority over them shall remain un-
impaired.[2] Even submission is not enough. The wife
faced with an unworthy husband, the child oppressed

---

[1] Cf. Burke's panegyric on chivalry " that proud submission, that
dignified obedience, that subordination of the heart, which kept alive,
even in servitude itself, the spirit of an exalted freedom."

[2] *Family Secrets* (1797). This book, like the rest of the author's
later work, but unlike his other novels, was published under his real
name, S. J. Pratt. To avoid confusion, I have referred to him all
through as Courtney Melmoth, the name under which he first appeared
to the public.

by a tyrannous father, do more than obey. By an act of will they abrogate reason, quell discrimination, and not only accept but approve the fiat they bow to. " Where the author of my being is concerned," says Caroline Stuart, " I feel myself as having no judgment, no will, no reason, nor any of those faculties, which in every other circumstance of life I am free to exercise " ; while Fanny Burney's Mrs. Tyrold, only less extreme, " considered the vow taken at the altar to her husband as a voluntary Vestal would have held one taken to her Maker ; and no dissent in opinion exculpated, in her mind, the least deviation from his will." [1]   The comments of life on this attitude are various and amusing. We have here to do with dreams.

In different ages popular emotion has been focussed on different types. In the Renascence it was the man of will, in the early nineteenth century the defiant rebel, to-day, perhaps, the defeated man. The modern reader is often called upon to follow the fate of the under-dog, sometimes to watch him, like Mr. Polly, find the release of a tardy self-assertion ; but submission is an attitude that no longer has much popular appeal. Yet its roots run deep ; and though it is not possible to refer to any one cause the eighteenth-century disposition to find pleasure and profit in contemplating it, it is possible to make out some of its sanctions. Its most cogent association was with the Christian virtue of humility ; but behind that lies the sentiment of a patriarchal authority older than record, known to eighteenth-century readers chiefly in the terms of Roman fatherhood and the fifth commandment. Voluntary submission to law is the basis of society, ordained both by reason and revelation ; while, to leave on one side these deeper significances, the practice of the stage kept alive the picturesque aspects of the attitude. Youthful splendour abased, hardihood return-

[1] v. *Camilla*, Ch. I.

ing to its allegiance, the bending of the plumed crest, these were the spectacles that moved the eighteenth-century audience ; and a forgotten drama reached its climax when Charles Kemble, falling at Philip's feet, with accomplished elegance embraced his knees. Nor were the boards of the theatre the only stage on which this posture was exhibited. The penitent criminal, from the moment when he appeared before his judge in deep mourning, to the moment when with his bound hands he pulled down his hat over his face, was expected to conduct himself with exemplary humility. Fortitude was out of place ; it was his business to show that he was both ashamed and afraid, since this public witness to the laws he had transgressed was the only amends now in his power.[1]

There are too many penitents in eighteenth-century fiction, and novelists drew too heavily for their effects on the passions of shame and contrition. The sensitive reader learns to skip those orgies of abasement, in which the bystanders, if we believe their epistolary effusions on the subject, found a " pleasing " and sometimes an " aweful interest." The situation is dealt with in all degrees of intensity, from the blush of noble youth under reproof to the self-conviction of the criminal, and the prodigals range from the young man, who has overspent his allowance, to Cain, who is brought back repentant to die in the tents of Adam and be buried beside Abel.[2] When Blifil " betook himself at last to confession," Fielding, after a disdainful glance, turned his attention to other matters ; but the superficial novelist has no notion of the guilt that injures the texture of the soul, and justifies

[1] The subject might be pursued. The penitent criminal, for instance, even if indirectly avowing his guilt, never pleaded " Guilty," since that was an insolent hardihood, savouring of suicide ; his endeavour should be to prolong his life in order to devote it to repentance ; v. the trials of Dr. Dodd for forgery and of Rev. J. Hackman for the murder of Martha Ray.

[2] v. The Death of Cain, by a Lady (1789).

his ignoble indulgences by assuming, without any discrimination, the purifying effect of pain. Usually the
penitent is received with signal mercy; indeed, the
complement of generous submission is the liberality that
accepts and rewards it, and the magnanimous autocrat,
whose energies pour forth in uninterrupted streams of
benevolence, is almost as necessary to vindicate the submissive as the tyrant to vindicate the rebel. In his hands
punishment becomes a sacred rite; and this conception,
which is general in French and English literature, in
children's books and in those for adult reading, may be
most conveniently illustrated by a passage from *Les Incas*
(1773). Here Marmontel imagines a type of punishment
which could only be effective if those who suffer and those
who inflict were alike consistently noble. The erring
son, whom his father reluctantly accuses at the Feast of
Palms, is condemned to a year's exile from the paternal
roof, during which time he is not allowed to use his
strength for the good of the State, by cultivating either his
father's fields or those allotted for the support of widows
and orphans, but is condemned to a shameful indolence,
and passes his days wandering near the threshold of his
home, without daring to touch it, until the year brings
round the Feast of Palms again, and his father's embrace,
publicly bestowed on him in the temple, restores him to
his place. This was the chastisement thought fit for
generous souls, and it was in this way that Mme. de Genlis
would have children rebuked. How much she relied
upon the natural generosity of childhood, and how heavy
a burden she laid upon it, can be seen in her *Veillées du
Château* (1784),[1] where little César voluntarily adds to his
own punishment to purchase his tutor's full forgiveness.
In such a scheme repentance and pardon, it will be seen,
are really assumed from the beginning, but they must

[1] Translated by Holcroft as *Tales of the Castle* (1785). Marmontel's
Incas was translated in 1777.

still be displayed in the interests of the public and of the picturesque.

The reaction from this attitude had set in before the turn of the century. The " philosophers " were in the van with their reasoned assertion of the importance of self-respect and independence, and extravagance is matched by extravagance when Mary Hays in her *Memoirs of Emma Courtney* (1796) declares that " *obedience* is a word which ought *never to have had existence.*" More important to the popular novel than philosophy, or an impulsive woman's travesty of philosophy, was that cult of passion which was triumphantly established during the last years of the century and culminated in the glorification of defiance. A little may be set down to closer contact with reality and a little to the growing taste for reticence, though neither of these considerations weigh very heavily in the popular novel. At all events, the excesses of submission cease to be admired, and the penitent, after contending for mastery with the rebel, is finally worsted.

II

The book I had been reading lay by my side. He took it up, and opened it where I had marked down the page. It was wet with tears. He regarded me with a look of inquiry, then, pressing the page to his lips, he exclaimed : " Gracious heaven ! what enchanting sensibility." —*The Liberal American*, 1785.

In the preceding pages the word sensibility has been used more than once. To the eighteenth century it was a significant, an almost sacred word, for it enshrined the idea of the progress of the human race. Sensibility was a modern quality ; it was not found among the ancients, but was the product of modern conditions ; [1] the heroic and tremendous virtues might be dying out with the

[1] Cf. J. Cradock (*Memoirs*, I, p. 63): " How much soever the ancients might abound in elegance of expression—their works are very thinly spread with sentiment." Here sentiment is practically equivalent to sensibility ; *v.* below, p. 93.

stormy times that evoked them, but modern security, leisure and education had evolved a delicacy of sensation, a refinement of virtue, which the age found even more beautiful. The human sympathies, which a rougher age had repressed, expanded widely, especially towards the weak and unfortunate, and the social conscience began to occupy itself with prisoners, children, animals and slaves. But the good in this cult, which was considerable, was accompanied by manifestations of folly that discredited its very name, which was laughed at, neglected during the greater part of the nineteenth century, and has only recently been revived, in a more strictly defined sense, as a useful part of the critical vocabulary. It is now our business, setting aside the modern usage, to display something of the vague and gleaming halo of associations that surrounded this mild moon of the eighteenth century. To display, rather than to define; we have to envisage a landscape, not to pursue an idea, and a landscape whose moonlight streams from no clearly discerned orb, but is filtered through mists, to fall upon and transfigure old fields and dwellings of the human race. Contemporary definitions, though they exist, are far to seek,[1] and it would be wasted labour to attempt to confine to distinct and precise meanings the words delicacy, sensibility and sentiment. They are not exactly synonymous,—sentiment, for instance, implies more of conscious thought and principle than the other two, and sometimes signifies an ennobled or even a platonic affection as distinguished from appetite,[2] while

---

[1] Cf. *Monthly Review* (Aug. 1799, p. 467); the reviewer wishes that novelists " would sometimes inform us what ideas they annex to the word sensibility," which ranges from compassion to " the irritable weakness which shrinks from the common duties of life."

[2] Cf. Graves, *Plexippus*, II, p. 27 (1790): " There is no *true* love but sentimental love, as you call it "; and the review of *Letters of Yorick to Eliza* in the *Gentleman's Magazine* (1775), where the letters are described as " expressive of the most tender and (we trust) sentimental friendship."

delicacy, besides being a less comprehensive word, is
often used in a purely moral sense,—but they overlap
inextricably, and no novelist troubled to be precise about
them. Sensibility was the most popular word, as it was
the only one to be degraded by its popularity, though
attacks were launched at the other two as well; and
sensibility is the word adopted by historians to indicate
this phase of taste.

If, however, strict definition is unprofitable, it is profitable enough to note how this moonlight of sensibility
touches and alters familiar features of the landscape;
how it blends with humanitarianism, for instance (though
not all humanitarians were sensible,—witness John
Howard), reinforces the feminists in their plea for a more
exalted notion of woman and of love, and helps to illustrate
the cult of the noble savage,—for what better evidence
can there be of the innate goodness of the human heart
than spontaneous sensibility? We hear of sensibility
as a means by which the unphilosophical mind can know
virtue, an instinctive moral tact;[1] we also hear of it as a

[1] v. Frances Brooke's *Emily Montague*, I, p. 225 (1769): "Women
are religious as they are virtuous, less from principles founded on
reasoning and argument, than from elegance of mind, delicacy of
moral taste, and a certain quick perception of the beautiful and becoming in everything. This instinct, however, for such it is, is worth all
the tedious reasonings of the men." Cf. also her *Excursion*, II, p. 156
(1777). Mrs. Griffith in *Lady Juliana Harley*, II, p. 288 (1776),
derives both modesty and tenderness from sensibility. Hannah
More affixed a poem on *Sensibility* to her *Sacred Dramas* (1782) in
which she thus defines her subject:

> Sweet sensibility! thou keen delight!
> Thou hasty moral! sudden sense of right!
> Thou untaught goodness! Virtue's precious seed!
> Thou sweet precursor of the gen'rous deed!
> Beauty's quick relish! Reason's radiant morn,
> Which dawns soft light before Reflexion's born.

Cf. also Andrew Macdonald's play *Vimonda* (1787, Act IV, p. 64,
1788 ed.), where sensibility = conscience.

> My heart Dundore empoisoned . . .
> Robbed me of all the heav'n-born sensibility
> Which once could shake my frame at thoughts of guilt.

dangerous elegance, tending to enervate the mind and seduce it into " refining away " its happiness ; at times it is " an inexpressible and melting softness," at times an active philanthropy : it allies itself easily with premonitions and supernatural intimations,[1] and no less easily with the simplest domestic virtues. Its constant quality was an immediacy of sensation outrunning thought ; it was, said Mary Wollstonecraft, " the result of acute senses, finely fashioned nerves, which vibrate at the slightest touch, and convey such clear intelligence to the brain, that it does not require to be arranged by the judgment ; "[2] but this is to ignore the delusions of vanity and sick fancy to which less enthusiastic writers pointed.

The best-known and in some ways the best storehouse of sensibility is Mackenzie's *Man of Feeling* (1771), but it is far from comprehensive. Indeed, no one can judge of the compelling vogue of the sensible heart who has not pursued it outside its proper reservations and found it functioning vigorously and unexpectedly in the alien terrain of the picaresque. Thomas Bridges devotes a good deal of the third volume of his *Adventures of a Bank-Note* (1770–1) to the sensible heart of Mr. Villiers, of whom we are told that " tears cours'd one another down his manly cheeks, and form'd a rapid current o'er his garments," and the description, in whatever mood it was penned, was not intended to be read as parody. In the huge variety-programme of the picaresque there was room for a few serious turns ; in the next chapter the scene has

---

[1] *E.g.* the " presaging gloom " which the heroine of *Julia de Roubigné* feels on entering her new home. Sensibility is also expressed by the surprising intimations of reverence felt by characters in fiction in the presence of unknown relatives, or before the pictures or graves of these; v. *Ermina ; or, the Fair Recluse* (1773), *The Prudential Lovers ; or, the History of Harry Harper* (1773), and Miss Lee's *Recess* (1783). Bage especially notes the absence of these intimations in the case of *James Wallace* (1788) : " nor does the instinctive principle, by which these secret ties have been so often felt (in books) before they were known, seem to have operated in the least."

[2] v. *Cave of Fancy*, printed in *Posthumous Works* (1798).

changed, and we hear the cheerful undertaker whistling homeward with his fee in his pocket; " his tune indeed was the Babes in the Wood, but that to him, I suppose, was a merry tune, because it exhibited the idea of two buryings at once."

Tears, the " briny flood of humanity," [1] were as much valued in the eighteenth century as in the Middle Ages, though for different reasons. To weep was not to show contrition, but—the phrase is frequent—" to give convincing testimony of one's sensibility," and " by sensibility I understand," wrote Harriet Lee, " a certain tender sympathy of disposition, which, tho' originally deriv'd from the passions, is meliorated into something gentler and more pleasing than those." [2] By " meliorated " Miss Lee probably means softened and refined in its expression ; she might have added " subtilized," for one trait of sensibility is its delicate responsiveness to minute stimuli. Here we are, of course, on Sterne's ground with his cult of the trifle, ground that had often been travelled by poet and lover, but had never before been so mapped and popularized as it was now. It is from the small things that life takes its colour, said Mackenzie, and the sensible writer at his best did not require catastrophic events or violent emotions. His " curiosity " did not pry into abnormalities, like that of the seventeenth century, but was directed towards the tremulous vibrations of the mind under the normal shocks of grief, pleasure, anxiety, or indignation. He does not stretch his characters on the rack, but tickles them with a feather or pricks them with a pin. It is a matter of associations, and the nerves respond to the least twitch on the spider-fine filaments of memory and pity. There is a characteristic passage in *Julia de Roubigné* (1777), where the young man who has said farewell overnight to the woman he loves, looks into the

---

[1] v. *Sentimental Magazine*, No. 1, p. 6 (1773).
[2] v. *The Errors of Innocence* (1786).

room where they sat, as he goes in the morning. " The chairs we had occupied were still in their places ; you know not, my friend, what I felt at the sight : there was something in the silent attitude of those very chairs, that wrung my heart beyond the power of language." This is what Mackenzie calls reading Nature " in her smallest character," and his books consist chiefly of interpretations of this minuscule. The sensible heart, when it is stricken, turns consciously to trifles for its solace. " To ruminate over the unimportant bustle of an anthill," writes the author of *Wanley Penson : or, the Melancholy Man* (1791) ; " to spread himself on the grass, and trace the little minims of nature, like the native Americans, exploring their unbounded forest ; and to moralize if a thwart straw impeded their intent progress ; to pore over a brook, and, emulative of the universal Benefactor, feed the minnows with crumbs from his pocket ; these unlikely means were what nature adapted to relieve his mind, by giving just such a play to its functions as they found a pleasure in indulging." [1]

Sensibility of this high-strung sort is the dower of most heroines and many heroes. " 'Tis the magnet which attracts all to itself," wrote Mrs. Brooke in *Emily Montague:* " virtue may command esteem, understanding and talents admiration, beauty a transient desire, but 'tis sensibility alone which inspires love." The incident which gives birth to liking is usually some effusion of the sensible heart,—an act of charity or an overflow of sympathetic emotion at the theatre,—and the most " insinuating " address that could be made to a young lady was to compliment her on the tenderness of her

---

[1] The discouraged and patient humility of *Wanley Penson* is very close to the *Man of Feeling*. His end is equally distressing. His melancholy is the result of the loss of his beloved by drowning. He at length transfers his heart to her friend and is in a fair way for happiness, when the first lady returns as from the grave, and at the first sight of her, he dies of shock.

passions. In health heroines have an expression of "animated sensibility," but it is the languid beauty, the over-susceptible emotionalism of sickness, that is considered most appealing. And here we touch a vein of morbidity, similar to that which made seventeenth-century artists delight to paint the extreme of beauty in the extreme of pain. That face is more pleasing, we hear, which has been slightly pitted with small-pox, perhaps because our sense of its beauty is made poignant by mortality's sign-manual,[1] while a "hectic" confers a complexion more delicate than that of health. Men were attracted to this precarious loveliness, not only because it appeared spiritualized and removed from the coarse business of life, but because it appealed to their compassion. Witness Melmoth in *Emma Corbett*. "The feeblenesses to which the tender frame of woman is subject, are, perhaps, more seducing than her bloom. The *healthy* flower looks superior to protection, and expands itself to the sun in a kind of *independent* state ; but in nursing that which *droops* (sweetly dejected) and is ready to fall upon its bed, our care becomes more dear, as it becomes more *necessary*." The odium of this false refinement must, however, be shared between the sexes, for Sophia Lee ascribes to one of her heroines in the *Recess* "a feminine helplessness which is, when unaffected, the most interesting of charms."

The chief weakness of sensibility, its tendency to relax the mind and suffer it to luxuriate in induced emotions, was clearly apprehended, not only by the hard-headed, but by sensible writers themselves, who anxiously distinguish between the true quality and the counterfeit.

---

[1] This argument can hardly have applied with the same strength to the looks of men, though even here an appearance of ill-health was found attractive. Miss Bell Fermor's admirer in *Emily Montague* was "marked with small-pox, which in men gives a sensible look." It probably modified the appearance of self-confident robustness which overwhelmed sensitive women and antagonized spirited ones.

" Sensibility under proper restrictions, is one of the most pleasing and interesting virtues, which inhabit and give a gentle polish to the mind," wrote Mrs. Bonhote in her *Parental Monitor* (1788). She emphasizes the restrictions, and so did Mrs. Radcliffe and, later, Miss Edgeworth. Not only must one guard against false sensibility, rooted in pride and artifice, but against that excess of genuine emotion, which " is but a mode of our pervading dissipation," [1] and must in the end exhaust the heart it agitates. It is not our duty to keep our wounds open, or even to nurse our sensitiveness, if thereby we become incapable of the general business of life. " I knew a family," writes Catherine Talbot, " good, agreeable, sensible and fond of each other, to the highest degree ; but where each was so delicate, and so tender of the Delicacy of the rest, that they could never talk to one another of any serious business, but were forced to transact it by means of a third person, a man of plain sense, and a common friend to all." It was against this impracticable delicacy that Mrs. Jane West (Prudentia Homespun) set her face in that embryo *Sense and Sensibility*, *A Gossip's Story* (1796), in which the moral, that the imaginary duties of false refinement are never practised but at the expense of solid virtues, is enforced by the contrasted temperaments and fates of two sisters, Marianne, who wrecks her own happiness by her romantic emotionalism, and Louisa, whose fortitude and sense sustain her through trouble and win the heart of the man she loves.[2] Mrs. West's tale is very simply and naturally

---

[1] *v.* Preface to Isaac d'Israeli's *Vaurien* (1797).

[2] The studied moderation of Jane Austen is thrown up by contrast with her predecessors. There is nothing extravagant in Mrs. West, but Louisa's trials are more spectacular than Elinor Dashwood's, including as they do the loss of her fortune and attendance on her dying father, while Mrs. West's Marianne drives her follies to a more catastrophic conclusion than Miss Austen's. The setting of *A Gossip's Story*, a small northern market-town, with a society of spinsters of limited means, clerical and medical ladies, and one big house, is an embryo *Cranford*, and the resemblance is increased by the

managed, but it fails—indeed it does not endeavour—to conciliate sympathy for the culprit. That was done in the extravagant but rather pleasing *Victim of Fancy* (1787) by Elizabeth Sophia Tomlins,[1] a full-length portrait of an amiable enthusiast whose sensibility cost her life. The book is not ill-written ; something of charm is conveyed in Theresa Morven's heedless ardour for all that is good and great, her tears over Milton's grave, and her quixotic search for and defence of the maligned author of *Werter*. Her excesses blend the noble and the ridiculous, and she perishes under the wear and tear of her feelings.

The votary of sensibility valued emotion for itself, without stopping to consider whether it sprang from an adequate cause ; indeed, it was a mark of the most refined sensibility that the cause should appear at first blush inadequate. Hence springs in the first place a lack of proportion, and in the next place all the insincerity of stoked-up feelings and self-complacency. The sensible heart seeks an occasion to indulge itself in a shower of tears, since tears are, axiomatically, purifying, and a very small occasion can be made to serve. The tiny spring releases the accumulated stores of pity, or generous indignation, or of the sense of human fellowship. The individual—be he victim or philanthropist—is never seen merely as such, but by a generalizing habit of mind becomes a type, a grand hieroglyphic of human destiny. It is the body of human wrongs, the general habit of human patience, momentarily linked to the spectator's consciousness by the object before him, that evokes the

---

benevolent irony with which the author records the fluctuations of opinion, and the ways and means of gossip.

[1] Miss Tomlins published anonymously *The Conquests of the Heart* (1785), *Victim of Fancy* (1787) and *Memoirs of a Baroness* (1792). She signed *Rosalind de Tracy* (1798). The B.M. has the French translation only of her second book, *La Victime de l'imagination, ou l'enthousiaste de Werther*, by A. G. Griffet de Labeaume and F. Notaris. Paris, L'An III.

overwhelming response. The sculptured urn under the trees is instinct with a universal experience of loss and loneliness ; the old soldier, filling his pipe sparingly with three fingers of his maimed hand and then plodding forward with his head bent against the rain, is Tom, or Dick, or Harry, a unique being with a personal history, but he is also a " son of sorrow," kin to Lear's " loop'd and window'd raggedness " and to all the outcasts of the world. So far, of course, the process is not only legitimate, but it is that of the great poets, notably Wordsworth, though there is little in the style of the apostrophes and adjurations, the litanies of petitions, that flow from the sensible heart on one of these encounters, to recall the discipline of great poetry. But the flaw that so often vitiates the sensibility of the eighteenth century is its egoism ; it is difficult to find a passage that is quite clear from this taint. Tears are too facile, too enjoyable, and the sensible heart is too much like an Æolian harp, designed to be susceptible and placed in the position where it will be most affected. One longs for a little toughness ; one meets instead with complacency. Of this danger the majority of eighteenth-century writers cannot have been much aware ; they give themselves away too handsomely. Again and again we find that enormity of self-gratulation with which the weeper at once luxuriates in the beguiling softness of tears and compliments himself on his capacity for shedding them, seeing in his mind's eye not only the object of his attention, but himself in a suitable attitude in front of it. " Weep," says Mrs. Radcliffe, inviting the reader to approach *The Ancient Beech-Tree*,

—" if grace
And grandeur ever touched thy heart, adore
And weep—weep tears of deep delight, and tears
Of gratitude that thou canst weep such tears." [1]

---

[1] Published posthumously in *Gaston de Blondeville*, etc. (1826); written much earlier, probably before or soon after 1800.

There is plenty of this complacency in *The Man of Feeling*, together with the ironical humility which so often accompanies it. The sensible man feels that he is an advanced type of being, of finer clay than the rest of the world, and though he pays for his superiority by weakness and anguish, he does not find the price too high, but regards with gentle scorn the low pleasures of the unthinking world. Superiority, however, is not a very amiable feeling ; moreover, all the strength of practical competence was on the other side. This, then, was to be disarmed by humility. With what heart-wrung whimsicality does the Man of Feeling forestall his critic in his confessions of weakness ; with what delicate sarcasm does he assent to the verdict of the world and head a chapter in which Harley expresses his disquiet about English behaviour in India : " The Man of Feeling talks about what he does not understand."

Egoism betrays—or, rather, proclaims—itself in other ways. When Ignatius Sancho, the negro, wrote to Sterne, recommending slavery as a subject for his pen, he called him " an Epicurean in Charity," and the charity of many a sensible heart suggests rather a calculated method of evoking pleasurable emotion than the spontaneous movement of justice and pity. Then there is the word " luxury," in itself a millstone that should have sunk many an author. " Great G—d ! " cries the silly young man who wrote *A Brother's Advice to his Sisters*,[1] " unless I have greatly offended thee, grant me the luxury, sometimes to slip a bit of silver, though no bigger than a shilling, into the clammy-cold hand of the decayed wife of a baronet." The reviewer was amused ; would not a knight's widow do ? But he left the major heresy unattacked ; indeed, it passed for orthodoxy ; and one of the main attractions of Courtney Melmoth's *Shenstone-Green* (1779) is the sympathetic and benevolent Mr.

[1] Quoted by the *Critical Review*, Dec. 1775, p. 464.

Seabrooke, who revels in " pretty severe pangs " during a touching scene, and goes to bed at four o'clock in the afternoon, in order that he may not, by seeing inferior objects, " blunt the divine edge of [his] present sensasions." [1] Grief of this barbless and ideal kind was felt to be pleasurable, and very naturally we find in the books of the time a cult of distress. " Go on, I insist upon it ! I love to weep, I joy to grieve ; it is my happiness, my delight, to have my heart broken in pieces," cried Brooke's Lady Maitland on a more serious occasion, and the novelists did go on, encouraged by critics who were willing " to forget every violation of the laws of Criticism " in return for " that divine pleasure which the tears of virtue only can bestow." [2] " Distress " was a technical term in criticism, and authors set themselves, like Lady Ann Lindsay composing *Auld Robin Gray*, to " kill the cow," which, in polite life, meant to get the heroine to the point when she finds herself penniless in a hackney-coach in London, with nowhere to drive to, with a rising fever and an injured reputation. The next step, of course, is distraction. Sometimes she dies. It became the fashion to conclude a novel with a funeral. " The heroes and heroines must all be buried," said the *Monthly* in 1787. Or the author conciliates all tastes by providing a hearse for one pair of lovers and wedding-bells for the other.

[1] Cf. *Juliana* (1786) by the author of *Francis the Philanthropist*: " Never before have I revelled in such luxury of tears " ; J. Thistlethwaite's *Man of Experience* (1778): " pity . . . the greatest luxury the soul of sensibility is capable of relishing " ; Mary Heron's address to sensibility as " luxurious woe " in *Sketches of Poetry* (1786) ; and the letter from Chremes, *Gentleman's Magazine*, May 1791, giving an account of an affecting scene of Village Distress, a visit to a young labourer, who has lost his wife and is left with seven children, because " it might yield to some of your readers a portion of that luxurious pity which I felt." Cf. also the dismissal of the bereaved parents at the end of Mrs. Brooke's *Lady Julia Mandeville* (1763), to " indulge in all the voluptuousness of sorrow " ; and the *Younger Sister* by Anne Dawe (1770), where a scene of abject humiliation inspires in the onlookers " a pleasing kind of distress."

[2] *Gentleman's Magazine*, March 1773, on the tragedy of *Alonzo*, performed at Drury Lane.

Mrs. Charlotte Smith is a very pretty hand at distressing her heroines ; moreover, her methods are delicate and probable, whereas many novelists were driven by the exhaustion of all natural situations to base their embarrassments upon " artificial refinements and false morals." [1] As Mrs. Barbauld [2] pointed out, there was a crying need for a " new torture or nondescript calamity " in the world of fiction, and the need was the more difficult to supply because distress, in order to be pleasing, must avoid awakening disgust.   Pity must always be associated with love and esteem ; no idea must be admitted which destroys " the grace and dignity of suffering," and even scenes of poverty must be so chastened as to leave the imagination an amiable figure to dwell upon.   We do not, remarks Mrs. Barbauld, see the ruined Belvidera " employed in the most servile offices of poverty," and one realizes how daring it was of Miss Burney to let Cecilia discover Henrietta Belfield washing up ; but Henrietta, of course, is not the heroine, and Cecilia, who is, never touches a dishclout ; for her is reserved that most touching of heroic distresses—distraction.   French distresses, in Mrs. Barbauld's eyes, compare favourably with the overdone violence of the English Melpomene ; but there were not wanting among the better English writers some who cultivated the " little affecting incidents," and arranged compositions in distress that have the delicate hues of water-colours.   In the *Man of Feeling*, for instance, there is a scene where Harley, thinking that Miss Walton is walking with an accepted lover, stands alone by the gate into her grounds.   He hears her dog bark, and at once the poignant words dart into his mind—

> " the little dogs and all,
> Tray, Blanch, and Sweetheart, see, they bark at me."

---

[1] *Critical Review*, April 1796, on the *Fugitives*.
[2] Then Miss Aikin ; *v.* her *Inquiry into those kinds of distress which excite agreeable sensations* in the *Miscellaneous Prose Pieces* published by herself and her brother in 1773.

" His resolution failed ; he slunk back, and locking the
gate as softly as he could, stood on tiptoe looking over the
wall till they were gone.   At that instant a shepherd blew
his horn ; the romantic melancholy of the sound quite
overcame him !—it was the very note that wanted to be
touched—he sighed ! he dropt a tear !—and returned."
This is a deliberate composition in sensibility, and, though
nothing can exonerate it from the charge of tampering
with the emotions, it is skilful enough to deserve a serious
comment.   There were things to be learnt in this fashion,
and the novel learned them ; occasionally a light stroke
touches the source of tears that were not dried five
generations ago.[1]

The *Man of Feeling* was an exceedingly popular book,
and one can imagine that the perusal of it was often undertaken as a sort of drill to keep the sensible heart in training.
Sensibility was the mark of a valuable mind, and the
achievement of a long process of civilization ; but each
sensible heart, exposed to the roughening contact of daily
life, felt it necessary constantly to test its own reactions,
to make sure that it was still humane, that it had not lost
ground.   The same intention can be traced in those
scenes of cumulative pathos by deathbeds and at partings,
where stroke after stroke is delivered until the reader's
heart is in an appropriate state of softness, and the novelist
too often, forgetting his discretion, demeans himself like
a lusty cook beating steak.   The reader soon recognizes
the subjects that sensibility most gladly embalms.   The
majority are domestic, such as the gap in the family
circle, or restoration after illness.   Children are very
touchstones of sensibility ; and if a mother is indifferent
to their " confiding innocence," we may take it as a very

---

[1] *E.g.* in Mrs. Radcliffe's *Mysteries of Udolpho* (1794), Emily's
return home after her father's death, and her parting with Valancour,
with his fear that he will not be able in her absence to remember her
face.

bad sign; she can hardly end well. Then there is the theme of the widow's mite, the loveliness of small acts of charity, and closely linked with this the loyalty of the humble. Sensibility broods gratefully over the alms-deeds of the poor,[1] and over the half-articulate devotion of servants, where the candle of love throws its beams through a grotesque lattice of mis-spellings and mispro-nunciations. Sensibility becomes the interpreter for dumb animals, and, if space allowed, a touching and amusing collection could be made of passages in which they appear.[2] Sensibility, in a more elevated mood, expands itself in a vague and hopeful Deism and loves to contemplate the Christian priest, the enlightened Brahmin and even the humane sceptic at one before God.

The gestures in which sensibility expresses itself once more raise the question of the relationship of these books to life. Something must be allowed for the influence of the stage and of the emphatic style of acting developed in large play-houses; for it is not credible that any young Englishman, however penitent, indicated his state of mind by casting himself flat among the flower-beds of a public garden in Bath, as does Sir William Harrington.

---

[1] *E.g.* Extract from *A Brother's Advice to his Sisters, Monthly Review*, Sept. 1775: "I saw an honest negro not long since, as he was walking towards Deptford, at the rate of about five miles an hour, stop short, in passing an old sailor, of a different complexion, with but one arm and two wooden legs. It was my fortune, I say, to have the luxury to watch this worthy savage take three halfpence and a farthing, his little all, out of the side-pocket of his tattered trousers; wrap them in a bit of an old hand-bill, which held his tobacco when he was so rich as to have any; force them into the weeping sailor's retiring hand, with both his; wipe his eye with the corner of his blue patched jacket, and walk away so happy, and so fast—that I was obliged to put your friend Spot into a Canterbury gallop, to get up to the dog, in order to shake him by the hand."

[2] Among animal-lovers are Graham in the *Spiritual Quixote*, Benignus in *Liberal Opinions* and Handford in *Alwyn*. The case of post-horses is discussed in *Philo and his Man Sturdy* (1788) and the humane preparation of food is advocated in Dr. Moore's *Edward* (1796). Lady Mary Walker's *Munster Village* (1778), a description of an ideal community, provides a paddock for pensioned-off domestic animals.

On the other hand, contemporary letters and memoirs, especially those of women,[1] show a society very ready to weep and tremble, and to take credit for doing so ; ready too, it appears, to describe a simple gesture magniloquently. In the novels to kneel is nearly always to " prostrate oneself," while a hand-shake or a clap on the shoulder is an " embrace " ; and the anecdotes scattered in the pages of magazines are narrated in the same idiom. No doubt the transports of tears, the tottering steps, the embraces in which the participants " sink slowly together to the floor," and the constant male and female swoons are grotesque travesties of contemporary manners, but they cannot be wholly dismissed. The same conventionalized extravagance of bearing is found in the French novel, and the popular mind of Western Europe accepted it as a suitable expression of heightened emotion. The repression of feeling, though it was a mark of breeding in high life,[2] was not yet a universally accepted standard of behaviour. " Our parting from the amiable friends at the Hôtel de Lisson," writes a young lady in *The Convent : or, the History of Sophia Nelson* (1786),[3] " was such as it ought to be—the women applied their handkerchiefs to their eyes—the men shook hands, smiled, put on their hats, and drew them two inches lower than usual." Even reviewers were sympathetically affected, and a perusal of Mrs. Smith's *Celestina* caused the *Critical* reviewer to take off his spectacles more than once. These displays—and others of so amazing a nature that the author cannot even have stopped to visualize them—confirmed the reader's faith in the value of human nature. In *Augusta*,

---

[1] *E.g. Love-Letters of Mary Hays* (1779–80), ed. A. F. Wedd (1925) ; but *v*. also Richard Griffith, *Genuine Letters of Henry and Frances*, V, p. 279, where the author weeps while writing a poem to his wife, and her friend weeps on reading it.

[2] *v*. Ann Yearsley's *Royal Captives*, IV, p. 271 (1795) ; " I was not so highly polished as to affect indifference, and call it fortitude." Cf. also Mrs. Jane West's *Tale of the Times*, I, p. 51 (1799).

[3] By Anne Fuller.

or the Dependant Niece (1788) a middle-aged man, hearing
of his brother's death, throws himself upon the floor and
lies there for a quarter of an hour, while when Father
Arthur in *Family Secrets* reads an affecting letter, his
tears drop audibly upon it. Of tears we have already
seen much, and they will inevitably moisten the whole of
this book. Every author, including even Bage, who so
staunchly opposed convention in more important respects,
allowed " a sufficient Quantity of Slobbering, and Blessing,
and White Handkerchief Work." [1] One peculiarly
horrible manifestation of this cult may be called tear-
tracking. Tears of gratitude fall upon the hand of the
charitable, verge slowly towards the finger that extracted
the alms, and are suffered to dry there. Tears of sensibility are kissed off, rediscovered, and kissed off by a third
person. It is inconceivable to what lengths the pursuit
went, but Courtney Melmoth may be consulted, especially
the passage on the Carbines in *Emma Corbett*. Slightly
less blatant was the shamefaced sensibility which is, I
believe, peculiar to or at least most highly developed in
the English novel. Philanthropists whistle, cough, feign
to bully the object of their charity, or upset a board of
chessmen to distract attention from their too obvious
feelings. The outward signs of emotion are ludicrously
described. " How the devil shall I contrive to tell you
the rest of the story," writes the " humorist," Mr. Handford, in Holcroft's *Alwyn* (1780), " to make you caper,
and sing, and wipe your eyes, and rub your shins as a
Christian ought to do ? " It is plain, of course, that the
shame is itself a superior ingredient of the sensibility, and
part of the display ; there is no real concealment, as there
is none in the displays of reticence to which a later school
of novelists has treated us.

Sensibility must also be credited in part with a particular
style of dialogue, chiefly found in sententious or pathetic

[1] *v.* G. L. Way's *Learning at a Loss* (1778).

passages, and marked by a sophisticated simplicity. In trying to describe it, one thinks of primary colours and common chords. Ideally simple emotions are postulated, expressing themselves in language of the utmost transparency, and the author, discarding realism, gropes for some primitive rectitude and succinctness of speech. In Thistlethwaite's *Man of Experience*, for instance, the hero meets an old friend and hears of his misfortunes. The dialogue then proceeds in this fashion :

" I will, if possible, relieve your distress.
      It is great, said Raymond.
      It shall be my study to lessen it, replied Honorius."

Inches of virgin paper on each side enhance the significance of these remarks, and the author aims at ideal dignity by means of elimination. A modern writer would probably have dealt in silences and awkward colloquialisms, but Thistlethwaite and his fellows, when they dismissed the elaborate verbiage current in their day, did so that they might overhear and echo the immediate shock of heartbeats. Such a style cannot, of course, be used except in the simplest situations,—or rather in situations that have been reduced to their simplest elements ; for it cannot coexist with any study of character, and has the effect of reducing the speaker to the typical " man " of the theorist. It is, however, susceptible of a certain noble swagger, best illustrated from the French novel. " Live," says the philosophic duellist in Baculard d'Arnaud's *Fanny, or The Happy Repentance*, to the villain whom he has disarmed ; " live, and enjoy the privilege of repentance."

It was not against this simplicity but against the excesses indicated above that the attack was launched, sometimes in the name of common sense and sometimes in that of true sensibility. " I hate unnecessary snivelling," wrote Andrew Macdonald [1] uncompromisingly,

[1] Andrew Macdonald (1757–1790) resigned a charge in the Scottish Episcopal Church to settle as a man of letters first in Edinburgh, then

and went on to state his suspicion of its purifying powers
and his preference for humour as a corrective weapon.
Even the apostles of sentiment and sensibility felt that the
words had been blown upon and the notions they conveyed contaminated. " I do not wish to make a *Parade*
of sentiment," says Clara Reeve in her stately way, when
chaffed by Hortensius on the high level of morality which
she requires in novels, " like some writers, who have
brought even the word itself into disgrace."   This was in
1785, and nine years earlier Dr. Cogan had represented
John Buncle Junior refusing to let the publisher put the
word " sentiment " on his title-page, since " at this
delicate æra of British refinement, when every *Cook-Maid*
talks sentiment, and every *Porter* boasts of sensibility,
the word is become so wretchedly prostituted to subjects
void of sentiment, that it must be thrown off among
exploded phrases."   It is indolence and vanity that
account for the sentimental style, and now even tavern-
tipplers pretend to relish it.

It is most instructive to watch the contrivances of
novelists who run with the hare and hunt with the hounds,
who provide all the attractions of sensibility and yet come
out ultimately on the side of common sense.   The usual
way is an epistolary connection between a hero of exquisite
sensibility and an austerely practical friend ; but the most
gigantic example of this compromise is Courtney Melmoth's *Family Secrets* (1797).   The book drips and reeks
with sensibility ; sensibility smokes round it like morning
mist ; Shelley's admired *Thaddeus of Warsaw* of the many
handkerchiefs is a dry book in comparison ; and yet
through the mist, at punctual intervals, we hear the rebukes
of the author or of his mouthpiece, John FitzOrton, like

---

in London.   Besides his novel *The Independent* (1784), from which
the quotation is made, he wrote verse, serious and burlesque (the
latter under the pseudonym of Matthew Bramble), sermons and plays.
His greatest success was the romantic play *Vimonda*, produced at the
Haymarket in 1787.

the clang of a great gong. Melmoth claimed that one of the aims of his book was to point out the danger of this abuse of emotion, and the loss of the sense of the relative importance of objects to which it leads ; and his claim cannot be denied. He and John are quite explicit about it. In Volume V (it is a very long book) John says of his sensible brother, " the disastrous Henry " : " As a man he has no character at all. It has evaporated in sighs and tears." But the reader who reached this salutary observation had done so through four other volumes of melting delights.

" O Harry ! Harry ! you have feelings only on paper," cried Mrs. Mackenzie to that successful lawyer, once the Man of Feeling. A writer is not bound to wear his heart on his sleeve in daily life, but the words, playful as they are, suggest an essential falsity which infected the whole cult of sensibility, and of which it perished. The heaviest discredit fell on it during the French Revolution. In August 1798 the *Anti-Jacobin Review* published a cartoon which includes the figure of Sensibility in a cap of liberty, weeping over a dead robin and trampling on a crowned and severed head. Feelings, runs the implicit argument, are a treacherous standard of behaviour ; over-indulged, they loosen the ties of moral responsibility, destroy the sense of proportion, and, by fostering egoism, induce a fundamental callosity of heart. " Mary Wollstonecraft could plead her feelings in justification of her concubinage and her attempted suicide," wrote Dr. Bisset ; " we doubt not that even Newgate has considerable supplies from these *victims of sensibility*." [1]

[1] *v.* review of Mrs. Robinson's *False Friend* in the *Anti-Jacobin Review*, May 1799, p. 39.

III

Our Ancestors placed their Amusement in Laughter, we place our's in Chastity of Sentiment.—Advertisement to the first number of *The Sentimental Magazine*, 1773.

In the days when even a Cossack chieftain was accommodated with a " settled melancholy," [1] and when it was—according to the popular novel—the most natural thing in the world to want to keep a beloved corpse unburied in an oratory hung with white satin, it is not to be expected that the pleasures of mirth could compete with the pleasures of melancholy. Humour in the English novel at the end of the eighteenth century is, with a few marked exceptions, scanty and crude. Didacticism and sensibility in league had gone near to choke it, and of these two sensibility was the more deadly, since from sensibility sprang that false refinement to which pictures of low life were distasteful and laughter barbarous. " Tears, tears, Mr. Web, misses must cry or it's nothing; write for the white handkerchief, dear Web, an' you love me," says the library-keeper in Melmoth's *Family Secrets* to his hack, for " fine light tragical reading " moved more nimbly from the shelves than " one of your heavy merry books." [2] Critics deplored the neglect of " the walks of humour and character," though some of them held that those eccentricities of conduct, in which the older writers had found so rich a source of mirth, had been filed away by the advance of social refinement, and were no more available.[3] Manners had become more decent and uniform; character in society was not often salient; and outside society there were only the " low," from which a large part, perhaps the majority, of the reading public

---

[1] v. *Siberian Anecdotes* by Rev. Thomas Haweis (1783).

[2] v. Bridges, *Adventures of a Bank-note*, III, p. 4.

[3] Cf. Cumberland, *Henry*, Bk. VIII, Ch. I (1795): " As the state of society becomes more refined, eccentricity of character wears away."

at this time had a fastidious aversion. The same discouraging view was taken in France ; broad humour and open passion are alike antiquated, and the modern reader must draw his amusement from the delicacies and ironies of sentiment. In England the brand of humour most acceptable was that which has a strong substratum of sentiment. Human foibles are noted in a mood drenched in benevolence, and promptly offset by some notable virtue ; whimsical characters are evolved, like Partington, the eccentric philanthropist of *Family Secrets*, who abuses his friends, is ceremoniously polite to the objects of his contempt, and rails at the destitute with tears in his eyes and his hand in his pocket.

Graves in the novel, like Goldsmith in the drama, defied " the modern tapino-phoby or dread of everything that is low, either in writing or in conversation," and declared his belief that " as we sometimes find very low wit employed upon the highest subjects, so there is room for high humour (if the author had abilities) upon the lowest subjects." [1] There were few humorists, however, to prosecute his challenge, and, while we find plenty of coarse fun and satire, and a certain amount of whimsy, high humour is generally lacking. The usual tone of comic scenes at this period is unsympathetic. On one side we have farce,—horseplay and back-chat, quarrelsome families, the baiting of old maids and distraught foreigners,—on the other, a survival in the new form of the old tradition of character-writing. Most novels contain satirical sketches, scoffing in tone and antithetical in structure, of odd types and characters,—rich vulgarians, pedantic old gentlemen, hard-riding young women,— people whose external peculiarities and traits of character are ludicrously emphasized for our amusement. Certain humorous themes of long lineage do duty with much regularity ; again and again we meet the country squire

[1] v. *Spiritual Quixote*, I, p. 6.

in London, the old maid who would like to get married, the retired tradesman aspiring to taste, the hypocritical Methodist, and the out-at-heel troupe of actors.   It is remarkable that these characters, and the incidents in which they are involved, are often irrelevant to the story,— so much waste satiric material, that employs the hero's pen, fills up the stage-coach, perhaps, in which he travels, but makes no contribution to the plot.   Young ladies enliven their letters with smart, crackling ridicule at the expense of fops and boors and henpecked husbands. Good themes as these are, they began to crave some freshness and kindliness of treatment.   Least harsh among the comic figures of the period are the various Quixotes, philosophical, benevolent and amicable ; [1] they are of the breed of Parson Adams, though often sadly degenerated, and the ridicule they inspire leaves their amiable and respectable qualities untouched.   One reads with pleasure of the poor and stately baronet, Sir Joseph Dingle, of the *Flights of Inflatus* (1791), setting forth on his fly-fishing expedition accompanied by his maid-servant.[2]

The Quixotes are exceptional, since their comic foibles do to some extent motivate the plot in which they move. They do not stand like marginal grotesques, detached from the action or only jerked into it by the arbitrary will of the author.   Apart from them, even the best comic work of the period is of an incidental, episodic nature. The French surgeon in *Zeluco* (1789), the two Scots in the same book who fight a duel on the subject of the reputation of Mary Queen of Scots, the professional

---

[1] Mrs. Lennox's *Female Quixote* falls outside our period, but, besides the *Spiritual Quixote*, there are the *Philosophical Quixote ; or, Memoirs of Mr. David Wilkins* (1782), *The Amicable Quixote ; or, the Enthusiasm of Friendship* (1788), *William Thornborough, the Benevolent Quixote* (1791), and the *History of Sir George Warrington ; or, the Political Quixote* (1797).   The Quixotic model is constantly recalled, either directly or through Smollett or Fielding, in the various " rambles " that are published.

[2] *The Flights of Inflatus ; or, the Sallies, Stories, and Adventures of a Wild-goose Philosopher.*   By the author of the *Trifler* (1791).

hermit in *Columella* (1779), who is hired to sit outside his hermitage with a book and is more often found with a beer-pot, are lively and authentic figures, but they have little enough to do with the stories they are found in, and their brief appearances give no scope for depth of characterization.

Certainly bad luck beset the comic muse towards the end of the eighteenth century. The comic invention, the easy fluidity of the *Spiritual Quixote* runs thin in Graves's later books, though it does not quite dry up, and Fanny Burney's humour in *Cecilia* suffered from the same antithetical rigidity as her prose. Relief is to be found in obscure corners of fiction. In 1778 Gregory Lewis Way published *Learning at a Loss, or the Amours of Mr. Pedant and Miss Hartley*, a lively, gossiping, well-bred novel, which contains in the character of Sir Thorobred Rugg an original variation on the Tony Lumpkin type. We assist at the informal wash of this rowdy, clumsy, good-humoured young horse-fancier, and see him " dipping the corner of the Breakfast Cloth into his Tea-cup, and wiping himself with his dirty Pocket Handkerchief," throwing his legs into the seat of any chair that stands near him, and entangling his boots and spurs with the bars. These small gratifications tide the reader over to the 'eighties and the work of Bage and Dr. John Moore. Bage's cheerful sarcasms caught the critics in his first book, and there is a refreshing solidity and inventiveness in his handling of old types that fulfilled their expectations. It was obvious that the funds of humour were not exhausted. The unobtrusive fineness of Moore's observation was equally reassuring. A new spirit was moving in the novel, and the comic vision of life was being renewed and extended.

CHAPTER IV

THE FEMALE NOVELISTS

I

For a woman to expose the want of literary talent I conceive no reproach, provided she is not led to publish merely through self-conceit.—Mrs. INCHBALD, *A Simple Story*, 1791.

" THE easy productions of a fine fancy," said Sir Charles Grandison reassuringly to Emily Jervoise, " not made the business of life, or its boast, confer no denomination that is disgraceful, but very much the contrary."

The qualification should be noted, for Sir Charles is voicing the opinion not only of men but of women, not only of his own generation but of at least two generations to come. Let a woman write to amuse her leisure hours, to instruct her sex, to provide blameless reading for the young, or to boil the pot ; moral zeal was an accepted justification and poverty an accepted excuse ; but there was one motive which could neither be justified nor excused—ambition, the " boast " of conscious power, craving to perform its task and receive its reward. The proper attitude for a female talent was diffidence ; the proper field for its exercise, the narrow circle of her intimate friends ; and if for any of the permitted reasons she stepped outside the circle, let her at least sedulously avoid the disgraceful imputation of assurance. As a rule it was not difficult ; the hesitations, the tremblings and deprecations were sincere enough, for the literary ladies of George III's reign were unsheltered by any tradition and were painfully conscious of the " Disadvantages consequent from a common Female Education." Anonymity was the great resource, and only by the most prudent degrees was the veil dropped. Frances Brooke acknowledged her third novel, while Clara Reeve withheld her full signature until the publication of *The Exiles*, eleven years after her success with *The Old English Baron*, when she was in her sixtieth year. The fact that in many cases the authorship was an open secret only adds a fine point to the delicacy of the procedure.[1] " There always seems to be a degree of vanity and presumption in those who believe themselves capable of entertaining, or informing the public," wrote Clara Reeve, when, at the age of forty, she launched her first book, convinced at last by daily examples that her sex was not an insuperable bar to literary reputation.[2] Miss Reeve had some ambition, though she kept it well chastised ; a more emotional and even humbler neophyte is found in the authoress of *The Example ; or the History of Lucy Cleveland* (1778). " When I attempt to interest an impartial Public in favour of the following Work," she writes, " it is not from a vain hope, that it is deserving of the *approbation* of the *judicious*. —No, my hopes are better founded ; a candid, a liberal, a generous Public, will make the necessary allowances, for the *first* attempt of a young female Adventurer in Letters."

The necessary allowances were most frequently claimed on the score of distress. These female adventurers, it was made clear, wrote with their breasts against the thorn of poverty, and, if the thorn were removed, would cease

[1] A good many women, who would not put their names to the title-pages of their books, signed their prefaces ; *e.g.* Maria Susanna Cooper in the *Exemplary Mother* (1769 ; new edition 1784). On the other hand, where distress was the motive of publication, and the author appealed in this fashion to her friends, the name was sometimes very fully given ; e.g. *The Old Maid ; or, History of Miss Ravensworth*, by Mrs. Skinn, late Miss Masterman of York (1771) ; *Moreton Abbey; or, the Fatal Mystery*, by the late Miss Harriet Chilcot of Bath, afterwards Mrs. Meziere, Authoress of *Elman and Ethlinda, a legendary Tale* (1786). Even the modest " Author of——" savoured of pretentiousness to some critics.

[2] v. *Original Poems on Several Occasions*, by C. R. (1769).

to write. Sarah Fielding's plaintive address to her readers
has often been quoted, and to this may be added that of
Mrs. Eliza Parsons, who took up her pen for the support
of eight dear fatherless children, assuring her patrons that
inclination had no share in her feeble attempts to entertain
the Public.[1]

Diffidence was the only wear, but it did not suit all the
women equally well. Mrs. Griffith, already popular and
respected, might " presume once more, though with
extreme timidity, to solicit the indulgence of the public
to this further attempt," [2] and Miss Reeve might mask her
growing self-confidence decently under her zeal for
education, but Miss Burney, to the surprise and approval
of her reviewer, did not plead the privilege of her sex,[3]
while Mrs. Brooke, in the person of Maria, heroine of
The Excursion (1771), dares to depart a little, if not very
far, from the convention. Maria is a poet, though she
has kept the secret even from her sister. Now, driven
to put her tragedy on the market, she sits reading it
through before submitting it to an eminent critic for his
advice. " Diffident as she was by nature, that enthusiasm
inseparable from true genius broke through the veil which
modesty would have thrown over the merits of this piece."
Maria beholds her work and sees that it is good ; and the
eminent critic confirms her opinion. This is a more
natural air than Emily Jervoise breathed.[4]

The whole question of the relation in which women
stood to literature was receiving a good deal of attention
in the 'seventies. It was, of course, part of the wider,
perpetually re-canvassed question of the learned woman.
That a woman should write was not new ; there had

[1] *v.* her *History of Miss Meredith* (1790) and her *Mysterious Warnings*
(1796).
[2] *v. Lady Juliana Harley* (1776).
[3] *v. Monthly Review*, Dec. 1782, on *Cecilia*.
[4] There are a few petulant prefaces, but they did not avail. The
Monthly told Mrs. Cowley (May 1780, p. 378) that her " *Deprecation*
was evidently written in the hour of insolence and vanity."

always been single spies ; but soon after the middle of the
century the battalions advance, and before a generation
is over, women of all ranks are writing, from the Duchess
of Devonshire and Lady Craven down to the Bristol milkwoman and a farmer's daughter of Gloucestershire. Dr.
Johnson commented on the change ; in his youth, he said,
the woman who could spell an ordinary letter had been
considered all-accomplished, but now " they vied with
the men in everything." Chief among the liberating and
stimulating forces was the gradual improvement in the
education of middle-class women ; [1] in the second place
we need not hesitate to put the popularity of the novel.
Not that the women who now began to write confined
themselves to the novel; they wrote history, poetry,
treatises on education, moral essays and even sermons,
though this was felt to be going rather far ; but it was the
novel that gave the vast body of them confidence to make
the plunge. Here, as they apprehended it, was a new
and unexacting literary form, hedged round by no learned
traditions, based on no formal technique, a go-as-you-
please narrative, spun out in a series of easy, circumstantial
letters, such as a young lady might write to a school-
friend before domestic cares absorbed her. It did not
look difficult ; even the plot need not be so strictly premeditated as it is in a drama, or in Fielding's elaborate
comic epic in prose ; one could start with a rough sketch
of a group of characters, and ideas for their future relationships would surely present themselves. The process
was little more than a methodizing of the day-dreams that
exercise a young woman's fancy, patched with a few
scraps of realistic and malicious portraiture from her
immediate surroundings. In this way it could be done,
and in this way it was done time and again, for of the
epistolary novels, which stock the shelves of the circulating

---

[1] v. the conversation from *The Irish Guardian*, quoted in the
Gentleman's Magazine (1775, pp. 535–6).

libraries, the majority must, on external and internal evidence, be assigned to women. The picaresque, the survey of manners,—these were the masculine preserves, and it was a long time before any woman invaded them ; but in the epistolary novel of domestic morals they were at home, sharing their portion only with such arrant Richard-sonians as Thomas Hull and the inevitable book-sellers' hacks, who now added female impersonation to their bag of tricks. " We suspect," wrote the *Critical* in April 1778 of the *Memoirs of the Countess D'Anois*, " that Madame la Comtesse may be found in some British garret, without breeches, perhaps, but yet not in petti-coats ; " and there is evidence that eight years earlier the fraud was already an old and paying one.[1] Women were supposed to constitute three-quarters of the novel-reading public, and this was probably true, for the establishment of circulating libraries, which catered especially for their leisure, conspired with the failure in the succession of male novelists of power and seriousness to push back the novel from the position which Fielding had claimed for it and to debase it into a form of female recreation. Women, to complete the link in the argu-ment, liked to read what women had written, to meet in books with a reflection of their own interests and point of view ; it was a new pleasure, and gave such plentiful occupation to " your female novel-writers, your spinning-jennies " (as C. H. Wilson [2] pleasantly called them), that in 1773 the *Monthly Review* remarked with meaning that " this branch of the literary *trade* " appeared to be " almost entirely engrossed by the Ladies." [3]

[1] Cf. *Gentleman's Magazine*, 1770, p. 274 ; *Monthly Review*, April 1774, p. 327, and *Critical Review*, April 1774, p. 317. The motive of the impersonation was to benefit by the acknowledged superiority of women in imagination and fancy, and to " preclude the severity of criticism."

[2] *The Wandering Islander*, I, p. 71.

[3] Cf. *Monthly Review*, Dec. 1790, on *The Denial* : " Of the various species of composition that in course come before us, there are none in

The novel, then, offered an outlet to the imaginative, an instrument to the didactic and a resource to the straitened. If we seek, as at times we must, to visualize these early adventurers, it is the first type that provides us with the fewest clues, for they almost invariably hid themselves under the mantle of the second. Mrs. Radcliffe, scribbling alone at midnight, emancipated romance, not from moral responsibility, of which she was very careful, but from this apologetic attitude; her influence, however, was not felt until the 'nineties, and for the earlier part of the period we have no full-blown romantic and can only accept, in the place of one, the figure of that dignified and self-reliant old maid, Miss Clara Reeve, seated in her library, shuffling her slips like a research student, while the biddable Hortensius jumps up to consult her references for her.[1] There is an air, if not of romance, at least of leisure and enjoyment about the picture; Miss Reeve, though her didactic leanings were very strong, did write primarily to please herself. Lady Mary Walker wrote, we are told, in her nursery, among the children who were the original motive of her authorship.[2] Mrs. Griffith had, as Mrs. Woolf may be pleased to know, " a room of her own," at least in the absence of a novel-writing husband. As for the poor soul whom need drove to market her talents, we see her among the stage-coach company on the road to London in Mrs. Bonhote's *Rambles of Mr. Frankly* (1773). " The female writer sat and eat her meal with silent humility—yet sighing." Her husband is in gaol, and she is on her way to sell her second novel, her first having brought her praise but no cash. But we are not reduced to fiction for evidence of these sad and

---

which *our* writers of the male sex have less excelled, since the days of Richardson and Fielding, than in the arrangement of the novel. Ladies seem to appropriate to themselves an exclusive privilege in this kind of writing."

[1] v. *Progress of Romance* (1785).

[2] v. *Letters from the Duchess de Crui and others.* By a Lady (1776).

squalid Muses. Sarah Emma Spencer, sending her *Memoirs of the Miss Holmsbys* (1788) into the world, adds that they were " written by the bedside of a sick husband, who has no other support than what my writing will produce ; "[1] while in the history of Mrs. Skinn we have a typical case of the circumstances that drove a woman into authorship. The *Gentleman's Magazine* printed her obituary in 1789. She had been Anne Emelinda Masterman, granddaughter and heiress to H. Masterman, Esq. of York, who disinherited her for a false step committed before she was sixteen. She married Mr. Skinn, an attorney, and on his death Nicholas Foster, Esq., an officer, the son of an Irish baronet, who abandoned her in poverty. For ten years this beautiful and talented woman supported herself by her pen, her needle, and by keeping a day-school ; at forty-two she succumbed and died at Margate in great distress. The obituary speaks of ill-health induced by poverty and exquisite sensibility. Poverty is sufficiently evident, but *The Old Maid* inspires a hope that the second curse was spared. One notes that up to about 1780 the majority of women writers were married. There were, of course, notable exceptions, women of spirit and a conscious literary bent, such as Frances Moore (later Mrs. Brooke), Elizabeth Carter and Frances Burney, but, generally speaking, only the encouragement of a husband or the desperate hardihood of adversity gave a woman the resolution to face print. It was a state of affairs that was soon modified, as the " British fair "—every woman writer, whatever her age or circumstances, was " fair " to her critics and her public—grew in collective and individual self-confidence, and by 1790 there were a good many spinsters in the field, while the practice of anonymous publication, though still frequent, was no longer general. Scotland was behind England in assimilating the female author. Mrs.

[1] v. *Monthly*, Feb. 1789.

Marishall's tears over her novel-writing daughter were soothed by the assurance that such behaviour was not uncommon in England, but forty years later a " female literary character " was still " a sort of phænomenon " north of the Border, and Elizabeth Hamilton, who had written novels while she lived in the south, was very conscious of the " dangerous distinction of authorship." [1]

There is a remarkable solidarity about the attack of the women on the literary world, and the old rubbed military metaphors, that run almost unconsciously from the historian's pen, have at least this justification, that the women marched shoulder to shoulder. " They seem to be animated with an emulation for vindicating the honour of women in general," wrote the perceptive *Critical* in 1776, " rather than for acquiring to themselves the invidious reputation of great accomplishments." The point will emerge more clearly when the stock themes, the common code of ethics in their novels, fall to be considered. At present it is enough to point out that they lost no opportunity of advertising each other's wares. The literary squabble between Mrs. Cowley and Hannah More in 1779, which led the latter into the " unsexual hardiness " of writing to a newspaper, as well as that in 1785 conducted by Miss Seward and Miss Reeve in the comparative decency of a monthly magazine, may prove that the women were getting accustomed to the care of a literary reputation, but they are not typical.[2] Far more characteristic is the passage in the *Irish Guardian* (1775) where the company at a masquerade slips into discussing

---

[1] *v.* Miss Benger, *Memoirs of the late Mrs. Elizabeth Hamilton* (1818). The passage is from the account of a friend who first met Elizabeth Hamilton in 1804.

[2] The Cowley-More dispute, which involved a question of plagiarism, appeared in the *St. James' Chronicle*, and was reprinted in the *Gentleman's Magazine* for August 1779. In 1786 Miss Reeve's relative valuation of *Pamela* and *Clarissa* caused Miss Seward to attack her in the same magazine, and there was an exchange of hostilities (Jan.–Feb. 1786, pp. 15, 16, 117).

" Mrs. Rowe, Mrs. Carter, Mrs. Lennox, Mrs. Griffith, Mrs. Brooke," or the compliment to Miss Lee in *The Victim of Fancy* (1787) and her appearance in the Pump Room scene, or Miss Reeve's quiet triumph as she adds Susannah Dobson's *Life of Petrarch* to her list of books on mediæval romance,—" a name," as she says, " that will not disgrace the list, a writer of my own sex."

The female contribution to literature was viewed by the critics with sympathetic indulgence. There was a very real belief in the civilizing function of woman in society, and to this was added the hope that womanly delicacy and purity, imported into literature, might supplement the robust virility of eighteenth-century utterance. The world of the novel, in particular, seemed incomplete; let the women now speak of their experience; let them contribute their native sense, their elegant simplicity, to the common stock, and complete the revelation of human nature. The contribution, it may be repeated, was to be emphatically feminine. The *Monthly* reviewer, expressing his sincere admiration of " the excellences of our female writers," insisted on the recognition of sex in minds, and chid Miss Aikin and her fellow-authoresses for treading too much in the footsteps of men, while Miss Roger's *History of Miss Temple* (1777) set him brooding on the possibilities of a love theme, handled by a woman writer.[1] The female heart, it appears, experiences " the delicate sensibilities of the tender passion, in a degree of refinement of which the rougher sex is seldom capable "; moreover, the female mind combines the power to " unfold sentiments of elegant love " with an instinctive care for perfect decorum; therefore " we naturally expect the

---

[1] Feb. 1773 and Aug. 1777. In 1792, on the other hand, the reviewer rejoices that women novelists are " gradually taking a higher and more masculine tone," and approves of the politics in Mrs. Smith's *Desmond*. But by then the *Monthly* had become markedly liberal in tone, and Holcroft and Mary Wollstonecraft were among the reviewers.

most lively and touching delineations of this passion from the female pen." The men, in fact, expected to enjoy a glimpse into that ideal world of the affections, which they hoped was inhabited by their woman-kind; and to some extent they did enjoy it; the love-scenes of most of the novels are conventional, but there are occasional touches of delicate veracity that carry into the novel the movement of a young girl's heart. Such is Lady Helen's involuntary cry on first seeing Erskine: "Oh! my dear, how insignificant are half the human race, compared with what they ought to be ";[1] and such is the moment when Cecilia sits lost in thought after Delvile's departure, "looking at the door through which he had passed, as if, with himself, he had shut out all for which she existed."[2]

Delicacy in a woman writer was a *sine qua non*, and a flaw in it forfeited the special consideration that women confidently claimed and critics seldom failed to show.[3] Indeed, so sensitive to pollution was this fine effluence of womanhood that, when Mrs. Cowley published a *Monologue in Honour of Chatterton*, the *Gentleman's Magazine* felt obliged to point out, " with all due deference to creative genius," that it was " not an unexceptionable subject for a female pen." Delicacy which, on its negative side, meant abstention from the least shadow of coarseness,[4] expressed itself positively in those fine

---

[1] v. *The Errors of Innocence* by Harriet Lee (1786).

[2] *E.g.* Elizabeth Blower's *Maria* (1785): " He seemed to penetrate the inmost folds of my heart: but at the same time inspired none of that embarrassment one usually experiences when under particular observation; my soul seemed to submit itself with pleasure to his scrutiny, as conscious the heart of its judge beat with sentiments congenial to its own, as if certain of candour and lenity."

[3] v. *Critical*, June 1770, p. 474, on *The Unhappy Wife*.

[4] The critics' standard of delicacy is not easy to define. They register no protest when a girl writes of a man on his wedding-day: " With what greedy impatience did Seymour explore the beautiful symmetry of his wife's person." On the other hand, the *Critical* (Feb. 1775) reviewer objected violently to a simile in Cumberland's

analyses of sentiment which were often compared to the French.[1]   In literature, as in life, a woman's strength was held to lie in heart, not head.   Sympathy, imagination, spontaneity, simplicity—these were the qualities expected of her, and for these the critics awarded her high marks.   Faults of judgment were expected and passed over tolerantly,[2] while discursive reasoning on " topics that require investigation and labour " was, in some quarters at least, definitely discouraged.   No woman could be expected to make any valuable contribution on such subjects ; " proficiency in any science can only be the result of much severe application and study ; perhaps more than a female's constitution can bear " ; and meanwhile there was also the danger to her moral balance, lest she should become " most intolerably proud and self-consequential." [3]   Exceptions, however, could upset even these well-grounded views, and Mrs. Catherine Macaulay, historian and bluestocking, who, after grappling publicly with the question of copyright, went on to metaphysics,

---

Battle of Hastings " which we presume to say even a princess of those rude days would have been too delicate to use."   The simile is :

> " I saw your hero dart into the fight,
>   As a trained swimmer springs into the flood."

" We do not doubt," concludes the critic, " that if Matilda's eyes had ever, *by accident*, been gratified with the sight of a swimmer springing into the flood, the young lady had more judgment than to use it in her common conversation, *by way of simile*."   Gratified ! *v.* also the *Monthly Review* (April 1771) on *Meditations by the late Mrs. Jean Stuart.*   Mrs. Stuart turns roundly on the scoffer, crying : " *You lie*—the Lord is a shield."   The reviewer asks : " Do not the two words printed in italic, in the latter part of the foregoing extract, imply something rather too indelicate and masculine for the pen of a lady ? "

[1] Cf. R. Griffith's *Genuine Letters*, I, p. 138 ; and *v.* for an example Miss E. Blower's *Features from Life* (1788).

[2] Cf. R. Griffith, *The Triumvirate*, I, p. 37 (1764)—" sense of the right feminine kind, for it consisted rather in a quickness of apprehension and a delicate taste, than a strong judgment "; and Clara Reeve, *Original Poems* (1769), *To my friend Mrs. —— on her holding an argument on the natural equality of both sexes.*

[3] *v.* the discussion between Fanny and Charles on Learned Ladies in Dr. Cogan's *John Buncle, Junior*, Letter X (1776).

obviously fell outside all categories. " I would have statues erected to her memory," writes Lord Lyttelton to Mrs. Peach ;[1] " and once in every age I would wish such a woman to appear, as proof that genius is not confined to sex . . . but . . . at the same time . . . you'll pardon me, we want no more than *one* Mrs. Macaulay." There speaks the old Adam, who puts charm and learning in opposite scales and then throws the whole weight of his masculine prepossessions in with the former to make the latter kick the beam ; he speaks, indeed, with extorted generosity, endeavouring to correct an instinctive bias, but there is no doubt that Dr. Cogan's Fanny [2] would have detected here too " a lurking Mahometan creed."

With all the encouragement meted out to women, there was as yet no question of judging them by the same standards as men. Novelists fell into three classes—men, fair authoresses, and Grub-street hacks ; and, with such rare exceptions as Mrs. Macaulay and Miss Burney, the critical vocabulary, when it is applied to the work of women, is always comparative. To say that a novel is " in the main correctly written " is to refer not to structure and proportion but to grammar and spelling ; at other times the critic deigns himself to correct inaccuracies ; Mrs. Parsons, it appears in her *Mysterious Warning* (1796), constantly writes *neither, or*, whereas " *neither* should invariably be followed by *nor*."[3] In the main

---

[1] v. *The Correspondents, an Original Novel* (1775). The book professed to be the correspondence between Lord Lyttelton (*d.* 1773) and Mrs. Peach, who afterwards married his son. Horace Walpole wrote on July 7th, 1775 : " I think one cannot doubt the letters being genuine." Lyttelton's executors, however, promptly disclaimed them, and Walpole accepted the disclaimer (Aug. 3rd). The identifications—only initials had been used in the book—were not challenged. The letters are therefore evidence, not of what Lord Lyttelton and Mrs. Peach certainly thought and wrote, but—having regard to Walpole's original acceptance of them—of what they might well have thought or written, what was typical of their rank, education and characters. In this sense they have been quoted here and elsewhere.

[2] v. *ante*, p. 126, *n*. 3.

[3] v. *Critical*, April 1796.

critics prided themselves on honouring the large drafts made on their " candour," and refused to " point their critical cannon " against a woman, especially a woman in distress. Towards the end of the century this sort of chivalry declines ; reviewers begin to take credit for strict impartiality, and the " philosophesses," in particular, are felt to have forfeited all right to special consideration.[1] Even before their appearance provocation was often extreme, and courtesy stretched a point or two. " A plain story, told in very plain language, and may be read without the trouble of laughing, crying or thinking," wrote the *Monthly* reviewer of *The Thoughtless Ward* by a Lady (1777), while the *Critical* dismisses *The Noble Family* (1771) in this fashion : " Humanity prompts us to hope that Mrs. Austen, of Clerkenwell, does not trust to her pen for her subsistence. As a writer she is no object of criticism ; as a woman she is entitled to candour." In the last resort the exordium : " Could we believe this novel to be the composition of a man, we should not scruple to say "—calls down on the poor fool floods of contingent rebuke.

II

The world that the women of George III's reign set out to depict is a limited one. Its centre is the home, its outlying provinces Ranelagh, the Opera, the debtor's prison and the convent finishing-schools of Northern France. It is dependent on an obscure male world of action and business, which its occupants can seldom envisage, but of which they feel the reverberations. It has often been remarked that Jane Austen's novels contain no scenes between men, and, while no other woman

---

[1] Cf. *Monthly*, July 1792, p. 339 : " The public opinion of literary merit has no connection with, and will very seldom be influenced in favour of, the private motives of the writer." *v.* also Rev. R. Polwhele's *Unsex'd Females*, p. 16 (1798).

accepts quite so logically the consequences of her limitations, roughly speaking the abstinence is typical. Man is seen in his domestic aspect as father, husband, son or lover ; if a merchant, we never accompany him to his counting-house ; if a farmer, his farm is kept out of sight ; if a soldier, he has resigned from the service " in consequence of disappointments " ; and this is just as well, for the male world is full of pitfalls for a female novelist, and Mrs. Radcliffe's Theodore de Peyrou, who deserts his regiment on the frontier to attempt the rescue of his persecuted Adeline, is promoted, after some intermediate tribulations, as a reward for his gallant conduct.

Nevertheless, it would be uncritical to stress too heavily the accidental limitations of the women's experience. Not one of them, certainly, was in a position to attempt the comic epic in prose, though Mr. Smith in *Evelina* proves that certain piquant dishes were well within their scope ; but the significant fact remains that these women controlled their servants and dealt with their tradespeople, and that they very seldom chose to write of either tradespeople or servants.[1] They were not, with the amazing exception of Jane Austen, primarily realists, though much that is real may be found in their works. They were moralists, satirists and dreamers. In their hands the novel was not so much a reflection of life as a counterpoise to it, within the covers of which they looked for compensation, for ideal pleasures and ideal revenge. To say that the foundations of the woman's novel are laid in malice and in day-dream is, of course, to exaggerate ; pages of quiet veracity spring to mind and contest the assertion ; but it is the exaggeration of a truth, and so far useful that it connects the domestic sentimental novel of the 'seventies with the Gothic romance of the 'nineties and shows them to be the products of the same mental

[1] Mrs. Charlotte Smith's servants are good; cf. *The Old Manor House* (1793).

soil. The themes and incidents of Miss Burney, for
instance, reappear in Mrs. Radcliffe's books, a little
obscured by the rich romantic setting but substantially
the same. Is Lord Orville much less a dream-figure than
Theodore de Peyrou ? Both are examples of the New
Hero of the lady novelists, that devastating blend of the
susceptibility of Saint-Preux with the morals of Sir
Charles Grandison and the devotion of the Grand Cyrus,
who corrects the perspective of the heroine's sketches,
defers implictly to her notions of right and wrong, and
receives the promise of her hand with a bosom thrilling
with the most delicate sensations of felicity. Orville, to
be sure, breathes a less rarefied air than Theodore ; but
he is respectful, he is refined ; there is no trace in him of
the brutal arrogance of the mere male ; he treats Evelina
with thoughtful consideration, and admires the beauties of
her mind as well as those of her person. He is the perfect
young man, whose " insinuating " manners we admire
alike at the eighteenth century tea-table, and in the
vaguely mediæval past, who performs miracles of tact in
sparing the embarrassment of young girls just launched in
society, and by his " seducingly respectful " bearing
restores their composure and increases their sense of their
own worth. Often enough his delicacy becomes effemin-
ate and his sensibility maudlin, but he was none the less
the expression of a deep need on the part of the women,
and an echo, reverberated and distorted through a
generation, of the plea for refinement which Tom Jones
heard from the lips of Sophia. He may profitably be
compared with the modern cave-man or Sheikh ; both
are the compensations of fancy and conditioned by
circumstances, for the dominated woman of the eighteenth
century indulged in the idea of sway, while the independent
woman indulges, for a short time at least, in that of
subjection.

Often the day-dream widens to embrace a group of

friends, who, in surroundings of natural beauty improved by taste, fulfil their social relationships with enlightened delicacy. It is chiefly at the beginning or end of a novel that we find these plots of enchanted ground, though even in mid-career a persecuted heroine will sometimes stumble into one. Once found, they are not lightly left; the benevolent guardians must be shown in action, the virtuous and cheerful poor must entertain their betters in their cleanly parlours, and youth must picnic in the mountains or wander by moonlight through gardens in the English style. Such pleasances of fancy are found equally in the romances and the novels;[1] Miss Reeve constructs an educational Utopia,[2] and Lady Mary Walker devotes a volume of *Munster Village* (1775) to Lady Frances's library and colleges, while, if we turn to the *Romance of the Forest* (1791) and the *Mysteries of Udolpho* (1794), we find the trait well-exemplified in the households of La Luc and St. Aubert and in Château-le-Blanc, where Mrs. Radcliffe delightedly erects a tower with windows giving on the four cardinal points and a magnificent view to be descried through each.

When the women forsake these idylls and elegies, and turn to study the outer world with its variety of creatures, the temper in which they conduct their inquiry is retributive. They are paying back old scores. A strong satiric vein runs through the domestic novel and, in the hands of Mrs. Radcliffe, penetrates even into the Gothic romance. In a generation whose humour mostly took the form of whimsical sentiment or of horse-play, the women show a keen sense of the ludicrous, but none of the charity of humour. They have taken notes of all the stupidities, all the selfish-

---

[1] They are found also in the novels of men, though not so frequently. Richardson had been a notable architect this way, and in our period there are Graves's *Eugenius*, Bage's *Mount Henneth* and the last chapters of Cumberland's *Arundel*.

[2] *v.* especially *The School for Widows* (1791) and the *Plans of Education* (1792), connected with it.

ness and clumsy motions of conceit with which for centuries their sex had been affronted. They observe with a scornful eye and record with a dry intolerance of phrase, and where their fastidiousness is offended they punish without mercy. The self-satisfied young man had as many shafts in him as St. Sebastian by the time the female authoresses had done with him ; but like St. Sebastian he recovered from the episode. He advances, " full of the idea of his own irresistibility . . . humming an opera tune, and casting a side glance at every looking-glass in his way," in gentle Mrs. Brooke's *Lady Julia Mandeville* (1763), but nothing worse happens to him than marriage into a family of rich vulgarians ; his progressive humiliations, culminating in Belinda's rejection of Sir Philip Baddely (" You can't be in earnest, Miss Portman," exclaimed the astonished baronet "), are more apparent to others than to himself, and he is never considered capable of reformation. Neither, we may remember, does Sir Willoughby Patterne reform.[1] Beside the fop, with his flashing white teeth,[2] stands the boor,

---

[1] The proposal of the conceited young man is a favourite scene, and Mr. Collins' proposal in *Pride and Prejudice* had a long lineage ; *v.* e.g. *School for Fathers*, II, p. 175 (1788) and Mrs. Smith's *Emmeline*, IV, Ch. I (1788).   It is sometimes found in a man's book when a fop is to be scourged, as in Moore's *Edward*, Ch. XCII (1796) ; (" This seems very unaccountable ! But pray, Miss Huntly," added he, after a minute's reflection, " have you formed a resolution *never* to marry ? ")   It should be added that one contemporary critic (*Critical*, Nov. 1785, on B. Walwyn's *Love in a Cottage*) is blind to this retaliation.   A male author, he says, has once more given examples of weakness and mutability in women. " The lions are, in their turn, painters ; but they do not seem disposed to retaliate : the tender texture of the female mind does not perhaps allow of any very lasting resentments."   I do not understand this gentleman's point of view, unless he refers to the ultimate repentance of libertines ; but that is another case, and very flattering is the woman who " fixes " them. Male conceit is heavily scourged by them, and seldom pardoned.

[2] Teeth are important as indications of character ; the hero's are white and even, the fop's flashing, the villain's blackened or yellow stumps.   A taste in gardening is an equally good criterion ; Madame Cheron in Mrs. Radcliffe's *Mysteries of Udolpho*, has a formal garden, whereas all the author's good characters, without consideration of time or place, have gardens in the English style.

often enough a country squire, bringing his day's bag and his hounds into the drawing-room,[1] or standing, as Mrs. Brooke saw him, back to the fire, with his hands in his pockets and his coat and waistcoat bundled up under his arms. His offence is a natural brutality, incapable of refinement, not quite so deadly in female sight, it appears, as the offence of the fop, at any rate less bitterly resented; but the tinge of melancholy, that distinguished so many of the idealized heroes of novel and romance, is to be set down to the reaction of fine nerves from the overbearing animal spirits of the boor.

But the shafts of malice are not loosed only against the other sex. The vulgar, insensitive woman made a broad target for them. Not to cite the Miss Branghtons, in whose portraiture relish contends with disgust, there is, in the midmost fortress of Gothic romance, Madame Cheron, etched by Mrs. Radcliffe with deadly precision.[2] " Hers was the blush of triumph, such as sometimes stains the countenance of a person, congratulating himself on the penetration which has taught him to suspect another, and who loses both pity for the supposed criminal and indignation at his guilt in the gratification of his own vanity." This is shrewd indeed, but it has something in it of that very triumphant detection which its author reproves; moreover, Madame Cheron, who is potentially a comic figure, is seldom treated comically; she bulks too large for mirth. During the first half of the book she is a butt for the arrows of contempt, and during the second she is hunted to a miserable death. After this Mrs. Radcliffe, relenting a little, does suffer the heroine to attend her funeral, but this is all the pity she shows. The power of overbearing vulgarity to inflict suffering is a consideration that intrudes on all the comic scenes of which it is an ingredient, and warps their mirth, for

[1] v. Anne Dawe's *Younger Sister* (1770).
[2] v. *Mysteries of Udolpho* (1794).

the spectacle of undefended sensitiveness cannot but be painful. There are scenes in the books of Mrs. Smith and Miss Burney—notably that where Cecilia is found in Belfield's room—which are distressing to read. But though lacerated delicacy is prohibited, by its own nature, from retaliation, the author is not, and Miss Burney frequently mortifies the vulgar by those rough-and-tumble methods which alone, she probably thought, could be effective.[1] Indeed, where their fastidiousness is offended, the women are not pitiful. Their laughter covers a sore, and they can scarcely regard with equanimity any of those qualities which undermine the dignity of woman, or of man in his relations with woman. The henpecked husband is as much an object of scorn as the presumptuous wooer ; the ninny tied to his mother's apron-strings is even more repulsive than the boor. The tyrant, on the other hand, is not ridiculed, nor is the seducer, for to be a victim, as these women saw it, is to gain rather than lose in dignity.[2]

This irritated fastidiousness, while it affords too narrow a basis for humour, induced in the women a fine exactness of record, which is their peculiar contribution to the technique of the novel. An admirable moderation disengages itself slowly from the tradition of boisterous caricature, inherited from satire and the stage and reinforced by the farcical breadth of Smollett, and in Fanny Burney the two veins will be found side by side. But guffaws, the overturning of coaches, with the accompanying indecencies of wigless pates and miry ditches, were not really the women's quarry ; their burlesque conforms to a prevailing taste, but of the better writers few except Fanny Burney practise it, for the crime that

[1] Cf. also Mrs. Johnson's *Gamesters* (1786), one of the imitations of Miss Burney.

[2] Andrew Macdonald in his *Independent* (1784) ridicules the seducer, on principle ; cf. *ante*, Ch. 3, pp. 109–10. Reference to Richardson on all these points will bring out his essentially " feminine " nature.

offends fastidiousness is in itself too heinous to need exaggeration, and vulgarity of mind and appearance needs no heightening to make the nerves tingle. Thus Mrs. Charlotte Smith, in whom the style is fully developed, having to describe the young tutor, the Reverend Lemuel Paunceford in *The Banished Man* (1794), does so with the utmost sobriety :

> " He was a punch figure of five feet, whose tight black clothes, knowing boots and splendid leathern breeches served only to make his redundancy of flesh more remarkable. He wore his hair high behind his round head, so that a collop of fat that was thrust from his short poll by the pressure of his neckcloth, seemed to support the spruce row of yellow curls that marked him (though somewhat to his displeasure) as being in orders."

This is nearer to Addison in spirit than to any of the great mid-century novelists, and, while it has a touch of feminine intolerance, it has none of the distorting vision by which Smollett would have changed the Reverend Lemuel into a grotesque and his collop of fat into a monstrosity.

Other similarities of predilection and experience link the domestic novels with the romances, but these must be briefly enumerated. The passivity of heroines [1]— and sometimes heroes—in a world where initiative is

---

[1] Very marked. In many books the heroine is entirely passive ; the plot is made by the activities of her family. There are exceptions. Miss Lee in *The Recess*, III, p. 28, laments this passivity, and envies men their resources and activity. " From your various disappointments in life, ever springs forth some vigorous and blooming hope, insensibly staunching those wounds in the heart through which the vital powers of the feebler sex bleed helplessly away." Heroes are passive too. Disinherited young men sit down and languish ; and when Charlotte Smith deals with the French Revolution, it is chiefly suffering, deprivation and exile, which attracts her. This is the great difference to be found between Mrs. Radcliffe and Scott, when the latter, as in *Rokeby*, uses her properties. In him suffering and suspense is terminated by decisive action.

too often a monopoly of the bad ; the cult of the pathetic, involving numerous and often irrelevant sick-beds ; the preoccupation with domestic scenes and with a prudential type of morality—these and kindred traits mark in some degree all that the women produce.   The romantic background was unfavourable to other themes that would probably, except for this, have been as pervasive. Children, for instance, those large families of which some modern readers complain, but which were a valuable contribution to the personnel of the novel, are out of place in a Gothic pile ; nor is it easy to express through a romantic heroine that anxiety about ways and means which so pathetically marks the books, where a scanty wardrobe begins the heroine's troubles, and a father's debts induce the catastrophe.   The novel, too, provides more room than the romance for the development of the " mixed female character," in which the women took a special interest.   The mixed female character, in their hands, is one which cannot be labelled good, dangerous or funny ; it is kneaded out of the common virtues and follies of human nature, but none of these is heightened for the sake of dramatic effect.   It is this absence of heightening that is the differentiating quality, the reliance on the power of unemphatic veracity to interest the reader.   The four great novelists hardly practised this method, and the women learned it slowly and applied it to small sections of their books rather than to the whole ; for it implies a faith in the value of unadorned life which is the faith of realism, to which, in literature at least, they were seldom courageous enough to adhere.   No doubt the limitation of their subject matter helped them —one is led to discriminate more closely with few objects in a small space ; at all events, in the hands of Mrs. Charlotte Smith, as later in those of Miss Edgeworth, though the ruthless treatment of dowagers, old maids and dissipated women of fashion still persists, by the side of it we find characters like Lady Ellesmere and Miss Jamima Milsington in *The Banished Man* (1794). Lady Ellesmere, a stupid, kindly woman, who has heard of the French Revolution vaguely for four years, but always forgets what it is about, and whose imagination is so dull that it cannot even be stirred by the departure of her son to join the allied forces on the French frontier, is notable because, uninteresting as she is, Charlotte Smith has thought it worth while to account for her. The explanation comes, without any bitterness, from the mouth of the son to whom she has just said good-bye. " As to ideas of danger," he says, " she has none. She has not a mind capable of figuring what she never saw. Imagination never oppresses her with its visionary terrors ; or if it did, the most terrific drawing would be erased by the home scenes around her ; and she would think more of what had happened at the next market-town. Such is the effect of living always in a narrow circle without any change of ideas." This impartial judgment about a character in whom the older novelists would have seen, if they saw anything at all, merely a source of ridicule, appears again in the figure of Miss Jamima Milsington. Miss Milsington is a woman of fashion, verging on middle age. She has not a large income, and she finds it convenient to live with her friends, and no harm to gratify their love of flattery. She is self-interested, husband-hunting, affected and sentimental. On the other hand, she is really elegant and accomplished, and kind-hearted when the cost is not too high. She betrays her partiality for the hero too openly, but goes courageously to wake him when the house is on fire (an office usually reserved for the heroine), and when she finds that he is already married retires with some remains of dignity and no vindictive feelings. To these proportions does Mrs. Smith reduce the legendary figure of the amorous old maid ; it is a humane and credible portrait. Other figures might be cited ; Mrs. Langston in Clara Reeve's *School for Widows* (1791), a cynical gossip, but good-humoured and capable of sincere liking ; or Charlotte Jones in *The Modern Fine Gentleman* (1774), an early example of the mixed female character, and, like so many, attractively sketched but not supported. Charlotte is an amateur blue-stocking, twenty-five years old, not bad-looking, untidy and kind, " bewilder'd in literature, absent, forgetting the common forms of good breeding, yet wishing to be civil to all." The subject is good, but it is soon dropped in favour of the heroine's sentimental distresses, and Charlotte is hurriedly married off at the end of the book. Abortive as many of them are, however, these attempts are evidence of a resolve on the part of the women to widen the circle of female portraits.

Something should be said of the themes of the woman's novel, though it is not easy to detach them for consideration from their moral code, which is the subject of the next section. Pursuit and endurance are their two main subjects, and these they expressed chiefly through the characters and incidents of Richardson, the pervasive quality of whose influence was strengthened, in their case, by a sense of gratitude. " Richardson is a writer all your own," says Hortensius to Euphrasia in *The Progress of Romance ;* " your sex are more obliged to him and Addison than to all other men-authors " ; and though Euphrasia (like King Henry when he received the news of Chevy Chase) remarks with dignity : " We have other redoubtable champions," she does not deny the fact. The domestic scene, often steeped in sentiment or melodrama but enlivened at times with a sort of patchy realism, was the main theme of these women. Their books do not proceed upon the level ; there are irruptions of crude romance and sudden touches of authentic observation that stand off from the faded background with an autobiographical sharpness. To conclude this section, the plots of two typical novels of the period may be briefly considered.

The Husband's Resentment ; or, The History of Lady Manchester, published anonymously, in 1776, begins with the case of Selena Belville, a poor but well-bred companion, dependent on the harsh bounties of Lady Lichfield. She attracts the affection of the middle-aged Lord Manchester, for whom she feels esteem but not love, and moved by misery, gratitude and a desire to revenge herself on Lady Lichfield, accepts his hand. In a few months the lover of her dreams, Lord Hastings, enters her life, but, though both are conscious and troubled, they remain virtuously silent. At this point the book plunges into the murk of melodrama. The incredible Lady Betty Mountague snares Hastings as her husband, and inflames Lord Manchester with jealousy of his wife. The hitherto reasonable Lord Manchester forthwith imprisons his lady in a lonely house, cuts off her hair, and feeds her on bread and water ; but Lady Betty dies, after a full confession of her crimes, and Selena is released, thanking Heaven on her knees that she is restored to her lord's favour. Then the book stumbles back in the direction of the real and lights unexpectedly on a new and significant theme. Selena forgives, as in duty bound, but she cannot feel or counterfeit confidence ; he, perceiving this, acquiesces in a temporary separation, and both set to work with good-will to build up a new relationship on the basis of friendship. But the end of the book is in sight ; the situation is no sooner sketched than it is obliterated by the death of the husband, and Selena, after the usual mysterious postponement of her inevitable felicity, is married to Hastings.

This novel, with its possible and impossible situations, its sensational folly and its tantalizing glimpses of something better, is not below the average quality. The Duchess of Devonshire's *Sylph*, published anonymously in 1779 and warmly praised by the reviewers for its originality and knowledge of *ton*, is on a higher level, and can be read even now for its liveliness and a certain freshness of touch, the gift of the amateur in letters. Julia Grenville, country-bred and not quite seventeen, marries Stanley, a young man of pleasure, who introduces her to the fashionable world and leaves her to her own protection. A former admirer, Woodley, disguises himself as a German baron and enters her circle, with the object of watching over her. His aim, however, is likely to be defeated by the strong mutual attraction they feel, and to counteract this he adopts a further disguise, and in letters signed " Sylph," and purporting to come from a Rosicrucian philosopher, acquainted by means of his commerce with spirits with all her thoughts, he directs her conduct, warning her especially against himself in the form of the Baron. Julia, although puzzled by the playful mystery, accepts the advice, and the situation is worked out with some delicacy, until the Nemesis of a gambler conducts Stanley to ruin and death, and enables Woodley to reveal himself, which he does with unnecessary—but inevitable—elaboration.

The praise accorded to this readable little book was broken by one note of doubt. Ought a young wife, asked the moralists, to take advice from any man but her husband? Might not the example operate harmfully? Was this quite the ideal of wifehood that the women wished to present? To understand these profound and delicate questions we must go on to consider the moral code of the woman's novel.

III

Remember, my dear Evelina, nothing is so delicate as the reputation
of a woman ; it is at once the most beautiful and most brittle of human
things.—F. BURNEY, *Evelina*, Letter 39, 1778.

The morality of the woman's novel has been termed
prudential, and nowadays the epithet is damaging.   Christ
in a modern poem [1] tells St. Thomas that prudence is the
deadly sin ; and we hear in the shut syllables of the word
the symbol of a cautious reserve, passing all generous
impulse through the sieve of public opinion.   But to the
eighteenth century, prudence had another sound.   Fielding, who held no brief for the self-regardful, considers it
as the quality without which " if a man doth not become
a felon to the world, he is at least a *felo de se*."   Prudence
is the duty a man owes society.   It is the candlestick of
the gospel, in which his virtue shines with a comely light,
whereas without the candlestick it might be lost under
a bushel or set the house afire.   And if the compulsion
of prudence lay strongly on men, it could not fail to lie
even more strongly on women—*quibus pretium faceret
ipsa fragilitas.*[2]   Prudence is essentially self-government
in the interests of the community, and it is well to use
ourselves to this liberal interpretation of the word in
dealing with the ethics of the women writers and with
their ideal of womanhood.   The interpretation will be
too wide for many of them, but the injustice will be less
than if we try to reduce the motives of women like Elizabeth Griffith and Frances Brooke wholly to fear and selfishness.   With prudence, then, the ark of female virtue, we
may begin our inquiry.

In the *Progress of Romance* Clara Reeve makes a quotation for which, as she ingenuously confesses, without any
suspicion of the magnitude of her crime, she has lost the
reference.   It is, however, a sentence that might be found

[1] Lascelles Abercrombie, *The Sale of Saint Thomas.*
[2] Pliny, *De Crystallo* ; quoted by Mrs. Griffith on the title-page
of her *History of Lady Barton* (1771).

in any issue of the contemporary literary reviews. " The great and important duty of a writer is, to point out the difference between virtue and vice, to show one as rewarded, and the other punished." Didacticism as the function and justification of art was a creed held, if possible, even more uncompromisingly by the women than by the men. They were most of them by necessity or choice educationists. They taught their own children or other people's ; they interested themselves in the village school; and they knew that by education alone could their sex claim its due place in the world. Moreover, they never forgot that the essential business of education is ethical, the enlightening and strengthening of the mind. In the novel they saw a supplementary instrument to direct tuition of great range and penetration, and they appropriated it to assist in the business of " good principling." " These ladies are all sentimental," says a character in *The Irish Guardian* (1775) of the female novelists, and adds, explaining the exact force with which she uses the word—" have all supported the cause of virtue, and, I hope, numbers have benefited by their labours." Many of them had written or were to write essays on conduct, unsweetened by fiction ; [1] with some, as with Lady Mary Walker, the fiction was an acknowledged afterthought,[2] a thin sprinkling of sugar on the solid fare of moral instruction. Amusement and edification overlap in every possible way. One of the heroines of the *School for Widows* keeps a school, which enables the author to insert a complete list of books suitable for the young ; Maria Susanna Cooper wrote a book, *The Exemplary Mother* (1769),[3] of which the title is a sufficient

---

[1] *E.g.* Mrs. Griffith's *Essays addressed to Young Married Women* (1782), Mrs. Bonhote's *Parental Monitor* (1788) and Miss Reeve's *Plans of Education* (1792).

[2] *v.* her *Letters from the Duchess de Crui* (1776).

[3] It was apparently popular. A " new edition " came out in 1784, with a dedication to the Hon. Lady Jerningham, and, as this dedication is dated 1779, there had probably been an edition in that year too.

description; and even the hacks found it necessary to parade a moral purpose on at least the first and last pages. Their lessons naturally refer chiefly to domestic life, for it was at once to vindicate the importance of woman in her domestic relationships and to instruct her how best to undertake and sustain them, that these women wrote. What follows is a composite portrait of ideal womanhood as their books develop it. Differences of opinion existed, of course, notably on the question of filial and wifely obedience, which the more romantic among the women drive to a picturesque height of fanaticism; but they are almost negligible beside the unanimity of the writers in principle and ideal.

In her essay on Charlotte Smith in *English Women of Letters* (1862), Charlotte Brontë's friend, Julia Kavanagh, makes a great point of the change effected by women writers in the portraiture of young girls. The " young woman," she says, was replaced by the " young lady," the girl who exists only to reward the hero by the girl who has intelligence to match her beauty. Miss Burney's heroines indicate the change—" not that they are very remarkable, but that they are something,"—while in Charlotte Smith's books the new heroine is fully evolved, a quiet, steadfast, sensitive girl, whose virtue is modesty and her strength endurance, whose character is ripened by adversity and love, and who solaces her worst hours with the contemplation of nature and the English poets. Miss Kavanagh overstates her case and post-dates the appearance of the new heroine by at least twenty years, but there is truth in what she says. The young girl of the woman's novel has an independent life; she is not just " the embodiment of beauty and the object of desire." She has her rational amusements,—her silhouettes and lessons on the harpsichord; sometimes she understands Latin;[1] she knows Shakespeare by heart and reads him

[1] This is rare, but *v.* Elizabeth Blower's *Maria*, I, p. 249 (1785), where Emilia reads and weeps over Lucan's *Pharsalia*. Miss Austen

with a starting tear ; and again and again she has to be warned by her elders against the delusions of romance— those amiable errors of a refined mind—and the perils of excessive sensibility.   Youth with its eager and rest- less susceptibilities is a state that these writers understand. " The common occurrences of life appear like enchant- ment to some minds," writes Mrs. Griffith, and recalls, through the mouth of Lady Barton, the halcyon days of castle-building, when fancy is still predominant over the first faint stirrings of passion ; and Harriet Lee, with the sympathetic knowledge of a schoolmistress still in touch with her own youth, dwells on the perpetual striving for intimacy, the craving for " the soft enthusiasm of congenial affections " that marks the adolescent girl.[1]

But the delicious dreams of youth disperse (to use a thoroughly characteristic simile) like the tinted vapours of morning before the light of the working-day.   The solid virtues—the " principling " on which the women lay such stress—remain.   There remains also that highest grace of the female character—delicacy.   Delicacy con- cerns itself with " the *beautiful*, the *becoming*, in the intercourse of life " ;[2] it is a spontaneous moral taste,[3] embracing but transcending propriety or decorum, of which Mrs. Radcliffe said that it included beneath its modest shade every grace which ought to adorn the female character.   Delicacy is defensive ; it is the reserve that

---

and other humorists mock the untaught genius for the arts displayed by these heroines ; it is ridiculous, but also significant.

[1] *v.* her *Errors of Innocence* (1786), which contains some per- ceptive remarks on girlhood, and the well-sketched but unsupported character of Lady Helen Spenser, " sanguine, impassion'd—keen, even to a degree of the sarcastic," masking her idiosyncrasy partly under the timidity of one brought up in seclusion, partly under assumed fine-lady airs.

[2] *v.* Mrs. Brooks, *The Excursion*, II, p. 156 (1777).

[3] Henrietta Belfield, in Miss Burney's *Cecilia*, is an example of this " intuitive integrity."   Cecilia and Mrs. Delvile are conscious reasoners.

is symbolized by the veil; but it is also sympathetic, a subtle perception of the emotions of others, expressing itself in a timid but penetrating compassion. In both its phases it was subject to foolish excesses, and was at times perverted to add a spice to the epicure's dish. We hear too much of " the visible contest of the purest affection with the terrors of a chastity yet unbreathed on," while a character in Mrs. James Keir's *History of Miss Greville* (1787) expresses the wish that his wife should feel passion, but never express it, since the turbulence of passion is incompatible with " that innate delicacy . . . which is inseparable from an elegant and truly virtuous female mind." Delicacy can also be a stumbling-block in the affairs of life. Adeline in the *Romance of the Forest* cannot receive her lover's vindication, simply because delicacy forbids her to mention his crime; while " breaking the news " is an orgy that calls for roasting at the slowest fires. To all this we can only say : *Corruptio optimi pessima*, and turn back to Mrs. Brooke or Mrs. Griffith.

Where, out of their own books, could the women find the picture of this, the peculiar dower of womanhood? There was, of course, Richardson, but to many of them Clarissa's delicacy seemed, as it seems to us, an ambiguous and ill-considered virtue. Richardson had their gratitude, but they did not go all the way with him. In Shakespeare, however, they discerned " the judge, the friend of womankind." [1] The dignity of Hermione and Queen Katherine, the essential delicacy of Imogen, Miranda and Desdemona, confirmed them in their sense of their own worth; more, Shakespeare alone among great poets had written nobly of the friendship of women. It was a point on which the women were sensitive and on which they were very glad to have so important an ally. The disbelief of unthinking men in the capacity of women

[1] *v.* Mrs. Peach in *The Correspondents*, p. 176 (1775).

for friendship, the serious conviction of thinking men, with which some women agreed, that such a relationship could not survive marriage, were slurs upon the honour of the sex, which they applied themselves to expunge, and it was a great advantage to them that in this contest they could fight behind the shield of so redoubtable a champion. " I shall ever love and honour his memory," wrote the supposed Mrs. Peach, " because he is the only poet (that I know of) who has delineated to perfection the character of a *female friend*." Celia is her favourite heroine, and it is to Rosalind and Celia that Lady Mary Walker points in her *Letters from the Duchess de Crui*.[1]

We must not, however, expect the claim that a woman is something *per se* to fill a large space in the novel at this period. The aim of every honest woman, said Mrs. Griffith, was marriage ; and, once married, unless her husband failed to do his part, she was his satellite. " As from our birth we are but *secondary* objects in creation," wrote Miss C. Palmer in her *Letters upon Several Subjects from a Preceptress to her Pupils who have left School* (1797), " subordination is the natural sphere in which

---

[1] The theme occurs constantly ; *e.g.* in Mrs. Griffith's *Lady Barton* (1771), where the heroine resolves to vindicate her friendship with her sister in the face of her husband's incredulity ; *Danebury, or the Power of Friendship* (1777) by a Young Lady, in which Emma sucks the poison from the wound of Elfrida ; Harriet Lee's *Errors of Innocence* (1786), where the friendship of Lady Helen Nugent sustains Sophia O'Brien through a loveless marriage (*v.* especially II, p. 11) ; Mrs. Anne Hughes' *Henry and Isabella* (1788) with its praise of " that lively, sweet and confidential affection by which two, three, or more . . . of sensible, virtuous and amiable women are united ; " and Charlotte Lennox's *Euphemia* (1790), in which occurs Mrs. Neville's definition of a friend as " a witness of the conscience, a physician of secret griefs." A few men added their testimony : *e.g.* Hayley in *The Young Widow* (1789) refers to Rosalind and Celia, and complains that female friendship has not been enough the subject of art. The correspondents of the epistolary novels are technical necessities, of no significance. There are also signs of the cloven hoof. The hero of *Anecdotes of a Convent* (1771)—by a woman—admires female friendship. " It is a noble sentiment in itself but when dressed in female softness is irresistible." Irresistible to whom ? Historically, female friendship was amply vindicated by the Ladies of Llangollen.

we were intended to move. This subordinate state does not degrade us. . . . The degradation is when we attempt to step out of that state." It is her relations with the other sex that are the real test of a woman's quality. The test begins before marriage. The tension between love and filial obedience, a favourite theme time out of mind, specially occupied the eighteenth-century novelists. Nearly all of them, men as well as women, came down heavily on the side of parental authority. By an overwhelming majority it was resolved that, while a parent ought not to force a child into a marriage repugnant to her, and while a child is justified in passively resisting such tyranny, nothing justifies her in carrying her resistance to the point of marrying against her parents' will. This had been the attitude of Sophia Western and was felt to be the common sense of the matter. The dissenters on the liberal side were few and not very heretical. " Parents should chuse our company," wrote Mrs. Brooke, " but never pretend to direct our choice; if they take care we converse with men of honour only, 'tis impossible we can chuse amiss." This is hardly revolutionary, except in so far as it tacitly rules out the marriage of family interest, which may perhaps have played a larger part in the novel than it did in real life. The few fanatics who deny that resistance to a father's will can ever be justified need not detain us; they may fairly be accused of holding their creed in the interests of their plot. But one point is worth emphasizing; moralists are ready enough to enforce the duty of parents, in their turn, to their children, but there is no sliding scale of obligation. " No demerit in a parent can absolve a child from that duty which has the double sanction both of God and Nature," wrote Mrs. Griffith. Children who marry against their parents' will are invariably consigned to misery; usually the love they trusted fails them and leaves them to poverty and disgrace, but even

if affection persists, it is embittered by remorse. Dis-
obedience, says Lady Mary Walker, seldom goes un-
punished ; it certainly did not in her books.   In short, the
rebel marriage was not in their eyes the vindication of love ;
it was merely the victory of passion over reason and duty.[1]

The women were very careful to distinguish between
love and passion.   They had nothing new to say, but the
cumulative weight of their testimony, the care with which
they elaborate their conception, has some significance.
Love should last ; and multitudes of disappointed women,
in whose eyes the young bride has become a victim, seem
to breathe through the stilted words and give them force.
The love " that looks on tempests and is never shaken,"
on what basis shall that be reared ?   It is strange to turn
back from our modern perplexities to the wistful confidence of their reply.   With sympathy and mutual respect,
they feel, it is—given the indispensable " principling "—
hardly possible to go wrong.   They hoped much from
the cult of sensibility, the effect of which was to induce
some measure of approximation in the ethical ideals and
emotional sensitiveness of the two sexes.   " A con-
formity of taste and sentiment alone can make marriage
happy," wrote Mrs. Brooke, and gave in *Emily Montague*
(1769) an attractive picture of a delicate affection [2] and of
a lover of " almost feminine sensibility,"—almost, because,
though approximation was desired, identity was not.
It is often a display of sensibility, at the theatre for
instance, which, contrasted with the unconcern of hardened spectators, attracts the young people to each other.
The heroine of *The General Election* (1773) falls in love

---

[1] Good heroines do not elope.   If the plot requires an elopement,
they are either borne away fainting or harassed to the verge of irresponsibility ; cf. Mrs. Smith's *Emmeline* (1788).

[2] Rivers writes of Emily (II, p. 50) : " The first moment I saw her
the idea struck me that we had been friends in some pre-existent
state, and were only renewing our acquaintance here."   This must
be an early version of a theme common in romantic love-passages
later.

with the hero at a performance of *Oroonoko*. " His sensibility," she writes, " was everything you can conceive of a rustic, except audible, and I believe even in that respect he did himself great violence." [1] Yet sympathy of tastes was a delusive attraction unless it was supported by sound moral principle. The repetition of the word is characteristic. No belief was more deeply ingrained in the common female consciousness than the insufficiency in man or woman of a mere good disposition. It is open to casualty ; caprice can sap and adversity destroy it. It yields or resists on impulse, has no motive to oppose to degeneration and, after a false step, suggests no means of recovery. Book after book enforces this lesson. Usually the culprits are husbands, dragging their families into debt and disgrace, and violently closing the scene with suicide, but at times a coquette pursues her devastating career, and at times a neglectful or too easy mother suffers her children to fall into error. To principle Mrs. Inchbald immolates the charming Miss Milner, dragging her from the arms of Dorriforth to tie her with pedagogic ruthlessness upon the altar.[2] Principle provides the groundwork of Miss Austen's novels, and forty years later, in Miss Brontë's *Shirley*, Mrs. Prior's first question after she has revealed herself to her daughter is whether she has received a proper principling. On this subject, they felt, there could be no compromise and no experiment. Safety lay in one thing and one only, a strict adherence to established moral values. Even the liberal spirit of Mrs. Charlotte Smith will be found faithful in the main to this allegiance, for her liberality expresses itself not in tampering with standards but in a greater tenderness to frailty, a less rigid distribution of justice.

[1] *v.* also *Female Friendship* (1770) and *Maple Vale, or the History of Miss Sidney* (1791), where Charles Beverley is attracted to Miss Fancourt because on first seeing Mrs. Siddons she " could no longer restrain her soft sorrow, and actually sobbed aloud."

[2] *v. A Simple Story* (1791).

They accepted their function of ennobling men very seriously. It was the rôle allotted to them by the men themselves. Even a cynic like Lord Chesterfield found the presence of women in society the best means of keeping up the level of breeding, while the Reverend James Fordyce [1] declared from the pulpit that the best guardian of the soul of man against vice was " the near and frequent view of Female Excellence." The possible ennoblement of women by men, though not excluded from consideration, was not stressed. In book after book we see the gentle affection of a woman spiritualizing the emotions of a man, and the women, unlike Sophia and Amelia, are very conscious that they must undertake this process.[2] Charlotte Smith, whose earlier books [3] are shrines of perfect womanhood—and the term is the more appropriate when we remember how many of her heroines are glorified through suffering—even ventured in *Desmond* (1792) to present the honourable, controlled love of a young man for a married woman as an ennobling experience and, indeed, a great compliment to the sex that can inspire this " sacred passion." Fashion drives all tendencies to extremes, and perhaps the hacks ministered to this particular ideal with tongue in cheek ; for besides much good sense and real delicacy we have such sallies

---

[1] v. *The Character and Conduct of the Female Sex, and the advantages to be derived by young men from the society of virtuous women.* A discourse in three parts delivered in Monkwell Street Chapel, Jan. 1st, 1776. By James Fordyce, D.D. Cf. Mrs. Griffith, *Lady Barton* (1771) : " a strong but chaste passion for a woman of merit, . . . than which nothing in nature more elevates the mind, improves the understanding, refines the manners and purges the affections of man."

[2] The conception of woman as the guide of man is elaborated in Ann Yearsley's *Royal Captives* (1795) in the relationship between Henry and Emily. She is his " dear instructress," drawing his thoughts to " that lambent, that eternal flame which ever encircles kindred minds," and consoling him by this spiritual union for their parting on earth.

[3] *Emmeline, the Orphan of the Castle* (1788) ; *Ethelinde, or the Recluse of the Lake* (1789) and *Celestina* (1791). In her later books the centre of interest lies in the man, but the woman, *e.g.* Monimia in *The Old Manor House* (1793), is always a carefully drawn portrait.

as the indignation of the lady in *Anecdotes of a Convent* (1771), who rebukes the too hasty development of her lover's suit, because it betrays a partiality for her person before he has had time to know her mind. Yet in all these thirty years I have met with but one plain heroine; in 1789 the author of *The Mental Triumph*—a lady— announced that she had " ventured to quit the beaten road, and to introduce her heroine, unadorned by exterior beauties, yet richly gifted by every mental grace."

On the question of the reformed rake there was a split of opinion among the women; prudence was opposed to the missionary spirit, experience to faith. The old proverb stated that a reformed rake makes the best husband, and this belief, while it was passionately combated in the name of common sense and delicacy by the sober-minded, proved very alluring to the amiable enthusiasts. Thus on the one hand Clara Reeve's *School for Widows* (1791) shows us the prudent, obliging (but certainly rather chilly) Mrs. Darnford quite unable to check her husband's ruin, while on the other Jane Timbury's *Male Coquette* (1770) is willy-nilly so refined by the pure girl, whom he has once insulted, that he is able to sit all night in a thunderstorm with her on his knee, without being moved to the least evil intention. Mrs. Keir compromises; a rake may be reformed, she declares, but a libertine in principle never; while Mrs. Brooke, as usual, is wise and moderate. Her rake reforms, glad at last to settle down to an orderly life, and, since his wife both loves and understands him, we feel that the *ménage* may last; but this is not the marriage of sympathetic souls, and the weight must fall heavily on the woman, aware against her will of her husband's roughened sensibilities and alarmed for his constancy.

Meanwhile the girl who bestows her company on a rake runs into grave danger; and, since the highly inflammable nature of the male is assumed by these writers with the crudeness of servant girls, the urgency of their warnings is not surprising. Yet " Virtue is not wholly comprised in chastity, which is only a concomitant," wrote Lady Mary Walker, and certainly the point needed to be made, for to most of the women chastity was the keystone of the whole moral character and necessarily involved it in its destruction. Chastity was the obligation of their sex and they transformed it into a privilege, raising upon a basis of physical integrity an austere and sometimes fantastic ideal. Clarissa might be their martyr (though some of them had their doubts), but Pamela was certainly not their confessor ; her honour, they felt, was an accidental quality with a market value ; the honour they revered was essential, rooted in the necessity of a pure nature, and passing fitly from the honour of a maid to the honour of a married woman. It is in a sense spiritualized ; it rises into the finer element of mind and bears its dazzling blossoms there ; but its root is in a physical state, and, if it is cut off at the root, the tree dies and the blossoms wither. A bride, who had suffered her future husband to anticipate the hour of wedlock, flies to a nunnery to save him from her " polluted embraces." This is certainly an extreme case, only to be matched by that of the young man who, having overcome his bride's resistance, and still loving her, doubts now whether he dare marry so frail a woman, thereby risking the stability of his household and sullying the sacred name of wife.[1] This dilemma he confided to a magazine, and though his letter may not be authentic, it indicates one current of popular opinion.

[1] Cf. Hugh Kelly's *Memoirs of a Magdalen ; or, the History of Louisa Mildmay* (1767). Sir Robert Harold writes : " I have succeeded, fatally succeeded, with this amiable wretch, and both of us must bid adieu to happiness for ever." They were on the point of marriage, but, on her yielding to him, he argues that, with so quick an appetite, she will soon lose her fastidiousness and accept other lovers. Happily she convinces him by a long course of severe penitence that he can safely wed her.

Within the bounds of reason—which do not contain either of the foregoing examples—there are, of course, different shades of sentiment. Mrs. Smith dared to marry an unfaithful wife to her lover, when literary convention prescribed remorse and a decline. Yet it is to be noted that the loss of chastity is irrevocable only in the upper classes. A servant or a shopkeeper's daughter may retrieve her virtue and make some honest man happy ; she is even justified in hiding her past if her present resolve is honest.[1] But all the Magdalens of gentle blood are tragic ; their delicacy forbids compromise or concealment ; they languish in a settled melancholy and descend, elegantly penitent, to the family vault. It is a clear case of *noblesse oblige*. Even the appearance of guilt, without its substance, brings Nemesis, because, as Lady Mary Walker says, it is culpable to be in a position that needs justification. On this assumption those many books are constructed that trace the heroine's progress from her first, almost venial, false step into the direst gulf of calamity ; as, for instance, the sad tale of Lucy Hamilton in *The False Step ; or, the History of Mr. Brudenel* (1771), who rashly elopes with one lover, discovers and repels his treachery but suffers in reputation, and, though happily married to Mr. Brudenel, is dogged by the consequences of her false step, sees her husband lose confidence in her, and dies of agitation.[2] No fable should be used, said the author of *The Spectre* (1789), criticizing Mrs. Smith's

[1] Cf. the story of Sukey Jones in Clara Reeve's *The Two Mentors* (1783).
[2] Cf. also *'Twas Right to Marry Him ; or, the History of Miss Petworth* (1774). Hebe Petworth, distressed by the approaches of her gross old guardian, is persuaded to elope with Euston. At the inn his behaviour becomes too familiar ; she flees, and continues to repulse him, in spite of his repentance and her affection, until he is wounded in a duel, when she marries him to save his life. Her friend approves her behaviour, while regretting her fate. " He marries a woman who has been severely tried, and found invaluable. She marries a man who has rendered himself totally unworthy of her ; and yet it will be *right* in her to *marry him*, if she ever marries at all "— because another husband would torment himself with suspicions.

Emmeline (1788), in which virtuous characters are forced into situations where transgression is inevitable and pardonable. The demand for the exemplary could go no further.

The supposed oblates of this rigid discipline (for again, as so often is the case of popular literature, its relation to life is problematical [1]) seldom complain of the different standard of morality applied to men. No delicate woman would envy such a freedom ; rather they glory in being measured by the stricter standard and, to some extent, warded from temptation, for they see in this behaviour not so much the effect of selfishness or mistrust as the recognition of their own finer fibre. " Every appearance of vice in a woman is sometimes (something ?) more disgusting than in a man," wrote Clara Reeve ; " which I think is a presumption that woman was intended to be a more perfect creature than man,"—a quieting and sustaining conclusion. There were occasional dissentient voices, however, even before the " philosophesses " came to startle their sex with a new scale of virtues. Elizabeth Blower,[2] who was considered by some critics a rival to Frances Burney, and is now rather unjustly forgotten, drew in her *Features from Life ; or, a Summer Visit* (1788) the picture of a happy marriage of some years' standing, wrecked by the cold subtlety of a coquette and

---

[1] Cf. Bage, *Mount Henneth* (1781). Cara, the Persian girl whom Foston saves from death after she has been ravished, is offered to him by her father as his wife, but diffidently questions how he will view her loss of honour. In English books she finds that " women who have suffered it, must die, or be immured for ever ; ever after they are totally useless to all purposes of society ; . . . no author has yet been so bold as to permit a lady to live and marry, and be a woman after this stain." Foston is applied to by the father and says : " It is to be found in books, Sir ; and I hope for the honour of the human intellect, little of it will be found anywhere else."

[2] Watts, *Bibliotheca Britannica*, gives the following list of Miss Blower's books : —*The Parsonage House* (1780), *George Bateman* (1782), *Maria* (1785) and *Features from Life* (1788). The B.M. contains only *Maria* and a French translation of *Features from Life*, *La Visite d'Été, ou Portrait de Mœurs* (1788).

by the irreconcilable ideals of the wife, who believes that
love cannot survive the shock to confidence of an acknowledged infidelity, and only comes to a truer knowledge of
her own affections beside her husband's death-bed.   The
" moral " of the book tells as much against her scrupulousness as his disloyalty, but its meaning is larger than its
moral, and is best apprehended in the scene where Mrs.
Conway, nursing her husband through a fever, hears him
betray his secret in his sleep.   Miss Blower, whose work
is far slighter than Miss Burney's, has a French delicacy
of touch of which her rival was not mistress, and here it
stands her in good stead.   Conway wakes, sees from his
wife's frozen look what has passed, and hides his face ;
she takes up the taper in stricken silence and leaves him,
withdrawing herself from these ruins of her happiness
which, she feels, can never shelter her again.   As the
French translator remarked, the authoress took the point
of view that the fault of disloyalty is the same in man and
woman, even if the consequences in the first case are less
serious.   Where so many women pitched their domestic
roofs so low, it is something of a relief to walk upright in
Matilda Conway's lofty if fantastic dwelling.

The ethics of wifehood, a state which the heroine enters
" with decent reluctance " and supported, at times, by
eau-de-luce at the altar—for at this juncture the two ideals
of delicacy and candour are apt to clash—assume the
beauty of submission, and are based on economic necessity
sublimated by Christian ideals.   To be a wife is to be in
a state of dependence, and it is better for both wife and
husband that the fact should be emphasized, since the
success of the marriage depends upon his generosity and
her obedience.   That amiable die-hard, Richard Graves,
felt that even pin-money was a deplorable institution, in
that it obscured the wife's dependence and undermined
" that mutual affection which arises from a sense of their
interest being inseparably united. . . . Separate purses

between man and wife are as unnatural as separate beds." [1]
It was not an ignoble ideal, though it contradicted the
modern conception of marriage at almost every point.
It assumed that woman was created primarily for wife-
hood· and motherhood, and that she owed a debt of
gratitude, which only the severest ill-usage could cancel,
to the man who rescued her from the useless—it is their
own word—condition of old-maidenhood, and undertook
her support and that of her offspring.   It encouraged the
woman to express her nature through her household and
appealed continually to the man's protectiveness and
generosity.   Anyone who doubts that these precon-
ceptions could nourish a frank and equal love should look
at the letters of Richard and Elizabeth Griffith, especially
those written just after their marriage.   But such ideals
must be imbibed in youth ; they must be breathed in
with the air and the whole mind must be unconsciously
tempered to them ; and even so there will be rebellion.
The Middle Ages had found themselves forced to dissociate " maistrye " and love, and had done so in the cult
of *l'amour courtois ;* and now the Puritan endeavour to
blend the two things, of which the great monument is
Paradise Lost, was to suffer modification.   New winds
were blowing.   If love and mastery cannot thrive together
let it not be love that withdraws.   " Whatever conveys the
idea of subjection," wrote that gentle rebel Mrs. Brooke,
" necessarily destroys that of love, of which I am so convinced, that I have always wished the word OBEY expunged
from the marriage ceremony."   But at present few voices
echoed her.   In literature the patron saint of wives was
Griselda, and this remains true of the books of self-
reliant women like Mrs. Smith.[2]   They had, perhaps,

---

[1] Cf. *The Relapse* (1779), where the lively heroine cries : " What
must the wife be, who would wish to be independent of her
husband ? "   The *Monthly* (March, 1780) ascribes the novel to the
author of *Indiana Danby,* i.e. a woman.

[2] Cf. *Letters between an English Lady, and her friend at Paris, in
which are contained the Memoirs of Mrs. Williams* (1770).   This book

been forced by circumstances into an independence which they were able to sustain but not yet able to enjoy, and gladly reverted in fancy to a state where what adversity demanded of a woman was not enterprise but that she should know well how to suffer. The only philosophy that a woman ought to lay claim to, said Mrs. Griffith, was resignation. It goes without saying that, even in the novels themselves, the artificiality of this ideal is apparent, and that the governing woman frequently managed to hold the reins, though she was admonished to do so secretly and with proper regard for decorum. As far as possible let her husband carry before the world the merit of her good works; if possible, let her even persuade him that he has deserved it. The relationship is not unlike that between a good prefect and an inadequate house-master.[1]

Such adroit competence cannot always be presumed, but all wives should bring as their dowry patience and loyalty. " Complaisance " is the quality most frequently praised in wives, a flexible deference to the husband's mood, a ready fund of encouragement for all his tastes, provided they do not transgress principle. In this temper she must bear the change of a submissive suitor into a masterful husband; and the thought that she has never failed in complaisance must strengthen her if she dis-

---

deals with the sufferings of a woman married to an attractive libertine, who tries to pull her down to his level, and makes her his scapegoat. Cf. also Mrs. Stafford in Mrs. Smith's *Emmeline* (1788) and Mrs. Elphinstone in her *Celestina* (1791); the latter endures with a " still and mournful acquiescence which served her in the place of philosophy." Mrs. Lennox's *Euphemia* (1790) puts up with the tormenting temper of a husband whom she has married out of filial duty, comforting herself with the thought that duty to a man one does not love is a higher ideal than sacrifice for a man one does; *v.* I. p. 63.

[1] This conduct is admired by men; *v.* Bancroft's Mrs. Conway in *Charles Wentworth* (1770) and Dr. Moore's Mrs. Barnet in *Edward* (1796). " To make her husband in reality a man of sense and benevolence was not in Mrs. Barnet's power, but she managed matters so as to make him frequently appear such." For a man's version of Griselda *v.* George Walker's *Cinthelia, or, a Woman of Ten Thousand* (1797).

covers him to be unfaithful. Above all, she must never recriminate ; let her be blind as long as she can, and afterwards patient, and if possible cheerful. No husband was ever won back by what Mrs. Griffith calls the " vain arts of eloquence." [1] " How meritorious are the soft, the gentle sufferings of a virtuous woman," cries Lady Mary Walker, " who never torments her husband with complaints, but patiently waits the return of his reason, which will lead him to a sense of his faults, and the injustice he has done her." Lady Mary, however, envisaged possible breaking-points. She could not admit that complaisance should extend to the simulation of fondness— (" This would be the profanation of love ; and a woman capable of such abject deceit, I should look upon as capable of the most determined baseness ")—and one of her characters, Mrs. Lee in *Munster Village* (1778), after fourteen years of miserable loyalty is finally so insulted by her husband's suspicions that she leaves him, quoting Milton's *De Doctrina et Disciplina*—an action that the authoress does not exactly approve, but finds excusable. At any rate, it is impossible to regain complete freedom,

---

[1] Complaisance, otherwise called engaging compliance, might be copiously illustrated. Mr. Sidley in *The Relapse* (1780) says to his wife : " When you see me grave, ask not the cause, but endeavour to amuse me." Complaisance is frequently expressed by the adoption of the husband's illegitimate children. The heroine of *Fashionable Infidelity* (1789), whose husband is amusing himself, has a locket made of his hair with the words Patience and Resignation on it. He sees it at the jeweller's, orders it to be set in diamonds, and all is well. Cf. also the truly philosophic behaviour of Mrs. Clayton in Mrs. Skinn's *Old Maid* (1771), who is sorry she ever married her husband, but displays no reserve or ill-temper, but, " all serenity and good-humour, only considers how to remedy the evils he has occasioned." Male comments might be added ; they are usually enthusiastic. Coleridge (*Anima Poetæ*) felt that the most important part of a female education was complaisance, " how to greet a husband, how to receive him, how never to recriminate." Grosley, however, in his *Tour to London* (1770, transl. 1772), considered that the complaisance of Englishwomen was a mask for despotic power ; while Holcroft in *Alwyn* (1780) remarked honestly : " Husbands are enchanted by mildness and acquiescence from their wives ; they feel their own superiority in point of strength ; they fancy it in point of understanding."

for the wife forced to leave her husband will rather be silent than justify herself at his expense ; she may break one tie, but she is still held by countless obligations. Ideally she would apply to wifehood the same severe standard as was almost universally applied to filial duty. " It is my principle," says the Duchess de Crui's correspondent, " that where duty is reciprocal the failure of it in one party acquits not the other from a failure in his." [1]

This ethic is copiously illustrated in the woman's novel. In the cruder books Griselda is treated with melodramatic baseness, until a convenient fever sets her free to a second and more prosperous bridal.[2] For a reasonable and attractive handling of the theme, one turns to Elizabeth Griffith's *Delicate Distress* (1769), a book that neither Lydia Languish nor any other reader should need to hide. It consists of letters, the principal correspondents being Lady Woodville and her sister, and Lord Woodville and two of his friends. Lady Woodville, a new-made wife, very much in love with her husband, becomes aware that, though he feels tenderness and means loyalty, he has been unable to overcome a former passion for a foreign countess, who now comes back into his life determined to recapture her lover. Lady Woodville, counselled by her sister, preserves in spite of her grief the most delicate silence. It is in silence that the crisis of her fate passes. Wrought to the height by the sight of her husband's anguish of mind and the thought of the child that is to be born to them, she feels for one moment an almost overwhelming impulse to plead with him ; but she controls herself, and

---

[1] Besides *The Duchess de Crui* (1776) and *Munster Village* (1778), Lady Mary also wrote *Memoirs of the Marchioness de Louvoi* (1777), which I have not seen. All three books were published anonymously, but the *Monthly* (April 1777), reviewing *The Marchioness de Louvoi* ascribes it to Lady Mary Walker, and the *Gentleman's Magazine* (Sept. 1778) gives her name in a notice of *Munster Village*, rebuking her kindly for a slip in the title of one of her characters and remarking : " This *an earl's daughter* should have considered." Cushing and Halkett and Laing give only her surname.

[2] v. *Olivia ; or, Deserted Bride* (1787) by Mrs. Bonhote.

the moment passes. We then learn from her husband's letters that the moment was crucial for him too. Wholly aware of her temptation—for silence has not been able to conceal her suffering from him—he is torn between pity and passion. Had she spoken, he declares, the tension must have broken, and his temporary resentment have balanced the scales against his wife. As it is, from this day both his will and his affection set towards her, and the problem might have been solved without the usual sick-beds, which, however, Mrs. Griffith liberally supplies. Safety and decency lie in silence. The husband who cannot forget a former passion is unfortunate but not culpable, provided he tries to hide it from his wife. Even the man who, through his infidelities, has lost his wife's heart can still preserve her esteem if he upholds her position in the household and keeps his amours secret. Blatancy is the unforgivable sin in the husband, as recrimination is in the wife.

Mrs. Griffith's next book, *The History of Lady Barton* (1771), deals with a failure in conjugal loyalty. The failure is as delicate as possible, no palpable disloyalty, but an involuntary wandering of the heart towards the perfect lover who has appeared too late. The fruit of this error is death, which she awards not as one meting out exact justice, but with a sad conviction of the power of one venial indiscretion to darken into tragic mistaking and doom. Cæsar's wife was often on the lips of both men and women in the eighteenth century, and a married woman might be called upon to resign the most innocent-seeming friendship. As for " Platonicks,"—" the whole system of nature must change, and the tyger and the lamb live peaceably together, before a sincere and disinterested friendship can exist between an amiable young woman and a man not nearly related to her, who has not passed his grand climacteric ";[1] and when Dr.

---

[1] *v.* Mrs. Griffith's *Essays to Young Married Women* (1782).

Fordyce[1] endeavoured to promote " an intellectual, moral and *spiritual* intercourse " between the sexes, the *Critical* reviewer found it " a sublime, but, we are afraid, a fruitless attempt." The liberty to call themselves the friends of men, who neither were nor intended to become their husbands, was one of the claims made by the campaigning women at the end of the century, and Rosanna, in Mrs. Mary Robinson's *Walsingham ; or the Pupil of Nature* (1798) writes to the hero that ten short weeks have animated her bosom with all the proudest energies of friendship.

Mrs. Griffith's last novel, *The History of Lady Juliana Harley* (1776), is also tragic, and the tragedy in this case arises from a forced and loveless marriage. As we have seen, opinion in both sexes was united against the tyrannous exertion of parental authority to force a child into a union repugnant to her, but on the wider question of the morality of marriage without love we meet with different views. The arguments on both sides are necessarily familiar, but the discussion is differentiated somewhat from those of the present day by the simple honesty with which what one may call the business point of view is taken. It was still possible at this time to speak of a young woman's " market " without intending disrespect or jocularity. The amiable young clergyman in Richard Graves's *Eugenius* (1785), who is paying his addresses to the least pretty of three charming sisters, accounts for his choice to a friend, because " though equally sensible and agreeable, yet from her external appearance he thought her less marketable than her sisters, and therefore more likely to listen to proposals from him." Meanwhile the

---

[1] v. *ante*, p. 150. Scotch and Irish girls, however, certainly enjoyed greater social freedom than English girls. In Scotland this freedom was connected with the system of mixed schooling ; cf. Warrender's reluctant, amused admiration of the tall Scotch girls, who kilt up their skirts and skip over stepping-stones in *The Modern Fine Gentleman* (1774) ; cf. also the air of freedom in Andrew Macdonald's *Laura* (1790) and—for Ireland—in *Delia* (1790). Neither country seems to have admired helplessness.

father of the three young ladies addresses them on marriage ; one should not, he says, marry *merely* to get a husband, " but if you like the man, and he can make you a proper settlement, and your friends approve of it, do not play the coquet, or refuse what every young woman should aim at, a comfortable establishment in the world." Neither man would have contemplated such a marriage remaining loveless ; identity of interest, they felt, was the best possible soil for love, where the root was fertilized by gratitude and kindness.   This was the point of view of a man whose office called on him to solemnize marriages and who had certainly thought on the subject ; and the majority—perhaps the vast majority—of his readers, men and women, agreed with him.[1]   Marriage for an establishment is respectable, especially when it obliges one's family ; it is foolish, even in a sense presumptuous, to refuse an " unexceptionable " man because he does not happen to inspire one with a romantic degree of attachment, and a parent is justified in putting some pressure on his child to incline her to consider her own interest.   The heroine of *Benedicta* (1791)[2] is admonished that, if a young girl approves of and likes a man, she has no reason for refusing him ; the distinction between friend and lover is frivolous, " chimera, or something worse," since no lady of delicacy and virtue can acknowledge passion as the basis of love.

[1] Cf. C. Reeve's *Sir Roger de Clarendon*, I, p. 25 (1793), and, for an extreme case, *Peggy and Patty ; or, the Sisters of Ashdale* (1783), in which Miss Waller thus addresses Miss Harvey : " Heroic Emma ! Incomparable girl ! what a noble pattern have you set our sex !—to conquer a passion for a man you love !—to sacrifice every tender feeling in his favour !—to give your hand in all the bloom of youthful beauty of eighteen years, to a man near seventy !—and all this from motives of pure duty and affection to oblige your parents (*one* of whom is not the most *tender*, in the world)—is a triumph, my charming girl, which renders you a very heroine indeed."

[2] *Benedicta* (Minerva Press), *The Siege of Belgrade* (H. D. Symonds) and *The Memoirs of Julia de M . . . a reclaimed Courtezan. From the French of Le Chevalier Rutledge* (Bentley, etc.), are all three dated 1741 (for 1791) on the title-page.   The *Monthly* (July 1791) points out the mistake in the case of the last two : " They were both struck in the same typographical fount."

The outcome of such marriages forms the theme of many books, and usually, even if the girl has been in love with another man, prudence and filial obedience are justified over inclination. The marriages of " neutral hearts," [1] as Bage called them, were considered to begin under better auguries than love-matches; expectation is not wound up too high, and there is a reciprocal wish to please.[2] There are exceptions. In *Miss Pamela Howard* [3] (1773) a woman marries to escape a position of dependence and acknowledges the justice of her consequent unhappiness. " A woman, she used to say, who makes a property of a man, who enters into the most sacred of engagements from motives of conveniency, deserves the fate I experience." Mrs. Griffith considered a marriage without " a union of hearts " to be no more than " a state of legal prostitution." [4] and the lover in *Memoirs of a Scots Heiress* (1791) defers his proposal from a sort of delicacy rather unusual at the time, remarking : " I cannot take up with affection resulting from my addressing her ; she must love me spontaneously." Even so, the difference between the two points of view must not be exaggerated. Both admit that love can be to a certain extent willed and achieved ; both deprecate the marriage where the achievement is unlikely ; both know that marriage for an establishment is a second-best, but this second-best is accepted by one party with placidity, by the other with wistful regret. Miss Austen, who arranges love-matches for her heroines and vindicates Fanny's refusal of Henry Crawford and an establishment, has drawn one of these mar-

---

[1] *Mount Henneth* (1781), I, p. 160.

[2] Cf., *e.g.*, Mrs. Bonhote's *Darnley Vale ; or, Emelia Fitzroy* (1789) and Mrs. Keir's *History of Miss Greville* (1787), both written to prove that a woman can withdraw her affections from their first object and become perfectly happy in a second attachment, even although she may afterwards discover that she was separated from her first lover by treachery.

[3] By the author of *Indiana Danby* and *The Relapse*.

[4] This was also the attitude of Henry Mackenzie (cf. *Julia de Roubigné*) and Henry Brooke.

riages of interest in the union of Charlotte Lucas and Mr. Collins. She had not much sympathy with Charlotte, but she did not let Elizabeth, however disappointed in her, quite condemn her. Beside Charlotte we must put the picture of Mrs. Strictland in Clara Reeve's *School for Widows* (1791), who, with an inheritance of a few hundreds, no particular gifts and no close relatives, allows her guardian to arrange for her a suitable but quite loveless marriage with a gentleman-farmer, and painfully learns enough patience and tact to live not uncomfortably beside her boorish spouse, until his death makes her independent. Miss Reeve finds her heroine exemplary and not ill-rewarded. She holds to her bargain, takes comfort in her children and, after the first revolts, finds even in her confined circumstances opportunities for charity and mental growth. The picture is done in sober tones, without satire and almost without humour, but there is a quality of unassuming realism about it, a simple attention to important things, that commands respect. The Collinses are not brought under the shadow of death, but the Strictlands are, and the final harvest of their imperfect intimacy is faithfully recorded. " I felt compassion and concern for the father of my children, thus dying in the prime of life," writes Mrs. Strictland. " I wished I had loved him more ! I wished that he had allowed me to love him ! I was awed, and frightened, yet I could not take any blame to myself."

Miss Reeve's book is otherwise noticeable for its picture of feminine strength and enterprise. Both her widows have been exemplary wives, blending submission and resolution in due proportions, but both have been tied to men immeasurably their inferiors, Mrs. Darnford to a spendthrift, Mrs. Strictland to a boor. Now, released from the unequal bondage, they show their full quality, the one in managing her son's estate, the other by the courage with which she declines a dishonourable shelter and applies herself to earn her own spare living. A third widow is introduced, whose story is more romantic, but at the end of the book she, like her friends, is still free. Miss Reeve would not spoil her moral by remarriages. " All of us have had our respective trials," writes Mrs. Darnford. " . . . We have all worked our way through them. I trust we are all the better for them ; and we certainly have the better title to the blessings that remain to us." Another courageous acceptance of the second-best.

The figure of the ideal mother will be readily deduced from what has been said. Sympathetically, systematically, she indoctrinates her daughters with the principles of female conduct, while grappling with her son's moral and religious difficulties, leading both, with no undue pressure, in the direction of virtue and rational pleasures.[1] The tyrannous, negligent or jealous mother is a necessary feature of many plots and a means of distilling the pure essence of filial piety, but she is seldom closely studied. The situation of dutiful daughters, fully aware of their mother's folly, was an interesting one, as we see in *Pride and Prejudice ;* but the writers were in the main unwilling to trench in any way upon the sacred idea of motherhood, and preferred to lay such trials to the account of an aunt or guardian.

There are still some points to be touched on before we leave the woman's novel. One concerns the use of the word " suitable " as applied to marriages, and that curious tariff of dowries and settlements that repels the unhistorical reader in Jane Austen. The theory of financial " suitability " is given by Clara Reeve in *Sir Roger de Clarendon.* A bride should bring her husband a dowry large enough to enable him to pay his younger brothers and sisters their portions under his father's will, without altering his

---

[1] *E.g.* Maria Susanna Cooper's *Exemplary Mother ; or, Letters between Mrs. Villars and her Family* (1769).

own style of living; in this way justice is done and the family prestige preserved. A grossly unequal match is seldom defended, though a rich young man with no brothers to provide for—a Darcy or a Bingley—may reasonably disregard the financial aspect of marriage. Even the heroines of romances are somehow enriched before they are wed,—though this procedure is perhaps too traditional to be significant. A certain generous imprudence in younger brothers themselves is, however, often condoned. If they can bear to live modestly, and the dowerless brides have courage and economy, let them venture; but even so, it is apt to come hard on the children. It goes without saying that in this respect thought grows gradually more liberal.

It is disappointing to find that the women's claim for the dignity of the old maid is not substantiated by any careful study of such a character. One feels that Clara Reeve, in particular, missed her chance. The time was not yet ripe for an unwooed heroine, but the sundry " good old aunts " who adorn the backgrounds of many novels are singularly unindividualized, and may fairly be classified under the two heads of elegiac and amorous. Lady Frances Finlay in *Munster Village* (1778) remains unmarried until the age of thirty-seven, in order that she may act as guardian to her niece and nephew and put into operation her princely scheme of improvements and philanthropic institutions on the family estate; but a faithful lover bides her time, and as soon as her nephew has reached his majority, she gives him her hand. Mrs. Keir does better with the sensible, mellow Miss Helen-Maria Stanley in her *History of Miss Greville* (1787), who corresponds with her nieces and nephews, views their problems with a kindly shrewdness, and expounds to them her philosophy and the art of preserving sweetness in old maidenhood. Hayley, whose *Essay on Old Maids* was, on the whole, considered a tribute, in spite of ambiguous

pages, supported his character as their advocate by introducing Lucy Audley into *The Young Widow ; or the
History of Cornelia Sedley* (1789). But the portraits are
sparsely sprinkled among the caricatures.

The question of the learned woman, on the other hand,
receives copious illustrations. The stock positions of the
men—the advantages of a little education in a woman,
the great disadvantages of too much, the necessity of
humility and concealment if her market value is not to be
spoilt, the admission that reading and botany need not
make her an incompetent housewife—are on the whole
shared by the women, and the comic figure of the female
pedant, fairly frequent in the men's books, sometimes
appears in theirs. The pretentious, the excessive, the
unwomanly were sure of their scorn, and, while they
approved of education, they had no use for the " merely-
learned " woman.[1] The test was in a woman's relation
with her environment ; her learning should increase, not
hamper her usefulness, and from this point of view they
lent a careful if not quite convinced ear to male warnings
of impaired charms, for the destruction of charm is a
certain hindrance to usefulness.[2] Politics were specially

[1] *v.* Mrs. Cox, *Burton Wood*, p. 230 (1783), and cf. for a masculine
point of view the portrait of the slovenly, undomestic, pretentious
writing woman in Johnstone's *Pilgrim*, II, Letter VII (1775).
[2] Cf. Dr. Gregory's *Legacy to his Daughters* (1774) on retiring
delicacy : " If you happen to have any learning, keep it a profound
secret, especially from the men, who generally look with a jealous and
malignant eye on a woman of great parts and cultivated understanding.
A man of real genius and candour is far superior to such meanness.
But such a one will seldom fall your way." Cf. also *The Disguise*
(1771), in which young men discuss learned women ; Graves's Miss
Careless, in *Plexippus* (1790), who talks politics and reads newspapers,
and " has counteracted the effect of her personal charms, by affecting
to know what, if a woman does know, it would be her interest to
conceal ; *Delia*, I, p. 167 (1790) ; *A Plan of Female Education*
(1797) by Erasmus Darwin—a great advocate for concealment ;
Rev. R. Polwhele's indelicate attack on the indelicacies of botany in
The Unsex'd Females (1798) ; and the *Critical's* review of Margaret
Bryan's *Compendious System of Astronomy*, in Jan. 1798, with its
anxious query : Is female education going too far ? If " our women
should be turned into men, who are to soothe the wrinkled brow of
care, and afford relaxation after the tedious hours of intense study ? "

dangerous. " Ladies seldom converse *sensibly* on the subject," wrote Miss Palmer to her pupils ; " and when they do, it does them no honour. . . . The government of a family is the only government necessary for a woman to be acquainted with." Bolder voices were raised, however. Hannah More disputed the necessity of concealment, since a woman's learning " seldom proves to be so very considerable as to excite astonishment," and Lady Mary pointed out the difficulty of it, where the mind has taken its tone from intellectual interests. The erudite Lady Filmer is her mouthpiece in that rational and moderate campaign on behalf of women's capacities, which she conducted under the transparent guise of a novelist in her *Letters from the Duchess de Crui.* " What a mistaken idea do men form of a learned lady," cries the author, and, adopting drastic measures for once, endeavours to disabuse them by introducing in her last volume a very accomplished lady, who explains the principles of Newton's philosophy to her lover.

The pageant of excellence passes and, overcome with so much virtue, we echo the *Critical*'s [1] wish " to see a female character drawn with faults and virtues, to see her feel the effects of misconduct, which does not proceed from a bad heart or corrupted inclinations, and to see her in the end happy, in consequence of her reformation ; in short to see a female Jones, or another Evelina, with faults equally embarrassing, yet as venial." The linking of Tom and Evelina gives a moment's blinding insight into the critic's sense of proportion. For the rest, such a plan required the comic sense, and the power of sustaining and elaborating one theme, and both qualities are much to seek in the women writers at the end of the eighteenth

---

Elizabeth Hamilton, in her *Letters of a Hindoo Rajah*, II, p. 328 (1796), says : " You know how female writers are looked down upon. The women fear, and hate ; the men ridicule, and dislike them."

[1] June 1788.

century; so that the nearest approach to a female Jones (*mutatis mutandis*) that could have been offered was Mrs. Brooke's Maria Villiers,[1] that impulsive young poetess, with her " wild and Pindaric " virtues, her warm heart and her social imprudence. And even here, as is so often the case, it is the statement of the theme that attracts; the working out is thin and the conclusion conventional.

One question must be asked, though it can be answered only by the most tentative suggestions. Is it possible to trace in the books of the men any response to the ideal of cultured delicacy put forward by the women? How far do they accept and admire the new heroine? In 1772 Richard Graves described Ophelia, the heroine of his *Spiritual Quixote*, as " a young woman of great good sense and delicacy of sentiment, and thoroughly versed in all the best writers in the English language, and even the translations from the classics." There is more than a hint of raillery in the description, but at least neither Richardson nor Fielding, neither Goldsmith nor Smollett, had concerned themselves about their young women's reading. So much for the culture of the understanding; for the even more important culture of the heart we may turn to Mackenzie's *Julia de Roubigné* (1777) and read Julia's opinion of wifely fidelity. It is not enough, she thinks, for a woman not to swerve from the duty of a wife; to love another more than a husband is an adultery of the heart, and not to love a husband with undivided affection is a virtual breach of the marriage vow. Richardson had dealt with virtue and Fielding with wifely loyalty, but the atmosphere here is quite different; and if it is argued that such spontaneous refinement can occur, in isolated cases, in any age, the answer is that here, and even more in Melmoth's *Emma Corbett* (1780), it expresses itself through the moulds of the woman's novel. " Does

[1] v. *The Excursion* (1777).

not the superiority of our attachment make you generously proud ? " writes Hammond to Emma, and we wonder if the young soldier has stolen his mistress's pen ; while Emma's love, with its instinctive reserve, its insistence on " that beauteous decorum, without whose graces, woman is both despicable and wretched," its dread of wounding delicacy even by too free a use of the terms of affection, is analysed by a mind wholly in sympathy with the woman's point of view.   It is unlike anything in the four great novelists, but it is very like the work of Mrs. Brooke and Mrs. Griffith, and as Courtney Melmoth, though a popular writer, is not specially open to the charge of insincerity, one may suppose that he was pleasing himself as well as his public.

The higher fanaticisms of the ideal are not found in the men's novels ; moreover, it is they who first deliver direct attacks on what they believe to be its corrupt parts. Towards the end of the 'eighties a more liberal spirit moves through English fiction, heartening the sinners and unsettling the rigid pose of the exemplary heroine.   It shows itself at first in little ways.   The heroines— *Benedicta* (1791) for example [1]—manage to combine more independence with their delicacy, and more warmth with their prudence ; authors claim sympathy for erring women without reducing them to abject humiliation.[2] But these mild deviations are forgotten beside the new course struck out by Bage and Holcroft.   Holcroft's concern was to stimulate the practice of female fortitude. His *Anna St. Ives* (1792) fighting successfully against her would-be seducer with resolution, shrewdness and self-

---

[1] *Benedicta* repeats Evelina's social blunder of refusing to dance with one man and accepting another, but she justifies herself ; she knew the characters of both men and chose to consult her delicacy in her choice.   The author admits that there are occasions when a girl who possesses the reality of virtue may prefer it to the etiquette of virtue, and laudably despise the opinion of the world.

[2] *E.g.* Mrs. Burke in *Ela ; or the Delusions of the Heart* (1787), praises the Griselda-like faith of an unmarried wife.

possession is certainly less pathetic than Clarissa, but she is certainly more admirable ; hers is that militant virtue which will oppose his desires to the limit of strength, but will also, if strength fails, endure and survive them. Bage's heroines yield to seduction or suffer violation, but preserve their mental vigour, and are restored to society, regretful, but without any of that " humiliation and abasement " which even Scott found indispensable.[1] In a few years Mary Hays was to define chastity as " individuality of affection," and Mary Wollstonecraft in her *Wrongs of Women* (1798) was to claim sympathy for an adultress. The moral landscape was changing, and when Bage praised in his Kitty Ross " a certain Amazonian goodness, so very much unlike the feeble, gasping, dying virtue of the generality of the sex," it is as though another ancient stronghold, half palace, half prison, with its hearth-fires, its sanctuary, its pleasant gardens and its grim encircling wall, were nodding to its overthrow.

[1] *v.* his *Memoir* of Bage in Ballantyne's *Novelists' Library* (1824). Scott's harshness—Kitty Ross, who occasions the comment, was sixteen at the time of her seduction and has lived chastely for many years before she marries—was due to reasoned conviction that the influence for good, exerted by women on society, is very great, and wholly dependent upon their personal purity.

CHAPTER V

NEW LIFE IN THE NOVEL

I

Novels are generally interesting in proportion as they excite our attention by what is new. I think the manners and customs of other countries and other times afford mines of such novelty as yet unransacked. The materials are easily acquired from our numerous books of travel.—SOUTHEY to Mary Hays, May 3rd, 1803.

IN the early 'eighties the novel begins to stir with new life. The yearly output increases; new themes, settings and characters appear, and the general level of relevance and coherence rises. The date must not be pressed. Melmoth, who had a journalistic flair for novelty, was writing in the 'seventies, and Holcroft's novel *Alwyn* came out in 1780; but it is still a few years before the improvement reaches the rank and file. By the time Mrs. P. Gibbes had published her book *The Niece; or the History of Sukey Thornby* (1788), this had occurred. *The Niece* was a book of the common type, published by F. Noble at his Circulating Library in Holborn for the ephemeral needs of his trade, and without any pretensions to survival; yet, if it is compared with a similar product of ten or fifteen years earlier, certain differences emerge. The book has one theme only, instead of six,—the exposure of an untaught girl to the interested scheming of servants,— which is worked out with some skill and no gross outrages on probability. Moreover, with the exception of one baronet, the characters are in the middle walk of life, merchants and plain gentlemen—a healthy sign. Lastly, Mrs. Gibbes in her remarks on dialogue shows some interest in method. Even very bad books have acquired a certain coherence and agility of movement,[1] while better ones are more substantial and a little less improbable. Mrs. Agnes Maria Bennett, a very popular novelist who appeared in the 'eighties, wrote versions of the Cinderella and Griselda stories [2] which, though they claim the indulgence awarded to popular literature, do not affront the reader's intelligence, while her *Juvenile Indiscretions* (1786), with its crowd of minor characters and its studied scenes of London middle-class life, has a solidity of conception that points toward the broad-based, well-stocked novel of the nineteenth century. As one follows out the work of Mrs. Bennett or of Mrs. Gunning [3] a change of accent becomes apparent; Smollett and Richardson are left behind; we are on the threshold of a new era, and Dickens and Thackeray are casting their shadows before. An antecedent of Dotheboys Hall is sketched in the cheap boarding-school of *Juvenile Indiscretions*, and Mrs. Gunning's aristocratic gatherings are pale anticipations of *Vanity Fair* ; while in those books that do not suggest such formidable comparisons we note here a stock character approached from a fresh angle, and there an old situation that has been varied, and everywhere signs, however slight, of the discovery that even in writing trash there are standards to be observed, much more then in the book that tries, however modestly, to reflect and criticize life. The change, it will be noted, preceded the French Revolution. That mighty influence, whose potency on

---

[1] E.g. *Fanny, or the Deserted Daughter* (1792), by a Young Lady; *Orlando and Lavinia* (1792).

[2] v. *Anna ; or Memoirs of a Welch Heiress* (1785) and *Ellen, Countess of Castle Howel* (1794).

[3] Susannah Minifie; she wrote novels in youth, in collaboration with her sister, M. Minifie, and alone, married in 1768 the brother of the beautiful Gunnings, and published nothing between 1769 and 1792. Then, a year after her separation from her husband, she finished *Anecdotes of the Delborough Family*, begun years before, and wrote *Memoirs of Mary* (1793) and *Delves ; a Welsh Tale* (1796). Her daughter also wrote.

our literature can hardly be exaggerated, need not be credited with the improvement in the standard of novels. The reading public, having glutted itself for a generation on the flimsiest wares, had reached the stage when it demanded something a little better ; it was educating itself in some small degree, for it is the tendency of any popular form of amusement to improve up to a point, and the change in taste is reflected in the novel.   Coincident with this natural development was the appearance of several writers of marked originality, Bage and Sophia Lee, whose *Recess* set the fashion for so much Gothic-historic work, at the beginning of the 'eighties, Charlotte Smith, Ann Radcliffe and Dr. John Moore at the end.   Filling the old forms with new interest and striking out new forms of their own, they drew the novel nearer to life, on one hand, and farther into the realms of imagination on the other, and proved that its possibilities, instead of being, as was feared, exhausted, had been as yet but scantily explored.   The women contributed romantic colour and a more conscientious standard of craftsmanship, the men brought back that humane breadth of view, which had scarcely been known in the novel since the death of Fielding ; and periodical critics, with this restoration in mind, grew more intolerant of extravagance and demanded nature and humour with greater insistence and a stronger hope that they might get it.   All this preceded the fall of the Bastille ; but when this fact has been remembered, we need set no bounds to the effect of the revolutionary atmosphere in stimulating experiment and emotion.

Gradually the novel—even the library novel—ceases to move within a traditional world and opens to the world without.   This remark must be understood in its most moderate sense.   There had always been novelists who found pleasure in contemplating the real—Richard Graves for instance—as there had always been aspects of contemporary life which thrust themselves into the most irresponsible novels ; even within the circulating library one cannot long remain unaware of debtors' prisons, Methodism, the state of the poor clergy, and the press-gang. On the other hand, there is no sudden demand for realism in the 'eighties, and no demand at all for realism unadulterated. What there is, is a gradually increasing proportion of common-sense, though its manifestations are partial, and the same book is liable to contain both common-sense and its antidote ; greater probability of detail, at least, if not of plot, notably in the matter of dialogue ; a wider range of character, though there is still little development and very little subtlety ; a much greater variety of setting ; a quicker reaction to contemporary events, especially in those books that accompany and comment on the course of the French Revolution ;[1] a little more integrity in winding up the end of a plot,[2] and the appearance of a few new and serious themes. Novelists are more democratic, and the convention of the exalted rank of heroes and heroines begins to wane. Elwina, in the *School for Fathers* (1788), is the daughter of a rich grocer, and George Walker's *Cinthelia* (1797) begins, a little defiantly : " Cinthelia, the daughter of a Tradesman in London." It was a change that critics had long demanded, largely on moral grounds, and did not fail to welcome. The business of the novel is to teach conduct by example, and that example is the most telling of which the circumstances correspond to the

---

[1] *E.g.* Mrs. C. Smith's *Desmond* (1792) and *The Banished Man* (1794) which reveal a distinct change in the author's attitude. *v.* also *Lindor and Adelaïde, a moral Tale. In which are exhibited the Effects of the Late French Revolution on the Peasantry of France* (1791), by the Author of *Observations on Dr. Price's Revolutionary Sermon* (an account of this book will be found in the *Monthly Review*, July 1791); *Adolphus de Biron* (1794) ; *The Parisian* (1794)—on the Duke of Orleans—and *Adelaide de Narbonne* (1800), including the murder of Marat.

[2] *E.g.* Helen Maria Williams' *Julia* (1790), where the catastrophe is neither evaded nor exaggerated, and Mrs. Lennox's *Euphemia* (1790), where the disagreeable husband is left alive.

reader's own, or are at least capable of being imagined by him. How could the trials of a countess instruct the milliner's assistant? The really instructive characters are those that can be " universally substituted," " and unless the reader can himself substitute or enter into the character, he cannot properly enjoy it," wrote the author of *Wanley Penson* (1791), with an apparent blindness to the modes of human enjoyment of which only a strict interpretation of the word " properly " can acquit him. Old predilections die hard, and the romantic interest in rank, though nowadays a little shamefaced, is not yet dead. Even moralizing critics were not quite free from it ; for when Mrs. Smith left her Monimia at the end of *The Old Manor House* (1793) just what she was at the beginning, the housekeeper's niece, the *Critical* reviewer complained that he had expected her to turn out " a very different personage." One notes, too, the fluctuation in the treatment of the prosperous tradesman. There was an old tradition of satire upon this subject, engendered between the contemptuous envy of needy literary men and the fastidiousness of their patrons, and this is perpetuated in the City scenes of Miss Burney and her imitators. This snobbishness is found in unexpected connections ; George Barnwell, Lillo's unhappy apprentice, reappears in T. S. Surr's novel (1798) in the most refined surroundings ; his uncle has become a knight, and he himself, forced reluctantly into trade by his father's death, never suffers the indignities of desk and stool, but performs a few gentlemanly duties in the house of one of the new speculative and fashionable merchants who live in Society. On the other hand, *The Citizen* (1790), by Mrs. Gomersall of Leeds, is designed to do honour to the business man who has acquired his wealth by strict mercantile method and dispenses it with careful benevolence. Mrs. Inchbald, herself a farmer's daughter, insists in *Nature and Art* (1796) on the value of the emotions of the poor and obscure, and draws a touching picture of the village girl Hannah Primrose. In her this was sincere enough ; but the humble heart has sometimes been fashionable, and is less reliable as a barometer of democratic feeling than the citizen.

The study of the novel in the 'eighties is largely a matter of following small clues, for a single sentence in a preface may convey some novelty in the author's outlook which the whole conventional narrative that follows fails to suggest. This is in some sort the case with the author of *The Amicable Quixote ; or, the Enthusiasm of Friendship* (1788), who declares that his interest is in exploring character and tracing its " undiscovered lineaments," but, lacking the skill to engage his characters in action, makes a rather disappointing business of his researches. His probing after variety and complexity of portraiture and his insufficient technique are typical of the time. The reader is continually stimulated by possibilities and promising touches, only to see the author relapse into the commonplace. What is remarkable about this new interest in character is that it is directed more towards the individual than the type and that it has a bent, soon to be emphasized, to the extraordinary in temperament and situation. Southey, in the letter to Mary Hays quoted at the head of this chapter, says that he has often thought out subjects for novels, turning on the development of a single character, as, for instance, of a man who accustoms himself to look at everything from a ridiculous point of view, till by laughing at everything he laughs away every good principle. Such curious analysis as this would require is not found in the 'eighties, but they saw the first examples of Charlotte Smith's careful record of motive and of Dr. John Moore's [1] unobtrusive psychology.

---

[1] Dr. John Moore (1729–1802) spent the first fifty years of his life chiefly in the study and practice of medicine, though he was deeply interested in history, literature and philosophy. He accompanied

His *Zeluco* (1789), and still more his *Edward* (1796) and
Mordaunt (1800), are full of observation, penetrating and
urbane ; he has a scientific interest in the development of
character, and introduces his persons with notes on their
parentage and the environment of their childhood.   The
growth of habit, the slow hardening of the crust of egoism,
are specially interesting to him, and Zeluco and Mr.
Barnet in *Edward* exemplify different ways by which a
man may reach a state of comparative insensibility to the
feelings of others.   National characteristics, as well as
those of individuals, come under his probe ; [1] the figures
of Signora Sporza, the French surgeon, and the two
Scots who fight a duel over the reputation of Queen Mary,
enliven *Zeluco* and reduce that villainous hero to his
proper proportions in the world of men ; and in these
portraits as in the less individualized ones of *Mordaunt*
Dr. Moore shows that for him the pleasures of impartial
and often amused dissection were superior to those of
satiric onslaught.   He is admirable when tracing, with
unlaboured irony and a total absence of comment, the
lines of self-protective argument that men spin, and
admirable in recording the conversations of harmless and
unconscious absurdity.   He commenced novelist late in
life, and his work has that harmony of texture which comes
from a reflective habit of mind, operating in mature years
upon the stuff of experience.   Open as he is to new
impressions, there are no crude novelties in his books,
and the quest for the extraordinary must be followed in

the young Duke of Hamilton on his travels from 1772 to 1778, and in
1779 published a *View of Society and Manners in France, Switzerland
and Germany*, followed in 1781 by a similar book on Italy and in 1786
by *Medical Sketches*.   Besides his three novels he published *A Journal
during a Residence in France* (1793) and *A View of the Causes and
Progress of the French Revolution* (1795).

    [1] *v.* the sub-titles of his novels, i.e. *Zeluco.   Various Views of
Human Nature, taken from Life and Manners, Foreign and Domestic ;
Edward.   Views of Human Nature, taken from Life and Manners,
Chiefly in England ; Mordaunt.   Sketches of Life, Character and
Manners, in Various Countries*.

other writers, for he never engaged in it, finding, perhaps, that the ordinary employed all his talents. There is no Titanic force about his Zeluco; he is a thoroughly wicked man who becomes wicked by natural means, by a bad education, a selfish nature and the opportunities of power. He is mean, base and dangerous, and quite untouched by grandeur; he conciliates no sympathy, and towards the end loses the courage with which alone he had extorted some admiration. There are acts of violence in the book, but they do not trouble the cool scrutiny of an author whose moral nature, unlike that of Fielding in *Jonathan Wild*, does not need the relief of a fierce irony, but constantly compels him to look still closer to his facts. With Dr. Moore, the scientist enters fiction.

Unimportant in achievement, as a rule, but significant for the change in taste of the last decade of the century, are those books which attempt to describe the reactions of character under the stress of a painful and unusual situation. *Elfrida, or Paternal Ambition* (1787) contains in Ellison a man who returns, after many years, to find his wife married to another; and the author has not been content to carry out the design in black and white, but in the husband's egoism, his cruel impulses and his returns of generosity, suggests, though she cannot support, an interest in the psychology of her subject. This is seven years before Godwin gave in *Caleb Williams* the first and finest example of his brooding dissection of morbid mental states, and excited enthusiasm in a generation which had begun to hanker for the abnormal and the complex. Even where a book does not touch the confines of the abnormal, it is often spiced with the unusual. Exotic types, of which the most frequent is the West Indian prodigal,—warm-hearted and arbitrary, if a man, licentious and cruel, if a woman,—appear with greater frequency; the Jew, abject abroad but resuming his dignity in his own house, often spending what he extorts from the thriftless in princely benefactions, ceases to be a comic figure and involves himself in mystery ;[1] and the majestic criminal, favoured also by German authors, begins to put a strain on our sympathies. New modes of experience were annexed to the novel, and authors, even when eschewing the highly coloured, are not afraid to build on exceptional circumstances. Mrs. Inchbald's Dorriforth, a Roman Catholic priest who inherits a peerage, is released from his vows and marries his ward, is a very special case indeed in Protestant England, but critics by now were prepared to welcome special cases as new sources of interest, and Dorriforth, who is a sufficiently imposing figure, was much admired. Analyses of sensibility are more individual than those of the mid-century, and a certain amount of attention is being paid to adolescence. Here, of course, we cross the tracks of the educationists ; but the account of the heroine's girl-hood in Mary Wollstonecraft's *Mary, a Fiction* (1788) and the few comments on youthful egoism at the beginning of Charles Lloyd's *Edmund Oliver* (1798) suggest a more mysterious unfolding of power than do the nursery stories of bland theorists like Miss Edgeworth ; omniscient guardians are replaced by the operations of nature and solitude, and we feel—very naturally in the second case—the shadow of *The Prelude*.

Novelty of character is accompanied by novelty of setting. The background of the English novel had been, with the occasional exception of the picaresque, pre-dominantly insular. Now the material amassed by travellers, the picturesque tours and descriptions of foreign countries, is applied to vary the scene.[2] Poets were ahead

---

[1] *v., e.g.*, George Walker's *Theodore Cyphon, or the Benevolent Jew* (1796). The Jew has nothing to do with the story ; he receives the confidences of Theodore, shelters him, and satisfies the public taste for the sympathetic portraiture of outcasts ; cf. Cumberland's *Jew* (1794).

[2] Defoe had made some use of travel books, though not in the

of novelists in drawing on these stores, but the poet, who carries less luggage than the novelist, was usually first in any fresh field in the eighteenth century, and one need not search long among the versifiers before coming on Lapland eclogues and Mexican idylls. Isolated novelists there are, indeed, who sketch a foreign background, and the most admired of them was Mrs. Brooke, whose Canadian scenes in *Emily Montague* (1769) are often referred to by reviewers;[1] but Mrs. Brooke had personal knowledge of the country she describes; it is another matter when novelists systematically plunder travel books in search of atmosphere. No doubt the war in America and the trial of Warren Hastings quickened interest in our distant dependencies,—not that the Indian and American scenes that now appear are always based on knowledge; a scant *décor* of diamonds and forests in the first case, and rebels and forests in the second, was frequently found sufficient,—but these events will not account for the Turkish and Siberian tales, the richly coloured Spanish and Italian and French Romances with which, in the 'nineties, the Press begins to teem, nor will they account for the new direction which this material takes; for the aim of the writer is no longer merely to inform but to excite, and curiosity is yielding to glamour. This does not mean that veracious accounts of foreign countries are not found in the novel, but that the impulse, which led the majority of readers to these books, is not so much the desire of information as the desire of colour. The change of attitude can be followed in those novels that contain Indian or American episodes. The Indian, like the Redskin, first entered fiction as a philosophic character, a blameless vegetarian and Deist, conferring

---

interests of the picturesque; cf. Paul Dottin, *Daniel De Foe et ses Romans*, p. 340. The motive of interest here is their connection with trade.

[1] They were imitated, according to the *Critical* (Nov. 1773), by the author of *All's Right at Last*.

upon his daughter some invaluable moral precepts and some enormous diamonds. As time went on, the diamonds became more important than the precepts, and Indian episodes can be divided into three kinds, the humanitarian (brutal soldiery and harmless sufferers), the informative (suttee, sacred bulls, English life at Calcutta) and the romantic, in which all this material is directed to other ends, and the young Englishman, aided by a humane Brahmin, rescues the devoted wife by a trap-door under the pyre. The most pleasing of these Indian tales is *Hartly House, Calcutta* (1789), and the most extraordinary *Rajah Kisna* (1786). *Hartly House, Calcutta*, which reads as if it were based on personal experience,[1] is a lively, various and well-written account of the life and manners of the English population in Calcutta, sent home to her friend by an English girl who has gone out with her father. Sophia has an enthusiasm for the " gentle Gentoo," and there is an unusual streak in the book in the influence of a young Brahmin, after his death, in regulating the girl's mind and subduing her vanity. But this is slightly touched, and the major part of the narrative deals with the English households, the country bungalows where the children are kept, the garden statuary, characteristically imported from England and consisting of figures of eminent British literary characters, the fashionable ladies who drive phaetons and pairs, with a gentleman companion lolling at ease beside them, and the theatre, where all the parts are taken by men. Sophia can sketch charming pictures, like that of the country-born lady smoking her hooka while under the hands of her friseur, an activity that claims Sophia's admiration,

[1] The book may have been written in part eighteen years or so before it was finished and published. On p. 142 there are references to the King's coronation (1760) and to an arrangement between the Government and the Company, to run for four years from 1769; whereas on p. 196 the departure of Governor Hastings (Feb. 1785) is mentioned, and on p. 265 the news comes that Lord Cornwallis (appointed 1786) is on his way to Calcutta.

because of the " genteel air with which she drew out the
soft fume, and puffed it forth, alternately " ; and she can
convey by her inability to keep her mind off the possibilities of sudden death something of the strain under
which Europeans lived in a fever-ridden climate to which
they had not learned to adapt themselves. *Rajah Kisna,
an Indian Tale*, which was briefly dismissed by the critics
as " Eastern nonsense," was certainly calculated to raise
astonishment rather than approval at the time of its
publication. It is a mythological story of fighting and
magic, handsomely furnished with oracles and apparitions,
ivory cars drawn by lions, silver cars drawn by leopards,
subterraneous passages and imprisoned princesses. I do
not know whether any fragments of Hindu legend have
been built into this fabric ; some of the names are familiar ;
at all events it is the work of a man who knew something,
perhaps at second-hand, of Eastern mythology, but
retained his taste for Western moral allegory in full force.
Its nearest analogue is Southey's *Curse of Kehama*, and,
like that, it is too supernatural to wake sympathy. The
author has modelled his story, as far as he can, on the
Æneid, and provides a Dido and an Æneas, a Troy and a
Carthage ; but his figures are of no use except to grace
his pageantry ; and the grand pitched battle between the
angelic and dæmonic hosts, with which the book ends, was
not calculated to conciliate the *Critical* or the *Monthly*.[1]

[1] Indian episodes appear in *Gilham Farm, or the History of Melvin
and Lucy* (1780), " fabricated to introduce some seemingly original
accounts of India," as the *Monthly* said ; *The Indian Adventurer, or
the History of Mr. Vanneck, a Novel founded on Facts* (1780), apparently
based on the life of a young German surgeon and trader in India ;
Bage's *Mount Henneth* (1781)—philosophical ; Helenus Scott's
Adventures of a Rupee (1782) ; *Juliana* (1786) ; *Zoraida, or Village
Annals* (1787), and Ann Plumptre's *Rector's Son* (1798). The last
book refers to Mrs. Kindersley's *Letters* and Hodges' *Travels in India*.
The Disinterested Nabob (1787) is full of information and local colour,
and manifestly anxious to vindicate the English, but it is impossible
to tell whether the knowledge is personal or drawn from books. The
story is poor and the book far less well-written than *Hartly House,
Calcutta*.

The American scenes in eighteenth-century novels are mostly connected with the war or with slavery, though there is a certain amount of mirth over the custom of " bundling," and the noble savage survives, adapted to romantic purposes.[1] They often occur in the books of women,[2] and are informed by an indignant pacifism, for the fratricidal quality of the conflict heightened their sense of the horrors of warfare. Some books adapt current anecdotes, like Melmoth's *Emma Corbett ; or, the Miseries of Civil War* (1780), which was both the first [3] and the best of the novels to draw its spring of action from " the assassination of America," though its American scenes are few and vague ; some, like George Walker's *Cinthelia* (1797), in which the heroine follows the camp, are arranged as a pageant of dreadful distress. The war is the great theme ; except in Gilbert Imlay's *Emigrants* (1793), which was written to promote American settlement and easy divorce, we see little of the normal life of the country, and must not expect any great degree of accuracy in the pictures of its conditions. There is one pleasant exception ; the popularity of American subjects stirred in Mrs. Charlotte Lennox, then an old woman, the memories of her youth, and in *Euphemia* (1790) she conducts that patient wife to New York, takes her up the Hudson to Albany with a Dutch skipper, shows her an Indian camp and the working of the Indian fur trade, and causes her to winter in Schenectady and Fort Hunter,

---

[1] *E.g.* in *The Adventures of Jonathan Corncob, Loyal American Refugee, written by himself* (1787), and in *The School for Fathers* (1788), where the noble and sentimental Logan stabs himself for love.

[2] *E.g. Georgina : or Memoirs of the Bellmour Family* (1787), by a Young Lady ; *Julia* (1790) by Helen Maria Williams ; Mrs. Smith's *Old Manor House* (1793) ; Mrs. Eliza Parsons' *The Voluntary Exile* (1795) and the anonymous *American Hunter* (1788).

[3] The American episode in Mrs. Catherine Parry's *Eden Vale* (1784), in which the lover and brother of the narrator fight on different sides in the war, with fatal results, was written years before the publication of the book in which it is included, and may have pride of place.

where the service is read in Dutch and Indian in the Mohawk chapel. *Euphemia* blends instruction and entertainment according to the old recipe, but by the end of the century not even the most northerly latitudes were free from the raids of romance, and in *Wanley Penson, or the Melancholy Man* (1791) we come on that strange and exciting story of the barbarous descendants of the old Norse settlers in Greenland, of their debased names, their half-forgotten and barbarized laws, and the great Latin Bible which they revere and cannot read.

It is not necessary to go through the various European countries which in turn became the scene of action in romantic novels, and are visited by the travelling heroes and heroines of which there are so many in the fiction of the 'nineties. Usually the south of Europe is favoured and Mrs. Radcliffe set the fashion for glowing Italian landscapes as a background for love scenes. The Prussia of Frederick the Great is the scene of one or two tales of simple domestic and military sentiment,[1] and the *Siberian Anecdotes* (1783) of Thomas Haweis, chaplain to Lady Huntingdon, testifies, by an odd mixture of history, romance and local colour, to a sense of the growing importance of Russia. " Some future generations perhaps shall till these plains, where elks and antelopes now graze undisturbed," says one of the settlers in Siberia ; " and that mighty empire of Russia, which seems fast emerging from barbarism, teem, like China, with population, and emulate her industry." The passion for travel made matters easy for the hack novelist ; he had only to

---

[1] E.g. *Valentine* (1790). There are some remarks on Greece in *The Spectre* (1789), and the very romantic *Radzivil, a Romance, translated from the Russ of the celebrated M. Wocklow* (1790),—probably written by an Englishman in Russia,—has a background of Poland and the central European countries, as has the *Siege of Belgrade* (1791), while *Phedora; or, The Forest of Minski* (1798) by Mary Charlton plays in Russia at the end of the seventeenth century, and the author refers in notes to a *Customs and Manners of Russia, Livonia, etc.,* and to the Appendix to Voltaire's *History of Russia*.

select his authority, transcribe liberally, intersperse a few love-scenes and market the result. *The Château de Myrelle* (1791) consists of a journey through France to Bath, Bristol and Weymouth, together with a birth mystery ; and *Louise ; or the Reward of an Affectionate Daughter* (1790), of a libertine, a faithful clergyman, and a tour in Holland and Hanover. " This turf they dig out in square pieces about a foot long, and six inches thick," writes the heroine informatively, " it is laid up in immense piles to dry, and is then brought here by water for sale— and when mixed with coals, burns very well." One turns the page. " Curse on the confounded obstinacy of that troublesome old fellow, your uncle ! " Better writers acknowledged the quarries whence they drew, and, if they did not, the critics often made their acknowledgments for them. *Orlando and Seraphina, a Turkish Tale* (1787) draws on the recently-translated relation of Baron de Tott, though, as the reviewer truly says, the European colouring is not thrown off ; Alexander Bicknell, a ready pen, plunders Savary and Volney for remarks on Egypt in his *Doncaster Races ; or the History of Miss Maitland* (1789).[1] Mrs. Smith in *Celestina* (1791) went to Ramond de Carbonnières, and Mrs. Radcliffe in the *Mysteries of Udolpho* to Ramond, Grosley and Mrs. Piozzi,[2] while Mrs. Mary Robinson, referring in her *Hubert de Sevrac* (1796) to Cox's *Travels in Switzerland*, calls them ingenuously " those beautiful and romantic descriptions, of which so many novelists have availed themselves." No wonder that Charlotte Smith, having painfully constructed yet another castle in *The Banished Man* (1794), wonders " if it would not have been better to have *earthed* my hero, and have sent him for adventures to the subterraneous town in the Chatelet mountains in Champagne,

---

[1] v. *Critical*, July 1789.
[2] v. my article *Ramond, Grosley and Mrs. Radcliffe* in the *Review of English Studies*, July 1929.

or even to Herculaneum or Pompeii, where I think no scenes have yet been laid."

Nearer home we can observe the slow growth of that regional interest in fiction which in a few years was to produce *Castle Rackrent* (1800) and the Waverley novels. Sketches of the national types of Great Britain and Ireland [1] are less persistently tilted towards mirth, and the travelling hero sometimes employs his descriptive pen on his own country, when his comments are the more graphic for being less studied than when he enters into competition with Claude and Salvator on their own soil. Such a comment is Alwyn's brief description of Kendal.[2] " Here every object is bleached, as it were, by time and simplicity." Country scenes are gradually freed from boisterous exaggeration on the one hand and school-room idealism on the other, though, in this kind, there is nothing so good in the 'eighties as Graves's *Spiritual Quixote* with its strong local colouring and its absence of sentimentality. One remembers the prolific mother to whom Lady Forester took a present of extra strong linen. " The poor woman turned it about, and surveyed it with some attention ; and, upon Lady Forester's asking her how she

---

[1] Smollett's Scottish types and scenes are imitated, *e.g.* in *The Prudential Lovers; or the History of Harry Harper* (1783). There is a pleasant picture of young Highland ladies, and a formidable one of a Scottish breakfast, in *The Modern Fine Gentleman* (1774), and the Highland scene is repeated, apparently at second hand, in *Fatal Follies* (1788). Scotland early became the land of romance, as the distractingly bad *William Wallace* (1791) of Henry Siddons—then, to be sure, little more than a school-boy—testifies. Ireland was less cultivated. The *Monthly*, reviewing *The Reconciliation ; or, the History of Miss Mortimer and Miss Fitzgerald. An Hibernian Novel.* By an Irish Lady (1783), complains of the absence of local colour. " We do not even meet with blunders." There are, however, *Anthony Varnish* (1786), *The Minor ; or, the History of George O'Nial, Esq.* (1787), and a pleasing picture of a young Irish peer in Miss Blower's *Maria* (1785). Welsh pride of blood and Welsh pronunciation are traditional comic themes, but there are a few local touches in Mrs. Bennett's *Ellen, Countess of Castle-Howel* (1794) and Mrs. Gunning's *Delves, a Welch Tale* (1796).

[2] *Alwyn, or the Gentleman Comedian* (1780), by T. Holcroft; published anonymously.

liked it ? she said it was pretty coarse, but she believed it
might do." Such strokes are rare, and they were not,
as a matter of fact, much encouraged by critics. " Readers
of taste," says the *Monthly* pontifically of *The Incognita,
or Emily Villars* (1784), " will be disgusted at descriptions
which enter too minutely into vulgar scenes, and at
dialogues which are degraded by the cant of provincial
speech." The *Monthly* may have been a little behind the
times. At all events, three years later the *Gentleman's
Magazine* welcomed in *The Happy Art of Teasing* " a
general picture of rural life, in all its gradations, from the
cultivated gentleman and lady, through the yeomanry,
independent and wealthy farmers, down to the common
ploughman and housemaid." [1] As for the cant of
provincial speech which, though it had been current on
the stage, had mostly been translated into literary English
in the novel,[2] its peculiar expressiveness, as the medium
of untaught intelligence, began now to attract attention,
and there are even sporadic attempts to suggest dialectal
pronunciation.[3]

The quickening interest of the novel-reading public in
history and the romance of the past is discussed in a
separate chapter ; it was one of the most marked developments of the novel at the end of the century, and had far-
reaching effects. Scientific discovery, on the other hand,
touches fiction but slightly. This is not surprising. To

---

[1] I have not been able to find this book.

[2] v., e.g., Cumberland's *Henry* (1795).

[3] The West of England dialect gets most attention ; it was Squire
Western's speech. There are touches in *The Histories of Lady
Frances S— and Lady Caroline S—* by the Miss Minifies of Fairwater
in Somersetshire (1763), Courtney Melmoth's *Family Secrets* (1797)
and Mrs. A. M. Bennett's *Welch Heiress* (1785). In *The Citizen*
(1790) by Mrs. Gomersall of Leeds a poor woman speaks dialect, and
a speech of the housekeeper at Grasmere is recorded by Mrs. Smith
in *Ethelinde*, I, p. 38 (1789), with a careful attempt to convey exact
sounds, while the same attempt is made by Mrs. Bennet with the talk
of the waggoner and the servant, Mat, in *Juvenile Indiscretions*, I,
p. 65 and II, p. 70 (1786). I have found one Americanism, " aloong "
in *Jonathan Corncob* (1787).

the general reader natural science was still an assortment of curious odds and ends of knowledge ; those which were profitable could be built easily enough into the structure of daily life ; those which were unprofitable— the majority—provided comic material, along with the collection of coins and butterflies. In Italy, geology and " Moses " were already clashing over the lava-beds of Ætna and setting up a discord which was to require the utmost efforts of poetry and philosophy to resolve ; but the shock of the challenge was not yet widely felt. Spectacular and sometimes tragic experiments were conducted nearer home. In 1774 Day was drowned at Plymouth, testing his submersible boat ; in 1783 Pilâtre de Rozier, the " most intrepid philosopher of the age," made the first free navigation in a balloon in company with the nervous Marquis d'Arlandes ; and in 1785 Lunardi, ascending from St. George's Fields, took with him Mrs. Sage, the first English Female Aerial Traveller, who promptly wrote an account of her trip in a *Letter to a Female Friend*. The magazines reported experiments in mesmerism and electricity, and warned their fair readers that " a lady who has her head surrounded with a wire cap, and her hair stuck full of metal pins, and who at the same time wears silk stockings, that is, stands upon silk, is to all intends and purposes an electrical conductor, insolated (*sic*) and prepared for collecting fire from the atmosphere." [1] Yet it is easy to see how unmanageable all this science and pseudo-science was for the purposes of fiction. It could not be treated seriously, for it was not focussed by any comprehensive idea. Heroes in the eighteenth century did not find themselves balancing the claims of marriage and scientific research ; nor did they agonize in the shipwreck of their faith. Even the comic possibilities were limited. " Scientific wit is an unwieldly weapon," said the *Critical*, reviewing *The*

[1] v. *Scots Magazine*, June 1773.

Philosophical Quixote ; or Memoirs of Mr. David Wilkins
(1782), a book in which a country apothecary makes
ridiculous attempts to apply the " late philosophical
discoveries " to medicine, and, believing rain-drops to be
charged with electricity, sends people similarly charged
out into a thunder-storm, in the hope of seeing the drops
repelled.[1] Some humour, too, of the old harsh sort, was
to be got out of figures like Bage's Miss Caradoc, who
kills cats in air-pumps and investigates the generation
of animals. More fruitful, though as yet little explored,
was the application of science to fantastic adventure. An
anonymous and very humble precursor of Jules Verne
published in 1786 *The Balloon, or Aerostatic Spy, a Novel,
Containing a Series of Adventures of an Aerial Traveller ;
Including a Variety of Histories and Characters in Real
Life,*[2] a book which, beginning with a thrilling plate of
Lunardi's ascent and a preface anticipating the use of
balloons in exploration and in war, and ending with a
summary of all the ascents in England up to date, offers
in the middle of the sandwich the story of a young
American, who is shipwrecked, meets a philosophic
recluse on an African island and with his help constructs
a smoke balloon, only to find himself and his balloon
taken charge of by Amiel, a " spirit of atmosphere," who
fills the balloon with gas, and takes the young man a jaunt
through Constantinople, Spain, Paris, London and Reading to Bristol, pointing out to him noted people of all
kinds, but particularly rogues—for here Amiel takes on
the rôle of Johnstone's Chrysal—and discussing political
conditions. One feels disappointed that Amiel cannot

[1] It sounds as if this character may have suggested old Holman in
Bage's *James Wallace* (1788), who electrifies his orchard to improve
the fruit ; but I have only the review to go on.
[2] The title is taken from the B.M. copy. The *Monthly* reviewed
the book in Dec. 1785 under a slightly different title, viz. *The Aerostatic Spy ; or Excursions with a Balloon. Exhibiting a View of various
Countries in different Parts of the World, and a Variety of Characters
in real Life. By an aerial Traveller.*

turn his balloon to something more exciting than the old satiric survey ; the passion of fear is only once aroused, and yet it was by way of fantastic terror that science was first reduced to the service of fiction. Science enters the novel masquerading, through the Tale of Terror, and having supplied magical accessories to Illuminists, at last, in Mrs. Shelley's *Frankenstein*, supplies a theme.

Frankenstein falls outside our period, but within it there are signs that the poverty of invention, from which the novel had long suffered, is diminishing. The authoress of *Memoirs of a Scots Heiress* (1791) introduces a new episode in the story of Miranda, the beautiful black girl, who is brought to England by her uncle and falls in love with a young Englishman. He proposes marriage from compassion and they actually approach the altar together, but poor Miranda, worn out by her struggles and the thought of the complex destiny she is bringing on her husband and her children, at the last moment repels him in terrified reaction, faints, and dies. The sentimentality of the scene should not blind the reader to the fact that this is a new subject in the novel, turning on new motives, and treated with seriousness. It is still, however, connected with love, and at this time the question is raised, whether it is not possible to write a novel without the tender passion. Mrs. Smith, at the end of the loveless first volume of *The Banished Man* (1794), pauses to assure her readers that there is a little love coming, and that hers is not " the experiment that has often been talked of, but has never yet been hazarded," a novel without love. Afterwards she added a note, stating that when the passage was written she had neither seen nor heard of a book called *Things as They Are*. This is Godwin's *Caleb Williams* (1794), the first novel to do without love-making. But if it is difficult, in a book of entertainment, to dispense with marrying and giving in marriage, it is possible to reduce it to a secondary level of importance.

This had always been the practice of the picaresque, and now it is extended to the serious, sentimental novel. One of the earliest examples was Courtney Melmoth's *Shenstone-Green* (1779), which appeared a few years before the general lift in the quality of fiction was perceptible and, in so blank a time, naturally attracted a good deal of attention.[1] The ex-parson had some seriousness of conviction ; he had thought and felt, and conveyed the results of these exercises in his novels, in a tone of flamboyant sentimentality. Nor was he content to embody them in casual dialogue or anecdote ; in his books the opinions are central and provide the plot—a simple refinement of the novelist's art not much practised at this time. In *Shenstone-Green* Melmoth returns to his old subject of unwise benevolence, but this time he is more concerned with the consequences to the recipients of the bounty than with those to the donor. The misguided philanthropist, Sir Benjamin Beauchamp, himself tells the story of his failure to establish in Wales a perfect society, secured by his munificence from poverty and dependent for its peace, not upon law, but mutual goodwill. The effusions of his enthusiasm are salted by a wryly cheerful admission of failure ; the laugh is against him ; human nature is more recalcitrant than he had thought to its own good ; and he can give full weight in his narrative to the attitude of Samuel Sarcasm, his loyal steward and the tenacious adversary of his schemes, who carries out his orders with repining and anger, but clings to his office to save what can be saved of his master's property. The story, allowing for some swampy patches, is told with liveliness and humour. Shenstone-Green is established and named in honour of the poet whose idea of " building a neighbourhood " had so inflamed Sir Benjamin's fancy ; the deserving and amiable poor of all

---

[1] The book is alluded to by other novelists, *e.g.* Bage in *Mount Henneth*.

classes are collected, classified and pensioned, " and happiness really resided with us almost a whole month." After that the idle hands find or make mischief, and the vanities of the world intrude. The tradesmen take to cock-fighting and the young gentlemen import race-horses; Shenstone's statue is defaced with notices; women of the town flaunt at the races and are taken into keeping. Meanwhile honest Henry Hewit, sole wise man in the Green, goes quietly back to his trade of master-mason and bricklayer, sure that work and even anxiety are better for him than idleness. Sir Benjamin, already half-convinced of his folly, cannot interfere, for the delicacy with which he has made his pensioners independ-ent of him has tied his hands. At last the establishment of a theatre, with its concomitants of expense, debts, suits and bailiffs, and the folly of a debating society, which allows a dispute on religion, bring about the catastrophe of Shenstone-Green. The settlement is handed over to Samuel Sarcasm to be run on more normal lines, and Sir Benjamin, disillusioned, but not irretrievably hurt in peace or pocket, withdraws to meditate on his experi-ence, admitting that human nature, as it is, needs the discipline of enforced work and the control of law, and that a society based upon delicacy and good-will is a chimæra.

II

While thou keepest always looking up at me, and I, down at thee, what horrid obliquities of vision may we not contract?—BAGE, Mount Henneth, 1781.

The greater number of human opinions seem to me to be swad-dling clouts for children.—BAGE, Barham Downs, 1784.

Robert Bage, paper-manufacturer in the Midlands, wrote six novels, which he published anonymously, Mount Henneth (1781), Barham Downs (1784), The Fair Syrian (1787), James Wallace (1788), Man as he is (1792)

and *Hermsprong, or Man as he is not* (1796).   He commenced novelist at the age of fifty-three, to take his mind
off business losses, and persisted in the soothing occupation through years of commercial and political anxiety.
He was warmly welcomed by the critics ; they found in
him something strong and unusual, a cheering exception
to the general run of novels ; they praised his characters,
his humour and philosophy, and, admitting that his
strokes were sometimes coarse and that he had more
genius than taste, found it a cheap price to pay for the
re-entry of a vigorous masculine mind into the novel.
Later the note of praise dropped to a lower pitch ; it had
indeed been forced up by contrast with the insipid
novels with which the Press overflowed, and a modern
reader, though pleased and interested, looks in vain for
that " thrilling, lambent fire " which the *Critical* detected
in Bage's first two books.   His lanterns shone bright in
that murky dawn, and were quenched as the day widened.

What Bage brought to the novel was a great increase
of intellectual content.   His active, liberal and independent mind had ranged through a variety of subjects,
and his books are full of thought.   They are indeed, to
use Mr. J. B. Priestley's classification of the far more
finished but not wholly dissimilar work of Peacock,
novels of opinion.   In the house-parties which, like
Peacock, he loves to assemble, from which his philosophers-
errant go forth and to which they return, bearing their
trophies of experience and philanthropy with them, the
talk turns from government to religion, from democracy
to sex.   There is nothing ponderous about these debates
and nothing dogmatic about the conclusions ; Bage has
no rigid system to compare with the moral stiffness of the
woman's novel.   Seeing that conduct must be to some
extent experimental and spontaneous, the best we can do
is not to choke spontaneity nor penalize experiment too
heavily ; to beware of submission, lest it engender the

vices of a slave, and of power, lest it lead to tyranny ; to
be slow to anger ; to look always to the points of similarity
between men rather than to those of difference ; and to
follow reason without fear but without fanaticism, remembering that the suffering of others can be too high a price
for our own mental integrity.[1]   This position he explains
with cheerfulness and moderation, in a forthright, short-
breathed style, broken with whimsy.   Less solemn than
the band of didactic novelists, he is, if not more convinced
than they, at least, in right of the scope and frankness of
his speculations, more honest ; he will distinguish between
ancient decencies and ancient follies, and whatever concessions he feels called upon to make, they will be no
blind immolations to tradition.   It is, however, necessary
to understand just how far his seriousness went and to
what extent it affected the structure of his novels.   It
was by no means the intense, the almost tyrannical
seriousness of modern art.   Unity of impression, a
religious verisimilitude, meant nothing to Bage.   The
novel was still a pastime, and no novelist required austere
endeavours on the part of his readers, or refused to
indemnify them for such efforts as they did make by a
liberal supply of providential coincidences and turns of
fortune.   Bage accepted the old framework without any
misgivings, and set out to amuse.   Patches of common
novel-material lie beside pictures of real life, and he does
not seem to have felt that one invalidated the other or
disturbed its effect ; they amused the reader in different
ways, of which he must be trusted to distinguish the
relative importance.   In the case of Bage's first book,
Mount Henneth, it is possible to maintain that the majority
of the adventures, the kidnapping, imprisonments and
the meeting with privateers, are illustrative of the author's

---

[1] Cf. *Man as he is* ; on the subject of compliments Bage says :
" We owe to society . . . not to sacrifice the vanity of others at the
shrine of our own."

opinions, that they are not there for the sake of their value as entertainment, but as they flow from a state of war, which he detests. In *Barham Downs*, also, while the story is not very significant, nearly all the characters reflect special moral ideas. But in the later books he tended more and more to express his opinions in conversation rather than in action, and except in *Hermsprong* the connection between opinions and story is very loose. He does not in his plots oppose two systems of ideas in sharp and sustained conflict, as Holcroft does in *Anna St. Ives* (1792); he seems to have felt that, unless one were an egoist, occasions for such a rigid opposition are not frequent. Action in his books, where it is relevant to opinions at all and is not simple story-telling, is less often an expression of these than an amused comment on them. Like Peacock again, if not to the same extent, he felt the disconnection between a man's ideas and his life, and nowhere is this more clear than in *Man as he is*, with its impulsive, convincible, blundering hero, and the tutor, who, having done his utmost on several occasions to persuade his charge of the criminal folly of duelling, himself makes ready to fight. Certain moral principles are exempt from this sceptical banter; circumstances do not imperil the value of benevolence or of independence.

Man as he is is Bage's best book. It is the most forward-looking. Where the other five are, at times, comparable to Peacock, but at times wholly of their age, this reads for whole chapters like a lighter-handed anticipation of Thackeray. There is Thackeray's scene—Spa, with its English visitors, its foreign noblemen, its adventurers and adventuresses—and, partaking somewhat too lavishly of its pleasures, there is the generous, dissipated young man, Sir George Paradyne, who is the pencilled outline of one of Thackeray's heroes. We move through Europe and back to England, losing and recovering our acquaintances as the crowds shift, aware, like Thackeray, of the irrational in society, though with less perturbation than he betrays. The story is slight, though natural enough, and variegated with the usual eighteenth-century insets. Sir George Paradyne, coming early into his inheritance, sets forth in life with the noblest intentions, chooses Mr. Lindsay as his travelling tutor in a tour through England, and, almost at the first stage, falls in love with Miss Colerain. She will not accept him until he has proved his worth in the world. Sir George takes his good intentions to London and the Continent, taints them with dissipation, is ashamed and sorry but cannot rally effectually. At last, ill and unhappy, he receives the reward he does not deserve, for Miss Colerain sees that she must supply the stabilizing power in his life, and that without her all his good qualities will go to waste. Round Sir George and Miss Colerain are grouped Bage's most interesting characters : Lady Mary Paradyne, Sir George's aggressive mother, who accosts her invalid son with the remark : " They say you are in a waste, Sir George "; Miss Carlill, the Quaker; Bardoe, the *nil admirari* Englishman; and Birimport, the returned " nabob," who will not discard his habits of autocratic command, but lives jealously secluded to avoid humiliations, re-establishing his sense of power by tyrannizing over his wife.[1] Birimport, particularly, with his perpetual *malaise* working out in a cruelty of which he is fundamentally ashamed, is finely imagined.

After the comedy and truth of *Man as he is* it is strange to turn to *Hermsprong ; or, Man as he is not*, for here the natural development of Bage's art is suddenly checked, or rather reversed. Hitherto he has been evolving a

[1] *v.* also the pedantic Catherine Haubert, whose learning is a balm for mortification in love; and, in *James Wallace*, the family of the successful oil-man, Gamidge, Sir Anthony Havelly, the fop with the Parisian coat and the real, though pedantic, scientific knowledge, and Squire Thurl, the Tony Lumpkin, recognized by all his acquaintances as an anachronism.

novel of manners and character, stripped of improbable turns of fortune and strengthened by a strong speculative interest. Now, forsaking the natural fluidity of this form, he writes a book in which the tendencious elements have stiffened into a bizarre framework.[1] *Hermsprong*, in spite of its touches of humour and pathos and a fairly lively cast, really belongs to what one may call the diagrammatic type of novel, and the mental process behind it is akin to that behind allegory. The author is visibly coercing his human agents ; they stand in symmetrical relations to one another, as representatives of this or the other system of ideas, and they pass through the action as through a formal dance, maintaining these relationships intact. They are ingredients in a pattern rather than individuals, and they are stripped of all complexities of character in order that the pattern may not be disturbed. On one side stands Hermsprong, bred among the American Indians to physical hardihood and moderation and instructed by his reason in honesty and a proper independence of mind ; on the other, the purple figure of Lord Grondale, swollen with tyranny and prejudice, supported by the sycophantic Doctor Blick. Between the two vibrates his lordship's daughter, Caroline Campinet, drawn to the side of unreason by what is good, not what is base in her, by an ideal delicacy of mind that yearns to render the most implicit filial duty and has to be tutored by Hermsprong and her friend Miss Fluart. There is a pleasant grotesqueness about this angularity ; the persons of the story are never at a loss, never, even in moments of crisis, fail to support their characters. One delights equally in the brisk exchange between Hermsprong and Lord Grondale over the body of the rescued Miss

---

[1] The *Monthly* reviewer preferred it, however, on account of its greater unity and of the figure of the hero, " a prominent and fine delineation of the accomplished, firm, frank and generous man, worthy to be impressed as a model for imitation." v. *Monthly*, Sept. 1796.

Campinet,[1] and in Hermsprong's subscription to his letter to his antagonist : " Obedient to the forms of politeness, I am your lordship's obedient servant." Even in this book, however, there is much that overflows the formula. Bage's practical sense and observation are never long dormant, and he has no taste for the fantastic heights of consistency to which the diagrammatic method can sometimes climb.

To test the difference in climate between Bage and the true perfectibilian dreamer, one has only to turn to L. S. Mercier's *L'An Deux Mille Quatre Cent Quarante. Rêve s'il en fût jamais* (1770),[2] translated into English by W. Hooper, M.D., as *Memoirs of the Year Two Thousand Five Hundred* (1772). In this " consoling dream " of a future that Mercier believed, in its essence, possible, when the vast majority of the human race shall act with a uniform and enlightened nobility, the author, like Bacon in the *New Atlantis*, makes a fine use of symbol and ritual. His most elaborate scene is the public trial and execution of a murderer. The man is condemned to death, but his voluntary submission to the sentence is required before it can be executed ; the alternative is a life of exile and

---

[1] Lord Grondale at once asks the rescuer his fortune and rank. " My fortune," answered the stranger, " Kings might envy ; it is equal to my desires. As to rank—I have been taught to distinguish men by virtue."

[2] Mercier published his book anonymously, but the authorship was known in England by 1781 (v. *Monthly*, Sept., p. 227). He published an enlarged edition in 1787. The book, which anticipates Mr. Wells's device in *When the Sleeper Wakes*, is full of interesting detail,—roof gardens and fountains in the streets of Paris, a literary censorship that forces the author of a noxious book to go about masked until he has retrieved his reputation, state-supported theatres, cheerful communal cremations, and the destruction of all that is pernicious in the world's literature, *e.g.* " Herodotus, Sappho, Anacreon and the vile Aristophanes." The first communion is replaced by a séance with the telescope and microscope, which is called the Communion of the Two Infinites. Observatories serve as churches. " On the day consecrated to the praise of the Creator, it is an affecting sight to see on our observatory the numerous adorers of God falling on their knees, the eye applied to the telescope, and the spirit in prayer, sending forth their souls with their sight, towards the Fabricator of these stupendous miracles " (Chap. XXI). There is also the usual flaw of these Utopias,—butchers are foreigners.

shame. The head of the senate adjures him to do justice
to society and condemn himself. He bows his head, and
with that resolve his guilt is atoned. The pastors strip
off his bloody shirt, clothe him in the white robe of reconciliation, and dismiss him to his death with the kiss of
peace. The bells of the city toll for him, and the populace
prays ; he is shot beside the corpse of his victim, his body
honourably bestowed, and his name re-inscribed on the
roll of citizens, whence his crime had blotted it. Is not
this a sort of sacred ballet ? The critic [1] who complained
of Mercier's " total ignorance of the principles of human
conduct " was beside the point ; the book was a dream,
not a scientific forecast. Mercier had cast aside the
burden of man's complex nature to design a pattern in
the ideal. The same effect of lofty and bloodless beauty
—for beauty it is—can at times be achieved in fairy tales ;
but neither Hermsprong, that philosophic Grandison, nor
Miss Campinet could figure in it, and the old innkeeper
who had served with Marshall Keith would break the
pattern to fragments.

It is certain that the French philosophic tale largely
determined Bage's course in the novel. Not that he was
the implicit disciple of Voltaire and Diderot ; his French
sympathies never obscured the sturdy English strain in
his work ; but they showed him what could be done in
the way of marrying philosophy and fiction. He would
probably not have written novels, he said, if he had had
books and opportunity for more serious work ; as it was
he managed to say what he had to say in this form, and
the English novel, which suffered as much from a paucity
of ideas as the French novel from an overplus,[2] benefited
exceedingly. His first reviewers praised his liberal
philosophy, though later, when liberal philosophy was
exploding violently into action across the Channel, it was

[1] v. *Monthly*, October 1772.
[2] Cf. F. C. Green, *French Novelists, Manners and Ideas* (1928).

found disquieting, and Scott, in his memoir of Bage, thought it necessary to include antidotes to his subject's morality. Bage's philosophy, in its connection with the common stock of progressive ideas that preceded and accompanied the French Revolution, has been studied by Miss Allene Gregory in her book *The French Revolution and the English Novel* (1915), and there is no need and no space to repeat the analysis here. It is enough to remember that a common creed is found, with individual variations, in the books of the English revolutionary group of whom Bage was the precursor; that all these writers believed that man could be, if not perfected, at least infinitely improved by the free use of reason in education and the abolition of crippling laws and customs; and that all of them saw in the novel a means of expressing this belief. It was not a new function for the novel, which had helped to disseminate one or two creeds already; it was the ideas that were new. For a few years they were given a sharp and challenging expression; then the menace of the reactionary forces became too formidable, and the prophetic voices, if they did not wholly cease, were content with a quieter and intermittent utterance. But though there is no need to rehearse the whole revolutionary testimony, it is worth while to glance at some of Bage's leading ideas, both as they illustrate the general quickening of thought in the 'eighties, and connect, by way of supplement or corrective, with the modes of thought and feeling already prevalent in the novel.

In the first place, he was no indiscriminate admirer of the attitude of submission. " Proud superiority " and " servile dependence " were ignoble bases, he felt, for human relationships. A man must be " free from the necessity of doing little things, or saying *little* words to any man." Moreover, humility is not always a grace; it can be " weak and enervating," and destroy the foundations of happiness, for " to be happy a man must think well of himself," and vanity is a great spur to virtuous action. The question of filial obedience occurs several times in his books and is a subject of debate between James Wallace and his friend Paracelsus Holman. One notices that the young people, though boldly " philosophical " in their talk, are quite moderate in their behaviour; even Holman, who roundly declares that his father is a fool and that he cannot be expected to love him, finds that the fool has a claim on his compassion which he cannot deny.[1] Duty, however, is reciprocal. " Merely for existence . . . I owe nothing," Hermsprong tells Miss Campinet. " It is for rendering that existence a blessing, my filial gratitude is due." Authoritative control must, in any case, cease when the children reach maturity, but wise parents will by then have won their children's friendship, and can rely on this. Wifely duty too has its limits, and Lady Bembridge will not follow a weak, vicious and unrepentant man into misery. " Servile compliance is a crime when it violates rectitude, and imbecility, at least, when it is prostituted to folly."

Some allusion has already been made to Bage's fearless dealings with the virtue of his heroines. His books were full of shocks for the conventional. A girl who has been ravished becomes the happy wife of another man; militant Clarissas defend themselves with sarcastic and resolved vigour; another young woman, chaste in mind, yet determines out of gratitude to become the mistress of the man who has preserved her from death, while vivacious girls claim the right to think, talk, and even jest about sex, since it is their prime concern. Bage's moderation, however, does not desert him in this last instance; the claim is conceded, but with the caveat that it is easy to lose the modesty of the mind. Critics who cried haro at this

---

[1] Cf. Holcroft's *Anna St. Ives*, where Frank Henley apologetically admits the " folly " that vice in his father grieves him more than vice in another.

relaxation of discipline, did not always notice that it is made possible by Bage's belief in the strength of will and faculty of mental growth in women. Kitty Ross is no Magdalen of the sensibility school, but a creature of " Amazonian goodness." [1] His liberal propaganda did not amount to a system. He felt that the custom of society punishes woman too much for an offence against chastity, and man too little, and in his books he redressed the balance a little. He pleaded also, through the mouth of Mr. Lindsay in *Man as he is*, for " a little more free-will to the sexes in the important article of their sexual conjunction " ; but he is no theory-monger ; others must find and invent new forms of life ; he but testifies to the coming of a spirit that breaks the old.

Bage's tolerance, his readiness to live and let live, is marked in all his books. It is the necessary and far from exorbitant price paid by a man in order that he may enjoy to the full the company of his fellow-beings. Youth, however, from a mixture of high and low motives, often refuses to pay this price, and so we have in *Mount Henneth* Mr. Foston's story of his own development from a bigoted young man blinkered by religious prejudice, into the tolerant philanthropist of his mature years. This educa-tion in philosophy replaces in Bage the widely popular theme of the education in morals, and is probably one of the signs of French influence in his work. As for the good which tolerance purchases, the free and kindly intercourse with different types of men, the mind which does not find delight in this is in no healthy state. In *Barham Downs* we have two types of solitary, and the attack is launched against both Sir George Osmond's anti-social pride and his brother's flinching sensibility. Tolerance is par-ticularly needful in religious matters ; indeed, bigotry is not only foolish but arrogant, for the basis of all religions

[1] Cf. Miss Wilmot in Holcroft's *Hugh Trevor*, whose intellect is awakened by her misfortunes and errors.

is the same, "the silent meditation of a contrite heart, lifting up its humble aspirations to the author and pre-server of all being," and the dogmatic superstructure is unimportant, temporary and probably wrong. This community of aspiration among men of good-will is illus-trated in *Mount Henneth* by the marriage of the Persian with the Jewish girls, and of his daughter with the Englishman. Bage liked these intermarriages, and liked too to trail his story through many lands, not for love of the varying background—he despatched the picturesque rather disdainfully—but in order to show reasonable men of all nations living in friendship together. The part of the merchant in furthering international amity was a source of pride to Bage, who regarded him as the prime civilizer, and is never tired of praising the mercantile virtues of keeping contracts and paying debts. One notes that the Utopia at *Mount Henneth* has a pronounced mer-cantile aspect, very different from the unsatisfactory feudalism of *Shenstone-Green*, and that it includes a dock and a glass-bottle manufactory. *James Wallace* is a novel of the trading and professional classes, and one of the most carefully wrought figures in it is that of Paul Lamounde, the Liverpool merchant, sound, gruff, shrewd and benevolent. The author was a democrat, who enjoyed giving gentlemen's daughters in marriage to honest merchants and lost a little of his usual serenity in con-templating the insolence of birth. A respectful treatment of the middle classes was, as we have seen, one of the things that the novel, stranded among night-cellars and the dimly realized drawing-rooms of the aristocracy, most required ; a whole world of circumstance, hardly touched as yet except by the satiric quill, lay among the counting-houses and quays.

Bage's personal character as a novelist is something more than the sum of his opinions ; it includes his unspoilt pleasure in the commonplaces of story-telling and his humorous gust in strokes of character. It is a vigorous character, uttering itself in a vigorous style. In the French translations of his work, his style is inevitably and deliberately flattened; the curt emphasis, the whimsical conceits, did not do in French and were smoothed out; his very strong vein of irony, on the other hand, tallied well with French taste and probably owed something to French examples. It is impossible to read in *The Fair Syrian* the Georgian Amine's account of her slavery without thinking of Voltaire.[1] Amine has cultivated apathy as the only means of bearing her fate, and her apathy, and the horrors and tyrannies through which she passes, are described with a high-wrought irony that obviously pleased Bage, as it threw up, like a varnish, the irrational absurdity of these tyrannies and of that apathy. In face of the generic sorrows of human kind, however, he drops his irony for a simpler speech. His deep sense of sorrow and the firmness with which he relegates it to its proper place in life, leading all his young tragedians back from their solitudes to the daily paths which must be travelled and are best travelled in company, are both the merits of a man who began novel-writing not in raw youth but in his full and wise maturity.

[1] I have seen only the French translation of this book, *La Belle Syrienne. . . . Traduit de l'Anglois. À Londres*, 1788. The translation naturally emphasizes the likeness, but does not account for it.

CHAPTER VI

THE STIRRING OF ROMANCE, AND THE HISTORICAL NOVEL

This same truth is a naked and open daylight, that does not show the masques, and mummeries, and triumphs of the world, half so stately and daintily as candle-lights. Truth may perhaps come to the price of a pearl, that showeth best by day; but it will not rise to the price of a diamond or carbuncle, that showeth best in varied lights. A mixture of a lie doth ever add pleasure.—BACON, *Of Truth*.

THE imagination of man is not satisfied with the contemplation of human nature and good sense. It craves first of all sensationalism, that crude intensification of life, and secondly romance, which is, in its simplest form, the suspension of the limitations of normal experience, and becomes, in delicate minds, the self-pleasing reverie of thought, shaping ideal forms of grandeur, beauty and happiness. When romance is ejected from the house of literature, it does not die of exposure, but is degraded; it finds shelter somewhere in the baser purlieus of that mansion, performs mean offices, forgets its breeding, and becomes crass and clownish. Here lies Havelok until maiden Goldborough perceives the royal signs on him; and then he is instructed and goes out to recapture his throne.

The middle years of the eighteenth century had been such a time of exile for the spirit of romance. Good sense had turned out of doors the high-flown and now faded pomp of the *Grand Cyrus*, in order that the novel might establish domestic tragedy and the comedy of manners on the model of Richardson and Fielding. Even the *Grand Cyrus*, however, did not expire as quickly as good sense hoped, for the recalcitrant human mind, especially the recalcitrant female mind, continued to demand the "mixture of a lie," and, since no new lie had been invented, the old one had to serve. It survived, however, in an apologetic, half-hearted way, heavily snubbed by reviewers, who are always fretful about resuscitations of the heroic romance ; [1] and its languishing existence is to be traced chiefly in the ridicule of Mrs. Lennox's *Female Quixote* (1752) and in the characters cast by later novelists in her mould.[2] Such characters—old spinster aunts and underbred girls who, like Arabella, have swallowed their antiquated reading whole and endeavour to act on it—extend into the 'eighties and, literary imitations as they are, must still have been comprehensible. Beside these faint ghosts we find occasional references to a still older romance ; Clara Reeve translated Barclay's *Argenis* and knew *Arcadia* and the Greek Romances,[3] but very few readers can have had access to these stores, and for the

---

[1] Cf. *Critical*, Feb. 1770, on *The Prince of Salermo* : "The author of this novel seems to have heated his brain by the perusal of old Italian romances"; and the *Monthly*, April 1773, on *The Test of Friendship ; or, the Royal Adventurers*,—" a tale truly romantic, and narrated in the unnatural, bombast style of the old chivalry books. We cannot conceive what could be the author's views in adopting this antiquated mode of writing, which has been exploded ever since fringed gloves and basket-hilted swords went out of fashion; and we are the more puzzled to account for the appearance of such a phænomenon, as he seems capable of producing something better." The *Monthly*, Aug. 1790, disapproved of James White's historical novel *Strongbow* (1789), seeing in it a revival of the old heroic fashion of engrafting " the extravagant legends of knight-errantry " on true history, as practised in *Cassandra* and *Cleopatra*.

[2] Female Quixotes whose eccentricity is the result of reading old romances, are found in the characters of Miss Southern, in John Potter's *Curate of Coventry* (1771) and Miss Williams in Herbert Lawrence's *Contemplative Man* (1771). In Mrs. Bennett's *Ellen, Countess of Castle Howel* (1794) occurs the belated figure of a woman of thirty-two, bred on heroic romances. A foreign version of the theme was provided by C. M. Wieland's *Der Sieg der Natur über die Schwärmerey, oder die Abentheuer des Don Sylvio von Rosalva*, translated in 1773 as *Reason Triumphant over Fancy*.

[3] *The Phœnix : or the History of Polyarchus and Argenis. Translated from the Latin. By a Lady* (1772). Cf. also her *Progress of Romance, through Times, Countries and Manners : with Remarks on the good and bad effects of it on them respectively ; in a course of Evening Conversations. By C. R.*, I, p. 85, 1785.

general public during the first half of our period there was very little romantic provision. They had the poets, of course, Ariosto, Tasso, Spenser and now Ossian; they had *The Castle of Otranto* and the *Old English Baron ;* and they had the Oriental tales, in which, however, the marvellous was too much blended with the grotesque, and too little reconcilable to Western sentiment, to satisfy much of their need, while in French hands the genre had been steeped in a cynical wit, very antagonistic to illusion. A vulgarized romance, to which we need pay little attention, was to be found in Richardsonian drawing-rooms. There flawless earls and iniquitous baronets compliment the reigning beauty to the rattle of teacups; the scene changes; Lothario abducts his victim in disguise from a masquerade, locks her in a deserted mansion and threatens horribly; we hear the thunder of post-horses across Britain and the clash of steel; Lothario, foiled and repentant, retires to the Continent to purify his mind, and the heroine, in a white lutestring negligée with silver spots, is supported at the altar by her peer, whose hair is " killingly dressed " and who " glews his lips to her hand." It is plain that this sort of stuff, even when supplemented by French episodes, complete with nunneries and *lettres de cachet*, is coarse nourishment for minds of any delicacy; and it is also plain that the contemporary setting of these tales threw their unnaturalness into such glaring relief as must have destroyed the pleasures of illusion to any but the most ignorant reader. A type of romance was needed that would thrill without offending the delicate, in which the fancy could expatiate without stumbling over self-evident absurdities. This was found in the tale of the past, the historical novel or Gothic Romance, for in their origin they are not easily distinguishable. The romantic mind desired rich colour and found it in the external pomp and picturesque incidents of the past; it also desired a murky sublimity, and found

it in the tremendous passions and invasions of the supernatural which it felt at liberty to postulate there. In the
Gothic [1] days of the Middle Ages and the sixteenth century—which, as Mr. Pearsall Smith [2] truly remarks, was
Gothic to the eighteenth—and in such buildings as
preserve in the modern world the traditions and
atmosphere of the past, romance found a new dwelling-
place, and for a generation was enthroned in a ruin.

The demand for colour and sublimity, however, invariably brought with it the demand for the marvellous,
and the critical world, which approved the first two
qualities in measure, looked askance at the third. The
whole question of romance in the eighteenth century,
fundamentally simple, is superficially complicated by the
ambiguous nature of that treacherous word which,
chameleon-like, takes its colour from its context and is
often used by a single author throughout the whole gamut
of its meanings ; for, while the æsthetic philosopher is at
liberty to narrow it down until it is capable of a sharp
definition, the literary historian is continually impeded
by contemporary implications, of which he must take
account, seeing that, vague and varying as they are, they
are full of significance for the study of popular taste. A
change in what we may call the intonation of the word—
the scornful or regretful or enthusiastic inflection that
accompanies it in the mind—is one of the chief signs of
the resurgence of the romantic mood.

[1] " Gothic " meant primarily barbarous, antique ; from its
application to architecture, it was extended to anything mediæval,
and could be applied to any age up to the reign of Anne. A vivacious
young lady in *The Example ; or the History of Lucy Cleveland* (1778),
calls " husband " a " gothic word," and James Penn in *The Surry
Cottage* (1779) describes duelling as a " gothic custom." The
extended use of the word was generally accepted, but the reviewer of
the *Gentleman's Magazine* (July 1778) quibbles at Clara Reeve's
description of *The Old English Baron* as a Gothic story, since our
ancestors who fought at Agincourt were not Goths. Miss Reeve
ignored him, however, and in *Sir Roger de Clarendon* (1793) refers
to the men of the fourteenth century as our Gothic ancestors.

[2] *v.* his *Four Romantic Words*, S.P.E. Tracts, No. 17, p. 10, 1924.

To the eighteenth-century moralist " romance " implied a seductive delusion, pathetic or ludicrous, according to the quality of the victim and the angle of the commentator. It is natural and graceful in youth, but no longer " respectable " in the adult, since it indicates the persistent immaturity of a mind that refuses to look on truth. To be romantic is to prefer the satisfactions of imagination to those of reason ; it is to remain wilfully blind to the real nature of man and the world, to insist on finding in daily life those figures of beauty and terror, at once grander and simpler than life, that haunt the mind in reverie ; it is, in short, to emancipate Fancy, that Cinderella of the eighteenth century, from the control of her stern sister, Judgment. An ignorant or vulgar mind will be satisfied with the beauty and terror of the circulating library, with melting heroes and villains whose promiscuous iniquity can hardly be crammed into a working day ; a more delicate one will see life in terms of ideal nobility, and will intensify and dignify every emotion it encounters.[1] Lovers who die of love are romantic, and so are perfectly contrite villains, and friends whose loyalty involves the complete renunciation of their own happiness. They are romantic because their motives are technically " purer " than it is possible for the motives of a human being to be ; and the youthful enthusiasm that credits their purity is itself romantic. " I am not romanticly (*sic*) or foolishly in love, my Dear," writes a young woman in *Anecdotes of a Convent* (1771), meaning that she has not pitched her expectations above the flight of common human nature. One notes the words with

---

[1] Cf. Graves's *Eugenius*, I, p. 24 (1785). Eugenius thus describes his own " romantic turn of mind." " I dignified the most familiar objects by viewing them through the mist of an enthusiastic imagination. What they called a hill, I called a mountain ; an old wood or copse, I considered a sacred grove ; and a neighbouring heath, overrun with broom and birch-trees, appeared to me a wild forest, which I fancied to be inhabited by nymphs and fauns, or by outlaws and robbers."

which " romance " is coupled. " A generous but romantic project," says Mrs. Smith of a lover's confession to his rival, and Miss Edgeworth, without the wistful intonation, suggestive of some unattainable ideal, speaks in a crescendo of " romance and error and folly." [1] " I lament when generosity becomes romantic," writes Mrs. Jane West,[2] from the standpoint of social utility, blaming the benevolence that seeks only to satisfy its own lofty notions, without descending to consider how far its activities are profitable. Romance is " hunting after shadows " ; [3] there is always something unreal in its assumptions, some artificiality or omission in its premises to invalidate the conclusion. In *Anna St. Ives*, Coke Clifton, exasperated by Anna's calmness and his own passion, speaks of " this tormenting, incoherent romance of determining not to have any," and Sophia King in *Waldorf* (1798) stamps a delusive system of philosophy as " romance." Romance is error on the border of vice ; or, less culpably, a lack of balance in a mind open to one class of sensations only. The prisoner, Maria, in Mary Wollstonecraft's *Wrongs of Women* (1793), ashamed of her emotional reactions over trifles, noticed " how difficult it was for women to avoid growing romantic, who have no active duties or pursuits." It was impossible that a word

---

[1] *v.* Mrs. Smith's *Ethelinde*, and the conversation between Belinda and Mr. Percival in Miss Edgeworth's *Belinda*.

[2] *A Tale of the Times*, III, p. 48, 1799.

[3] Cf. *Analytical Review*, June 1788, on *Edward and Harriet :* " Young women may be termed romantic when they are under the direction of artificial feelings ; when they boast of being tremblingly alive all o'er, and faint and sigh as the novelist informs them they should. Hunting after shadows, the moderate enjoyments of life are despised, and its duties neglected ; the imagination, suffered to stray beyond the utmost verge of probability, where no vestige of nature appears, soon shuts out reason, and the dormant faculties languish for want of cultivation, as rational books are neglected because they do not throw the mind into an exquisite *tumult*. The mischief does not stop here ; the heart is depraved when it is supposed to be refined, and it is a great chance but false sentiment leads to sensuality, and vague fabricated feelings supply the place of principles." Here romance is obviously closely akin to sensibility.

so variously and disapprovingly applied should preserve
any exactness of meaning.   It was, said Mary Hays, " a
vague term, applied to everything we do not understand,
or are unwilling to imitate," [1] and, in such cases, imposed
the same kind of slur as the word " singular," a hundred
years later.   " Romantic," in its general sense of extravagant, was applied to scenes in books where probability
has been sacrificed to produce some thrilling effect or
satisfactory conclusion.   Thus all sorts of recognitions,
escapes, providential reunions and resuscitations of the
dead count as romantic, however baldly presented ; and
the word was transferred to such incidents of real life as
lie outside reasonable expectation.   It is this sense of
extravagance, for which they perceive no adequate motive
and no adequate compensation, that accounts for its tart
flavour on the tongue of many a critic.   They flung it as
a rebuke to bring to heel a writer who forsook " nature,"
and the author of the *Providential Adultery* could not
flatter himself that he had pleased his judges, when he
was told that his book might be " termed a romance in
the strictest sense of the word." [2, 3]

The more liberal among the critics conceded that the
suspension of the laws limiting normal existence, in the
service of imaginative pleasure, was permissible ; the
pleasure thus obtained was certainly not of the highest
type, but it was legitimate, provided the romancer " knew
his place," and did not put himself forward as anything

[1] v. *Memoirs of Emma Courtney*, II, p. 14 (1796).
[2] v. *Critical*, Feb. 1771.
[3] " Romance " is not used in the modern journalistic sense, to
signify a love-story, though the companion term " novel " is.   " Our
Novel," says Frances to Henry in the Griffith's *Genuine Letters* (1757)
of their secret love-affair.   This is significant of the limited business
of the novel at the time ; as novel-themes grew more varied, this use
of the word becomes obsolete, and it was replaced by " romance."
It should be noted that when Henry in the later volumes of the *Letters*
uses the word " romance," it is always the ideal, unprecedented,
almost fantastic nature of his love for his wife, and hers for him, that
is uppermost in his mind, as when he dreads " lest the Romance of
our loves should dwindle into a Novel."

more than an entertainer. Ambitious romantic books worried them, and the *Monthly Review* blamed Godwin for his misjudged pretence of combining romance and philosophy in *St. Leon* (1800). To his plea that he has " mixed human feelings and passions with incredible situations, and thus rendered them impressive and interesting," the reviewer, losing patience, retorts : " Why imagine incredible situations and absolute impossibilities, in order to work on our feelings, passions and convictions ? . . . Of what use are such idle fictions to man in the actual state of his existence ? " At best, their attitude was permissive. Romance is a pastime, not a mode of experience ; its value is simply recreative, and when they make play with the tag " to elevate and surprise," it is in a tone of impatient irony. But outside these academic circles the word was more enthusiastically uttered, and its associations, though vague, were much richer. " Nothing met the eye but beauty, and romantic splendour," says Mrs. Radcliffe of Castle Mazzini, illuminated for a fête ; she would no doubt have been put to it to define the exact content of her epithet, but the excited throb of her voice is unmistakable. Romance implied enchantment,[1] and was the keynote of a spell. Egerton Brydges, that ardent and haughty advocate of romance as the pastime of elegant minds when " removed from the dull intercourse of common society," [2] constantly makes use of the two words together. In the forests of his ancient family seats, all distant sounds are romantic, and a hound, baying through the early morning mist, affords romantic music. His magic is compounded of exquisite and idyllic circumstances centring in the high-bred girl who, from her oriel window, gazes out on her ancestral domain ; and it is strengthened by an " energetic melancholy," rising from the sense of the antiquity of all that

[1] v. *Critical*, May 1799, on Isaac d'Israeli's *Romance*.
[2] *v.* Preface to his *Mary de Clifford* (1792).

he admires, and of its certain doom in a changing and vulgarized world. It is thus evocative, but not mysterious, for its elements are known. Mystery, however, that delightful stimulus of the imagination, was in many cases a predominant ingredient of the word, and it was specially used in cases where there was no fear that the mystery would be finally dispelled. In this sense it was applied by Governor Pownall to his treatise on pre-history, which he called *An Antiquarian Romance, endeavouring to mark a Line by which the most Ancient People, and the Procession of the Earliest Inhabitancy of Europe, may be investigated* (1795).[1] The theorists of the picturesque distinguished sharply between the romantic and the sublime; a romantic landscape is irregularly and wildly charming, and strongly stimulates the imagination, while falling short of the dignity and simplicity of the sublime; but the distinction was ignored by literary critics, who attributed sublimity to Mrs. Radcliffe, and were confused on this point by the question of supernatural awe. It is, however, a useful distinction to bear in mind. One element in the sublime is Necessity, and this causes it to lay a crushing weight on some spirits, who find here nothing to do but to submit, and in submission are painfully aware of the limits of their powers; whereas the romantic absolves them from that stern control, and evokes whatever of creative power they possess, so that about its crannies and its " sunny spots of greenery " even the most modest mind can be busy. Indeed, this freedom of delighted and easy co-operation is one of the gifts continually made by romantic artists to their audience. In that participation there is no suffering; for the grimmest sorceries dissolve at will, and the dreamer knows he dreams.

[1] Pownall's subject was the early history of the barbarian tribes who afterwards broke into the Roman Empire. He maintains that all early history is really romance, a reconstruction of the whole from confused and imperfect fragments, which does not " demand the reader's belief," because no proofs can be adduced.

So marked a taste on the part of the reading public, catered for by novelists on so large a scale, and often in so respectable a shape, ended by forcing the professional critics to reconsider romance. Or rather, they in their turn were affected by the spirit of an age craving for strong sensations and unfamiliar beauty. Younger men sat in the critic's chair, and behind the anonymous mask we see at times the features of Holcroft, Coleridge and William Taylor of Norwich.[1] This new generation, while they by no means accepted all the manifestations of popular romance, were willing to consider it in relation to a more flexible scale of values than the men they replaced. Less deeply committed to the didactic stand-point, they had more extended notions as to whither the " paths of nature " might lead the inquiring author, and did not halloo him back at the first sight of the marvellous. There remained a small band of irreconcilables, who, in the very height of the Gothic vogue, continued to lift up their voices in prophecy that the end of that deplorable episode was in sight, and that real life and manners were about to resume their claims.[2] These stalwarts could unbend a little over Mrs. Radcliffe, but even she was told that she was misapplying her talents, and entreated to devote them to the service of nature and truth.

The defence of romance in the novel, as it appears in the work of critics, amateur and professional, is a tentative extension of the defence of romance in poetry. The extension did not at first seem to be inevitable. Poetry, it was agreed on all hands, was exhausted and flat and needed fresh blood ; above all it needed " invention," to save it from degenerating into " mere morality, criticism

---

[1] v. C. Elbridge Colby, *A Bibliography of Thomas Holcroft* (1922) ; Garland Greever's *A Wiltshire Parson and his Friends* (1926), for Coleridge ; and J. W. Robberds's *Memoir* of William Taylor (1843).
[2] v. *Critical* on *The Italian* (May 1798). Coleridge was the reviewer.

and satire." [1]   A chorus of approval greeted Hole's
Arthur, or the Northern Enchantment (1789), which drew
liberally on " Gothic superstitions."   But it was by no
means clear to all that the novel required such a renewal.
Its sphere of manners and character was wide enough,
and every step outside carried it further from immediate
contact with life, and consequently weakened its moral
value.   The passion for the marvellous, however, could
not be ignored at a moment when it was vigorously over-
stepping the boundaries of verse ; and while conservative
critics denied or decried the pleasure of contemplating
the imaginary, others accepted it without demur, as a
taste " implanted from the cradle," the natural result of
human curiosity and love of novelty. [2]   Its results in
fiction, moreover, were often captivating ; in the modern
romance, said the *Monthly* reviewer, [3] " high description,
extravagant characters, and extraordinary and scarcely
possible occurrences combine to rivet the attention, and
to excite emotions more thrilling than even the best
selected and best described natural scene."   But in the
eighteenth century pleasure was seldom allowed to be its
own justification, and even the wild-fire of romance was
to be harnessed, if possible, to some useful purpose.   It
is something that it prevents insipidity, for the milk-and-
water of the sentimental novel curdles in these thunder-
storms ; something that it rouses curiosity in the young
reader and stimulates his faculties ; but the question
recurs, in what direction does such a stimulus impel the
mind ?   Does it not, asked the *Monthly*, [4] accustom it
" rather to wonder than inquire, and to seek a solution of

---

[1] *v.* Dr. Nathan Drake, *Literary Hours*, VI, *On Gothic Superstitions*
(1798).
[2] Cf. *Critical* on *Vathek* (July 1786) and on *The Castle of Hardayne*
(Sept. 1795).
[3] *v.* March 1797, on Mrs. Radcliffe's *Italian ;* and cf. Oct. 1797 on
The Count de Santerre.
[4] June 1793, on Heron's translation of the *Arabian Tales of Chavis
and Cazotte.*   Holcroft was the reviewer.

difficulties in occult causes instead of seriously resorting
to facts "? The marvellous, as Clara Reeve had
employed it, could be justified as an emphatic means of
drawing attention to the moral ; it filled the part of the
whale in the story of Jonah ; but not even disingenuity
could stretch this excuse into a shelter for the Gothic
Romance in its heyday. More and more clearly another
line of defence emerges. Let it be admitted that the
romantic and marvellous has no direct contribution to
make to ethics ; at least it exercises and strengthens the
imagination, which " may at length take bolder and more
successful flights." [1]   In addition, it gives great scope for
the portrayal of violent emotion, and by the middle
'nineties it was sometimes allowed that vigour and boldness may compensate for the lack of probability, while
the younger critics were speaking as if it were, at all events,
some merit to spurn the common bounds.

At the end of the eighteenth century, the bold writer
generally found himself attracted to the terrible, and the
imagination that spurned common bounds looked for its
peculiar satisfactions within the confines of the supernatural. Thus it is that the theorizing about romance is
inextricably interwoven with the vindication of the
importance of the terrible in art—a discussion that need
not be carried on upon romantic ground at all—while, on
the other hand, the attacks on romance nearly always
culminate in the charge that, by their puerile and
unphilosophic cult of fear, the romance-writers are
helping to keep alive " that superstition which debilitates
the mind, that ignorance which propagates error, and that
dread of invisible agency which makes inquiry criminal." [2]

The vision, that saw in the Gothic Romance a super-
numerary villain in the drama of civilization, was Hol-

---

[1] v. *Critical*, Sept. 1795, on the *Castle of Hardayne*.
[2] v. *Monthly*, Nov. 1792, on *The Castle of St. Vallery*. This was
Holcroft's first article for the *Monthly Review*.

croft's ; and the honourable extravagance of his warfare
with these faint shadows of the forces of darkness can be
corrected by a reference to *Northanger Abbey*.[1] For Miss
Austen is not at all angry or alarmed.   The perversion in
Catherine Morland's mind, due to her consumption of
Gothic Romances, is no more than a temporary unbalanc-
ing of the fancy, soon put to rights by her natural good
sense, a phase of adolescence that will not incapacitate
her for mature life.   Between the juvenile irresponsibility
of Miss Morland's tastes and the earnest disquietude with
which Holcroft regarded them, we seek for a middle
position ; and this is provided by the Suffolk physician
and enthusiastic literary amateur, Dr. Nathan Drake
(1766–1836), whose *Literary Hours*, first published in
1798 and reissued with augmentations, consist of critical
articles and illustrative stories, and are marked throughout by " an admiration for the terrible and gigantic "
which the *Monthly* reviewer found " too exclusive."
Much of what Drake says is explicitly applied only to
poetry, but he certainly meant that it should extend to
prose fiction ; if in one essay he draws his examples from
Tasso, Collins and Chatterton, in another he instances
Mrs. Radcliffe with equal reverence, and when he makes
up his own recipes, it is in the form of tales in prose.

Drake's central position [2] is that poetry cannot reach
its highest pitch without enthusiasm, especially, he
declares, showing his bias at once, that credulous imagination " which, seizing hold of the superstitions and fears
of mankind, pours forth fictions of the most wild and
horrible grandeur." These fictions alone are strong
enough to break up the limitations of polished poetry and
restore the fanciful, the terrible and the sublime.   It is

---

[1] Written in 1798.
[2] v. *Literary Hours*, II, *On the Government of the Imagination*, and
VI, *On Gothic Superstitions*. The references are from the 1798 edition ;
in the second and enlarged edition of 1800 the essays are differently
numbered.

desirable to draw on such beliefs as still retain a sufficient degree of credit to make them " an important and impressive machine beneath the guidance of genuine poetry "; and here Drake strongly advocates the advantages of Gothic (he means mediæval, not Norse) superstition, which " turns chiefly on the awful ministrations of the Spectre, or the innocent gambols of the Fairy " (he was not, however, keenly interested in innocent gambols, and promptly drops the Fairy), since this does not involve absurdity, as do exploded mythological systems, " but, floating loose upon the mind, founds its imagery upon a metaphysical possibility, upon the appearance of superior or departed beings." To fortify his position he calls, as all amateurs of the terrible did, upon Shakespeare and Ossian. The elder Hamlet, indeed, was the godfather of the Gothic romance, and the weird sisters rocked the cradle of the towardly child, while as for Ossian, it is probable that the eighteenth century had a fairer view of Macpherson's remarkable though flawed talent than we, who see in his book chiefly a trampled battle-ground. At all events, with his lyrical descriptions of nature and his flocking ghosts he entered very thoroughly into the history of the novel. To us Ossian's spectres are memorable chiefly for their number and their dignity, but Drake admired them for their abrupt force; to him they seemed to " rush upon the eye with all the stupendous vigour of wild and momentary creation." It is well though exuberantly said, and suggests clearly enough the sort of effect he admired, under the influence of which, if " well-conducted," he felt that " a grateful astonishment, a welcome sensation of fear, will alike creep through the bosom of the Sage and the Savage." The professional critics, he admits, have discouraged the introduction of supernatural agency, but they have reckoned without the public. Ghosts were a felt want; and " whilst they are thus

formed to influence the people, to surprise, elevate
and delight, with a willing admiration, every faculty of
the human mind," cries Drake in impressive climax,
" how shall criticism with impunity dare to expunge
them ? "

This ardent appreciation, so characteristic of its
moment, rested on no basis of æsthetic philosophy.
Drake writes " a welcome sensation of fear " and " a
salutary and grateful terror," without feeling obliged to
explain why fear is welcome or wherein lie the corrective
and pleasing powers of terror ; and this too is characteristic of the moment.   He was not unaware, however,
that the problem existed, for in his essay *On Objects of
Terror* (*XV*) he takes it up from the practical side and
discusses by what means terrible scenes can be controlled
so as to produce more pleasure than pain, when they are
deprived of the thrilling effect of supernatural ministra-
tion.   He finds the answer in Mrs. Radcliffe's technique,
her use of picturesque description and sentiment to relieve
the mind, and her stimulation of curiosity to overcome
disgust.   Fifteen years earlier, with no Gothic Romance
to press the question, Anna Lætitia Aikin, considering
rather more deeply the *Pleasure derived from Objects of
Terror*,[1] saw that this stimulation of curiosity was not
only a means of overcoming disgust but a positive pleasure.
The mind is stung with surprise, roused, kept on the
stretch ; imagination " rejoices in the expansion of its
powers.   Passion and fancy co-operating elevate the soul
to its highest pitch ; and the pain of terror is lost in
amazement." [2]   Like all theorizers of her time, she found
supernatural terror more easy to defend than natural

[1] v. *Miscellaneous Pieces in Prose, by J. and A. L. Aikin* (1773),
and cf., for the ascription, Lucy Aikin's *Memoir* prefixed to Mrs.
Barbauld's *Works* (1825).

[2] Cf. Mrs. Radcliffe's *Mysteries of Udolpho* (1794).   Emily, about
to explore the object beneath the black veil, feels a faint terror, " but
a terror of this nature, as it occupies and expands the mind, is purely
sublime."

terror ;[1] it led directly to religious awe, the "sacred effects of holy fear" and the "conscience personified" of which Courtney Melmoth talks in his plea[2] for some equivalent in literature to the impressive effect of Gothic cathedrals. Miss Aikin did not follow up this trail, however, but contented herself with pointing out that we derive more pleasure from scenes of terror when the circumstances are "wild, fanciful and extraordinary," whereas there is an overbalance of pain when they come "too near our common nature." In the famous fragment of *Sir Bertrand*, long ascribed to her but assigned by Miss Lucy Aikin to her brother, both kinds of terror are liberally applied.

Neither the inquiry nor the material that inspired it is new. Terror, perennially fascinating to the human mind, had long accumulated a stock of themes on which every generation drew to some extent, and we do not have to wait for the end of the century for slaughterous innkeepers, corpse-robbers, dungeons and ghosts. At that time, however, a natural reaction from a long period of sobriety in literature combined with revolutionary excitement and the growth of the reading habit in the lower middle classes to intensify the appeal of the terrible and increase the opportunities of gratifying it ; and society engaged on an exhaustive tour of the vaults. New sources of the TERRIBLE were explored with avidity, and German novelties in this line were imported in bulk.[3] A certain amount of sophistry invariably accompanies sensation-

[1] It is noticeable that Sergeant Talfourd in his *Memoir* of Mrs. Radcliffe, published with her *Posthumous Works* (1826), shifts his defence of her use of the terrible entirely on to supernatural ground.

[2] v. *Family Secrets*, I, ch. 46, 1797. The characters of the novel engage in a discussion of the use and abuse of the themes and method of ancient romances. Melmoth's argument is far too metaphorical to be clear, but it works out to an advocacy of themes that arouse awe, provided they are purged of the grossness of superstition.

[3] Cf. *Monthly*, Nov. 1795, on Schiller's *Ghost-Seer*. The principal new subject was "the pursuit of an influence over the invisible world."

alism when it invades the cultured classes ; and as neither
science nor social responsibility was an available plea in
the eighteenth century, recourse was had to the sublime.
Novelists and poets are full of vague allusions to the
elevating effects of terror ; the " dear, wild illusions of
creative mind," to which Mrs. Radcliffe addresses a
poem,[1] " rise sublime on terror's lofty plume," and the
critique of Veit Weber's *Sorcerer* in the *Monthly Review* [2]
begins with the remark that the " terrible and sublime,
perhaps, cannot be separated." The *Monthly* reviewer,
however, was a responsible critic and had scruples ; an
author ought not to raise disgust ; moreover, a taste for
the horrible and preternatural is a disquieting phenomenon
in literature, since such powerful stimulants " can never
be required except by the torpor of an unawakened, or
the languor of an exhausted appetite." No such consideration gave pause to Joseph Fox when he set out to gratify
his public with *Santa-Maria ; or the Mysterious Pregnancy* (1797). " Things MAY come out," he promises
them, " to chill—to make the sensitive soul thrill with
horror—to make the very hair stand perched on its native
habitual roost, where so long it had lain recumbent."
And the sensitive soul, tired of recumbent hair, bought
the book, and indulged in " the strange luxury of artificial
fear." [3]

Loose and misapplied as this jargon is, it had a respectable ancestry. We need trace it no farther back than
Burke's *Inquiry into the Sublime and Beautiful* (1756), a
book which coloured the impressions of many who had
never opened its pages. Terror to Burke is a sort of

---

[1] " Visions of Fancy " in *The Romance of the Forest*, I, p. 86 (1791).
[2] *v.* May 1796 ; also Feb. 1797, on *The Monk*; the latter review
is by Coleridge.
[3] *v. Monthly*, Nov. 1794, on *The Mysteries of Udolpho*, and cf.
Isaac d'Israeli's less ceremonious remark in his dissertation on the
marvellous in *Vaurien*, I, Ch. 11 (1797) : " The bulk of readers, the
only kind to which we moderns devote our lucubrations, seem now
much more pleased to be frightened out of their wits than to be
assisted in making a proper use of them."

mental athletics, the exercise of the mind's strongest
faculties, called forth by an appeal to the passion of self-
preservation ; the delightfulness of it lies in the expense
of energy, and " whatever is qualified to cause terror, is a
foundation capable of the sublime." These conclusions,
denuded of their safeguards and cut adrift from the
argument, circulated as catchwords, which, since they
correspond roughly to the emotional reactions detected in
themselves by amateurs of the terrible, were accepted by
them as a sufficient justification of their orgies. The
elevating power of the terrible, administered by such
hands as those of Joseph Fox, is a subject for scepticism ;
one cannot deny, however, that it was stimulating. The
imagination of the eighteenth century had been cramped ;
it required violent means to stretch it, and of these the
suggestion of terror, particularly of supernatural terror,
was the most potent. It roused dormant imaginative
energies, quickened sensibility and restored the sense of
the mysterious in life. It was subject, however, not only
to abuse, but to honest mistaking. If, when the Spirit of
God passed before the face of Job, the hairs of his flesh
stood up, might one not, ran the argument, by raising
the hair induce the vision ? In the 'nineties this
experiment was tried upon a lavish scale.

II

The ingenious defence of Mary Queen of Scots, being mentioned
t'other night at a card-table, a maiden lady, who would pardon murder
or sacrilege rather than any violation of the laws of chastity, . . .
cried out : " Oh ! she was an abandoned woman ! don't defend
her ; she had two *bastards* (*natural children* I suppose you'll call
them) by the Duke of Norfolk." I said I had never met with that
circumstance, even in Buchanan, or any history of those times.
" Oh ! " says she, " it's very true : I have just been reading an entertaining *novel*, which is *founded* entirely upon *that fact*."—GRAVES,
Preamble to Plexippus, 1790.

The dealings of the novel with the matter of the past are
naturally closely connected with and dependent on that

general increase of interest in the world of the Middle Ages and the Renascence, which finds so many expressions, literary and extra-literary, serious and jocular, in the eighteenth century. Antiquarians, topographers and literary historians are accumulating stores of information and surmise, and there is a strong though vague feeling abroad that these stores, heavy as they are, can somehow be made available for romantic fiction if the right method can be struck. The interest in the past is not in itself, of course, necessarily romantic, but in the unlearned it is predominantly so; and at a period when historical knowledge was partial and thinly spread, while the impressive relics of the past still filled the eye and served as a focus for easy imagining, when education had hung no weights on the dreamer's heels, and she could multiply dungeons to her heart's content and transport without misgivings, herself and her ideal lover, with all their varnish of modern sensibility fresh about them into the rust of the past; when, in short, the headmistress of a well-known girls' school [1] could publish a novel in which the Armada preceded the execution of the Queen of Scots, and escape censure, then we may conclude that " historical novel " and " romance " spell the same sort of entertainment. The foundation of these books lay in suggestion, not in knowledge. Their authors knew nothing of mediæval literature and very, very little of mediæval life; but from keeps and chancels, storied windows and broken tombs, there started forth such a flight of fancies, such entrancing spectres of tyranny and valour and romantic love, that they were compelled to embody them and set them in action. Sometimes they clustered round historical names and events, sometimes they were wholly imaginary, but the distinction between

---

[1] Miss Lee started a school in Bath with the proceeds of her play, *A Chapter of Accidents* (1780). The dates all through *The Recess* (1783-5) are manipulated—or ignored.

the two types does not amount to a difference, and it is not until the 'nineties that the historical novel proper begins to draw away from the romance.

Verse-writers, whose medium was less elaborate and sustained than the novel, went ahead of novelists, hanging their garlands of simple narrative on ancient landmarks up and down Britain ; for " localized romance " was in existence before Scott.[1] The tardiness of the novelists in following their steps was the more striking as they had in Leland's *Longsword, Earl of Salisbury* (1762) and Walpole's *Castle of Otranto* (1764) capital examples of the two kinds of fiction they were to cultivate, the romance built round actual facts and the romance *per se. Longsword*, which professes to be based on " ancient English historians," does indeed make occasional use of the data of history ; its main attractions, however, are monkish villainy and wifely truth, war, imprisonment and flight, together with a well-wrought scene of suspense and terror, which anticipates the methods of the Gothic Romance. It is flavoured to the eighteenth-century palate by a strong infusion of sensibility, and counts among its characters sententious nobles who bedew their armour with tears. In addition, it is adorned with a frontispiece, in which a monk succours a languishing warrior outside a Gothic church ; the archæological details of this performance do not inspire much confidence, but the romantic thrill is indubitable.

[1] *v., e.g.*, Thomas Percy's *Hermit of Warkworth : a Ballad in Three Cantos* (1771), which professed to gather up Border traditions; *Richard Plantagenet, a legendary tale* (1774), by Mr. Hull ; *Albert, Edward and Laura, and the Hermit of Priestland* (1783), three legendary tales by Miss R. Roberts, of which the first was written to illustrate the past of an old house at East Barnet, once belonging to the Knights of St. John. The same accretion of fancy round a familiar place is found in Mrs. Elizabeth Bonhote's *Bungay Castle* (1797), a romance. She had lived in youth within twenty yards of the ruins and, at the time of writing, owned the plot on which most of them stood ; the Gothic vogue gave her an opportunity of expressing her sentiment about them, though, like Miss Reeve, her real interest is in domestic morality.

The book seems to have been fairly well known, and it is mentioned by Clara Reeve in her *Progress of Romance*, but its posterity is lost in that of its far more influential successor, *The Castle of Otranto*. *The Castle of Otranto*, which it is so hard for us to take seriously, had for its author the seriousness of a plaything, and for its more single-hearted readers, especially after Walpole had fitted it with a theory, the seriousness of a manifesto. It really was, as he claimed, a new species of romance, and in writing it he did draw, however apologetically, upon the " great resources of fancy," which had been " dammed up by a strict adherence to common life," while refusing to relinquish the advances made by his own century in character-drawing. Theodore and the two young ladies carry modern sensibility into the Gothic past, which by this means becomes accessible to the readers. The basis of *Otranto* is architectural, and in this respect it is the true starting-point of the Gothic Romance; it is a bewitched and tragic Strawberry Hill, in which antique curiosities resume with terrific effect their primal use and life. All the prolonged delights of the later romance are here succinctly sketched—the " feudal arrangement " of the castle, the vaults, the caverns, the church; the thrilling mystery, upheld by hints and interrupted confessions; the suspense of Isabella's flight; the supernatural incursion; Manfred, that notable Gothic character, with his guilt and his defiance; and the garrulous servants whose chatter makes the abyss reverberate more hollowly. We have here the " penny plain " version of themes which appear in Mrs. Radcliffe as " twopence coloured," but we have also marks of a spirit that must be exorcised before the dreamer can really lose himself in the Gothic pile. Walpole's was no inexorable vision, but a light morning-dream, to which he never fully surrendered himself; the man of the world was always ready to take command and redress the balance by some faintly malicious comment or equivocal phrase. A similar blend of qualities can be found in the grotesqueness and ardour of *Vathek* and in the alternate parody and romance of James White's *Earl Strongbow* (1789). To the simple romantic mind there is something unsatisfactory in this dabbling in spells; not so did Anne Radcliffe, Regina Maria Roche and Isabella Hedgeland weave their sorceries, or any of that " illustrious train of English women, the literary magi of the present day " whom Courtney Melmoth cites in an interesting note to his discussion of romance.[1]

The pattern, then, was set. Romance was to find the materials for its new appearance in the past, and in a past which, though sometimes nominally historic, is really an elaboration of the impressions made by Gothic architecture on modern sensibility. It was, however, some twenty years before the pattern was standardized, and the interval was studded with a number of odd and abortive dealings with the past, which witness at once the attraction of the material and the groping incompetence of those who tried to handle it. It must be premised that the historical novel as we understand it, that union of exact knowledge and penetrating imagination, was not at this time possible; the historic sense was too little developed. A few authors —Clara Reeve was one [2]—make a point of not falsifying such historical facts as they knew, but none of them had any misgivings as to the nature of what they added. Private loves and vengeances replace political motives, and love, to which (to adapt Bacon) the novelist is more indebted than the life of man, accounts in Miss Lee's eyes for Essex' behaviour in Ireland and Sidney's death

[1] v. *Family Secrets*, I, ch. 46 (1797). Melmoth takes " romance " in its widest sense and instances " Sir Bertram's patroness " (*i.e.* Mrs. Barbauld, though Lucy Aikin says that the fragment was written by her father, not her aunt; *v.* her *Memoir* of Mrs. Barbauld), Miss Reeve, Mrs. Radcliffe, Mrs. Smith, Mrs. Cowley, Miss Burney, Mrs. Inchbald and Laura Maria (*i.e.* Mrs. Mary Robinson).
[2] v. her *Memoirs of Sir Roger de Clarendon* (1793).

at Zutphen.[1] Anachronisms of thought and feeling are innumerable and often delightful; a Highland clan in the Middle Ages shakes off the tyrant's yoke and resumes the rights of man; morning coffee and geology lectures are found in France in the sixteenth century; a mediæval seducer, anticipating later sophistications, tells his prey that "the emotions of the heart are involuntary and therefore cannot be criminal," and De Clavering, acting surgeon to the guard of Bungay Castle during the Barons' Wars, speaks of his gun and wears a wig.[2] It is even more astonishing to find a critic [3] praising James White's *Earl Strongbow* (1789), a book in which the conquest of Ireland is enlivened by parodies of the Parliamentary orators of White's own time, because the author has been "minutely attentive to every part of the costume." Without knowledge the historical novel cannot give, as it should give, an increase of imaginative life, it can only provide a means of withdrawing from that of everyday.

We must now pick our way across the years between *Otranto* and Miss Lee's *Recess*. Walpole's theme of an invasion of human life by the dead, to succour and punish, was taken up in 1772 in a high-flown little book called *The Hermitage : a British Story*. The author was William Hutchinson (1732–1814), a solicitor at Barnard Castle, Durham, known in later life as a topographer and historian; but this development could not have been foreseen by the reader of his British story, which is destitute of any sort of historical precision. The hero, Astianax, at a time when "the first vestiges of the Reformation had not yet taken place in this Kingdom," is beguiled by monkish treachery and, in spite of the protecting spirit of an ancestor who appears to him in the

---

[1] v. *The Recess* (1783–5).
[2] v. Mrs. Radcliffe's *Castles of Athlin and Dunbayne* (1789) and *Mysteries of Udolpho* (1794), Anne Fuller's *Alan Fitz-Osborne* (1787) and Mrs. Bonhote's *Bungay Castle* (1797).
[3] v. *Critical*, May 1789.

guise of a hermit, driven into the wilderness. Here he finds in a hermitage the embalmed figure of his ancestor, and, after fourteen years of penitent retreat, comes forth to quell the forces of evil and inter the hermit's remains in the family vault. The story, which, as the *Critical* reviewer [1] said, is " sufficiently romantic," is quite free from Walpole's hesitations. It is entirely serious and steadily didactic, and contains pages of prayers and admonitions, all intended to inculcate " resignation to the will of Heaven, filial reverence, and universal love." The style aims at the sublime by means of elaborate imagery, for Hutchinson, as his pastoral tale *A Week in a Cottage* (1775) shows, liked to tread the edge of prose and verse; it outraged his critics, but provides the literary historian with one more example of that baffled quest for colour and passion that goes on behind the eighteenth-century decencies.[2]

Five years later the ghost of *Otranto* stirs again, moving to a very sedate measure in that conduct-book with Gothic trimmings, Clara Reeve's *Champion of Virtue* (1777), reissued in 1778 as *The Old English Baron ; a Gothic Story*. This friendly and reasonable woman was nearly fifty when she published her first story, and, if she had ever submitted to romantic intoxication, she had long since recovered her balance. She still had a marked liking for romance, or " heroic fable " as she called it, but her strongest interest lay in the moral lesson that it adorned and enforced, and this she elaborated in homely detail. Indeed, it is this homely and practical streak that differentiates *The Old English Baron* from any other Gothic story whatever ; nowhere else do we find knights regaling on eggs and bacon and suffering from the tooth-

---

[1] *v.* Jan. 1773.
[2] *E.g.* " Over his whole soul affection lay bleeding. His eyes, as they dwelt upon the object, swam in tears ; while the blackness of hi mind, in mourning, absorbed the image from the aching optics, and never returned one fair refraction to the seat of love."

ache; and it is wholly characteristic of her that she did not set her scene in a vaguely mediæval Italy, but in England in the reign of Henry VI. Her theme, like that of all these eighteenth-century dealers in the supernatural, was divine retribution; for what other purpose, indeed, could they be justified in employing so mighty an agency? Mediæval demonology was exploded, and sorcery temporarily out of fashion as a literary subject, though it was soon to return, while the cheerful piety of the age of reason refused to conceive of supernatural powers of evil strong enough to overcome the virtuous. That is why there is no real terror in these books. The ghosts are permitted visitants, and innocence is a shield of proof. Miss Reeve, as a serious writer, was anxious to be as economical as possible with her supernatural appearances, and to restrain them " within the utmost *verge* of probability "; she probably had moral as well as artistic reasons for this, for she was a most conscientious woman; at all events, the result was fortunate, for in *The Old English Baron* we see the beginning of that refinement of ghostly effects, that reliance not on the prodigies of Otranto but on the ambiguous suggestions of dreams, falling armour and crashing doors which, waking in the reader vaguer and more disquieting fears than any defined spectre, was to be one of the sources of Mrs. Radcliffe's powers. For the rest, Miss Reeve has a good story to tell, and tells it competently in a series of brief, circumstantial little scenes; she has one fine romantic invention —that disused tragic suite of rooms, with its rusty locks and rain-soaked furniture, which was to become a regular feature of a Gothic residence,—a rather unusual villain, who neither repents nor expires in agonies, and a well-sustained mystery; but her keenest interest is in behaviour, and she is most herself in describing the Baron's handling of his refractory sons and the scene where he and Sir Philip Harclay discuss in a spirit of gentlemanly accommodation the terms on which the new-found heir shall receive his estate.

Such as it was, the book was thirteen times reprinted between 1778 and 1786. A second ghost story, *Castle Connor—an Irish Story*, was lost from the London coach in May 1787, and never retrieved. In her other novels [1] the moral interest overpowered the romantic and they are set in the modern world. She turned once more to the past, indeed, in the *Memoirs of Sir Roger de Clarendon* (1793) but it was in search of ethical instruction, not romance. She had once wished to write a history of the great men who lived in the reign of Edward III and now approached her task with something of an historian's sobriety and a determination to use up her material. The book indeed is not amusing; it makes few concessions to the trifling human demand for entertainment, and is wholly unlike the Gothic Romances in the middle of which it appeared. Miss Reeve's text was : " Let us now praise famous men, even our fathers who begat us." She saw in the fourteenth century the heroic days of pristine morality, and as such she described them, to rebuke her own degenerate age, to stimulate its ideals and to counteract the debilitating influence of pessimists and levellers. " In those days," writes the sturdy old patriot,

[1] Clara Reeve (1729–1807) : *Original Poems on Several Occasions* (1769) ; *The Phœnix* (1772) ; *The Champion of Virtue* (1777), reprinted as *The Old English Baron* (1778) ; *The Two Mentors* (1783) ; *The Progress of Romance* (1785) ; *The Exiles ; or, Memoirs of the Count de Cronstadt* (1789) ; *The School for Widows* (1791) ; *Plans of Education* (1792) ; *Memoirs of Sir Roger de Clarendon* (1793) and *Destination : or, Memoirs of A Private Family* (1799). The last book, mentioned in *D.N.B.* on the authority of Davy (*Athenæ Suffolcenses*), was published under her name and is clearly hers, by every testimony of style, subject-matter, and mental attitude. It shows the marks of old age in a certain relaxation and lack of proportion and emphasis, but is not drivelling. *Fatherless Fanny*, on the other hand, published in 1819—twelve years after her death—as by the author of *The Old English Baron*, with a garbled version of the preface to that book prefixed, is certainly not hers ; it belongs to a later generation in style and structure, and Fanny, who is five in 1798, has been married some time at the conclusion. Clara Reeve died in 1807.

" Christmas was kept as so solemn a festival ought to be. . . . They had neither tea nor coffee. . . . They rode with wind, rain, or snow in their faces, and were not afraid of the air of their own country." [1] Thus she made what she declared was her last literary voyage, sailing under her true colours, and the *Monthly* reviewer, at the end of an unfavourable notice, did not fail to record his concern that he could not " unreservedly applaud a work written by a lady who appears to be actuated by the best motives." At all times Clara Reeve extorts respect.

Meanwhile in 1776, the year before the *Old English Baron*, there had appeared Alexander Bicknell's *History of Lady Anne Neville, sister to the great Earl of Warwick ; in which are interspersed Memoirs of that Nobleman, and the Principal Characters of the Age in which she lived.* Here we touch an older, though not very fruitful, layer of the historical novel, for Bicknell's book was based closely on Prévost's *Histoire de Marguerite d'Anjou, reine d'Angleterre* (1740), and did not omit to borrow from the still older *Comte de Warwick* (1703) by the Countess d'Aulnoy.[2] The French had long been partial to historical settings

---

[1] For the ethical idealization of the past, as contrasted with the present, *v.* Mrs. Bonhote's *Bungay Castle* (1789); *e.g.* : " Night was night, and dedicated to its original purpose "; also, in a more playful vein, James White's *Earl Strongbow* (1789), where the hero's ghost remarks : " We handled the battle-ax, you wield the dice-box. We ran at the ring, you play at ombre. Our breakfast was beef and ale, yours is toast and chocolate. . . . We were a stately and robust race, you are an enervated and unmajestic generation."

[2] Prévost's book was put into English in 1755 and Mme. d'Aulnoy's in 1708. Nearly all Bicknell's story is in Prévost,—Gloucester's love and attempted murder of Lady Anne, her disguise at the Dauphiness's court as Miss Saunders, her return with Margaret of Anjou, and Somerset's passion. Many passages are verbally copied. Bicknell shortened the book, displaced Margaret as heroine in favour of Anne, slightly emphasized the love-interest, and deleted what criticism of Anne there was. The episode of the rivalry of Edward IV and Warwick for the Countess of Devonshire is from Mme. d'Aulnoy's *Earl of Warwick*, in which Lady Anne Neville does not appear. There is a MS. note in the B.M. copy of Bicknell's book : " Suppressed by the Neville family." This seems improbable, unless the book was felt to allude to some current scandal, which I have not traced.

for novels of sentiment; the settings had no picturesque value, and sometimes consisted of nothing but a few names,[1] but they allowed of a certain freedom of conception, and enabled the author to glorify the tender passion by bringing the great characters of history under its sway and exhibiting it as the cause of " the Most Memorable Actions of the Greatest of Men, and the most Stupendious Events in the World."[2] Prévost had supplied a good deal of straightforward historical narrative, and had cast his work in the form of a biography; Bicknell followed his example, and if ever the critics' dread of the confusion of fact and fancy in the reader's mind was justified, it was by the level, undifferentiated narration of these books. Bicknell dedicated *Lady Anne Neville* to the notorious Duchess of Kingston, prefixing the motto *Humanum est errare* and appealing for audience to " those whose exalted minds can rise above the restraints of Custom "; it was probably with the dedication in view that he selected for his heroine a lady whom Prévost had described as " as noble in her sentiments as she appeared irregular in her conduct," and whose delicate honour was quite unconnected with chastity. Journalist as he was,[3] and

---

[1] Cf. *The Duke of Exeter* (1789), which is either a translation from the French or an exact imitation. The book is supposed to play in the fifteenth century, but local colour is confined to one mention of the Lollards; the rest is sentiment seasoned with melodrama. On the other hand, Sophia Tomlins's *Memoirs of a Baroness* (1792; running title, *Baroness d'Alantun*), admittedly based on a French model and French fashions, contains a good deal of historical matter on Marshall Biron's conspiracy, by which both heroines are affected. On the subject of French historical novels, cf. F. C. Green, *op. cit.*

[2] *v.* translator's preface to Mme. d'Aulnoy's *History of the Earl of Warwick.*

[3] Alexander Bicknell (d. 1796) wrote in addition to the books mentioned an unacted drama, *The Patriot King : or, Alfred and Elvida* (1788), grammar, philosophical disquisitions on the Christian religion, verse and novels. Of these last, *Doncaster Races ; or, the History of Miss Maitland : a Tale of Truth*, was published under his name in 1790. Watts, *Bibliotheca Britannica*, mentions also *Isabella, or the Rewards of Good Nature* and *The Benevolent Man*, undated. The latter may be the *Man of Benevolence* reviewed by the *Monthly*, Nov. 1789.

not above fishing for profit in muddy waters, he had a real interest in history. In his next two books, *The History of Edward Prince of Wales, commonly termed the Black Prince, eldest son of King Edward the Third, with a short view of the reigns of Edward I, Edward II and Edward III, and a summary Account of the Institution of the Order of the Garter* (1776) and *The Life of Alfred the Great, King of the Anglo-Saxons* (1777), he greatly reduced, if he did not wholly eliminate, the proportion of fiction to fact, and appeared as a popular historian. Critics might scout his learning, but he was probably right in thinking that there was an audience for historical biography, if it were sprinkled with anecdotes and speeches and coloured up in the emotional scenes. Meanwhile he satisfied his romantic tastes with *Prince Arthur : an allegorical romance* (1778), a prose version of the first two books of the *Faerie Queene*. His books are significant for what they indicate, not for what they are; they suggest an approach to the historical novel through fact rather than through fancy, which was not seriously tried for many years; they are not novels, but they are the scaffolding for possible novels.[1]

French influences on the historical novel are not exhausted by Bicknell. A far more potent instance is the relation between d'Arnaud and Sophia Lee,[2] to whose *Recess* contemporary critics agree in ascribing the sudden popularity of that kind of writing. *The Recess* began to appear in 1783 and was completed in 1785, and in 1786 Miss Lee published a translation of d'Arnaud's *Warbeck* (1774), so that we may fairly presume a prior acquaintance

---

[1] A popular monograph of the same type, leaning towards fiction but stopping short of the historical novel, is Rev. Joseph Sterling's *History of the Chevalier Bayard* (1781).

[2] Sophia Lee (1750–1824), daughter of John Lee, the actor, and elder sister of Harriet Lee (1757–1851). After *The Recess* she devoted herself chiefly to her very successful school at Bath and to social life. She published a ballad, however, and an unsuccessful tragedy, and contributed to her sister's *Canterbury Tales* (1797–1805).

with that work on the grounds of date alone; other
grounds, however, are not wanting.[1] *Warbeck* is the
usual unharmonized mixture of historic fact and sentimental fiction, violently yoked together by love. Love
causes Warbeck to lose a battle, love induces him to make
his confession of fraud, while in Henry VII he has not
only an enemy but a rival. Miss Lee in her turn had
availed herself of this perilous licence, but she derived
more from d'Arnaud than this French alloy with which
to make the ore of history workable; she found also in
his taste for the morbid and sombre,—for tombs, prisons,
death and monastic atrocity,—a reinforcement of certain
elements of Gothic gloom, which were already apparent
in *Longsword* and *Otranto*, and lay plentifully to hand in
the English drama. " Let us fancy ourselves in a prison,"
writes d'Arnaud, working himself up; " let us descend
to the bottom of a dungeon, enlightened by a lamp, whose
glimmering rays serve only to discover horrors, which
darkness would conceal;—then turn our eyes towards the
miserable inhabitant of this gloomy recess, and behold a
young man of the most noble and interesting figure,
loaded with chains, pale and emaciated, weeping, throwing
himself on the damp earth, then rising and crying out in
agony, repeating incessantly: ' Ah ! dear wife ! dear
wife ! thou diest, and I am thy murderer.' " Isabella's
flight, Warbeck in prison, Longsword waiting for the
assassins, Edmund venturing the haunted room—we are
accumulating our Gothic data rapidly.

The Recess ploughed a deep track in the world of letters.
Miss Lee had a copious fancy, a strong dramatic bent and

---

[1] D'Arnaud was well known in England, in translation and in the
original; cf. D. Inklaar, *François-Thomas de Baculard d'Arnaud*
(1925), in which his influence, especially that of his " drames
monacales " is traced on Edward Jerningham (*v.* especially his poem,
The Funeral of Arabert, Monk of La Trappe), Miss Reeve, Mrs.
Radcliffe and M. G. Lewis. In *The Recess*, Matilda's escape from
the convent church in France and Ellinor's imprisonment at St.
Vincent's especially recall d'Arnaud.

an imagination capable of moments of intensity ; her style is deeply coloured by the rhetoric of the stage, and she shares the tendency of contemporary dramatists to force up her passions. Her book won the praise of novelty and deserved it, in spite of its affiliations to Walpole, Clara Reeve and d'Arnaud, by its colouring, its emotional quality, its scale and the invincible ingenuity with which it sweeps into its labyrinthine plot all the better-known characters of Elizabeth's reign. Twin daughters of Mary, Queen of Scots, and the Duke of Norfolk, alike lovely and unfortunate, are bred up secretly in underground chambers inside a ruined monastery. Matilda's fate is to wed Leicester secretly, to endure agonies of suspense at Elizabeth's court, to see him murdered, to be kidnapped to Jamaica, to be eight years imprisoned there with her daughter, and, on returning, wealthy and free, to find her sister insane. For Ellinor's life has been knit with that of Essex ; she has known her share of prison and persecution, in which the chief agent of her woe has been the Queen, has fled to Ireland in male disguise and been Tyrone's captive ; Essex's catastrophe has unhinged her reason, and Miss Lee conceives an effective scene when she brings her, an unconscious accuser, into the bedroom of the dying Elizabeth. " Consummate misery," writes Matilda, " has a moral use " ; it had at least for Miss Lee an artistic attraction, and she does not abandon Matilda until hers is consummated in the death of her daughter Mary, who, privately affianced to Prince Henry, has given her heart to Somerset and is poisoned by his wife. " We wish this mode of writing were more frequent," said the *Critical* of the first volume, finding the great shadows that fell across this book delightful after the perpetual insipidity of " Sir Charles Beverley or Colonel Beville." It speedily became more frequent and critical enthusiasm waned as speedily. This had been conditional on the preservation of " costume " and, within easy limits, of historical character, that is, on the instructive qualities of the work ; with these they were willing to accept a strong infusion of the Gothic, but Gothicism without costume was another matter. Nor were Miss Lee's imitators of a kind to evoke much enthusiasm.[1] In 1787 Anne Fuller sought to follow in her steps with *Alan Fitz-Osborne, an Historical Tale.* " I mean not to offend the majesty of sacred truth by giving her but a secondary place in the following pages," she wrote, in a skittish preface. " Necessity, stronger than prudence, obliges me to give fiction the pre-eminence ; but . . . I have preserved her genuine purity as unblemished as circumstances would admit." Circumstances admitted a little disconnected information about the Barons' Wars, but the main attractions of this historical tale were of quite another cast. " It too often happens in this novel," wrote the *Critical* moderately, " that the men are jealous without reason, and the wives murdered without examination." It does indeed ; and the bleeding spectre of Matilda, who appears at her murderer's bedside in a thunderstorm, tears the coverlet from his grasp and, drawing a dagger from her heart, lets the life-blood drip upon him from the point, is the pre-dominant memory retained by the reader of the days of Henry III. Miss Ballin's *Statue Room ; an Historical Tale* (1790) was cut more closely to pattern, and followed the vogue set by Miss Lee for illegitimate and unacknowledged children of the great. Her heroine is Adelfrida, a daughter of Henry VIII and Catherine of Aragon born

---

[1] Mrs. A. M. Mackenzie was much praised for her *Monmouth* (1790), *v.* the literary conversation in *Orlando and Lavinia* (1792), where it is placed second to *The Recess.* I have not been able to read this or any other of her historical novels. She published *The Danish Massacre* (1791), *Mysteries Elucidated* (1795),—this played during the reign of Edward II,—and *The Neapolitan ; or, The Test of Integrity* (1796)—this under the *nom de plume* of Ellen of Exeter. Watts mentions an undated *Feudal Events.* She was still writing stories in the early nineteenth century, conforming to the German and other fashions ; e.g. *Martin and Mansfeldt; or, the Romance of Franconia* (1802) and *The Irish Guardian ; or, Errors of Eccentricity* (1809); *v.* also p. 80, *n.* 1.

after their divorce, who is imprisoned and loathed by Elizabeth—always the persecutor in these stories,— marries, rather oddly, the Duke of Alençon, is poisoned by her disappointed rival and expires, leaving her husband to die of grief and a daughter, Romelia, to carry on the family traditions. This she does by becoming the wife of Henry Seymour, son of Lady Catherine Grey, firing a pistol at Elizabeth at a masquerade, and perishing of heartbreak.

By 1790 the fly-leaves of novels, particularly those published by William Lane at what was presently to become the Minerva Press, are full of advertisements of Legendary Tales, Old English Tales, Historical Stories and Historical Romances. The two types of historical novel, the " familiar history," as the *Critical* [1] called it, in which known characters, in the intervals of historic events, are involved in fictitious incidents of a kind supposedly suitable to their historic characters, and the novel that " connects the outline of history with a chain of events in domestic life," [2] are already evolved ; but as early as 1788 the *Critical* [3] is describing this type of fiction as the " bow of Ulysses," which requires " strength as well as address to bend." What the novelists brought to their task, on the other hand, was mostly violence and ingenuity. There is, however, a promise of better things in the anonymous *The Minstrel ; or Anecdotes of Distinguished Personages in the Fifteenth Century* (1793). [4] The book is romantic enough, for the minstrel, whose adventures involved so many distinguished personages, is a girl in disguise, fleeing from one lover and seeking another, and the story is properly

[1] March 1786, on *The Recess*.
[2] v. *Critical*, March 1788, on *Alan Fitz-Osborne*.
[3] v. Dec. 1788, on *The Castle of Mowbray*.
[4] I have found no trace of the author; but she also wrote *The Cypriots ; or, a Miniature of Europe in the Middle of the Fifteenth Century*; v. *Critical*, June 1795.

equipped with hermits, a ruined castle and a ghost.   But
from the moment Eleanor assumes her carefully described
disguise we are aware of a difference in the author's
attitude.   The past is romantic to her, but it has other
attractions beside those of romance ; in particular, it was
the scene of a social life varying largely from that of the
eighteenth century.   There are suggestions of this kind
in Miss Reeve's *Sir Roger de Clarendon*, but they never
amount to more than casual remarks.   *The Minstrel*,
however, takes us into the smoky huts of peasants, brings
us to the Duke of Suffolk's almshouses at Ewelme, and
introduces us as spectator at the manumission of a villein.
We listen to the professional secrets of a pardoner, and
hear a priest at Ewelme recount his experiences at the
fall of Constantinople.   There is no depth of learning in
all this, but the attempt to tell the tale against a substantial
background, and to enrich the scene with characteristic
figures, does definitely foreshadow the method of Scott ;
and *The Minstrel* is the first historical novel of which so
much can be said.

In most cases learning approached the historical novel
unaccompanied by the graces.   Vast " cultural " com-
pilations, dressed in an incongruous and transparent
domino of fiction, stalk across the Channel.   Barthélémy's
Jeune Anarcharsis (1788) [1] is welcomed, and so are
Meissner's *Alcibiades* (1781–8) and *Bianca Capella* (1785),
and a home product, tailored on the same pattern, was
Miss Ellis Cornelia Knight's [2] *Marcus Flaminius ; or a View
of the Military, Political and Social Life of the Romans : In
a Series of Letters from a Young Patrician to his Friend, in
the Year 762 from the Foundation of Rome, to the Year*

---

[1] Translated first in 1791.   Meissner was read in French translations.

[2] E. C. Knight (1757–1837).   She had already published *Dinarbas*
(1790), a recension of *Rasselas* from a cheerful point of view, and later
produced a *Description of Latium* (1805) and a romance, *Sir Guy de
Lusignan* (1833), while her *Autobiography* was published in 1861.

769 (1792). Less laborious than these impressive exercises are the books in which historical backgrounds, often painted in ideal hues, give freedom and dignity to philosophic fiction, and names are borrowed from remote ages to lend an impression of substance to kings and kingdoms conceived in the author's brain.[1] These magnanimous and solemn affairs are of foreign origin, though they were known and translated here. In England we find (though we have to look for him before we find him, so well has oblivion done its work) a characteristically national product in the freakish and delightful work of James White, the one cheerful historical novelist of the time, who saw his subject alternately from the angles of romance and contemporary parody, and, while inclining more and more to mirth, still kept the end of the gold thread of beauty in his hand.[2] Such a man, however, has no posterity, though he has brothers up and down the ages ; Peacock, if he knew him, must have found something to enjoy in him.

Meanwhile the critics were vibrating between conscientious distrust of the historical novel and an admission of its charm. They had welcomed *The Recess* chiefly because it was so marked a change from the tedium

---

[1] *E.g.* Haller's *Usong*, translated in 1772 at the request of the Queen ; the *Bélisaire* (1767) and *Les Incas* (1773) of Marmontel, and *Télephe en XII Livres* (1784), in which the author displays his exemplary tyrant and benevolent autocrat in the shapes of Minos, King of Crete, and Pandion, King of Thebes, and regards the Initiates of Eleusis as idealized Illuminés.

[2] His novels were *Earl Strongbow : or, the History of Richard de Clare and the beautiful Geralda* (1789), *The Adventures of John of Gaunt, Duke of Lancaster* (1790), and *The Adventures of King Richard Cœur-de-Lion* (1791). He also wrote verse, political tracts and translations ; *v.* my article, *A Forgotten Humourist, Review of English Studies*, April 1927. For the absence of humour in the usual historical novel cf. *Monthly*, Sept. 1800, on *A Northumbrian Tale* : " The young men, except it be sometimes ' a squire of low degree,' never relax from the dignity of dullness, either to smile themselves, or to occasion a smile in others. The figures are all cut in wood ; and if Chaucer had not written, we might have been impressed with a belief that the English of those days were men of immovable muscles."

of the stock novel; and one may find, after search, one or two other novels that wrung from them a cautious expression of pleasure. But they considered the whole genre artistically unsatisfactory and apt, by its confusion of fact and fiction, to mislead the young mind in its search for truth.[1] In 1776 the *Monthly Review*, faced with Bicknell's *Lady Anne Neville*, solemnly warned all novelists off historic ground, while the *Critical*, less drastic but equally concerned, endeavoured to delimit *licentia poetica* and to distinguish supplementary fable from actual falsehood. One feels that these critics, with their anxiety lest the young and incautious reader should imbibe heresy from these uncanonical books or, even more perniciously, have his palate so depraved as not to relish the wholesome plain fare of history, are somewhat out of touch with their readers, and the impression is confirmed when the *Monthly* reviewer asserts that the reader of Marmontel's *Incas* will have to be so much on his guard to disentangle truth and fiction, that caution will inhibit enjoyment.[2] Not with this detective rage are historical novels commonly read. Oddly enough, we very seldom find a protest against that sentimentalizing of political action which seems to us the worst flaw of these tales; the novel was still too closely associated with love for this fault to be avoided; nor do the critics see clearly that the difficulty of harmonizing the historical and fictional parts of a narrative is more than half solved when the hero of the story is fictitious and, though deeply affected by

---

[1] Cf. C. Reeve, Preface to *Sir Roger de Clarendon* (1793): " To falsify historical facts and characters is a kind of sacrilege against those great names upon which history has affixed the seal of truth. The consequences are mischievous; it misleads young minds eager in the search of truth, and enthusiasts in the pursuit of those virtues which are the objects of their admiration, upon whom one true character has more effect than a thousand fictions." Cf. also the *Monthly's* description (June 1787) of *William of Normandy. An historical Novel*, as " a monstrous and misshapen birth, and such as criticism turns from in terror and disgust."

[2] *v.* May 1778.

historical events, does not himself initiate them. As the vogue increases, the critics yield to the current. They still hoped that a little information would stick to the ignorant novel-reader ; they lost patience with James White, whose anachronisms were deliberate, and who was puddling the fair well of truth in the interest of humour ; and they showed some predilection for the informative, classical compilation, though even these, they admitted ruefully, were misleading unless authenticated by minute references. It was fact that troubled them ; in character they were prepared to allow of high colouring, and in plot they passed Sophia Lee's multitudinous extravagances with the compliment that they were " near approaches to romance, without trespassing on probability." [1] Again and again they take occasion to remark that whatever merits a book may have, the objections to the species are insurmountable ; and when a feeble voice is raised for the defence, its tongue is disingenuous. Thus the reviewer of *The Minstrel*, pleased with the book, suggests that our interest is more keenly excited by stories founded on a truth than by those known to be completely fictitious. It is a lame argument when applied to *The Minstrel*, and it is unlikely that he had bestowed much thought on it ; it was the fiction—the romance—that seduced him.

Here we must leave the historical novel, born but not yet licked into shape. Deeper knowledge, wider humanity, an intenser imagination were needed before great work could be done in this sphere ; the sense of change and continuity, of the sameness and the difference in the characters of men in different circumstances, must be far more nearly balanced than they were in the minds of these romantic fugitives, before the mistrusted type can justify itself.

[1] v. *Critical*, March 1786.

CHAPTER VII

THE GOTHIC ROMANCE

I

Even in the present polished period of society, there are thousands who are yet alive to the horrors of witchcraft, to all the solemn and terrible graces of the appalling spectre.—NATHAN DRAKE, *On Gothic Superstitions*, 1798.

THE Gothic Romance was the predominant literary fashion of the 'nineties and extended, amid the outcries of critics, well into the next century. Like the beanstalk, it shot up overnight into redundant vegetation, and enterprising novelists thronged its stem. There are two stages in its development; in the first Mrs. Radcliffe, influenced possibly to some small extent by French sensationalism, but certainly working in the main from English models—Walpole and Sophia Lee and the Elizabethan dramatists [1]—established it in popular favour; in the second it was powerfully affected by translations of German stories, beginning with *Herman of Unna* (1794).[2] The characteristic figure of the second stage is Matthew Gregory Lewis, and the characteristic book his *Monk* (1795). The difference between these two phases must not be over-emphasized; English and German romance-writers are equally the progeny of *Otranto* ;[3] they are equally concerned with prisons, ghosts and

[1] *v.* C. F. McIntyre, *Ann Radcliffe in Relation to her Time*, Chap. II, 1920.

[2] Translated as by Professor Cramer, *i.e.* the author of *Hasper a Spada*; actually by Benedicte Naubert; *v.* C. Müller-Fraureuth, *Die Ritter- und Räuberromane* (1894).

[3] *v.* Müller-Fraureuth, *op. cit.*, and Rudolf Fürst, *Die Vorläufer der modernen Novelle* (1897).

escapes, and equally convinced that a large part of the spell of romance consists in imaginative terror. The German *Ritterroman*, however, is often susceptible of political meaning; not only is its anti-clericalism more virulent than the picturesque iniquities evolved by English authors, but it is strongly marked by idealism of the feudal past and the Holy Roman Empire. Walpole's sedate ghosts would have been insufficient to inspire its popularity; they were supplemented by the enthusiastic and boisterous mediævalism of *Götz von Berlichingen* (1773). The usages of chivalry, therefore, which were not much attended to in England,[1] where the focus of national feeling was the reign of Elizabeth, are very prominent in the German stories, and the authors make great play with vigils and accolades, feudal loyalty and the baffling of the recreant knight. It is from Germany also, refuge of Jesuits and stage of swarming societies of Freemasons, Illuminati and Rosicrucians, that the thrilling theme of the vast secret society emerges, closely linked with that of alchemy and natural magic. The ancient figure of the noble outlaw—at least as old as Robin Hood, in England—receives a fresh colouring and a more philosophical interpretation from Schiller's *Robbers* (1781), and Karl Moor, speedily at home in the German romance, presently finds his way to England.[2] Schiller made another contribution to the personnel of the romance in the character of the Armenian in the *Ghost-Seer* (1789); and in general these magico-political

---

[1] James White speaks of a great noble's house as the school of chivalry in *Earl Strongbow* (1789), and there is a sketchy trial by combat in *The Old English Baron* (1777). According to the *Critical*, Aug. 1797, *Memoirs of the Ancient House of Clarendon* (1796) delineated feudal manners, while the *Monthly*, April 1798, welcoming *The Knights ; or Sketches of the Heroic Age*, writes : " Not many romances of knighthood have as yet diversified the literature of the circulating libraries."

[2] There is a philosophic outlaw of a desiccated kind in the character of Raymond in Godwin's *Caleb Williams* (1794), and the defiance of, and ultimate submission to, a law capable of injustice is emotionally rendered in George Walker's *Theodore Cyphon* (1796).

romances, in which the forces of superstition, veiled in seductive illusion, are opposed to the doctrines of enlightenment, are a German type, springing from German conditions, and, though influential in England, are not imitated.

Beside *The Old English Baron* or *The Romance of the Forest* the German *Ritter-, Räuber- und Schauerromane* are very crude products. The ideal elements of the English romances are wholly lacking; terror is coarsely material and love a theme for jocularity, while the delicacy, dignity and moral scrupulousness of Mrs. Radcliffe's method are replaced by a heavy-handed grotesqueness, a strained emotionalism and violent assaults on the nerves. The reader who will turn from the Inquisition scenes in Mrs. Radcliffe's *Italian* to those in Lewis's *Monk*[1] will sufficiently perceive the contrast. German terror is frequently hideous, for the authors detail protracted butcheries that bruise the mind to contemplate; and this violence is met by a stolidity on the part of the characters, quite different from the English heroine's trembling fortitude. There is no twilight in these books, no insinuated mystery or gradual acclimatization of the soul to dread; the authors work by sudden shocks, and, when they deal with the supernatural, their favourite effect is to wrench a mind suddenly from scepticism to horror-struck belief. Their ghost-seers are not sensitive girls, but self-sufficient young men who are confronted by a real ghost when masquerading as a sham one. The

[1] *The Monk* was begun during Lewis's stay in Germany and finished under the influence of *The Mysteries of Udolpho*. Georg Herzfeld, in *Herrigs Archive*, CXI, has shown that two-thirds of the book are taken, almost word for word, from a German romance, *Die Blutende Gestalt mit Dolch und Lampe, oder die Beschwörung im Schlosse Stern bei Prag*, in which the two themes of the devil's compact and the spectral nun are already united, though the hero of the former is an old nobleman, not a monk. The technique of the ghost-scenes is completely German. Thus the story of the bleeding nun is first introduced in a burlesque tone, and this heightens the effect of what is to follow by violent contrast. The English or Radcliffian method was a slow darkening of the scene.

ghosts too are grotesquely horrible and so definite in outline that they are frequently perceptible to touch. Indeed, the literary supernaturalism of Germany was far more closely connected with folk-lore than that of England, and all sorts of imps and sprites, which were considered by English authors too puerile and extravagant to bear a revival in fiction, find their way into the German romance,[1] while the great devil himself, though a figure of European importance, is reintroduced to the British public through a German adaptation.[2]   Sorcery, too, is a German theme, and witches as well as ghosts are sometimes introduced in the full light of the eighteenth century, for the literary timidity that caused William Taylor of Norwich to transfer Lenore's spectral bridegroom from the Seven Years' War to the Crusades had no counterpart in Germany; and certainly in this matter the German authors had logic, if not discretion, on their side.

There is a scene in W. H. Ireland's *Gondez the Monk* (1805) in which a solemn session of Inquisitors is interrupted by the yelling spook of the Little Red Woman, a damned witch, come to summon the villain to hell; and no better illustration could be found of the way in which the lurid and vehement spirit of the German *Schauerroman* broke into the Gothic Romance. Its vogue was intense and brief, and was assisted by the vogue of Kotzebue on the stage, and stricter judges found romances and plays alike tainted by moral laxity and free thought. The German novel, wrote William Taylor in 1798, was known for its " bloated magnificence of diction, extravagance of imagination and wild eccentricity of adventure." He had spent his efforts in an endeavour to introduce English readers to the new German literature, and might well feel sour to see them frustrated by the invasion of this tenth-rate stuff. Meanwhile in the Gothic Romance the strains of English and

---

[1] *E.g.* Ch. H. Spiess' *Petermänchen* (1791).   [2] E.g. *The Monk.*

German influence lie side by side; and Mrs. Radcliffe, outraged, as it seems, by this vulgar mishandling of her effects and anxious to dissociate herself from the mob, dropped her pen. But the guilt of the degeneration should not be laid wholly at the German door, for though without the *Schauerroman* there might have been a little less crudity and horror in the Gothic Romance, it must equally have perished of over-elaboration and over-emphasis, and all the consequences of the endeavour to outdo its first models. Even in the hands of its finest exponent, it was precariously balanced over the abysses of the ludicrous and disreputable, so that a movement in any direction must confound it. It was a folly, run up without any consideration of the needs of reasonable beings, a glaring and picturesque façade on the edge of a precipice, uninhabitable by flesh and blood, or even by authentic ghosts. Such as it was, however, it was for the time being immensely stimulating to the cramped fancy of the age.

We have now to follow two trails that continually cross each other. We have to trace in the Gothic Romance those situations and characters in which the eighteenth-century notion of the romantic was expressed, and to define as far as possible the sort of thrill they yielded; and in so doing we shall turn frequently to the work of Mrs. Radcliffe, which is often the best illustration of them. But Mrs. Radcliffe herself is something more than a purveyor of romantic thrills, and her establishment of Gothic Romance does not exhaust her services to literature. Her work demands separate treatment, and treatment as a whole, if its significance is to be understood. To this crossing of trails, and to some consequent repetition, we must resign ourselves.

II

What ardent imagination ever was content to trust to plain reasoning, or to the evidence of the senses ? It may not willingly confine itself to the dull truths of earth, but, eager to expand its faculties, to fill its capacity, and to experience its own peculiar delights, soars after new wonders into a world of its own.—MRS. RADCLIFFE, *The Italian*, 1797.

Ann Radcliffe, mighty enchantress of Udolpho, Shakespeare of Romance-writers and first poetess of romantic fiction,[1] has during the last ten years resumed her proper place in the eye of criticism, and her very real though limited talent is no longer obscured by critical amusement, or by the excess of its own charms. The importance of her novels as a contribution to fiction has never been doubted, but recent studies,[2] cutting through their redundancies to the vigorous imagination that inspired them, have put the reader in position to understand, even if he does not wish to echo, the exuberant praises shed on her by contemporaries who, like Crabbe Robinson, weighed her against Scott, or, like Mrs. Barbauld, preferred the temptation of La Motte by the Marquis de Montalt to that of Hubert by King John. More and more one sees in her the focus of all the romantic tendencies of her time. She collected, combined and intensified them, harmonizing her work by picturesque beauty and quickening it with fear and awe. What in others had been timid and tentative, in her is bold and assured. Others had paddled toy-boats in the edge of the perilous seas ; her great ship takes the tide with its flags floating and its mistress aboard ; for she was unashamedly romantic, and did not pretend that she provided romance

[1] So termed by T. J. Mathias, *The Pursuits of Literature* (1794), Nathan Drake, *Literary Hours* (1798) and Scott, *Memoir* of Mrs. Radcliffe prefixed to her works in Ballantyne's *Novelists' Library* (1824)
[2] Especially C. F. McIntyre, *op. cit.*, and A. A. S. Wietens, *Mrs. Radcliffe—her Relations towards Romanticism* (1926).

in the interests of instruction. Only Sophia Lee had dared such a voyage before, and she had sailed under the countenance of the long-suffering and much-abused muse of history.

The function of Mrs. Radcliffe's books [1] was to exercise and recreate, in the first place, the mind of the writer and secondly that of the reader. They are the day-dreams of a mind at once fastidious and audacious, capable of energy and langour, responsive to beauty and to awe, and tremblingly sensitive to imaginative fear.[2] They are also the work of a conscientious craftsman, whose technique is always respectable, and whose development in power and self-knowledge from the pallid *Castles of Athlin and Dunbayne* (1789) to the assured romantic splendour of *The Italian* (1797) is interesting to follow. Her audience was ready for her. Her themes were not new; [3] but never had mountains and spectral music, defenceless beauty and the Inquisition, ruined manors, vaults, pilgrims and banditti been adorned with so much unfamiliar gorgeousness; never had there been such ample provision for the romantic mood, so pure in quality and so respectable in form. Here was romance that could be enjoyed by statesmen and head-masters without embarrassment. Here, moreover, was a novelty of technique which did effectively make of her books a new kind of fiction. Isolated anticipations, it is true, can be found of her lyrical and pictorial effects, while her handling of suspense and terror derives straight from

[1] *The Castles of Athlin and Dunbayne* (1789), *A Sicilian Romance* (1790), *The Romance of the Forest* (dated 1791 ; but C. F. McIntyre remarks that it was not announced until 1792), *The Mysteries of Udolpho* (1794) and *The Italian* (1797). The posthumous *Gaston de Blondeville* (1826) appears to have been written just after the turn of the century, and the verse romance, *St. Alban's Abbey*, published in 1826 together with *Gaston de Blondeville* and a collection of shorter poems, a year or two later.

[2] This is not inconsistent with Talfourd's description of her smilingly handing chapters to her husband, which he shuddered to read. She had then exorcised the fear by embodying it.

[3] *v.* Appendix III.

the scene of Isabella's flight in the *Castle of Otranto*, but even here the systematic lavishness and resource with which she elaborates these hints deserves the name of originality, while her plot is all her own. " She gave a new emphasis to action," writes Miss McIntyre, " not action in and for itself, as in the picaresque novel, but action as bringing about complications, and resolving them." She excited in her readers, by combinations of suspense, mystery and surprise, the sort of interest that continually strains to the outcome of a scene. For the first time reading was an exercise to be undertaken with bated breath, and it was to this tension that Coleridge referred in the *Critical* when he called the *Mysteries of Udolpho* " the most interesting novel in the English language." [1]

At four generations' distance it is the antitheses of Mrs. Radcliffe's nature that charm attention—her child's fancy and her woman's melancholy, her enthusiastic romance and demure satire, her voluptuous colouring and the chaste propriety of her phrase.[2] Her own generation was less sensitive to incongruity than ours; they recognized and responded to her perfectly sincere taste for the " dark sublime," and were not disturbed by such absurdities as the sixteen lines of poetry, carved by Valancour on the stone postern, or Alleyne's unusual achievements with a small knife. Her anachronisms of fact were not noted, while her anachronisms of sentiment added to her popularity. She was a Conservative, staunchly clinging to old ideals in the turbulent flood of new ones. Her heroines are quietly devout and " tremblingly jealous of propriety "; her nobles are benevolent

---

[1] *v.* August, 1794.
[2] *E.g* of Laurentini di Udolpho, who persuades her lover to poison his wife : " She suffered all the delirium of Italian love." Talfourd, whose *Memoir* certainly reflects in part Mr. Radcliffe's attitude towards his wife's work (*v.* Miss Mitford's *Letters*), praises her because she " has forborne to raise one questionable throb, or call forth a momentary blush."

and her servants humble and attached. When the Marquis de Montalt tempts La Motte to evil he does so by means of the subversive tenets of the " new philosophy," the relativity of right and wrong, and the exemption of the strong spirit from the laws which control and support the weak. The French Revolution, by shaking the foundations of society, had engendered an atmosphere of insecurity and excitement that quickened the nerves of literature, and in this nervous quickening Mrs. Radcliffe participates deeply; but she stood scrupulously aloof from the liberal speculations that accompanied it, and found occasion, undeterred by the antique setting of her tales, to testify a disapproval of them and a loyalty to ancient values which must have conciliated many readers. Her books, like those of all popular authors, are full of links with the talk and reading of the day; indeed, the student of the age who takes them for his field will find most of its characteristic tendencies reflected there. Through the mouths of sixteenth-century Frenchmen and seventeenth-century Italians she imparts her opinions on education, medical treatment, religious toleration, gardening and the humane treatment of animals, and even distantly salutes the new science of geology. These things did not make her fame, but they are characteristic both of her conscientious mind and of the catholic appetite and happy digestion of the romantic mood.

Her romances have a strong family resemblance. They play, for the most part, in glamorous southern lands and belong to a past which, although it is sometimes dated, would not be recognized by an historian. In all of them a beautiful and solitary girl is persecuted in picturesque surroundings, and, after many fluctuations of fortune, during which she seems again and again on the point of reaching safety, only to be thrust back into the midst of perils, is restored to her friends and marries

the man of her choice.   In all of them this simple theme
is complicated by mystery and involved at some point in
terrible, often supernatural, suggestions.   It would be
possible to classify all the ingredients of Mrs. Radcliffe's
romances under the two headings of Beauty and Terror,
and such a classification would have the advantage of
keeping well in view the cause of her enormous popularity.   It is this harmony of beauty and terror that causes
Dr. Drake to compare her to Shakespeare.   Beauty
refines terror, connects it with dignified associations and
prevents it from verging on disgust; terror in turn
heightens beauty, like the thundercloud impendent over
so many scenes in eighteenth-century engravings.   Such a
harmony is found in *The Italian* in the chapters that deal
with Ellena's imprisonment in the mountain convent of
San Stefano and her escape with Vivaldi.   The magnificence of the mountain scenery; the rich pomp of the
church and the tyranny it fails to conceal; the valiance
of the lovers and their fear, culminating in the dreadful
minutes spent waiting in the remote stone cell, where
the straw mattress, seeming still to retain the pressure of
a prisoner's body, forces the imagination to dally with
the horrible, but never defined, doom with which Ellena
is threatened; the momentary relief, soon quickened by
renewed apprehension, when at last they begin their
flight through the blazing moonlight;—these form an
interwoven texture of beauty and terror, to which the
reader's mind responds in fluctuations of anxiety and
satisfaction.   There had been nothing like it in the novel
before, or, rather, nothing on such a scale, for short
experimental passages in the same tone will be found in
Charlotte Smith, and perhaps such a fusion was the aim
of Miss Lee's *Recess*.   Mrs. Radcliffe's work, however,
had the force of a new revelation.   The spirit of poetry
mastered prose fiction, and enthusiasts were not afraid
to cite *Hamlet, Lear* and *Macbeth*.

The indispensable elements for producing such an effect were scenery, a Gothic building (or two, or three) and the sensitive mind of a girl, attuned to all the intimations, sublime or dreadful, that she can receive from her surroundings.[1] It was this preponderance of atmosphere over passion, or, rather, this reduction of passion to be no more than a component part of the atmosphere, which, together with the fact that we never behold the naked form of terror, but always its image obscurely reflected in the victim's mind, differentiates Mrs. Radcliffe's books from Walpole's *Castle of Otranto*, to which her debt is otherwise capital and perfectly authenticated. She did not contemplate violence with pleasure, although she was aware that the traces of violence past, and the shadow of that to come, deepen and enrich a romantic setting. Moreover, she had all that passivity which is so marked a trait of the women writers : her heroines feel, but they do not initiate ; they can resist but do not attack ; nor are the heroes or villains very enterprising, with the exception of Vivaldi and Schedoni in *The Italian*. In her first book there is fighting, but she speedily recognized her unfitness for this vein, and thereafter what violence is necessary is enacted behind the veil of time and distance, and often doubly veiled by the obscure narration of the witness. When Theodore is fighting a duel with one leg chained, we stay and tremble with Adeline in the room above ; when siege threatens at Udolpho, Emily is removed, and only catches a glimpse by torchlight of the abandoned battle-ground on her return. Indeed, it has often been remarked that nothing very terrible

---

[1] *Gaston de Blondeville* is in some ways an exception to these statements, for though it is composed of the same elements as the other romances, with the addition of antiquarian and historical detail, they are differently handled. The book simulates an ancient manuscript and is deliberately naïve ; the hero and ghost-seer is a middle-aged merchant, and the ghost is real. The book is interesting to students of Mrs. Radcliffe, but has no bearing on the history of the Gothic Romance, as it was not published until 1826.

happens at Udolpho after all; there are brawls, a soldier is killed, and an old woman worried into her grave by a harsh and selfish husband; but these things, in the shadow of that Gothic masonry, half-lit by those perpetually failing lamps, acquire a monstrous hue. It was not so at Otranto, where dreadful things really happen and happen often, where the action begins with Manfred's crushed son and ends with his bleeding daughter, and the castle itself, however carefully sketched, is no more than a necessary frame in which the actors move. We may say, with truth, that the primary inspiration of Walpole and of Mrs. Radcliffe was, like that of Chatterton, architectural. Both started by asking themselves what sort of incidents suited such imposing scenes. But from this point their paths divided. Walpole's mood was dramatic; he concentrated on the passions and actions of his characters; Mrs. Radcliffe's was mainly lyric and elegiac, and action was chiefly important to her for its picturesque qualities, and as it changes the scene or modifies the atmosphere. It is highly significant that the mysteries of Udolpho are nearly irrelevant in Emily's career, and that the most famous of them—the Black Veil [1]—is entirely so; it is explained to the readers only as an afterthought, and never explained to Emily at all. Mrs. Radcliffe's aim was to make her heroine pass through alternate patches of beauty and terror; Udolpho is a grandiose bit of chiaroscuro, and Emily leaves it much the same as she enters it. Even her delineations of character, on which she spends some pains, are not completed by action. Orsino, as he is described in the seventeenth chapter of the *Mysteries of Udolpho*, is of the stuff of Jacobean tragedy, but he is merely a picture to hang by the wall, a portion of the scenery, who never

---

[1] For the source of this famous veil—or rather of the object which it concealed—v. my article *Ramond, Grosley and Mrs. Radcliffe* in the *Review of English Studies*, July 1929.

engages in any deed commensurate with the promise of his appearance.[1] The *Romance of the Forest* and *The Italian*, it should be admitted, are much better constructed, while in Schedoni, in the latter book, we have at last a character effectively agitated by passion and will, whose actions are the mainspring of the plot. Her other characters may, without great injustice, be compared to the figures of landscape painters, those groups of banditti, or lovers, or haymakers, whose function is to focus and enhance the sentiment of the scene. The characters and conflicts of Emily and Montoni and Vivaldi and Adeline are not the centre of interest; the centre of interest is impersonal; it is the southern landscape, whose fullest effect is to be elicited by the happy musings of lovers or by their terror-stricken flight; it is the castle or the convent, for complete expression of which we require both the victim and the tyrant. The *raison-d'être* of her books is not a story, nor a character, nor a moral truth, but a mood, the mood of a sensitive dreamer before Gothic buildings and picturesque scenery. Story and characters are evolved in illustration of this mood; and Emily at Udolpho and Adeline at Fontan-ville Abbey are, as it were, organs through which these grim places speak, placed there to receive and transmit the faint rumours that cling about them, comparable with their trembling sensibilities to Aeolian harps. When all is said, however, a novel is neither a picture nor a lyric, and something more than attitude went to Mrs. Radcliffe's figures. There is dramatic tension in the scene at Udolpho where, as Emily sits at dinner among

---

[1] " Orsino was reserved and haughty, loving power more than ostentation; of a cruel and suspicious temper; quick to feel an injury, and relentless in avenging it; cunning and unsearchable in contrivance, patient and indefatigable in the execution of his schemes. He had a perfect command of feature and of his passions, of which he had scarcely any, but pride, revenge and avarice; and in the gratification of these, few considerations had power to restrain him, few obstacles to withstand the depth of his schemes."

the fierce guests, the poison rises hissing in Montoni's glass, and in a moment swords are out. Satire pleasantly ripples the romantic surface in the pictures of La Motte and Madame Cheron, and a touch like that of the elegant Marquis, swearing grossly at Adeline's escape, taking pleasure in inventing and expressing the foulest abuse, has a reality that cannot be reduced to the picturesque. For the rest, she provided sufficiently interesting variants of the beautiful and unprotected heroine, the " sensible " and gallant hero, the benevolent guardian and the Gothic tyrant, and filled up the background with soubrettes, brigands, ecclesiastics and faithful servants; and all these people develop, in her later books, a power of appropriate gesture and resonant phrase that carries them triumphantly through their strong scenes. It is not life, but it is coherent fantasy.

Romance to Mrs. Radcliffe implied dignity and remoteness, and her cult of both qualities was conscious. The homely and the grotesque were alien from her muse. She included a little comic relief, on the model of Shakespeare and Walpole, but it is never allowed to touch her chief characters. Perdita, we know, was sea-sick, and Sophia Western tumbled from her horse in a muddy lane; but Adeline and her sisters, though their lives are endangered by land and sea, are never discountenanced in this fashion. In the same way the scenes that Mrs. Radcliffe borrowed from the accounts of tourists— notably from Grosley's *New Observations upon Italy and its Inhabitants*—are subjected to a softening touch. There is no dirt in the Naples of *The Italian*, and the passage of the Alps is achieved by Emily in a chair, not a wheelbarrow.[1]

---

[1] Graves has many amusing remarks on the dignifying quality of the romantic mood; *v.* p. 210, n. 1, and cf. the quips in *The Spiritual Quixote* and *Plexippus*. When Wildgoose meets an old friend, Graves writes : " They then embraced (in the language of romance), or, in plain English, took each other by the hand with great

Remoteness, with its consequence, obscurity, has been considered by Professor Abercrombie in his lectures on Romanticism. He does not instance Mrs. Radcliffe, but she provides an admirable illustration to his text. She was herself a theorist. " To the warm imagination," she writes, " the forms which float half-veiled in darkness afford a higher delight than the most distinct scenery the sun can show." [1] To describe is to limit and circumscribe the operations of the reader's fancy, but to suggest is to stimulate it by the intimation of a grandeur or a terror beyond the compass of words.[2] This principle she carried as far as it would go. Her books are full of the half-revealed, of objects that are betrayed sufficiently to excite curiosity but not sufficiently to allay it, of hints and traces that lead the mind into a region of vague sublimity. Her heroine's beauty gleams through a veil and a slouched hat shadows her villain. The crowning grace of her landscapes is mist, and music, to exert its most delicious power, must be breathed invisibly on the air.[3] Fontanville Abbey is first seen at twilight, when the desolate La Motte family shelter in the half-explored building; and, indeed, none of her Gothic edifices are ever fully known, even to their inhabitants, whose steps are always liable to stray, as in a dream, into unfamiliar apartments and down crumbling stairways. This deliberate recourse to suggestive obscurity is most noticeable and most important in her dealings with terror. It is a

---

cordiality." Also : " The company sat down to (what in romance would be called) a cold collation, which in plain English was a good quantity of cold ham and fowls, cold tongue, orange cheese-cakes, and other portable provisions of the best kind." Of Plexippus he says : " I would give the name of romance to my hero, though his real name was Philips."

[1] v. *Mysteries of Udolpho*, IV, p. 12.

[2] Cf. Isaac d'Israeli, *Vaurien*, I, p. 183 (1797) : " It is by concealing that we exhibit objects to the imagination."

[3] v. *A Sicilian Romance* : " The musicians were placed in the most obscure and embowered spots, so as to elude the eye and strike the imagination."

point that has been much investigated in theses on the
Gothic Romance. Briefly, Mrs. Radcliffe approached
the terrible with all the tremors of a highly-strung nervous
system. Not for her the crude vigour of Otranto or the
piecemeal manifestations of the good Alfonso; these
portents, as Scott suggested, are somewhat too definite
in outline; like the crash of the falling helmet, they stun
rather than stimulate the imagination. She is the poet
of apprehension. Her theme is not the dreadful happen-
ing—very often nothing dreadful happens—but the
interval during which the menace takes shape and the
mind of the victim is reluctantly shaken by its impendence.
Sources of and parallels to her devices can be found in
the Elizabethan drama, but the drama has no room for
the slow subjection of the mind to terror. For that we
must wait for the psychological novel, towards the development of which Mrs. Radcliffe made a contribution
in her analysis of fear. Her procedure can be traced in
those chapters of *The Romance of the Forest* that lead up
to and include Adeline's discovery and perusal of the
manuscript; or at even greater length in those describing
Emily's sojourn at Udolpho. A sensitive but spirited
girl is brought to a Gothic building and exposed to its
influence. She is lonely, helpless, in unhappy circumstances and presently threatened by real peril, and her
reasonable fears gradually sap her defences against the
unaccountable terrors with which her surroundings and
the confused stories of ignorant servants inspire her.
Her nerves are subjected to a series of slight, harassing
attacks, in which intimations of earthly and ghostly terror
are blended. One notes the delicacy of means by which
these effects are evoked, a sigh, a moving light, an unfamiliar tone of voice, the reflection in a mirror of a
cloaked and striding figure. Thus her senses are excited
and her reason is bewildered, and she is delivered over to
the " mystic and turbulent promptings of the imagina-

tion." It was no small achievement, in an age of rough-and-ready assaults on the sensibilities, to trace Adeline to the point when she sits reading the prisoner's manuscript, at midnight, by her failing lamp, and, shaken by mysterious sympathies, dare hardly raise her eyes to the mirror, lest she should see another face beside her own. In thus tracing the growth of fear, Mrs. Radcliffe takes a few steps in the direction of that science that was to become the guiding light of fiction a hundred years hence. Her innovation was noticed by her contemporaries, and Mary Hays in the preface to *Emma Courtney* (1796) ranks her among those writers who, by tracing the progress and consequence of one strong, indulged passion, have afforded material for philosophers to calculate the powers and estimate the motives of the human mind. Her study of abnormal mental states, however, is strictly limited by the bias of her own tastes and opinions. Of all the passions she studies only fear, and fear, through the intervention of her sense of dignity, never reaches such a pitch as to deprave the fearful. Her heroines are timid but steadfast. They have no enemy within; they are sure that innocence will be divinely shielded, and they never doubt their innocence. Those pits of agony into which Maturin cast a glance, where lie the souls of those who feel an involuntary pollution darkening their minds and dread lest their natures should conform to those of their persecutors, were beyond her scan. Under the pressure of fear Adeline, Emily and the lovers of *The Italian* remain devout, merciful and essentially courageous. Beyond this point terror ceases to be " a pleasing luxury," and dream passes into nightmare.

Terror does not play a large part in *The Romance of the Forest*. In this book Mrs. Radcliffe first reached her full strength, and to do so she retrenched on the exuberance of *A Sicilian Romance* and concentrated on a smaller field of incident. There is, as always, flight and pursuit, but her fancy lingers gladly with the lovely waif, Adeline, in the glades of Fontanville Forest and the mountains of Savoy, and the book was admired for its idyllic charm rather than its thrills. Darker threads, however, are woven into the fabric, and Adeline's finely-imagined dreams, when she is unwittingly brought near the room where her father was murdered, provide, with Vivaldi's dreams in the prison of the Inquisition, the only instances in the books published in Mrs. Radcliffe's lifetime in which the intimations from the twilight side of our nature are justified. The supernatural continually fascinated her imagination, but in most cases reason and prudence induced her to disown its promptings. In *The Mysteries of Udolpho* she devoted herself to elaborating at Udolpho and at Château-le-Blanc an atmosphere of supernatural awe. There is certainly too much of this, seeing that it is all a cheat, that Laurentini di Udolpho is still alive, and that smugglers were responsible for the disappearance of Lorenzo and the shaking of the black pall. She makes the mistake, as Coleridge pointed out in his review for the *Critical*, of raising expectation so high that it cannot be satisfied. In *The Italian*, which is altogether better wrought than the more popular *Mysteries*, the supernatural suggestions are slight and fade away before the more substantial terror inspired by monastic tyranny and the Inquisition. On this ground also she preserved her delicacy of taste and her cult of obscure suggestion. Where precision would lacerate the imagination she is impressively vague, and Vivaldi in the dungeons of the Inquisition hears nothing but a distant groan, sees only some undefined "instruments," and though once stretched in preparation on the rack, never feels its strain. The secret of the effect of these slight touches on the reader lies, of course, in preparation. On the one hand, there is the picturesque elaboration of scenes appropriate to dreadful incidents—dungeons and caves and moonlit ruins; on the other, there is a skilful though too lavish employment of suspense. The mind is first disposed to contemplate the terrible, and then worked into a fever of fluctuating emotion. Walpole had shown how this was to be done in the famous flight of Isabella through the vaults, and there are similar though briefer passages in *Longsword* and *Ferdinand Count Fathom*, where the intended victim hears murderers plotting his end. Mrs. Radcliffe bettered this instruction. If there is suspense in *Otranto*, in *Udolpho* everything is suspended. Perils threaten and withdraw; lovers part and meet and part again; mysteries are suspected and explained, but the explanation is misleading; false trails are laid; confessions are interrupted—if only by the dinner-bell; sudden knocking alarms us—even if it is only the servant.[1] The sophisticated reader soon finds these shocks tedious and refuses to answer to the cry of " Wolf, wolf," while even at the height of her fame, critics advised her to bridle her ingenuity; but it was just this sustained command of the reader's nerves that was new, at a time when even the best novels were short-breathed, and one recalls that Henry Tilney read *The Mysteries of Udolpho* in two days, his hair standing on end the whole time.

It is the vice of her method that scenes of raised excitement, where suspense is continually heightened by mystery and unexpected incidents, must be followed by patches of flat explanation. Her ingenious plotting was, however, on the whole, much admired. Like Walpole, though to a far greater degree, she roused, baffled and finally satisfied the detective interest in her readers. In *The Romance of the Forest* three mysteries are mooted,

---

[1] Cf. W. Dibelius, *Englische Romankunst. Die Technik des englischen Romans im achtzehnten und zu Anfang des neunzehnten Jahrhunderts* (*Palaestra XCII and XCVIII*), 1910, for an elaborate exposition of Mrs. Radcliffe's methods of composition and of their relationship to those of Fielding and Walpole.

that of Adeline, that of the Abbey and that of La Motte,
and in the end all three run together in the hand of the
Marquis. Providence, however, is the elucidator, not
the persevering ingenuity of man, and for a modern taste
there is too much chance and too many futile mystifica-
tions in these books. Their appeal was not intellectual
but emotional. The reader is not invited to unpick a
knot, but to enjoy the emotion of mystery; the knot,
indeed, is not unpicked at all; at the appointed hour an
incantation is breathed over it, and it dissolves, for the
methods of an enchantress are not those of Sherlock
Holmes.

Those who do not read Mrs. Radcliffe are apt to
exaggerate the proportion of terror in her books. Her
popularity did not rest wholly on a shudder; indeed, for
chapters on end the shudder is in abeyance, while the
heroine and other good characters enjoy the view or tour
leisurely among the stupendous objects of nature. Mrs.
Radcliffe was an enthusiast for natural beauty. Travelling was the romance of her life, and where she could not
go herself she sent her heroines, taking the works of
landscape-painters and the accounts in picturesque tours
and vivifying them with her glowing imagination. It is
possible to trace some of her steps, for she did not spurn
local colour though she transcended it, and odd little
scraps of fact are woven into her itineraries. The travelling hero is as old as Jason, who did not, however, travel
for the sake of the scenery. The travelling hero, new
style, was evolved by Charlotte Smith in *Celestina* (1791)
when she sent Willoughby to ease his wounded heart
among the Pyrenees, and based her account of them on
Ramond de Carbonnière's *Observations faites dans les
Pyrénées*. The travelling heroine, suggested by Mrs.
Smith in *Emmeline* (1788), became Mrs. Radcliffe's preserve; Julia flies and is pursued through all the wild
beauties of Sicily, Adeline visits Switzerland and Lan-

guedoc, while Emily tours in the Pyrenees, crosses the Alps, visits Venice, and passes months in a castle among the Apennines. Descriptions, infected with picturesque terminology, but beautiful in their mannered way, flood the romances with colour. More than that, they reflect and enhance the emotions of the principal characters. Mrs. Radcliffe was deeply read in the poets. Tasso, we know, was a favourite author, and she knew the English poets and Ossian, and, like Charlotte Smith, who precedes her so closely that one cannot be sure of their literary relationship, she sought to adorn prose fiction by the same lyrical interpretation of nature that she admired in them. The scene reflects the emotions of her characters, or ironically contradicts them; it darkens towards a catastrophe or spreads into sunny safety. A flexible harmony of colour accompanies the action; it is beneath a lowering sky and beside a wind-ruffled lake that Ellena walks to church on her fateful marriage-morning, while the changing aspects of Fontanville Forest keep pace with Adeline's changing fortunes, as its lawns darken with the coming storm and its trees are stripped by the wind. From the divine order of nature the persecuted heroine draws fortitude, purifying her soul in the beauty of frequent dawns and sunsets. There is, indeed, an excess of these glories, and the reader turns with approval to the sobriety of Mrs. Charlotte Smith's English scenes and the structural rightness of their introduction. Both women proved that the sensibilities and the methods hitherto associated with poetry could perfectly well be applied to prose fiction and would enlarge its scope. The immediate inspiration was certainly Ossian, for whom they felt an enthusiastic loyalty. The showers and sunbeams and flying mists that clothe the Ossianic hero and foreshow his destiny had been specially praised by Blair in his *Introductory Dissertation*, and it is to Ossian that Mrs. Smith refers in that scene in the autumnal woods where Fitz-Edward meets the betrayed Adelina.

Mrs. Radcliffe was certainly a poet, though her verses, with their confused colouring and lack of outline, are the least satisfactory expressions of her spirit, and even in prose her style is hardly supple enough to convey her emotion. The informal notes in her diary are more transparent, and occasionally in her novels she strikes out a phrase which by its concentrated imagery stands out from its context; such are the " gasping billows " of the storm in which Emily is wrecked, and Vivaldi's reproach to Ellena, when she weeps as she promises to marry him : " Should your tears fall on my heart now ? " There are other passages where the lyrical quality is apparent in the feeling, though often blunted in expression. Her sense of the transitoriness of human beauty and joy is poetic rather than didactic, and there is a passage in *The Italian* where Vivaldi, going to Ellena's house, is assailed by a sudden irrational fear that she is dead, which is parallel to one of Wordsworth's *Lucy* poems. The exultation of Ellena in her mountain prison, Valancour's dread lest he should forget the face of his beloved, Adeline in the Alps, walking, as it seems to her, over the ruins of the world, are passages to be matched in the poets, but not elsewhere in the prose fiction of the eighteenth century. She was indeed, as Scott called her, the first poetess of romantic fiction. She liberated fancy and quickened colour, and fancy and colour, thus restored, were not long confined to the Gothic Romance. She lived to read and admire the Waverley Novels, for which she had helped to prepare the way.

III

It appears to me that every creature has some notion—or rather relish of the sublime.—MARY WOLLSTONECRAFT, *Mary, a Fiction*, 1788.

Turning through the library novels of the 'seventies and 'eighties, before romance was triumphantly established by Miss Lee and Mrs. Radcliffe, one notes the recurrence, in sentimental or didactic contexts, of certain themes which, treated baldly enough, were nevertheless associated in the readers' minds with some sort of romantic thrill, and by a suggestion of force and strangeness fostered that universal human relish for the sublime, which Mary Wollstonecraft detected in the most imperfect shapes. Most frequent among these themes are Gothic mansions, convents and penitent hermits. They are often irrelevantly introduced and summarily treated. Abducted girls and erring wives are imprisoned in Gothic piles, even where nothing further is made of their possibilities; it was felt to be appropriate. Even more significant is the fact that the hero's ancestral home is usually Gothic, and occasionally described at some length, though again nothing happens there; but it was felt to be a suitable home for a hero. The Gothic fashion has effected a lodgment in the novel, though at present in a singularly dry and allusive way. The reader, one assumes, appreciated the allusion, and carried over into the novel something of the atmosphere of rich melancholy in which poetry, followed at some distance by drama, had bathed the Gothic building.[1] Ghostly hints, traces of faded violence and quenched revelry had invested these feudal remnants with an allure that was quite different from though not altogether

---

[1] Contrast Andrew Macdonald's play *Vimonda* (1787) with his novels, *The Independent* (1784) and *Laura* (1790 ?). The former is thoroughly romantic and spectacular, with a Border castle, a gloomy oratory, moonshine and a supposed ghost. In the novels the Gothic setting is only once used, and that is to stage a practical joke.

antagonistic to the " curiosity " of the antiquarian. A new source of emotion had been unsealed, and novelists were trying to take account of it, though without much notion as yet how this was to be done. As a rule they provided the castle and left the rest to the reader, conscious that in a modern novel they could not imitate *Otranto*, and hoping that the simple word " Gothic " would release the spell; and if it were not for the frequency of these abortive suggestions, and the gloss provided by contemporary poetry and pictures, it would not be easy to deduce from these early novels how dominating an image was the Gothic castle in the fancy of the age. Henry Mackenzie, who had strong leanings to the picturesque and cultivated atmosphere, staged Annesley's narrative in *The Man of the World* (1773) in a ruined chapel on a heath, where an old soldier sits over a brushwood fire in partial shelter from the storm, and the house that Julia de Roubigné enters, with a sinking heart, after her marriage, is " a venerable pile, the remains of ancient Gothic magnificence "; but it is Charlotte Smith, herself a poet, who first begins to explore in fiction the possibilities of the Gothic castle, and her *Emmeline* (1788) is the first heroine whose beauty is seen glowing against that grim background, or who is hunted along the passages at night. Castle Mowbray, however, contributes little to the plot and is soon left behind.[1] The complete exposition of the Gothic pile was in the hands of another poet, Ann Radcliffe, who, mindful of Otranto, of the *Old English Baron*, of Castle Mowbray (probably) and the ruined battlements of Ossian (certainly), together with all that her eye had seen in the fields of her own country and in pictures of foreign lands, fused all into a grandiose vision of the vast,

[1] Mrs. Smith continued to provide castles and aged mansions in her novels, notably Castle Rochemarte in *Celestina* (1791) and Rayland Hall in *The Old Manor House* (1793), but her predominant interests were not romantic, and in *The Banished Man* (1794), in which two more of these edifices were described, she complained that her material was exhausted.

intricate, sinister and superb hold, established at the heart of her story, indeed itself the heart, radiating atmosphere and suggesting incident.

The castles of Gothic romance, unlike those of mediæval romance, are never new. The tale may play in bygone centuries, but they are more ancient still ; usually, too, they have at least one ruinous wing, for decay was Gothic and picturesque, and the romance-writers wished somehow to combine in their architecture the attractions of tyrannous strength and of melancholy. Hence all the absurdities of feudal chiefs, who fail to keep their castles in repair, and mansions that fall to ruin in less than twenty years. Ossian's lament for Balclutha rang in the ears of the age, and on some ruined wall in every Gothic domicile the thistle shakes its lonely head and the moss (literally, Mrs. Roche assures us) whistles to the wind. The eighteenth century thought much of death and decay, from churchyard-poets to philosophers, who broke open coffins, prized apart ankle-joints with their walking-sticks, and sent minutes of their researches to the *Gentleman's Magazine*. Decay was part of every romantic spell, the noiseless slipping of life into oblivion. It was consonant with the cult of the dim and the half-seen ; and, from this angle, the defaced tomb of an unknown knight has superior attractions to the fully-authenticated resting-place of an historical character. When the romantic asks : " What have these old walls seen ? " he does not want too precise an answer.

Mingled with the melancholy and awe, inspired by a Gothic building, was a gentle thrill of complacency. It is not usually explicit in the Gothic romance, for obvious reasons, but it is liberally attested elsewhere. There is a castle in William Hutchinson's pastoral *A Week at a Cottage* (1775), whose " disconcerted walls stand sullenly and brave the wrath of Time." It is a record not only of tyranny but of the expiration of tyranny ; it is " an object

now for Pleasure's Eye," and its nodding battlements
" now domineer not, but adorn the Place." To the hero
of the Reverend James Thomson's *Denial, or the Happy
Retreat* (1790) the ruins of a castle " demonstrate the
stability of the government, the progress of civilization,
the security of property and the safety of the subject."
The romantic thrill was superimposed upon this groundwork of complacency; and perhaps not enough has been
made, as an ingredient in the attraction of romance, of
the charm of recovery, the breaking as well as the binding
of the spell, and the return, with full hands, to a familiar
world.

The degradation of the Gothic castle, when every hall
is the scene of deeds of violence, and the heroine makes
her way through dungeons littered with rotting bones,
relying on, and inevitably finding, a secret door, need not
be illustrated. The dim veils of romance were torn, and
the author, often under German influence, set out to hit
hard and often. Gothic architecture suffered from over-
production, and Mrs. Roche in *The Children of the Abbey*
(1796) provided no less than four edifices, a Welsh
mansion, an Irish castle and convent, and a Scottish
Abbey. Mrs. Roche and Mrs. Isabella Hedgeland
imported Gothic scenery and effects into tales (pro-
fessedly) of contemporary life, but Mrs. Hedgeland, at
least, fails to keep her footing, and towards the end of
The Ruins of Avondale Priory (1796) the portcullises
thicken, the two guilty dowagers assume a feudal complexion, and we overhear an ancient warder saying
" Methinks."

Castles and convents (to which we shall presently turn)
bring with them the theme of imprisonment, perennially
attractive to the romantic mind. What the realist has to
say about prisons is soon said, or was, before minute
psychology came into fashion. It was said by Smollett
when he described Peregrine Pickle after several months

in gaol, desperate, squalid and mulish. For the romantic mind, however, the significance of a prison is inexhaustible. It is the dark frame that enhances whatever emotions are displayed within it; it is the supreme test of virtue and the expiation of the penitent; it provides that recess (otherwise sought for on desert islands, in Arcady or the pale allegorical realms), that limited fragment of being, secluded from the complexities of social life, where consciousness is forced back on itself, friends are left alone with their love and enemies with their hatred, criminals with their guilt and saints with their God.[1] It is the instrument of tyranny and the occasion of love's triumph, as King Lear, ceasing to envisage earthly reality, believed; it is the secret altar of resignation and the secret shambles of the butcher, a charnel-house when shame corrupts there, but turned by the breath of the virtuous to an enclosed garden of lilies. The romantic minds of the eighteenth century made little use of the advantages of a prison in shaping a plot, and did not much study the ingenuities of escape. Their style was broadly emotional; prison and prisoner were not so much the factors of a problem as a symbolic picture. Godwin's *Caleb Williams* (1794) is the first novel to give a circumstantial account of an escape. Before writing it he had prepared his mind by reading criminal literature and, without sacrificing the symbolic quality of the situation—indeed, in him it is stronger than ever, reinforced as it is by his social theories,—he imported into it a keen interest in the practical aspects of escape. There is more than a suggestion of this double appeal in Holcroft's precise account of the conditions of Frank Henley's imprisonment in *Anna St. Ives* (1792), but Frank does not contrive to break prison; and we see the influence of both models in George Walker's description of his hero's imprisonment in a madhouse in *Theodore Cyphon; or, the Benevolent*

[1] Cf. Chaucer's treatment of the prison in *The Knight's Tale.*

Jew (1796), and of the persistence, ingenuity and suspense of his flight. These stories pleased the philosophers because they illustrated the power of mind over circumstance, and they pleased the public because of their strong narrative interest. It is, however, only at the end of our period that the attention of the novelist was turned to the prison-breaker; the early romance writers, who were mostly women, saw in the prisoner one more example of their favourite virtue, patient fortitude.

Contemporary events reinforced the imprisonment theme. The philanthropy of the eighteenth century cast an eye of curious horror at those grim dungeons which Europe had not yet fully outgrown. Prison conditions in England were bad enough, worse in some cases, as John Howard declared, than the corresponding conditions abroad, but the treatment meted out to serious criminals, more particularly State offenders, was nothing like so atrocious. The English public was kept in mind of the happy contrast. From time to time the *Gentleman's Magazine* overflowed with revolting details of foreign judicial procedure, while the reviewers of the *Monthly* and the *Critical* are sure to quote similar accounts in full, whenever it falls to their lot to review a book of travel. Thus English readers learned that, in Denmark, Count Struensee and Count Brand lay for weeks, weighted with iron, on the stone floor of their cells. They heard of Frederick the Great's punishment of Baron Trenck, and were soon to read in Trenck's own memoirs of the Saxon fortress of Königstein, and of the disloyal Secretary who had languished there for thirty years, without seeing the light of day. They turned to Spain and saw the Inquisition re-established and the enlightened Count Olivadez a prisoner in its dungeons, and found later in Trenck's memoirs the passage where Olivadez, escaped into safety at Paris, shows the author the marks of the torture on his body. In Portugal the fall of the Marquis of Pombal not only consigned members of his party to ingeniously hideous deaths, but raised as from the dead their long-imprisoned predecessors, clothed in rags and half-starved, together with a son of the Marquis of Tavora, who had grown up in solitary imprisonment since he was five years old, knew no language and was " in every respect in a pure state of nature." [1] In France, meanwhile, a few miles away, not yet abolished if largely disused, were *lettres de cachet,*[2] oubliettes, monastic prisons, seigneurial rights over body and life, and, summing up this whole world of abused power in two thunderous syllables, the Bastille, of whose rigours they learnt much from such books as the highly-coloured *French Inquisition* (1715) of Constantin de Renneville and the more sober and recent *Memoirs of the Bastille* (1783) of Linguet, on which Mrs. Radcliffe seems to have based the manuscript of the prisoner in *The Romance of the Forest.*[3] There were descriptions of Russian punishments, illustrated at times with plates at which the reviewer's heart sickened, anecdotes of the slave-trade, and, to fill in any possible gap, such revivals of the bloody past as Lithgow's account of

[1] Cf., e.g., *Gentleman's Magazine*, 1773, p. 515 ; *Scots Magazine*, 1772, p. 161, and 1777, p. 217 ; the account of the Venetian dungeons where prisoners stand twelve days up to the knees in putrid water among corpses in Helenus Scott's *Adventures of a Rupee* (1782) ; *The Memoirs of Henry Masers de la Tude, during a confinement of thirty-five years in the State Prisons of France* (1787) ; Trenck's *Memoirs*, translated by Holcroft (1788) among others ; Helen Maria Williams's account in her *Letters written in France* (1790) of the discovery at the Bastille of chained skeletons in subterranean dungeons, to which, or to similar material, we may trace the irrelevant chained skeletons in, e.g., *The Castle of Count Roderick* (1794) ; and the extract from Mariana Starke's *Letters from Italy* in the *Critical*, 1800, retailing the anecdote of the French soldiers, during the siege of Mantua, who found a nun fettered in a dungeon under a deserted convent. It is unnecessary to remark that it is not the authenticity of these tales that matters, but their imaginative effect.

[2] Very frequent in English novels that deal with French parental tyranny, *e.g.* Mrs. Smith's *Celestina* (1791).

[3] *v.* especially the disappointment of both prisoners that the high window, to which they manage to climb, gives only on a blank wall. With so much material, however, one cannot venture a definite ascription.

his experiences in the hands of the Inquisition at Malaga, reprinted by the *Gentleman's Magazine* in 1776.   And presently came the Terror to provide sensation hot and hot.

It will be readily seen how all this material lent itself to the purposes of the terror-monger, whose dreadful compositions in dripping dungeons, stained instruments, and putrid or mangled flesh increase in number and violence as the public temperature rises with the insecurity and excitement of the French Revolution.[1]   But physical horror was not the emotion that the first Gothic romance-writers tried to raise.   They had to preserve the dignity of the human body and bear witness to the supremacy of the soul.   With the selective licence of romance, they left dirt and vermin out of account, ignored tedium, and defied the power of unremitting oppression to produce imbecility of mind.   The secretary, of whom Trenck tells, was more like a wild beast than a man after his thirty years' imprisonment, but the Marchesa Mazzini [2] walks out of her subterranean cell with collected piety, and, for all we hear to the contrary, as neat as a new pin.   Prolonged imprisonment in secret vaults occurs often in these books, and once more contemporary journalism provides sources and illustrations of this theme.   Louis XVI released an unhappy prisoner, whose guilt was having spoken ill of the late King, from a forty years' captivity in the Bastille.[3] The reverberating fall of that fortress [4] set other rumours afloat, and Lord Massereene, an Irish peer, who had been imprisoned for debt in the Châtelet, in the first place, and,

---

[1] Cf. Lewis's *Monk*, and, for a more moderate treatment of the theme, Ann Yearsley, the Bristol milkwoman's *Royal Captives* (1795), a story of real power and deep feeling, though both naïve and melodramatic in expression.   The plot is founded on the mystery of the Man in the Iron Mask.

[2] v. Mrs. Radcliffe, *A Sicilian Romance* (1790).

[3] v. *Scots Magazine*, 1774, p. 321.

[4] In 1789, *The Memoirs of Charles Townly, written by himself*, appeared, containing a good section on the hero's imprisonment in the Bastille; before the end of the year, the book was provided with a new title-page, *The Bastille ; or the History of Charles Townly*.

on attempting to escape, transferred to a dungeon under the Seine, where " his beard grew to a most immoderate length," landed at Dover, and, jumping out of the boat, fell on his knees, kissed the ground thrice, and exclaimed : " God bless the land of liberty." [1] In fiction, the victim of such an imprisonment is usually presumed dead by the world, and the tyrant has thus a free field for his revenge or his lust. We are not to imagine, however, that ten years or so can weaken the divine authority of virtue, and Stephen Cullen, who exposes the hero's mother to the solicitations of an Abbot for nearly twenty years, preserves her unsullied to the end.[2] " The patience of this lover we cannot but admire," said the *Critical*.

It was the Marchesa Mazzini who set the fashion in England for these returns from the dead, but an earlier example is found in the history of the Duchess of C—— in Mme. de Genlis's *Adèle et Théodore* (1782).[3] Mme. de Genlis declares in a footnote that this story of a jealous husband who imprisoned his wife for nine years in a subterranean cavern, without light, is true in its essentials, and that she has met the lady. However this may be, she alone makes some faint attempt to trace the effects of such an imprisonment. The Duchess cannot bear the slightest light, and has almost forgotten how to read and write ; her greatest consolation has been the weak whisper of thunder that penetrated to her during the heaviest storms. Mrs. Radcliffe did not repeat the extravagant situation ; in her next book she resisted the temptation to resurrect Adeline's father, and thus left unspoilt the authentic, if rhetorical, pathos of the manuscript which his daughter

---

[1] v. *Gentleman's Magazine*, 1789, pp. 66 and 752.

[2] v. *The Haunted Priory : or, the Fortunes of the House of Rayo. A Romance founded partly on historical facts* (1794). This book was published anonymously. In 1796 appeared *The Castle of Inchvally : a Tale, alas ! too true. By Stephen Cullen, Author of the Haunted Priory*.

[3] *Adèle et Théodore, ou Letters sur l'Education* (1782), translated in 1783 as *Adelaide and Theodore ; or, Letters on Education*.

finds.   She had set a fashion, however, and it was followed to such an extent that the experienced reader of the Gothic Romance hesitates to believe in the death of anybody, especially if it be a parent or a wife.   Yet Mme. de Genlis's suggestions were not taken up, and no attempt was made to procure the willing suspension of our disbelief until 1798, when Harriet Lee, according to the *Critical*, judiciously varied the trite incident by the derangement of the sufferer.[1]   This " decline of intellect is finely conceived," wrote the reviewer;   " it is the probable effect of long and solitary confinement."   It is;   but nothing illustrates more clearly the wilfulness of eighteenth-century romance than its reluctance to consider the fact.[2]

A similarly wilful bias, this time in the direction of melodrama, is obvious whenever the story approaches a convent.   The dealings of the literary men of Protestant England in the eighteenth century with the institutions of the Roman Catholic Church are a little disingenuous. They are very conscious of the picturesque attractions of convents, vows of celibacy, confession and penance; they are seduced by the emotional possibilities of the situations that can be based on these usages;   but they seldom fail to make it quite clear that they regard the usages as superstitious and irrational, and, if they did, there was not wanting a critic to blame this " attempt to gloss over the follies of popery, or to represent its absurdities as sacred." [3]   Thus Mrs. Radcliffe, having intro-

---

[1] *v.* her *Canterbury Tales*, Vol. I, *The Frenchman's Tale.   Constance* (1797).

[2] Ellis Cornelia Knight in her optimistic continuation of *Rasselas*, *Dinarbas* (1790), devotes Rasselas to solitary confinement for months, without books or conversation.   He sustains himself by studying the scenery.

[3] *v. Critical*, March 1792, on Mrs. Mary Robinson's *Vancenza*. Mrs. Robinson, who was liberal and " philosophic " in her sympathies, was very careful to make this clear in her next romance, *Hubert de Sevrac* (1796).   Critics sometimes refused to accept an author's premisses, if these were based on Catholic usages;   thus the *Critical*, reviewing Mrs. Bennett's *Agnes de Courci* (1789), denied

duced a monk's tomb as a picturesque property in *The Romance of the Forest*, is careful to express through the mouth of Louis La Motte her real opinion of monasticism. " Peace be to his soul," soliloquizes the young man; " but did he think a life of mere negative virtue deserves an eternal reward ? Mistaken man ! reason, had you trusted its dictates, would have informed you, that the active virtues, the adherence to the golden rule, ' Do as you would be done unto,' could alone deserve the favour of a Deity, whose glory is benevolence." From Addison's *Theodosius and Constantia*, however, to Jerningham's *Death of Arabert, Monk of La Trappe* (1771), the conflict of love and vows was a recognized source of pathos, and Mrs. Radcliffe seized on it in *A Sicilian Romance* when she made the nun Cornelia die at the high altar in her lover's presence, in " a fine devotional glow." [1] Mrs. Radcliffe's convent is one of those odd affairs, imagined by Gothic romancists, where monks and nuns in adjacent buildings are shepherded by an abbot. Jerningham, who, as a Catholic, should have had more discretion, yet introduces Arabert's mistress into La Trappe, where she lives as a monk, unknown to her lover.[2] Ignorance enhanced the charm of this material. There were no convents in England, and though a certain number of English girls attended French convent-schools, where

---

the enormity of a breach of celibacy. There is in some novels a mild plea for a " Protestant nunnery " (e.g. *Indiana Danby*, 1765), but the motive is not so much religious as social ; such an institution would be a centre of good works and a means of disposing unmarried women.

[1] On the other hand, the Catholic Mrs. Inchbald dealt with the theme in *A Simple Story* (1791) discreetly and delicately. Dorriforth, though charmed, does not love till released from his vows ; it is the Protestant girl, unaccustomed to associate a sacred prohibition with any man, who is enmeshed.

[2] Jerningham was educated at Douai, though he later became a Protestant. La Trappe captured English imaginations ; cf. George Keate's *Sketches from Nature* (1779). There were also French handlings of the subject ; v. Baculard d'Arnaud's *Comte de Comminges*.

there were also to be found poor Englishwomen living cheaply as parlour-boarders, such information as they could supply did not seriously affect the readiness of the novel-reading public to believe that any extravagance could happen in such a setting ; [1] moreover, to set against authentic accounts, such as Father Isla's *Fray Gerundo de Campazos* (translated in 1772), there were the secret violences divulged by Baculard d'Arnaud and Jean Gaspard Dubois-Fontenelle.   Out of two pictures, both hailing from Catholic countries, the Protestant public were bound to choose the more lurid, thus providing themselves not only with emotional excitement, but with a thrill of that warm complacency which always stole through a British bosom when meditating Continental tyrannies.

Dubois-Fontenelle's *Effects of the Passions, or Memoirs of Floricourt*, translated in 1788, though written some twenty years before, was a fine anthology of monastic horrors for the nascent Gothic Romance to draw on.   The author, who had failed to get his anti-ecclesiastical drama *La Vestale* past the censor, but had nevertheless seen it enjoy a good circulation, packed into his novel as many strong situations as it would hold.   We begin with Floricourt's beloved, Julia, who has been forced into a convent by her father.   The lovers meet and plight their troth in the burial vaults under the church ; their attempted escape, however, is frustrated, for Floricourt is late at his grisly trysting-place, and Julia, having dropped her lamp and overcome by terror, is on the point of death when he finds her, and expires in his arms.   The second volume shifts to secular prisons, but the third presents us with the story of M. and Mme. Vareuil. Vareuil, made a monk at fourteen, is detected in lewd

---

[1] A few quietly-authentic convent settings can be found, though the story they enclose is frequently improbable.   This is the case with *Anecdotes of a Convent* (1771) by the author of *Memoirs of Mrs. Williams;* here the plot is concerned with a boy, bred up in a convent as a girl, and believing himself to be one ; the author declares that the story is true.

offences, subjected to inhuman discipline and finally immured for life in a secret and devilishly ingenious dungeon (the monastery possessed at least four of these). The walls are undermined by flood, and he escapes and marries in England, but years later is lured back and recaptured. His wife follows him into the monastery, where she lives disguised as a monk, and at length effects his escape from a subterranean iron cage, only to see him die in her arms of exhaustion. These are the effects of the passions of love and cruelty, and for all the theatrical extravagance of the story, there is in it a sense of frenzied beating against the bars, of possible agonies and possible perversions of the human mind, which differentiates it from the English treatments of such themes. Some vestige of reality, some trace of true indignation, are discernible under these hyperboles; but they are not discernible in the *Monk*.

It was the asceticisms of conventual life that attracted the English imagination, and now the range was extended from Addison's melancholy resignation, which by no means fell out of use, to include these French savageries. An alternative line of treatment—the ribald—is perennial and universal, and hardly needs comment, except to observe that, when the salt of humour evaporated, the lasciviousness of priests, monks and nuns added an ugly ingredient to the hellish brew of the sensational writer. In the 'seventies a recalcitrant daughter is often imprisoned in a nunnery, and exposed to the unkindness of a bigoted, venal abbess; but by the 'nineties she is exposed to much more than that.[1] "Nunnery-tale books" had been a well-known class before the Gothic Romance came to give the material a more picturesque turn. They had been, as a rule, scandalously indecent;

[1] For priestly villainy v. *Santa Maria, or the Mysterious Pregnancy* (1797) by Joseph Fox. A priest, now penitent, confesses to drugging and violating nuns, and then suffering them to be buried in a state of trance.

but the union of lasciviousness and terror, outlined in many anecdotes, recorded in travel-books and made current by the reviews, was first thoroughly worked by M. G. Lewis in *The Monk* (1795). This scandalous book (" Yes ! the author of the Monk signs himself LEGIS-LATOR," wrote Coleridge in the *Critical;* " we stare ! and tremble ") is pervaded by a sort of excitable heat. Lewis lets his fancy dwell on amorous encounters among the corruptions of burial vaults, on an imprisoned mother, caressing her putrid babe, on the forcing of innocence and the state of a man after torture. He acknowledged that he was inspired by *The Mysteries of Udolpho*, and Mrs. Radcliffe must have felt that he had both stolen and debased her thunder. She had herself touched on monastic themes in her early work, *A Sicilian Romance*, and in Germany, whither she went to look for copy for a new book, she had caught impressive glimpses of conventual life—a nun in prayer under a pointed arch, black-cowled monks striding under the cliffs at Boppart—which she still wished to embody in it ; she had also, it seems, read *Herman of Unna*, and seen in the baldly-described incident of a girl's captivity in a mountain-convent an opportunity for her picturesque pen. Whether or no the further stimulus of Lewis's *Monk* was needed to complete *The Italian*, at all events in that, the last romance published in her lifetime, she made a gallant attempt to redeem the subject of monastic tyranny, and to treat it in a manner that should be quite terrible and yet consistent with perfect delicacy. In *The Italian* there is no lust and no luxurious cruelty ; in place of them there is bigotry and ambition. There are no scenes of blood, but there is that " dreadful hieroglyphic," the straw mattress of the unknown dead nun. The lovers break no vows, for Mrs. Radcliffe did not care for rebels, and turned aside from the criminal, unless uncommonly majestic. But there is the Church of the Dominican Convent, with

Schedoni in silent penance; and there is San Stefano, that stately nightmare among the Apennines, with its airy prison, its secret cells and the gorgeous pomp of its pilgrimage shrine. There is also, towards the end of the story, a good abbess who governs her convent in enlightened fashion, and this, no doubt, Mrs. Radcliffe felt, kept the balance true. The material is carried to the highest pitch of the picturesque. It has, of course, no religious bearing, for what religion there is in *The Italian*—and Mrs. Radcliffe, reticent as she is, sometimes lets her quiet faith become apparent—is undogmatic and uninstitutional. Nor does she develop the psychological aspects of her subject, in which direction alone there was a possibility of advance. Failing this, it hovered in other hands between the picturesque and the sensational. It did not lose favour, however. In particular, the living tomb of the unchaste nun continued to provide a " grateful horror," and was handled by Sir Walter Scott in *Marmion* [1] in the best romantic manner. He knew better, however, than to introduce it into a novel, and the *Monastery* is a human place.

The display of ecclesiastical tyranny in *The Italian* is not completed until Vivaldi has been led through the dungeons of the Inquisition at Rome, and has stood trembling among masked familiars before his judges in their black-draped hall. And here we have to record one small but delightful act of defiance on the part of the Shakespeare of Romance-writers. Grosley's *New Observations on Italy and its Inhabitants* had been her stand-by in certain sections of *The Mysteries of Udolpho*, and still, apparently, lingered in her mind. But Grosley had belittled the power of the Roman Inquisition in the most unromantic way; for over a hundred years, he said, it had passed no capital sentence; " everything there is trans-

---

[1] The convent scenes of *Marmion* are very like those in Mrs. Isabella Hedgland's *Baron's Daughter* (1802), which also play at Lindisfarne; but the material was common.

acted in private by spiritual and pecuniary penalties."
Now Grosley was in Rome in 1758, and it was in that very
year—for she dates *The Italian* with superfluous exactness
—that Vivaldi heard the groans of the tortured and was
himself bound on the rack.[1]   It was inevitable that the
Gothic Romance and the later Tale of Terror should turn
to the Inquisition for material.   It had always filled a
large place in the English imagination, which was familiar
with its outer forms, its espionage system, the silent
removal of its victim by night, the black-hung torture-
chamber, the great crucifixes, the candles and the hooded
attendants.   From   being   the   object   of   Protestant
abomination it had become the object of philosophic
disapproval; or, rather, both emotions combined in the
eighteenth century to make this theme an eminently lively
one.   The picaresque found room for it,[2] and in 1771
there came out a book which in its subject-matter though
not in its treatment anticipates some of the most thrilling
features of the Gothic Romance.   This is the *Adventures
of a Jesuit ;* and the noticeable thing about it is that, in
the character of Don Bertram de Torres, it provides an
early sketch of the powerful, ubiquitous man of mystery,
who thrusts himself into the hero's life to act in some sort
as his guardian, and, after assuming a variety of disguises,
turns out to be a familiar of the Inquisition.   The tale
is a puzzle rather than a mystery, for the author does not
know his own mind, and misses opportunities all through
the book; but the material was there, and it needed only
the romantic vision to colour it.   Here, as in many other
cases, the curiosity of the eighteenth century had peered
into a subject which the romance-writers were to com-
mandeer; they knew the facts, but limited their imaginative participation, and kept their defences up; whereas

[1] Cf. my article, " Ramond, Grosley and Mrs. Radcliffe," *Review
of English Studies*, July 1929.
[2] *v., e.g.,* Charles Johnstone's *Chrysal ; or, the Adventures of a
Guinea.*

the romance-writers first filled these terrors with life, and then deliberately exposed their sensibilities to them.

One need not assume that Mrs. Radcliffe knew *The Adventures of a Jesuit*, although in *The Italian* she does link the Inquisition—not, it is true, very closely—with the figure of a man of mystery, the confessor, Schedoni. The plan of that book, the first half of which is dominated by Schedoni, who, in the second, summons up the dread society to fill the scene, and himself shrinks before it, is much closer to the plan of certain German romances, which became known in England between 1794 and 1796, namely, Schiller's *Ghost-Seer, or Apparitionist*, Cajetan Tschink's *Victim of Magical Delusions, or the Mystery of the Revolution in P——l, a magico-political tale*, and Marquis Grosse's *Genius*, on the second translation of which was bestowed the famous title *Horrid Mysteries*. To these we may add, though the likeness is not so close, Benedicte Naubert's *Herman of Unna*.[1] All four concern the activities of powerful secret societies (if the Inquisition may be included, for the sake of expediency, in such a description), and in the first three the appearance of the society is heralded by that of a mysterious, austere and yet attractive man, who ultimately proves to be an associate of the society. The pattern was Schiller's,[2] and the theme, with its political and magical ingredients, was of common interest to Western Europe. At the end of the eighteenth century, rumours of secret societies and widespread conspiracies flew thick. Great changes were in progress, and men of liberal sympathies and men tenacious of ancient forms of life were alike prone to see something

[1] The order of translation was :—*Herman of Unna* (1794), ascribed to Professor Cramer ; *The Ghost-Seer* (1795) ; *The Victim of Magical Delusions*, by P. Will (1795) and *The Genius*, which was twice translated in 1796, as *The Genius : or the Mysterious Adventures of Don Carlos de Grandez*, by Joseph Trapp, and as *Horrid Mysteries* by P. Will. Only the first half of *The Ghost-Seer* was translated in 1795.

[2] No connection with *The Adventures of a Jesuit* need be supposed. Such resemblances as can be detected are inherent in the subject.

monstrous and abnormal in each other's activities. Many
strands went to form this web, which shimmers with
different colours as it is viewed from different angles.
The Jesuits, whose Order had been suspended by the
Pope in 1773, had found refuge in Prussia, where Protestant imaginations credited them with persistent activity.
The Spanish Inquisition, reduced at one time to a mere
College of Inquiry, had been re-established in its full
powers some five years later. This was an ominous sign
of the gathering strength and oblique methods of the
forces of reaction. On the other hand, Conservatives
saw in philosophers and reformers banded conspirators
against Church and State, and their apprehension
increased to panic under the pressure of the French
Revolution. A fantastic element enriched the confusion
in the stories of occult powers, their practitioners and the
discipline required for initiation. Here we are on
debatable ground, on the confines of magic and science,
of moral idealism and charlatanry, of all that is most
seductive to the imagination of man and most perilous
to his reason. Cagliostro might grow old in his Italian
prison, but the philosopher's stone did not lose its attractive power. Rosicrucianism was a beneficent mystery
or a sinister deceit. Freemasonry either liberated the
spirit of man and forwarded the era of his perfection, or,
by relaxing moral restraints, plunged him into cynical
debauchery. The enthusiasts for hidden wisdom do not
express themselves through the novel,—or, at least, no
such novels reached England before the turn of the
century; rather, we find the skilled intriguer, making
use of this false glamour to lure an ardent young man to
initiation in order that he may commit his will and all his
resources to the service of the society. Freemasonry and
Illuminism were constantly associated with infidelity and
political liberalism, but the attractions of natural magic,
the mummery of magic-lanterns, explosive powders and

combined mirrors, could be adapted equally well to the purposes of the reactionary party. We have thus a shifting phantasmagoria of bewitchment, from which there emerges the notion of some widely-ramified secret society, subversive in its aims and formidable in its strength, wielding or simulating occult powers by means of which its ignorant tools are controlled, but in its ultimate nature, when the last grades are passed, sceptical and anarchic. Germany, which, owing to the tolerance of Frederick the Great and the tyranny of other governments, seethed with societies, where prophets appeared who practised animal magnetism, professed to raise the dead, or to live a thousand years upon a tea,[1] was a fruitful bed for these fantastic ideas, but even in England, where elemental spirits and natural magic were not taken very seriously, the disturbed atmosphere of the revolutionary period caused the idea of a grand political conspiracy to take root, though in shallow soil, and to bear some astounding fruits. Thus there were found English adherents to the theories of Abbé Barruel, who, in his *Memoires pour servir à l'histoire du Jacobinisme* (1797–8), maintains that the French Revolution was due to a threefold interacting conspiracy of the philosophers against religion, the Freemasons against kings, and the Illuminists (an inner ring of sceptics, using the superstitious lower grades to further their secret aim) against organized society. This theory gave the Jacobins an ancestry reaching back through the Knights Templar to the Manichees; and certainly, in comparison with bearing blame oneself, it must have seemed almost tolerable to have been undone by so far-reaching, long-prepared, diabolically ingenious a conspiracy. We had also extravagances of native growth, for John Robison, Professor of Natural Philosophy at Edinburgh, produced *Proofs of a Conspiracy against all the Religions and Governments of Europe, carried on in the*

[1] Cf. Lady Craven's *Memoirs* (1826).

Secret Meetings of Free Masons, Illuminati and Reading Societies (1797), which proofs are adduced in favour of the same contentions as Barruel's. We need enter no further into these superficially intricate, but really over-simplified, explanations of a vast political change. Barruel's and Robison's books were published just after the translations of the German stories, but they serve to show how receptive the reading public was to this new form of romantic terror.

As a literary theme the secret society takes many shapes. Schiller dealt with the Inquisition, Tschink with a political conspiracy, while the writers of chivalric romances found equivalents in the past in knightly brotherhoods and especially, as in *Herman of Unna*, in the Secret Tribunal of Westphalia. The aim of Marquis Grosse's society is impressively vague. The title *Horrid Mysteries*, by which the romance was known to Shelley and Miss Austen, obscures the intention of the author, whose skill is chiefly seen in the changing aspects, now sinister, now seductive, under which the society appears to the young hero, as he alternately breaks its chains and submits to them again. All the books have in common those heart-shaking moments, when the ground rings suddenly hollow under a young man's feet, when incidents, believed fortui-tous, are seen to be pregnant with disquieting meaning, and he gropes onward, to find his energy baffled at every point, until he is precipitated into the appalling, though still only half-understood power of the society. Such moments as these invited imitation, although the German theme as a whole was not naturalized in England, and as many of them as would bear transplanting were reset by Mrs. Radcliffe in the Inquisition scenes of *The Italian*. Meanwhile in Schedoni, whose towering figure commands the earlier part of the book, we see clear traces of the man of mystery,—the Armenian, the Irishman, Grosse's stranger with the petrifying eye,—who first enmeshes the hero; and through this channel the German romances made a picturesque and influential contribution to English literature, for Byron, whose heroes trace their lineage on one side through Milton's Satan to Prometheus, did not disdain to borrow for them a physiognomy of more recent invention. The face that is the frozen mask of extinct passions, the piercing eye that none can endure unabashed, the supple charm of bearing which at need replaces the accustomed austerity,—these are the mark of Schiller's Armenian, and to these Grosse added the convulsions when the exhausted passions momentarily revive. Mrs. Radcliffe blurred the outlines with Gothic gloom, and, by dissolving the close connection between her man of mystery and her society—for Schedoni has no voice in the Inquisition, by whose aid he hopes to work—left him in lonely dignity.[1] It was an attractive legacy, and was not allowed to rust.

Mrs. Radcliffe does not conciliate our sympathy for her criminal, majestic as he is, though it is plain that, in common with her age, she felt the attraction of great energy of character, and saw that this can be most easily expressed in a conflict with the forces of organized society. Schiller's *Robbers*, we are told, was one of her favourite books. The attitude of the romantic mind towards guilt was undergoing an important change of fashion during the last ten years of the eighteenth century. Whereas the favourite subject of contemplation had been repentance and expiation, the interest now shifts to the passionate excesses that precede them, and presently repentance ceases to be the most popular sequel to crime, and yields to a picturesque defiance. English narrative verse during the last thirty years of the century had been full of hermits, exceedingly contrite (mostly with good reason) and not

---

[1] The connection between the *Ghost-Seer* and *The Italian* in point of incident, especially in the first meeting of Vivaldi and the monk, has often been noted; I have not seen any allusion to Schedoni's expression, which seems to be modelled on the Armenian; *v.* Appendix IV.

always old; they even overflowed into the novel, and John Potter's *Curate of Coventry* (1771) seems to have included a penitent libertine, a peer of the realm, domiciled in a hermitage somewhere on the road between Coventry and London. This was in the eighteenth century; [1] but romance, with its excursions into the past, gives a much wider scope to the activities of the hermit. He buries himself in the Syrian wilderness, after failing to get killed in a Crusade; he retires to caverns and vaults beneath ruined castles, where he achieves remarkable feats of engineering and the applied arts; he is found, a generation after his transgression, in gloomy contemplation of the embalmed relics of his victim; if, however, he is summoned to resume his old place in society, he reappears very little the worse for wear, and takes up his duties with a chastened melancholy. He never submits to the discipline of a regular order, for by a curious convention, while hermits, even ex-criminals, are virtuous, monks are not. This distinction is even more heavily emphasized in the German romances, where the bad eminence of the monastic orders is shared by castle chaplains. It is, at root, one more instance of anti-Roman prejudice. A monk is part of the organization of the Church of Rome; so is a chaplain; but a hermit need not be so considered. He secludes himself at the bidding of his own conscience, and in the haze of romantic melancholy which envelops

---

[1] A representative list of hermits in the novel has some interest. Fielding's Man of the Hill in *Tom Jones* might be taken as a starting-point. John Potter's *Arthur O'Bradley* (1769) contains the recluse Bentley, who lives in a wood, in a hermitage built of roots, while in *The Spiritual Quixote* (1772) we find the conscience-struck solitary, Graham, inhabiting a rock-perched dwelling. *Female Stability* (1780) by Miss Palmer is provided with two hermits, one penitent and one pensive. Mr. Albany in *Cecilia* (1782) must be considered as a sub-type. In *Zoraida, or Village Annals* (1787) a penitent lives in a cave, and in Anne Fuller's *The Convent : or the History of Miss Sophia Nelson* (1786) a sentimental young recluse retires to a cave in a wood. All these are books that play in England in the eighteenth century. In *Maria, or the Vicarage* (1796) we find a Polish count keeping sheep in Switzerland, with a broken pitcher and Locke on the *Human Understanding* in his cell.

him creeds and churches are easily confounded. Nevertheless, even here the usual parenthetical warnings against superstition are not wholly lacking.

Repentance, however, attractive as it was, had never wholly satisfied the desires of the reading-public. Who is it that repents? Not common human wilfulness, but a baron " black with complicated guilt," or a " supereminently villainous " knight. More and more, as the century draws to its close, readers of all kinds, from the cultured Dr. Nathan Drake to the mere novel-taster, no longer content with the compensations of sensibility, groped towards the colossal, the impassioned, the dark sublime. They wanted to see great forces let loose and the stature of man once more distended to its full height, even if it were stretched on the rack. They wanted to see him ablaze with destructive fire or tempered by his will to an icy ruthlessness; they wanted to see him stride over the laws of man and affront the laws of God; they wanted vehemence and tumult, and measureless audacity and measureless egoism, Othello, in fact, and Richard III, and Satan, and Pierre, moving through the intrigue of a novel and engineering its effects; and when audacity was defeated, they did not want the defeat to be met—as they began to realize—by an abject collapse; rather let irreconcilable pride still brave the lightning. The rebel, a figure never far from human sympathies, is entering on his most prolonged period of popularity. The full development falls outside our limits, but already in the 'eighties there are unmistakable signs of what is coming. On the one hand, the conventional moral ending wholly fails to cover (it was probably not intended to cover) the sympathetic excitement roused by the aspect of uncontrolled passion. It was exhilarating in a circumspect world to feel that the human mind was after all capable of this abandon, that it had something to show akin to the destructive glories of those storms in which amateurs

of the picturesque delighted.[1]   On the other hand, something like the will-worship of the Renascence is again
warming popular imagination.   To be sure, the first and
most careful study of the complete egoist, Dr. John
Moore's *Zeluco* (1789), is quite devoid of the romantic
glamour of guilt.   Moore was as sound a moralist as Dr.
Johnson himself, and Zeluco is no " archangel ruined,"
but an undisciplined and selfish man, whose nature
hardens in craft and cruelty as it loses in courage, and who
has no resource against boredom but in the gratification
of his sense of power.   Yet such a figure, though not
romanticized, was meat for the romantic mood.   He is
the man apart, who will not share the destiny of common
man or his charities; and presently romantic sentiment
was to make much of his loneliness, to throw over his
crimes and his defiance a mantle of specious majesty, to
heighten his momentary twinges of remorse to an aching
malady, and to cancel his failure in courage.   Zeluco is
not, of course, the only model, but he is the first adequate
portrait of this character in the novel.   Shakespeare and
the later dramatists contributed much and Milton more,
while painters—Salvator Rosa and Caravaggio—supplied
the picturesque of the figure.   Thus it grew, by traceable

---

[1] Cf. *Death's a Friend* (1788) by the author of *The Bastard*.   The
hero unwittingly falls in love with his niece, and, on discovering the
relationship, gives the rein to his emotions in solitude, is brought near
suicide, begins to recover, and is killed in a duel.   His first letter
exhibits his state.   " You condemn the impetuosity, the madness
as you term it of my passions and affections.   I glory in it, and more
than equally despise your cool, philosophic, calm indifference.   I
was born to feel every sensation in the most violent extreme, and
though I suffer at this time agonies, which your constitution keeps
you exempt from and ignorant of the force of, I would rather be
their eternal victim than be capable only of lukewarm emotions."
There was felt to be something laudable in this point of view.   A
cult of passionately indiscreet heroes develops.   Mrs. Robinson's
Walsingham (1798) loads himself with voluntary and involuntary
transgressions.   Passionate excesses were considered a sign of a rich
nature.   Charles Meadows in Ann Plumptre's *Rector's Son* (1798),
being present with his estranged Amelia at a Methodist sermon, " drew
a knife from his pocket, and darting a wild and furious look at her,
plunged it into his breast, exclaiming : " Traitress, this is your deed."

degrees, towards its culminating incarnation in the hands of Byron. We do not follow it farther than those of Mrs. Radcliffe, whose Schedoni—mysterious tyrant of himself and others—is never allowed to establish a claim on our sympathy, though he does on our admiration. Black was black to Mrs. Radcliffe, and white was white, and there must be no tampering with them; but great force of will, however perverse its channel, was a stimulating spectacle to her, and her thrilled response gave to Schedoni (and in a less degree to Montoni in the *Mysteries of Udolpho*) a vitality and consequently an influence much greater than those of her other characters.

The craving for Titanic passions was fed by German drama—which for the English public meant Kotzebue and the early Schiller—and the German novel, and grew with what it fed on. "The author delights in the enormous," wrote the *Monthly Review* [1] of Schiller; and German taste, as represented by the work that found its way into England, came to connote wild extravagance of sentiment and incident, passion wound up to the highest pitch, horror, grotesqueness, and the expression of all these qualities in inflated language.[2] A favourite theme was the abnormal conflict, frequently conditioned by oaths or mysteries, between kinsmen or friends; in *The Robbers* brother is set against brother, and in *Herman of Unna* friend stabs friend, reluctantly carrying out the orders of the Secret Tribunal. "In general it may be remarked of this class of stories," wrote Taylor of the latter book, "that, by familiarizing characters of a stronger sinew than are common, crimes of a bolder enormity, and modes of coercion which the tolerance of a polished age has

[1] Feb. 1797.
[2] The first—very small—instalment of German fiction to be imported gave a quite different impression. Of *Henrietta of Gerstenfeld*, translated in 1787, the *Critical* wrote: "Is it in consequence of our common ancestry that we feel a congenial warmth for everything of German origin? Or do we only approve of their writings because of the strong, sound, good sense which is observable in every page?"

renounced, they tend to suggest a revival of the heroic in virtue and in vice, and to prepare the general mind for contemplating, with complacence, a sort of characters, the influence of which may not prove very compatible with the " monotonous tranquillity of modern states." [1] Germany soon rivalled Italy as the land of romance ; by 1792 a heroine's accomplishments include German,[2] and a year later the Minerva Press had discovered Central Europe.[3]   It was in Central Europe, a few years later, that St. Leon [4] met Bethlem Gabor, that gigantic misanthropist, and, while feeling the effects of his superhuman hatred, still recognized in him " the sublime desolation of a lofty soul."

We have seen the romantic mood, in its dealings with prisons, tyranny and guilt, reshaping for its own purposes material which, in its naked ghastliness, it is not tolerable to contemplate.   As a rule the romance-writers betray no misgivings.   Author and audience have entered into a mutual compact of non-realization, as they do in the modern murder-story.   But there was one subject which did, at least at first, demand some consideration, and that was the supernatural.   Romance deals gladly with the supernatural, finding it accommodating material, equally stimulating and obscure ; it was a necessary part of the atmosphere of old castles, and there were precedents for it in Shakespeare and Ossian ; but the whole sense of the age of enlightenment had been against the propagation of superstition, and, in spite of *The Castle of Otranto*, the subject was surrounded with embarrassments.   The conscience of the writer, the appetite of the reader, the jocose associations with turnip-ghosts and horse-play, the anxiety of critics lest youth should be misled and

[1] v. *Monthly Review*, Sept. 1794.
[2] v. *Orlando and Lavinia*.
[3] v. Mrs. Parsons's books, *The Castle of Wolfenbach ; a German Story* (1793), *The Mysterious Warning, a German Tale* (1796), and many others.
[4] v. Godwin's *St. Leon* (1800).

ground lost in the fight with barbarism,—all fell to be considered by the serious writers who were the pioneers of the Gothic style. Miss Reeve allowed the minimum of supernatural agency; Miss Lee did without it; Mrs. Radcliffe was lavish in supernatural suggestions, but explained them nearly all away afterwards. It was this compromise, so unsatisfactory to later generations, that was most popular in its own. The explanations preserved " probability," and readers could indulge in romantic sensations without " hoodwinking their reason ";[1] and, since sensibility had taught them to dissociate the value of an emotion from the validity of its cause, they did not resent being cheated into their tremors. Critics pointed out the danger of bathos in these explanations,[2] but on the whole they preferred them to the authentic supernatural, and were not very ready to extend to prose fiction the licence enjoyed by poetry of introducing the real ghost. The best defence of the explanatory method, however, comes in the next generation, as the result of a deliberate effort of sympathy on the part of Sergeant Talfourd, Mrs. Radcliffe's biographer. What matters, he writes, is not the objective truth of the apparition, but the tremblings of the human spirit in its supposed presence, since these are the " secret witnesses of our alliance with power which is not of this world." These affinities are implanted in our nature and lend dignity to an emotion which, though cheated in the specific instance, is of deep

---

[1] v. Coleridge's review of *The Mysteries of Udolpho*, in the *Monthly Review*, Nov. 1794 : " The reader experiences in perfection the strange luxury of artificial terror," he writes with some disingenuousness, " without being obliged for a moment to hoodwink his reason, or to yield to the weakness of superstitious credulity." Cf. d'Israeli, *Vaurien*, Bk. I, ch. xi (1797) : " Of our miraculous writers, there have been a few who have so far felt a reverence for venerable nature, as modestly to explain supernatural appearances by natural causes ; and assuredly their ingenuity deserves commendation, while their torture excites compassion."

[2] v., e.g., *Monthly*, Oct. 1795, on *The Abbey of St. Asaph, Critical*, Appendix, April 1796, on Mme. de Genlis's *Knights of the Swan*, and May 1796 on *The Rose of Raby*.

significance. It is a subtle plea, and a generation of romantic poetry had gone to shape it; even so it could by no stretch of charity apply to any other of the Gothic romances. Mrs. Radcliffe alone is not shamed by its grave echo.

The first notable scene of the explained supernatural precedes our period by a few years, and is one of the fruitful experiments of Smollett. Melvil, in *Ferdinand, Count Fathom* (1753), lamenting his lost Monimia in a church at midnight, hears " a few solemn notes issuing from the organ, which seemed to feel the impulse of an invisible hand," and presently sees a white figure, whom he takes for her spirit. It is, of course, Monimia in flesh and blood, and Melvil, restored to happiness, is soon partaking with her of a small but elegant collation in the vestry. Smollett, who had used the mock-supernatural for the purposes of farce, here gives the situation a serious turn, develops its picturesque aspects and embalms it in " atmosphere." Under this treatment it yields a delicious shudder. Smollett's experiment was not forgotten, though for some twenty years it was but sparely imitated.[1] Then, with the appearance of Gothic Romance, it becomes suddenly fertile. Lights flicker in uninhabited wings; doors clash and bells toll, spectral voices sound from hidden passages; vague figures flit along the battlements; icy hands greet us in the dark. And all these manifestations, before the book ends, are strictly ascribed to natural causes, and thus reason is satisfied. At most, we are left with a dream, a justified premonition, vague hauntings from the confines of our nature, which reason did not intercept. This was Mrs. Radcliffe's method, and with writers who made any pretensions to literature

---

[1] Examples of the explained supernatural, handled romantically, before Mrs. Radcliffe are found in a passage in Miss E. Blower's *Maria* (1785), where the heroine wanders about an old castle by night, and *The Spectre* (1789), where the hero is followed by his betrothed, whom he believes dead, but who acts the part of his coloured valet by day, and at intervals appears as a ghost.

it remained the most popular. Occasionally, however, it was abandoned in favour of Miss Reeve's stately, deputed spectres. Such a variation is to be found in Stephen Cullen's *Haunted Priory* (1794), a book which, in spite of many and serious flaws, has real poetic force in its supernatural scenes. It tells how the young heir of the house of Rayo is supernaturally led to discover and avenge his father's murder; how, riding alone on Christmas Eve through the moonlit Sierra Morena, he follows a figure of more than human size into a dark plain, surrounded by mountains, fights his way through a sudden storm, comes to a lighted church, and cuts a path with his sword through brambles to a low side door; how, kneeling in the garnished, empty church, he hears voices of invisible beings celebrate the midnight Mass, until lights and music are swallowed up in darkness and hideous noises, and he falls into a deep slumber, crossed by dreams, in which a mailed figure demands vengeance of him and presents him with a key; how he wakes in the morning to find the church a ruin and the key in his hand. The sequel of the adventure finely maintains the suspense. As the avengers march through the darkness, the rattle of armour and the tramp of a single footfall go before them. They toil feverishly among the rubbish of the dark chapel to find the entrance of a vault, while strange sounds awe and encourage them, and the old Baron, father of the murdered man, tears up the stones with the strength of his youth, until the vault is revealed, and within it he finds the armour of his dead son, while a few inches under the floor lie his bones and skull, split, like that of the phantom, by an axe. The critics did not like this book, but it has passages of incomplete poetry that induce the reader to piece out its imperfections.

Righteous vengeance is the business of all Gothic ghosts, but there were other possibilities latent in the supernatural, which were soon to be explored. The assumption that some portion of supernatural power can be passed over to a mortal at once suggests a new range of situations, in which normal human emotions are warped by this strange ingredient, and in which the struggle of the individual will to assert itself against the levelling laws of nature is raised to a titanic pitch. In its crudest form this assumption gives us stories of witchcraft; subtler versions are the legends of Faust and the Wandering Jew. To handle these legends successfully, however, requires a fantastic seriousness, a bold and disciplined imagination and the power to perceive symbols, and there was no novelist working in England in the 'nineties who had these qualities. Godwin's *St. Leon* (1799), which turns on the possession by a French nobleman of the elixir vitæ and the philosopher's stone, has the merit of conceiving occult powers as tragical to their possessor, since they estrange him from his kind, and overburden and often debase his human qualities. It is a disappointing book, nevertheless. The imaginative psychology, which should have reconciled the reader to the marvellous in the book, actually throws it into higher relief, for the subtlety, which is at times apparent, does not discount the laborious and prosaic movement of the analyses. Moreover, the poignant and unfamiliar situations, which were what attracted Godwin to the theme, are so artificially induced, and conducted with such narrative incompetence, that sustained interest is impossible. The romance did suggest, however, the range of subject and emotion which could be achieved by a judicious mixture of the occult, and while older readers scoffed, some of the younger men greeted it with enthusiasm.

It is not necessary to pursue any further the enumeration of the favourite themes of eighteenth-century romance. The most important have been mentioned. It will readily be assumed that Gothic authors appropriated and refurbished the old stock-in-trade of the sentimental novel, that families are scattered and symmetrically re-assembled, that parental tyranny took a more feudal shade, lovers languished in fetters, and heroines eloped through subterranean passages. It is not uninteresting, however, to notice the themes on which no romantic light has yet fallen. Gypsies, for instance, remain mere thievish vagrants; there are no eighteenth-century anticipations of Borrow or Watts-Dunton, nor do they share the glamour of the philosophic outlaw. Desert islands, the *tabulæ rasæ* of philosophic novelists, had so far yielded little fairy gold. Piracy, which was grimly real, played no part as yet in the romance, but slavery in Algiers, which was equally real, did. It is not always easy to find reasons for the selections and omissions of the romantic mood, and chance must be allowed to count for something.

Finally, it may be repeated that, as regards the sympathetic characters, the " reverie " quality of romance is never lost. Barbaric nobles may revel " in the wild glare of Gothic luxury," incredible monks perpetrate atrocities in noisome vaults, but the characters through whom we participate in this highly-coloured life are not in the least Gothic. They are projections of eighteenth-century ideals. It is amusing to watch the authors ignoring the illiteracy of the Middle Ages. Taste demanded accomplishments in a hero, and would have looked upon horsemanship and woodcraft as poor substitutes for modern elegance. Accordingly, every hero is provided with accomplishments, even if the story has no place for them ; and Nathan Drake was entirely true to his age when in his sample Gothic tale, *Henry Fitz-Owen*, he attributed to Henry, whose function is to outface complicated enchantments by dauntless courage, " what were rare attainments in that age of anarchy and ignorance (viz. the fifteenth century), the elegant accomplishments of the scholar and poet."

CHAPTER VIII

PHILOSOPHERS AND CHRISTIANS

She soars a flight more than mortal; but she leaves a luminous track.—HOLCROFT, *Anna St. Ives*, 1792.
Innovations are dangerous; theoretically it may be all perfection, but practically it is a different affair.—SOPHIA KING, *Waldorf*, 1798.

THE last decade of the eighteenth century saw an increase of intellectual energy in the novel. This energy, though pouring itself into literary form, was extra-literary in origin. It did not express itself in depth of characterization or significance of form, but, taking its source from the ethical, social and political views of the authors, streamed through the novel as through a well-worn channel of access to the public. Its torrential passing did not much modify the channel. Setting aside Godwin's *Caleb Williams*, we find little that is new in the literary aspect of these books. Form, incident and character are, with few exceptions, and allowing for the general improvement in standard, much the same as they have been for the last twenty years. What has altered is the attitude of the writer to these incidents and characters. A passionate revision of moral values underlies these books; the writers proclaim a gospel, and proclaim it in the form most likely to reach a large audience, using prose fiction as the Franciscans used popular songs; nor should their basic sincerity be impugned because they wrote for a living, nor, in Godwin's case, by his craving thirst for fame. They believed, and their belief could not fail to contribute something to the development and importance of the novel, which had always had preaching proclivities, but in which the intellectual life was now quickened by advocacy of a speculative and revolutionary system of morals.

Hitherto English fiction, though more than sufficiently didactic, had been poor in ideas. Not so the French, whose lively experiments in accommodating all sorts of moral and social notions to the business of story-telling were welcomed and approved in England, but not imitated. Mercier's *Memoirs of The Year Two Thousand Five Hundred* has already been mentioned; there were other importations, for the staleness of the English novel enhanced the charm of these philosophical fantasies. Thus we find Mercier's dream of the future followed in the next year (1773) by *The Man of Nature*, translated from the French, with the usual omissions and deviations, by James Burne. The hero of this book, who begins his memoirs with the arresting remark: "At the age of twenty, I learned that there were other beings in the creation besides myself," was, as a seventh and last child, devoted by his parents to the tutelage of nature, which meant that he was shut up for the first fifteen years of his life in a wooden cage, containing "a small bandbox of pasteboard, a fly, some straw, a stone," where food was supplied to him invisibly; and later decanted on to an uninhabited island, accompanied only by a dog, where he develops the purest monotheism, by the spontaneous processes of the unperverted reason, and sheds delicious tears at the sight of a hind suckling a fawn. After some years he meets a recluse philosopher, who marries him to his daughter, and instructs him in French, Latin, philosophy, arithmetic and mensuration. At length, at the age of thirty, he is reclaimed by his father, and, after a probationary and disapproving tour of Europe, assembles a ship-load of the virtuous, and retires, fortified by the newest ideas in education, to his island, where he founds and governs a republic. Another fantasy on the growth

and rectitude of the untutored intellect was translated in
1775 by Miss R. Roberts as *The Triumph of Truth ; or,
Memoirs of Mr. de la Villette*.[1] In this book the point
at issue is whether the movements of conscience are
divinely inspired or the relics of impressions inculcated
in childhood. To convince a sceptical and libertine
husband, a mother allows her only daughter to be brought
up in an artificial solitude, attended only by a dumb
servant and taught from specially prepared books, from
which all religious ideas are excluded.   Nature, however,
is invincible ; the death of a little playfellow at the age of
twelve starts the child upon a career of " just reflection
and unprejudiced inquiry," which ends by establishing
the truths of natural and revealed religion, and converting
her father. A favourite pastime of the French intellectuals
was the construction of ideal states, and between 1784 and
1787 were published the six volumes of Grivel's *L'Isle
Inconnue, ou Mémoires du Chevalier de Gastines*, a rework-
ing for philosophical purposes of the Robinson Crusoe
situation. The Chevalier—for the French Crusoe is no
commoner—is cast on an island with his betrothed wife
and large supplies from the wreck. He builds an altar,
composes a marriage service and weds her in the sight of
God. They have twenty-three children, whom the
Father (he is always honoured with a capital letter) causes
to intermarry, thus founding a state, in the history of
which are illustrated all the functions of law-making, war,
trade and justice.[2] The book was not translated, but it
was known in England, as were the less astounding but
equally stimulating tales of Voltaire.[3] These have a
traceable influence on the English novel through Bage,
but there is nothing among our home-grown products to

[1] For an account of this book, v. *Critical*, April 1775.
[2] Another Crusoe-book, though without philosophical content, was
Zelia in the Desert, translated by A Lady in 1789.   The Crusoe is
female, and the substance idyllic and sentimental.
[3] *E.g.*, in translation, *L'Ingénu, or the Sincere Huron* (1768), *The
White Bull* (1774) and *Young James, or the Sage and the Atheist* (1776).

match the engaging formalism, the amiable grotesqueness of the Crusoes and Men of Nature, and these secluded prodigies of the French imagination are described here partly to show the influences to which English fiction had long been exposed and to which in a decade of political excitement it suddenly became accessible, and partly for the sake of contrast. Bage's *Hermsprong* has, as we saw, enough rigidity of pattern to recall French analogues, and the same may be said of Mrs. Inchbald's *Nature and Art* (1796), a variant on the contrast between primitive virtue and the corruptions of civilization; but with the English writers life will keep breaking in, and the basic diagram of their books is obscured by scenes of pathos and humour.

The speculative element in the English novel of the 'nineties is conveniently focussed in the little group of revolutionary novelists and their opponents. The " philosophers " were a compact body, well known to each other, all Londoners (with the exception of Bage, who stands apart in more ways than one), and all sympathizers with the French Revolution. The anti-philosophers, on the other hand, are scattered, united only by common alarm and indignation, launching their attacks sometimes from remote country vicarages, sometimes from a London bookshop. In both parties there is a common faith in the essentials of their creeds, and a good deal of variety in the minor tenets. It is as social and political theorists that they have mostly been approached by modern historians; [1] ranged with Tom Paine or with Burke, they bear witness to the ferment of thought and emotion in England during the early days of the Revolution, and serve as a rude porch to the poetry of their own generation and the next. This approach is, up to a certain point, inevitable. All these novelists had axes to grind,

[1] *v.* especially Allene Gregory, *The French Revolution and the English Novel* (1915), and B. Sprague Allen, *Analogues to Wordsworth's Borderers, Publications of the Modern Language Association of America*, XXXVIII, 12 (1923).

and incident and character serve them as grindstones.
Their purposefulness outpaces the accustomed didacticism
of their period. Richardson and Fielding are didactic,
and so is the swarm of their imitators, but they are
primarily novelists of character, manners, or, at the
lowest level, incident. *Clarissa* does illustrate the misconduct both of parents and children in relation to
marriage, but *Clarissa* is greater than its moral. The
propaganda novels are not and cannot be greater than
their morals.

It was under the impact of political events that
English philosophic liberalism found utterance in the
novel, and it was by the impact of political events that it
was bludgeoned into silence. Setting aside Bage's earlier
novels as a detached prelude, we may confine the whole
development in about half-a-dozen years. The first
full-blown revolutionary novel is Thomas Holcroft's
Anna St. Ives (1792), and this was followed by Godwin's
Caleb Williams (1794) and by Holcroft's *Hugh Trevor*
(1794–97). Mary Hays's *Memoirs of Emma Courtney*
came out in 1796, and Mary Wollstonecraft's posthumous
Wrongs of Women in 1798. This concludes the revolutionary testimony; the prophetic voices cease or are
heard talking carefully of something else; the air, however, is vibrant with echoes. The anti-revolutionary
novel begins in 1791 with *Lindor and Adelaide, a moral
Tale. In which are exhibited the effects of the late French
Revolution on the Peasantry of France.* This was aimed
against the revolutionary party in France [1]; but the
Vindication of the Rights of Women (1792) and the *Enquiry
concerning Political Justice* (1793) soon concentrated the

---

[1] v. *Monthly Review*, July 1791 : " The enemies to the Revolution
are made in every way amiable. . . . The favourers of the Revolution, on the contrary, are distorted in body and corrupted in mind."
A prior talks the young peasant Lindor out of his love of liberty, but
he falls a victim to a band of enraged villagers. The book made
much of the disadvantage to the poor of the disappearance of
benevolent seigneurs.

attack nearer home, and Isaac d'Israeli's *Vaurien* (1797), George Walker's *Vagabond* (1799), Elizabeth Hamilton's *Memoirs of Modern Philosophers* (1800), the Reverend Charles Lucas's *Infernal Quixote* (1800) and Dr. Bisset's *Douglas ; or, the Highlander* (1800) are pointed at revolutionaries on English soil, and do not shrink from adding personalities to their weapons of offence. By 1800 the forces of conservatism had the vantage of sun and wind, and the "philosophers," who had families to keep, had ceased to advocate their systems openly, and were restricting their efforts to the exposure of social conditions.

The novel, then, had for the first time been the arena of a serious war of ideas. Critics were alive to the new development. When Mrs. Charlotte Smith [1] introduced representative discussions on French politics into her novel *Desmond* (1792), they took notice of it as something fresh and on the whole laudable,[2] though tough conservatives found it an indecent action in a woman. The advantages of the appeal by means of fiction were soon perceived. In 1793 Gilbert Imlay, in his Preface to *The Emigrants*, declares that he is writing to turn the attention of his readers to "the important political questions now agitated throughout Europe," and that he has chosen the novel as the most effectual means of doing so [3]; and by 1796 the *Monthly Review*, noticing Walker's *Theodore Cyphon*, remarks that "it was formerly thought sufficient

---

[1] Mrs. Smith, like Mrs. Inchbald and Mrs. Mary Robinson, stood on the fringe of the revolutionary circle, and, without being "philosophic," was liberal in her sympathies.

[2] Contrast the *Critical's* review of *The Reveries of the Heart* (1781), eleven years earlier, when the reviewer was "greatly and disagreeably surprised to find, that this vehicle, in the shape and appearance of a novel, was only made use of, by a verbose and violent pedant, to convey to the world his political sentiments on the present state of our public affairs."

[3] Assistant Professor R. L. Rusk (v. *Indiana University Studies*, No. 57, 1923) thinks that Imlay really put his book together when in Europe ; in which case, the adoption of the novel for his propaganda may have been due to the example of the revolutionary circle with which he was in touch.

for a novel if it afforded a few hours of innocent amusement. . . . Of late, however, it has been discovered that
a novel is a very effectual and interesting vehicle for truths
and speculations of the utmost importance, in moral and
political philosophy; and men of very superior abilities
have employed their time and talents in cultivating this
species of writing." The novel of propaganda was a
recognized species; its nature had become apparent, and
in 1800 the friendly *Monthly* put a finger on the weakness
perpetually inherent in it. The philosopher who makes
use of fiction to substantiate his theories by an appeal to
human nature, said the critic, is like a physician who
produces cases to bear out a new method of treatment;
but there is one great difference; here the cases themselves are matters of invention.[1]

There is indeed in many of these novels,—in all the
most " philosophical,"—a retrocession from life, as it is
observed by the unprophetic eye. The writers turn
away from manners and character to spin mythologies out
of their own brains. There is certainly some arrogance
in such a preference, but the brains were not ignobly
furnished. The process is irritating to some very good
judges; Professor Saintsbury, for instance, can find no
good word for *Caleb Williams*, and dismisses Holcroft's
novels as a " desert of dreary declaration and propagandist
puppet-mongering." This is dashing to those who
regard Holcroft's crusades with some tenderness. *Anna
St. Ives* is by no means a good book; it is even, with
regard to the main development of the novel, a deformed
book, since the hero and heroine act consistently according
to their enlightened reason, with a conscious loyalty and a
self-control that are complete in Frank and almost complete in Anna; yet there is a peculiar sweetness in it.
Holcroft's young people take up poses of angular heroism,
a little reminiscent of Andersen's tin soldier, and hold

[1] *v.* review of *St. Leon*, Sept. 1800.

the hope of oblivion, accepts the friendship of Frank and Anna, and acknowledges his duties to society. This bed of remorse is quite unlike any that precede it in the eighteenth century. The young people do not preach humility to the penitent; rather they endeavour to ease him of his sense of guilt and to persuade him that his sick disgust refers to a man who no longer exists. He is not even indebted to them for pardon, for in forgiving him they are acting on behalf of society. Let him then cease to torment himself, and join them in furthering the approach of " that state of society, when personal property shall no longer exist, when the whole torrent of mind shall unite in inquiry after the beautiful and the true, when it shall no longer be diverted by those insignificant pursuits, to which the absurd follies, which originate in our false wants, give birth, when individual selfishness shall be unknown, and when all shall labour for the good of all." We leave Clifton in a state something short of entire conviction, but full of respect for the idealists; and we leave them about to consult the good of society by marrying each other.

Holcroft's " romance " was followed a few years later by a book which has less of the diagram about it. In *Hugh Trevor* (1794–7) philosophic virtues are mixed to a greater degree with human frailty, and work among types that are at once more stubborn and more realistically described. Nevertheless, they are the same virtues proceeding from the same principles. Hugh, after years of arrogant and passionate error, reaches the position occupied by his friend Turl, and that is the position of Frank Henley, while the development of the trickster Wakefield parallels that of Coke Clifton. There is a good deal of biographical interest in the book, for the experiences that had made Holcroft a philosopher were inevitably drawn on for the *enfances* of his hero, and he still clung to his belief that it is necessary for a male child to be " steeped in misery," and thus case-hardened; there

are also some authentic scenes and characters from the
" low life " which Holcroft knew by experience, and some
highly satirical scenes and characters from the high life
with which he was less well acquainted.   The philosophic
novelist is attracted either to fantasy or satire ; sometimes,
of course, to both.   Holcroft had not constructed a
Utopia on a desert island or in the future ; his Utopias
are modestly confined to single households, and sometimes to households of a single member ; but he had
brought ideal characters from his private mythology into
contemporary London, and irradiated the atmosphere with
them.   In *Hugh Trevor* there is less radiance than in
Anna St. Ives, and consequently more satire.   The Law,
the Church, the University, the politician, are trussed for
judgment.   The whole moral system of mankind must
be reformed and erroneous habits of thought eradicated,
and nowhere are they more firmly established than in the
old professions ;   nowhere is the gap between ideal
function and actual activity wider.   Yet it is the mistake
of the cynic to believe that, because virtue is everywhere
imperfect, no virtue exists, and from this mistake Wakefield is freed by the sight of the struggling virtue of Hugh
Trevor.   The novel ends in the old evasive way, which
Holcroft afterwards admitted to be a mistake.   Hugh
inherits money and himself joins the privileged classes.
One theme, the possibility of intellectual growth in all
men, is satisfactorily illustrated by a number of characters.
The other, the moral importance of the profession chosen
for a young man, is unfinished ; Hugh does not come to
terms with society ; he is lifted above its pressure.[1]

---

[1] *The Memoirs of Bryan Perdue* (1805), Holcroft's last novel, shows
a great decline in quality.   He holds the same ideals, but is forced
by circumstances and failing powers to a sarcastic and tedious expression of them.   Once more, it is despair that is the chief sin and lets
in all the others ;   and once more he proclaims his faith in the nature
of man :   " I am firmly persuaded that goodness can never be wholly
driven from the human heart.   It is the necessity of man's nature to
be good."

Two years after *Anna St. Ives*, and in the same year as the first instalment of *Hugh Trevor*, appeared William Godwin's *Things as they are ; or, the Adventures of Caleb Williams* (1794). The book instantly made its mark, was received, translated, hated and admired. It has been a question with Godwin's critics, how far he betrays an extra-literary purpose. From the point of view of the contemporary reader, the question was unimportant. *Caleb Williams* was, as Godwin declared, the offspring of the temper of mind in which the composition of *Political Justice* had left him ; the same vein of thought, the same schematization of life, the same " *incessant* energy of mind " [1] runs through it ; this was evident, and inquiry went no further. To the literary historian, however, the inquiry is not quite nugatory. How far was the resemblance between the two books willed, how far inevitable ? To what extent did Godwin deliberately have recourse to the novel as a secondary means of propagating his philosophy ? What, in short, was the relative importance of story and philosophy in his mind ? The *Critical* gave a summary answer to these questions by recommending him to omit the political reflections, and a more recent judge,[2] refusing to class *Caleb Williams* as a full-fledged *tendenz-roman*, has decided that Godwin's interest in social conditions fades before his interest in psychological states. This is probably true ; he omits to notice, however, that the psychological states spring to a large extent from social conditions and from the moral ideas connected with them, and that all of them, with the possible exception of Caleb's passion of curiosity, are conceived in relation to the notion of power, and illustrate different forms of tyranny, slavery and assertive independence. There is certainly a strong narrative interest, and the book is full

[1] Mrs. Inchbald's comment; *v.* C. Kegan Paul's *William Godwin*, I, p. 139.
[2] *I.e.* Johannes Meyer in *William Godwins Romane* (1906).

of prison and pursuit; but it is upon two planes; there are stone walls and thief-takers, but the killing prisons, the unescapable hunters, are prejudices, those erroneous values which the new philosophy endeavoured to expose. Moral right and wrong raises intense feeling in the characters of the story, even in so unimportant a person as the footman who smuggles tools to Caleb in prison, while the emotions of Caleb, and of Godwin himself, rise not so much from a contemplation of individuals as from an abstract consideration of the relationships between men at large. " I saw my whole species as ready, in one mode or other, to be made the instruments of the tyrant," says Caleb. Lastly, though Godwin spoke of the book in different tones at different times, ranging from " a general review of the modes of domestic and unrecorded despotism by which man becomes the destroyer of man " to " a paraphrase on the story of Bluebeard by Charles Perrault," some special weight is to be allowed to those comments which fell from him at the time of composition. Chief of these is the title, which has now almost slipped from memory behind the sub-title. Godwin called his book *Things as they are ;* it is an arraignment of society on a criminal charge.

The " philosophical " meaning of the book may be epitomized thus. A noble-minded man, in obedience to inherited prejudice and false ideas of honour, does violence to his own nature by committing a murder; other iniquities become necessary to conceal the act, and he becomes the inflexible persecutor of an innocent man. The innocent man, living in a state of society in which the machinery of justice can be wrenched by the rich to their own ends, is at length debased by the suffering, which at first taught him fortitude, in his turn persecutes his persecutor, and forfeits his peace of mind. Both have maimed themselves, and the result is the loss to society of two richly endowed minds. There is a sort of cold passion [1] about this exposition, a ruminating and intellectualized indignation, which occasionally breaks forth into indictment, but is present mostly as a stifled desperation underneath the rapid, even flow of Caleb's narration. It is an oppressive book to read. Its first readers found it exciting as well, and Mrs. Inchbald called it " sublimely horrible—captivatingly frightful." It is sustained unflaggingly; and seen from this aspect, the book falls into another sequence of development, and is noticeable for its anticipation of the modern detective story. It has, what so few contemporary novels have, unity of structure and of atmosphere. Godwin has described how he constructed his novel. Determined to write a tale that should " constitute an epoch in the mind of the reader," and seeking for a powerful and absorbing subject, he evolved the situation of flight and pursuit in the last volume, and from that point followed his theme backward, projecting first the motive which could account for such a persecution, and then the circumstances which invite our sympathy for the persecutor as well as for his victim. Every incident is directly relevant to the main theme, and there is no relief. The development of the story is never checked and never runs into blind alleys, but keeps the highway with gathering impetus.[2] It is this control of the story by one strong interest that wholly differentiates *Caleb Williams* from the romances of Mrs. Radcliffe, which also effected an improvement in the structure of the novel, but in a more superficial way. Her dealings in mystery and mystification necessitated a measure of control of her plot, a

---

[1] Cf. *Caleb Williams* : " Passion in a state of solemn and omnipotent vehemence always appears to be coolness to him in whom it domineers."

[2] There are dropped stitches, notably the omission to explain the contents of the famous box, but the emotion informing the book carries one past them. In *St. Leon*, on the other hand, where the emotion is artificially worked up, the inconsistencies of the narrative are glaring.

technique of complication and resolution, but it is intermittent, and she turns from the highway to dream in
wayside arbours.   Critics have noticed the relationship in
which *Caleb Williams* stands to the Gothic Romance;
indeed, the two types of fiction are frequently found
linked in contemporary comments.   Both were, in the
derogatory sense, romantic, and sober realists disliked
equally the material marvels of Mrs. Radcliffe and the
moral marvels of Godwin and Holcroft.[1]   In matters of
detail, to which modern critics point, there is a good deal
of similarity in material, with a marked difference in its
application.   Godwin has mystery and suspense;   he
has a suffocating atmosphere of impending calamity;   he
has prison scenery, a lonely house in a forest, and a
philosophic robber.   These were matters of fashion
which, knowing the novel market, he picked up casually
and used for his own unique purposes;   at times they had
for him a cogent meaning, but it was not a Gothic meaning.
Mystery is not valuable in itself, but as the stimulus of
Caleb's mental growth;   prison and woodland provide no
scenic background, and the purpose of suspense is not to
enchant the reader;   it is the intellectual repercussions
of these conditions that are studied;   they are the agents
in the psychological development of Caleb.   " The thing
in which my imagination revelled most freely was the
analysis of the private and internal operations of the
mind," wrote Godwin in 1832.   From this brooding
dissection of morbid mental states, to facilitate which he
turned from narration in the third person to narration in
the first, grows the unity of atmosphere in the book.
There is not much dialogue, and little emphasis on the
single scene;   but a continuous probing commentary

---

[1] The expression " moral marvels " is used by Coleridge in his
review of *The Monk* for the *Critical,* and is there applied, not to
Godwin, but to the gross flaws in Lewis's psychology; it expresses
very well, however, the attitude of unenthusiastic readers to *Anna
St. Ives* and *Caleb Williams.*

winds itself round incident and character, and the very impartiality with which the inquiry is conducted—as in the case of Tyrrel, where the root of his almost fascinated malevolence is seen to be wounded pride—adds to the oppression. Godwin's " metaphysical dissecting-knife " lays bare the movements of intense, lonely, self-involved and tormented minds,—for poor Emily Melvil is the only spontaneous character among the egoists,—and in this respect *Caleb Williams* extended the scope of the novel. Moreover, the force of the delineation has prolonged its cold, tough life to the present day. It is the only one of the philosophical novels that does not need resuscitation, for, though torpid, it is still just alive.

Anna St. Ives, *Hugh Trevor* and *Caleb Williams* are the cardinal novels of the " philosophic " school. In them the new light shines in the most concentrated and dazzling degree. But there is an outer ring of minor fiction in which certain recurrent characters and situations reflect the illumination. Among others, our old friend, the noble savage, receives fresh adornment, for one tenet of the philosophers was the unnecessary and vicious elaboration of society, and the original benevolence and rectitude of unperverted man. Mrs. A. M. Mackenzie in *Slavery ; or, the Times* (1792) follows an old plan in bringing her African prince to England and suffering him to comment by a standard of absolute integrity on what he sees there.[1] Henry, the hero of Mrs. Inchbald's *Nature and Art* (1796), is no savage, but he has been bred by his father with philosophical simplicity among savage tribes, and returns to England to ask embarrassing questions about wigs, compliments, battles and charity. Bage's *Hermsprong* (1796) is older and more sophisticated, but he too, though

---

[1] A novel, *Berkeley Hall, or the Pupil of Experience*, came out in 1796, in which the advantages of the life of nature are exemplified by means of Red Indians, mermaids and dwellers in the Arctic and Antarctic. I have not seen the book, and it is not easy to make out from contemporary criticisms or more recent references exactly what point of view the author of this Lucianic-sounding fantasy took.

without idealizing savage life, has learned savage virtues, and especially imitates the devastating directness with which savages, it appears, are accustomed to reason. The radical disingenuousness of these debates between the perspicuous savage and the civilized man, thick-sighted with inherited prejudice, as they appear in French and English philosophic fiction, is amusingly exposed by Lucas in his *Infernal Quixote* (1800); the subject is religion.

> " The Reasoner begins," writes Lucas, " —declares the religion of the Men in the Moon, or the Cape— and one by one picks out the most prominent virtues of Christianity, which, with a long feather, naked feet, and plenty of Nature, becomes a very pretty picture, and assumes a most pleasing appearance. The *Logician of Christianity* is nonplussed ; his virtues are already taken from him, and he cuts but a pitiful figure. But the most common method of the REASONER is to write a dialogue upon the subject between himself and the savage. He, very kindly, for Christianity, the Savage for himself. Oh ! how the Savage cuts him up."

The quip was merited. But the unimpeded workings of nature and the purity of the untaught mind can likewise be seen in children, and scenes in which a child unconsciously shames the hypocrisies of its elders are frequent in philosophic fiction. Childhood scenes in themselves were by no means new ; there was a famous and much-imitated one in *Tom Jones*, and the educationists were filling books with the carefully-supervised activities of little masters and misses ; but to the philosophers the child was an epitome of their central doctrine, and in its natural sallies and its response to environment they read the proof of the perfectibility of man.[1]

A less artificial and very popular character was the

[1] *v.* the childhood scenes in *Nature and Art, Hugh Trevor* and *The Victim of Prejudice.*

victim of society; and of these victims incomparably the most frequent was the fallen woman. This character, again, is not new; what is new is the attitude that shifts all guilt from her to society, that sees in her first imprudence only the impulse of uncalculating affection, and in the sequel only the tyranny of hypocrites and the unco' guid. The subject is capable of great pathos, as Mrs. Inchbald proved by her picture of Hannah Primrose,[1] whom she traces from her proud position of village beauty to the time when she stands in the dock and hears sentence of death pronounced on her by her first corrupter; such pathos, however, is often achieved by loading the dice heavily against the victim. Mary Hays [2] in her *Victim of Prejudice* (1799) takes as her heroine the daughter of a woman who, driven by her seducer to prostitution, fell at last to murder and ended her life on the scaffold. Young Mary, courageous and impassioned, puts up a brave fight against her inheritance of shame, but the death of her guardian exposes her to the power of Sir Peter Osborn, who traps and violates her, and when, maintaining that her mind is uncontaminated and superior to her body, she refuses to become his mistress and tries, even in the humblest ways, to earn her living, pursues her with calumny and false charges of debt. Mary's health and spirit are broken by prison, and we leave her declining to an early grave, wretched with the sense of her wasted energies and unfruitful talents. She is called the victim of prejudice, but the title is a misnomer, for it has taken more than prejudice, more even than exceptional mis-

---

[1] v. *Nature and Art.*

[2] Mary Hays (1760–1843) was the friend of Mary Wollstonecraft, Godwin and the Lambs. She published *An Enquiry into the Expediency and Propriety of Public Worship* (1792), *Letters and Essays, Moral and Miscellaneous* (1793), *Memoirs of Emma Courtney* (1796), *The Victim of Prejudice* (1799), *Female Biography* (1803) and other works, including history for children. Information about her early life will be found in *The Love-Letters of Mary Hays* (1779–1780), ed. A. F. Wedd (1925), and *The Fate of the Fenwicks. Letters to Mary Hays,* ed. A. F. Wedd (1927).

fortune, to victimize her. To destroy Mary, Miss Hays has had to invent a villain of the most Gothic kind, luxurious, persistent and incapable of pity; and test cases, to convince us, must not be provided with Gothic accessories.[1]

Another victim of society is the philosophic outlaw, whose virtues are too immitigable to function in the crooked paths of society, and who administers a purer justice in woods and caverns. This self-conscious person is of German provenance, as we have seen. Closely allied and at times identical with him is the noble criminal who has taken the law into his own hands and himself executed his vengeance. The new philosophy was unjustly supposed to endorse his action, and George Walker, the London bookseller and novelist, having extracted the full charm from his sympathetic self-avenger *Theodore Cyphon* (1796), is careful to provide the necessary antidote by bringing him, a willing sacrifice, to the gallows, and causing him to vindicate the law in his dying speech. This character, who is strongly attracted to Gothic surroundings, is only shadowed forth in the 'nineties; his full development came later.

Conspicuous as the male philosophers are, it was the women in the revolutionary circle who focussed the horrified attention of the conservative public. The ethics of the woman's novel, that established harmony of submission, delicacy and self-control, were rudely shaken. Mary Wollstonecraft in her *Vindication of the Rights of Women* (1792) had said that independence was the soil of every virtue,[2] and had based delicacy on candour instead of concealment. She had written *Mary, a Fiction* (1788) in which " the mind of a woman, who has thinking

[1] For a much more convincing treatment of the victim of society *v.* Mary Wollstonecraft's Jemima in *The Wrongs of Women* and Mrs. Wilson in d'Israeli's *Vaurien.*

[2] Cf. Ann Yearsley's *Royal Captives*, II, p. 86 (1795): " No woman can be virtuous that is not self-dependent." The self-dependence, however, is not necessarily economic.

powers, is displayed," and had exhibited the development of these powers as consequent on the most unconventional behaviour. She had spoken freely of passion and saw in it an educative force. She had not embodied these views in any novel commensurate in achievement with Holcroft's or Godwin's, but at her death she left an unfinished narrative, which was published by her husband, entitled *The Wrongs of Women*, designed to show the disabilities under which women labour in society.[1] The book is very definitely a novel of propaganda; its plot is conditioned by the abuses it sets out to expose, and it suffers, as propaganda novels are apt to do, from violence of incident and character-drawing. We feel that the author has endeavoured by all means to get all the wrongs of women into one story, and even Maria's landlady has suffered from the inequality of the law. Crude as it is, *The Wrongs of Women* is deeply interesting. Ostensibly absorbed in her extra-literary purpose, the author can only express this through her own vivid sensibilities. The narrative is informed with a proud sense of the dignity of mind; it is because matrimonial despotism degrades the mind that it is the greatest of the wrongs of women, while in this degradation lies the worst sting of poverty. Maria, the victim of marriage, and Jemima, the victim of poverty, meet and exchange sympathy in a private madhouse, where one is prisoner and the other wardress. Jemima, a waif, brutally mishandled in childhood, has been "drenched with the dregs of human misery"; Maria, gently bred, has suffered all that befalls a woman of strong and delicate sensibilities, united to a cold, mean, and unscrupulous man, from whom the law will give her no release. Now at last, renouncing loyalties which her reason does not approve, she recovers the

---

[1] *Posthumous Works of the Author of a Vindication of the Rights of Women* (1798); in four vols., of which two contain *The Wrongs of Women; or, Maria. A Fragment.*

freedom of her soul, and turns again to life in search of happiness. The book here trembles constantly on the verge of a beauty which is in the author's mind but not within the compass of her craftsmanship. Maria receives as her lover a young man who is her fellow-prisoner, and in that grotesque madhouse, set in its desolate, leaf-strewn garden and haunted by the images and sounds of insanity, her precarious idyll develops, clouded by uncertainty of her husband's intentions and by more wounding uncertainty of her lover's strength of heart. About a third of the book was written, and two drafts exist of the end. There was to be a great scene in court,—the philosophers were fond of trial scenes, as in them prescribed law and natural morality can be most sharply opposed,—when Maria, charged with adultery, was to voice the sufferings of her sex; for the history, as the author said, was to be considered rather " as of woman than of an individual." Her plea was to fail, and the verdict to go against her; her lover was to prove false, and in despair she was to take the way that Mary Wollstonecraft herself had tried to take. In one version the book ends with her suicide; in another she is recovered, and resolves to live for her child.

Godwin's *Memoirs* of Mary Wollstonecraft—delicately referred to by an adversary [1] as Godwin's *History of the Intrigues of his Own Wife*—was a work which many of its readers failed most signally to understand. Obloquy was heaped on her grave, and a priest of the Church [2] found something singularly and providentially appropriate in the manner of her end. She had maintained the equality of the sexes; she had denied the false morality " which makes all the virtue of women consist in chastity, submission, and forgiveness of injuries "; [3] she died in childbed. It was awfully satisfactory. This dis-

---

[1] Rev. Charles Lucas in *The Infernal Quixote* (1800).
[2] Rev. R. Polwhele in *The Unsex'd Females* (1798).
[3] v. *Wrongs of Women*, II, p. 150.

pensation, however, did not quench liberal thought on the question of marriage and of female virtue.[1] By the end of the century the relaxation of the marriage tie, which in Godwin's *Political Justice* had appeared as the logical result of the abolition of property, and as matter for speculation rather than immediate action, had been bathed in sentiment by the German drama. The savage *Anti-Jacobin Review* lumped all innovations together. A poisonous infection spread, it appears, from Rousseau, who condoned the loss of chastity in his Julie, through the chilly speculations of Godwin and the recorded struggles of Mary Wollstonecraft to the shameless Mary Hays, who defined chastity as "individuality of affection." The same poison, stirring in German veins, produced *Werter*, with its dangerous expense of sympathy on the hero's infatuation for a married woman, *Stella*, with its amicable composition between a wife and her husband's mistress, and the plays of Kotzebue with their forgiving husbands. The forgiving husband was what stuck most in the reviewer's throat, for he was imperilling the structure of society.[2]

It will be remembered that some twenty years before a reviewer had expressed a desire to read a delineation of the tender passion by a female pen. At last the female pen, dipped in candour and courage, was giving such a delineation, and male critics, with few exceptions, were recoiling in distress. In 1796, two years before the *Wrongs of Women*, Mary Hays published her semi-autobiographical novel, *Memoirs of Emma Courtney*, and at once stepped into the pillory beside her friend Mary Wollstonecraft, where her short, unlovely form received

---

[1] *v., e.g.,* Gertrude St. Leger, heroine of Mrs. Robinson's *False Friend* (1799), who is an enthusiast for Mary Wollstonecraft.
[2] Continued French importations kept the subject in view. Jean Baptiste Louvet's *Emilie de Varmont, ou le Divorce Nécessaire ; et les Amours du Curé Sévin* (1790), translated in 1798, was a strong plea for easy divorce and clerical marriage.

its full share of mud-slinging. It is an odd, pathetic, ludicrous and, for moments, noble book. It was also widely misunderstood, for Miss Hays was supposed to be condoning the state of mind she describes, and to describe which she drew valiantly on her own history. *Emma Courtney* is the picture of a girl of strong, undisciplined emotions, restless for want of an object for her affections, resentful because in her isolation she feels shut out from the movement of life, who finds in philosophy not a means of regulating her feelings, but a sanction to indulge them, under the specious colour of reason and candour. The new philosophy especially valued energy of character,—to energize, a favourite word of the revolutionaries, was caught up and turned to mirth by their opponents,[1]—and Emma, holding that " the mind capable of receiving the most forcible impressions is the sublimely improvable mind," indulges in all the wild enthusiasm of her character. Her aggressiveness, her comic and distressing pursuit of a reluctant man, her adherence to " the unequivocable language of sincerity " through strange scenes of expostulation, though clearly based upon painful experience, are so ludicrous in their effect that we cannot blame Mrs. Elizabeth Hamilton for burlesquing book and author in the character of Bridgetina Botherim in *Memoirs of Modern Philosophers* (1800). Bridgetina's account of her importunate sensibilities and the fermentation of her ideas, her convenient habit of dressing up her own desires as measures of general utility, her inflexible love-letters—" I will inspire sympathy ; " she writes, " nor can I believe it compatible with the nature of mind, that so many strong and reiterated efforts should be made in vain," [2]—are fair satire, indeed, at times

---

[1] Cf. Mrs. Elizabeth Hamilton, *Memoirs of Modern Philosophers* (1800), where the philosophic Utopia in Africa is described, with " each congenial Hottentot, energizing in his self-built shed."

[2] Cf. *Emma Countney :* " Permit me then to hope for as well as to seek your affections, and if I do not, at length, gain and secure them, it will be a phenomenon in the history of mind."

hardly an exaggeration of the original; but Mary Hays's " mischievous chimæras " cannot be dismissed by laughing at them. She had courage and she strove for truth, and in blaming a " *distempered civilization* " for her misery she had some justification, if not as much as she thought. Finally, she had an honourable determination to benefit by her experiences, however disastrous. Her Emma is left a bereaved and prematurely old woman, but she can still employ herself in the services of her adopted son, for " it is not to atone for past error, by cutting off the prospect of future usefulness." Mrs. Hamilton, on the other hand, was obliged to kill off her poor penitent Julia.

The mixture of farce and tragedy in *Memoirs of Modern Philosophers* is a fairly successful endeavour to combine two lines of attack. On the one hand, a series of situations is contrived that makes nonsense of the philosophical harangues of Bridgetina by putting her assumptions to the test of practice; on the other, Julia, an ardent, lovely, imperfectly-educated girl, is dazzled by this jargon when she hears it from the lips of the scamp Vallaton, becomes his victim and perishes. Mrs. Hamilton [1] has humour, moderation, and a good word for what she found good in the works of Godwin and Mary Wollstonecraft, but she was convinced that they would become engines of mischief in the hands of a bad man, and, like many of her generation, she was appalled at the thought of this accession to the power of unscrupulous evil. The emancipated philosopher, or, more frequently, the ambitious man to whom philosophy is a tool to be used and dropped as occasion serves, rode the imagination of the time as he rode that of the English Renascence. Mrs. Hamilton

---

[1] Elizabeth Hamilton (1756–1816) was sister to the Asiatic scholar, Charles Hamilton, and was urged by him to write. Her first considerable work, *Letters from a Hindoo Rajah* (1796), was composed after his death and commemorates him in the character of Percy. *Memoirs of Modern Philosophers* (1800) was followed by *Letters on Education* and other educational works. She did not marry, but adopted the dignified " Mrs." in middle age.

had already introduced the philosophers, Mr. Axiom, Mr. Puzzledorf and Mr. Vapour into her *Letters of a Hindoo Rajah* (1796), and had traced the evil effects of their disinterested philosophizing on a servant, who, misled by his master's theoretical opinions on property, takes to robbery, and on a young sceptic, who has seduced his cousin, and commits suicide when he hears of her death. In *Memoirs of Modern Philosophers* both farce and tragedy are keyed up higher, and the folly of Mr. Myope, the philosopher, and Glib, the dazzled country bookseller, who see in Vaillant's account of the Hottentots the true philosophic state, is balanced by the premeditated iniquity of the adventurer, Vallaton.   Mrs. Hamilton, like Mrs. Jane West,[1] confined her villain to domestic life and engaged him particularly in the pursuit of a woman.   In the books of d'Israeli, Lucas and Walker, though their scope is far wider, lust is invariably in some measure the concomitant of the new philosophy, since relaxation of principle must, they believed, lead to immoral action; and in 1798 the *Critical*, reviewing Charles Lloyd's *Edmund Oliver*,[2] was constrained to point out that Godwin is not necessary to account for a seduction.

The point of similarity in the anti-philosophic novels is their opposition to the doctrines of *Political Justice*. They advocate the sanctities of domestic life and the ancient ties of gratitude and obligation, which the new

---

[1] Mrs. Jane West's *A Tale of the Times* (1799) illustrates " the alarming relaxation of principle that too surely discriminates a declining age " by the ruin of Lady Monteith through the malign and hypocritical Edward Fitz-Osborne; the process, carefully annotated by the author, begins in conciliating her vanity by the suggestion that elevated souls need no other impulse to virtue than its loveliness, and ends in decline on her part and suicide on his.

[2] The book is intended to show the dangers of modern philosophy, —callousness or a mad experimenting spirit; the passionate and energetic Gertrude, a person of " wild luxuriance," disgusted by her father's rigid Catholicism, yields herself to " loose and declamatory principles," takes a lover, is deserted by him and poisons herself in delirium.   Her mental bankruptcy is contrasted by the pious deathbed of a devoted mother, and by a peaceful domestic circle in the Lakes.

philosophy, as expounded in Godwin's treatise, endeavoured to transcend. They are anti-Godwin, anti-
Holcroft, and anti-Wollstonecraft, but they are not
necessarily anti-reform. George Walker, whose *Vagabond* (1799) is devoted to ridicule of Godwin's theories,
had previously exhibited in *Theodore Cyphon ; or, the
Benevolent Jew* (1796) examples of private and domestic
tyranny far worse and less explicable than anything in
Caleb Williams. The book, indeed, with its Tyrrel-like
persecution by a squire of his tenants, its hero's imprisonment in a private madhouse, its lonely house resorted to
by smugglers, and its long sequence of flight, disguise
and escape, is modelled closely on *Caleb Williams*, with
reminiscences of *Anna St. Ives*. It has the same interest
in ingenuity, the same suspense, though Theodore's
evasion of pursuit by climbing a gibbet and clinging round
the dead body is a cut above anything that Caleb attempts.
The theme of the book, like that of so many of this period,
is oppression, and it shares with others the characteristic
that, while any melodramatic passions will do to provide
the cause, the methods of oppression are carefully and
realistically traced. Walker is a reformer, with an eye to
abuses in the marriage and penal laws ; on some of these
his plot turns, and he also contrives to sweep in poor relief,
the press-gang system, and the shameful immunity of
private madhouses. Moreover, he is full of liberal feeling
on rank and religion and shares the pacifism of the philosophers. But, liberal as he is, Walker knows exactly
where he stops, and he stops short of perfectibility. His
moral, explicitly drawn, is the evil effects of passion when
supported by power, and this tells equally against the
enduring flaws of human nature, which he does not hope
to abolish by education and the organization of society.
Nor does Theodore digest his own errors with philosophic
equanimity ; his murder, however deeply provoked, was
a crime, and he atones for it in grief and humility.

There are two astounding villains in his book, of an exuberant, inexplicable and unparalleled iniquity. They gave the author himself pause, and he admitted that the picture was overcharged; he hoped, indeed, that the brothers Cyphon, uncle and father to Theodore, did not exist, but their superlative baseness " must be attributed to the necessary defect of this species of composition, which crowds into one person the vices or virtues of many." This unnatural compression and consequent intensification of colouring, which is apt to afflict the propaganda novel, is even more damaging in anti-revolu- tionary than in revolutionary fiction; for the ogres of the revolutionists are at least vast and aged systems of law and custom, whose force is admitted, and whose lack of dis- crimination cannot be quite denied, while the ogre of the conservative was the philosopher himself, and the author in tracing the most complicated and dreadful catastrophe to this single figure, can hardly keep incredulity at bay.

The false philosopher is not confined to contemporary Europe. As early as 1792 Miss Ellis Cornelia Knight, in her laborious historical novel, *Marcus Flaminius*, had shown him, in the guise of a Greek scholar taken prisoner after Teutoburgium, undermining the morals of a Ger- manic tribe by the same arguments which he afterwards applied to Georgian youth. Discipline is subverted, reverence destroyed, and the outcome is national disaster. But his proper field is Europe at the end of the eighteenth century, and there he looms tremendous. All ages of the world, said d'Israeli in the preface to *Vaurien*[1] (1797), show examples of foolish metaphysical speculation, but his own is the first to unite politics and metaphysics and to take up with the doctrine of man's perfectibility. It is the political consequences of the new philosophy which chiefly concern d'Israeli and Lucas, though its domestic

---

[1] *Vaurien: or, Sketches of the Times : exhibiting views of the philosophies, religions, politics, literature, and manners of the age* (1797).

consequences are not forgotten. They saw that the natural ally of the infidel is the fanatic, since both support private judgment and would prefer anarchy to authority; [1] and they believed that an intelligent, ambitious and unscrupulous man, conciliating the enlightened few by his revolutionary theories, could so hoodwink and lead the ignorant many as to overturn social order and induce a state of chaos, in which he might satisfy his ambition and his greed. This nightmare—it is, of course, another aspect of the conspiracy-mania—plays a part in *Vaurien*, in *The Infernal Quixote* (1800) and in George Walker's *Vagabond* (1799). D'Israeli's Vaurien, using the English philosophers as his tools, plans a massacre and a revolution in London; Lucas's Marauder is a guiding spirit in the Irish Rebellion of 1798; and Walker presents the No Popery riots as the outcome of philosophical intrigue. In all cases, the worst consequences are averted, but they have been envisaged, and the books are darkened with apprehension.

Vaurien is the best of these novels. It is a serious and satirical conspectus of intellectual and social follies at the end of the eighteenth century, and it has wit and understanding, as well as scorn. " I have chosen the *form* rather than *matter* of a novel," wrote d'Israeli, mindful of old conventions; towards the end of the second volume, however, the form got out of hand, and he huddled up the end as best he could. His real subject was the character of an age equally disfigured by scepticism and by fanaticism, an age " in which extravagance wrestles with extravagance; the imagination wanders astonished and half-delighted, but calm sense looks around and retires in horror." On this stage appears Vaurien, the perfectly equipped adventurer, philosophic when it steads him and anti-Christian at all times, luxurious, but able to do without luxury, passionate but controlled, full of

[1] This point, best illustrated in Lucas's *Infernal Quixote*—the term Quixote always denoted enthusiasm—is well brought out by Allene Gregory, *op. cit.*

vast romantic projects for which men are too feeble instruments, in short " a vicious and great man, capable even of virtue." Beside this figure, whose Titanic imagination we credit, though he does little to confirm our faith, Lucas's Marauder is the mere stuff of melodrama, in spite of the easy, pleasant writing of the book. He is a diabolist, an emissary of Hell, as the prologue explains, to conquer for his master the yet unconquered island of Britain. The contrast between Christianity and the specious philosophic virtues which can be so easily assumed as the mask of evil, sketched by d'Israeli, is diligently elaborated by Lucas in the parallel histories of Wilson Wilson and Lord James Marauder; the new philosophy is reduced to its lowest terms, to vanity, hypocrisy and self-interest, and the cause of Christianity is supported by Wilson Wilson even in its outworks, the liturgy and the payment of tithes.

The Infernal Quixote is a serious book, thick-sown with monitory calamity. No less serious in its intentions, though lighter in its expression of them, is the Vagabond (1799) of George Walker, who, by no means eschewing the tragic incidents with which his fellow-campaigners make their points, yet chose to conduct his warfare chiefly by farce and caricature. The book is fantastically satiric. The speculations of Political Justice are put to the test of action with rough literalness,[1] and Fenton lets both his mistress and her father burn to death while wondering which it will be most to the benefit of society for him to rescue. From the first pages the inconsistence of philosophers is exposed. They have endeavoured to generalize, and have consequently stunted, their natural emotions. Dr. Alogos, who could hug a Tartar to his breast and divide his little property with a Greenlander, has no such

---

[1] These practical tests of theories formed part of the method of The History of Sir George Warrington ; or, the Political Quixote (1797), published as by the Author of The Female Quixote—a catchpenny device. Miss McIntyre gives an account of this book; I have not seen it.

impulses in favour of his countryman, a poor soldier to whom he refuses a farthing, assuring him that " in a state of nature there is no necessity for soldiers." The end is high fantasy. Alogos, Fenton, a young student who has graduated in the new philosophy at the cost of being sent down from Oxford, and Stupeo, the tutor who instructed him in the principle that " all crime arises from some possessing what others want," emigrate to America, which they find less congenial to philosophers than they had hoped. Wandering in the wilderness of Kentucky, they begin to suspect that the state of nature is " not conducted on philosophical principles." Their disillusionment is complete when they reach a remote country of philosophers, and find that civilization, paralysed by the doctrine of equality, has stagnated among the vestiges of a once thriving state. Alogos and Fenton are converted from their " deviation " and return to England ; Stupeo, who sees nothing but perfect freedom in this chaos, is burnt by Indians.

Without some proportion of the ludicrous and the mean, the philosopher, as Walker may have felt, was in danger of attracting a romantic halo. His strangeness, his aloofness, the voluntary asceticism he sometimes practises, are eminently romantic qualities. Such a development was a foregone conclusion ; it had been indicated in *Vaurien*, and it was amusingly demonstrated in a book published the year before *Vagabond*, *Waldorf*, *or the Dangers of Philosophy*. *A Philosophical Tale*, by Sophia King (1798). This narrative, which it would be foolish to classify as a novel of extra-literary purposes, testifies to the vogue of the philosophical anti-hero. The young lady, who must, according to her own account, have been about sixteen at the time she projected this egregious fiction,[1] had somehow evolved or borrowed the notion of

<hr>

[1] She had already published *Trifles from Helicon*, and followed up *Waldorf* with *Cordelia ; or the Romance of Real Life* (1799), *The Victim of Friendship* (1800), in which, according to the *Anti-Jacobin*

distinguishing between the speculative and the practical
philosopher.[1] Waldorf, an impulsive youth, passes
under the influence of the emancipated Lok, puts into
action his purely speculative notions, proselytizes, and
heaps his path with victims. The advantage of this
conception is that it allows of the integrity of the philosopher, who is Waldorf's devoted friend and dies of grief
after his suicide. The calamities of this story are heaped
up by the unsparing hand of youth, and described in
distressing rhetoric.[2] Youth has at all times been willing
to exercise its imagination by the contemplation of
corruption, and Miss King finishes her lurid chronicle
in fine spirits ; those of the cast who are left alive—two
in number—have become confirmed misanthropists ;
the rest are food for worms. These are the dangers of
philosophy. What was death to Lucas and d'Israeli is
play to her.

The *Anti-Jacobin Review* is a good guide to these
fighting novels when they are approached simply as
documents on the history of social morality, and not as
subjects of literary criticism. The doctrinal parts of
each, however negligible in bulk, are thrown into high
relief by the review. Two pages in Charles Lloyd's
Edmund Oliver, which is otherwise anti-Godwin, express
the pacifism of the author, who was of Quaker stock, and
on this small but stout peg the reviewer hangs a bitter
animadversion, while practically ignoring all the rest.
This was intentional, for the *Anti-Jacobin* never con-
descends to the business of literary criticism unless the

Review, she confessed to seventeen years, and *The Fatal Secret, or
Unknown Warrior* (1801), in the preface of which she called herself
a "weak sapling of nineteen years' growth." Her taste was for
melodrama, and she appears to have been a friend of Rosa Matilda
(Charlotte Dacre Byrne), and included some of her poems in *The
Fatal Secret*.

[1] The subject occurs, though not centrally, in T. S. Surr's *George
Barnwell* (1798).

[2] *E.g.* "The eyes of Waldorf seemed bursting with the majestic
energy of intellect."

book in hand had passed its moral and political tests with a wide margin of safety. " On the style of her writings it is needless to remark," says the reviewer of Mary Hays; " who stays to admire the workmanship of a dagger wrenched from the hand of an assassin ? " [1] Not daggers only but little pen-knives were wrenched from the hands that held them. The *Anti-Jacobin* clique, thinking no child too young to be inoculated with revolutionary virus, kept their eyes on children's books; sure enough, the philosophers were undermining the nursery, and *Prince Abdal and Princess Selima, or Virtue Rewarded* was black-listed, on the information of an indignant father who had taken it up to amuse himself at tea-time and had come on the damning sentence : " This action put an end to a war proceeding from ambition and a combination of Princes, for the purpose of destroying liberty." Nor did the review confine itself to castigating books; it subjoined to every important notice an account of what the other reviewers said, and very often it is here that the force of the attack is concentrated; for the two big literary reviews, the *Monthly* and *Critical*, had distinctly liberal leanings, and the *Analytical*, published by Johnson, the friend of Godwin and Mary Wollstonecraft, sprang from a hotbed of anarchy. The *Anti-Jacobin* dealt faithfully with them every month, hooted with exultation when the *Analytical* was discontinued, and bestowed suspicious approval on the reform of the *Critical*. Even the *Monthly* had to play for safety, as reaction set in more and more strongly; but it was not allowed to forget its past.

The *Anti-Jacobin* could praise its friends, and foremost among them was that melancholy, refined and stubborn Tory, Egerton Brydges, whose *Arthur Fitz-Albini* (1798) comes in for a torrent of approbation. Fitz-Albini, the

[1] The reviewer was Rev. W. Heath; *v.* the interleaved copy of the *Anti-Jacobin Review* at the B.M.

projection of Brydges's dream-self, the fine flower of
centuries of specialized breeding in a stock which has held
the manors he now holds since the Conquest, cleaves to
all those loyalties which the philosophers assailed, to
glory, rank, faith and spotless honour, and falls the victim
of his own noble susceptibilities in a coarsened world.
The *Anti-Jacobin* found the picture inspiring; it certainly
has the precarious beauty which belongs to a way of life
that knows itself doomed and, wrapped in its pride,
resolves to perish with its differentiating qualities unim-
paired.   The book is steeped in sumptuous melancholy;
light falls through heraldic windows into the oriel where
the heroine sits studying her genealogy, while the hero,
exquisitely beautiful and proud, rides through the
autumnal woodlands of his demesne.   There is a dawn of
hope for them, but Jane dies from the mere touch of
vulgar malice, and Fitz-Albini drags on his life in that
state which the eighteenth century called " utter derelic-
tion of the faculties."   An England reeking with
vulgarity and democracy was no place for these choice
souls.

From the literary point of view these novels of propaganda are seldom valuable.   What is good in them is
independent of their purpose, stray scenes and characters
in which the author, relaxing his fervour, allows his
observation play.   At other times his purpose weighs him
down.   Character becomes type, incident settles into
illustrative rigidity, and we pass through tracts of argument and sarcasm to a mechanical tragedy.   There is
little room for the flexibility of life when the world is
portrayed as the battle-ground of systems.   Yet it was
something for the novel to mount the hustings, to come
closely in touch with contemporary feelings and fears,
even if it expressed them in terms of mythology; and for
the historian these books have still the interest that
attaches to the track of old dangers and old debates.

CHAPTER IX

THEORY AND TECHNIQUE

I

I know not whether the novel, like the épopée, has any rules peculiar to itself.—MRS. GRIFFITHS, *The Delicate Distress*, 1769.

THE reader who turns from Fielding or from the modern novel to the narratives of the seventeen-seventies will notice at once a complete absence of that preoccupation with form which marked *Tom Jones* and strongly marks the whole novel-writing world to-day. The moulds into which the novelist of 1770 ran his work were, in the main, those bequeathed to the craft by Richardson and Smollett. The epistolary novel first and foremost, with the easy-going picaresque as a bad second, between them cover his choice. Love-stories were detailed " in a series of letters "—the most common of sub-titles up to the end of the 'eighties—while the " adventure " or " history " was loosely modelled on *Roderick Random* or *Peregrine Pickle*, with a preference for the autobiographical hero. Precept and experiment were alike thin-sown, while the professional critic was ready to talk about anything rather than form. The general attitude was expressed by Herbert Lawrence in *Christopher Crab* (1771) when he rejoiced that " no modern Aristotle has stept forth, and laid down Rules for the Conduct of History " (*i.e.* personal history), and then proceeded to interpret this freedom as a release from responsibility rather than a stimulus to investigation. Dramatists, when they turned to the novel, made the most of the absence of discipline, and

stretched themselves at random, carelessly diffused.[1]
Critics and novelists were agreed as to the material of the
novel; it was to consist of character, manners and sentiment; it was to endeavour to display character in action,
and it was to be guided (not too overtly) to an instructive
close; but they were not deeply interested in the shaping
of the material. *Tom Jones* was admired, but rather as
The Bard was admired; it was ingenious and laborious,
but it raised the question whether such elaboration was
really worth while, when taste could be more cheaply
gratified. The reviewers paid attention to the moral,
probability and characterization of a novel, in that order,
and always chastised a bad style, but they were seldom
tempted to go further, or to apply general principles of
composition to the shapeless narratives that poured from
the press. There are honourable exceptions; Mackenzie
and Jenner are solid enough to be measured by the
universal standards of unity and proportion, but it would
have been waste of time to apply them to the ephemeral
products of nameless novelists, sponsored by Lowndes,
Bell and the Nobles.

During the 'eighties and 'nineties, however, we remark
a growing interest in form, both among the better novelists
and among the critics. In part it is the leaven of Fielding
working in the lump; in part, perhaps, French influence,
though English literature has always shown itself very
well able to resist this; but more importance must be
assigned to the general slow rise in the standard of the
popular novel, of which we have spoken. A significant
figure meets us at the outset of the 'eighties, in the person
of Holcroft, who, in the preface to his first novel, *Alwyn ;
or, the Gentleman Comedian* (1780), differentiates between
the romance and the novel on formal lines, without consideration of material. By the term romance he understands not only the mediæval romantic narratives, but the

---

[1] There are exceptions; *e.g.* Holcroft, Mrs. Inchbald.

anti-romances of Le Sage and Smollett, in which he
rightly sees a continuation of their form; and this he
defines as a fictitious history of detached and independent
adventures; " if the incidents be well marked and related
with spirit, the intention is answered; " we do not look for
interconnection or relevance to a main theme. But " a
novel is another kind of work. Unity of design is its
character. . . . A combination of incidents, entertaining
in themselves, are made to form a whole; and an unnecessary circumstance becomes a blemish by detaching from
the simplicity which is requisite to exhibit the whole to
advantage." Holcroft, like Fielding, approached the
novel by way of the drama and applied something of what
he had learnt in one form to the other. We find him
predisposed to critical investigation, with *Tom Jones* in
his mouth. On the other hand, a no less significant figure
is Bage, who approached the novel with no theories at
all, but was so far aware of them by the time he had
reached his fifth book, as to introduce a lady novelist,
from whose pen " may be expected, one day, that great
desideratum of this most favoured production of the press,
canons of criticism; for want of which, I must needs say,
after Mrs. Holford herself, there is rather too much
heterogeneity." One takes the measure of his unper-
turbed interest by this sentence. *Hermsprong* (1796),
which followed four years later, has some traces of formal
experiment, though Bage has not troubled himself to be
consistent, and some relevant strictures on the author's
own work, put into the mouth of a critic.

Meanwhile the reviewers are beginning to talk about
unity and relevance, and to blame the introduction of too
many episodes. The *Monthly* reviewer in particular
becomes insistent about structure and the dramatic
display of character, pointing his remarks by references to
Fielding. What he says is not new, but the emphasis and
painful clearness with which he expounds it at every

opportunity suggests a man with a mission. The novel has come to stay, and it has got to be licked into shape. Cumberland's *Arundel* is the text for an attack on didactic exposition in the novel; Mrs. Bennet's *Agnes de Courci* for one on the delusion, from which both novel and drama suffered, that " *perplexity* of fable " is necessary, whereas, by forcing character into the secondary place, it destroys, in some degree, " the very *essence* of such a composition " ; *Man as he is* is blamed for its digressions and the German Veit Weber praised because he " steadily attends to that unity of end and that climax of interest which are so perpetually neglected in English works of art." [1] In the 'nineties the *Critical* joined in the campaign. The vineyard certainly needed labourers. Witness the plot of *The Church of St. Siffrid* (1797) which the *Critical* [2] found " rather too complicated ; for there are three persons who appear to be married twice over ; and afterwards it is discovered that the priest who performed the ceremony had never taken orders ; the marriages, therefore, at which he officiated, are annulled. So many invalid marriages being thus introduced, create some confusion, and a degree of intricacy by no means agreeable to the reader." Plot must not be too complex, then, but, on the other hand, a very slight plot jeopardizes the claim of a book to the title of novel. *Zeluco* is " a series of conversation pieces " and the *History of Philip Waldegrave* is compared to " an agreeable but desultory conversation," since the story is no more than a vehicle for the miscellaneous observations of the author.[3] Twenty-four years back, when Bancroft had packed his various note-books into a thin portmanteau of fiction, not a critic had noticed that the result differed in any way from a *bona fide* novel. But it is time to leave the critics and turn to the practitioners.

---

[1] April 1789; Feb. 1790; March 1793; Dec. 1796. The hand is not always the same, but the critics of the *Monthly* show a general interest in form.
[2] Sept. 1797.   [3] v. *Critical*, Jan. 1797 and March 1794.

II

During the 'seventies the epistolary novel was at the height of its favour. It was stamped with the authority of Richardson and the more recent successes of Rousseau and Madame Riccoboni, and it preserved, if only to the eye, that suggestion of authenticity which could no longer delude but still pleased the public.[1] During the 'eighties it loses ground, though not to any marked extent. In the 'nineties the decline was quicker, largely owing to the influence of the Gothic Romance, which demanded a less cumbersome mode of narration, but romance-writers, like Mrs. Mary Robinson, still recurred to the " series of letters " when they turned to the modern novel. It was not, however, until the turn of the century that the fashion had subsided enough for the real nature of the form, its difficulties and its advantages, to emerge once more ; for we are not to suppose these were present in the minds of many of those who used it. They spoke indeed of its aptness for the record of emotion—(" I think Letters," says Mrs. Parker,[2] as she sits down to read a sequence to her friends, " wrote while the heart is yet agitated with the passions they describe, are much more affecting than cold Narrative ")—but they had not the subtlety to avail themselves of it, or of the possibilities latent in it for character differentiation. On the other hand, they knew, and shamefully abused, the opportunities that letters give for suspense. The husband of Melmoth's Emma Corbett, writing from America to his father-in-law, ends his letter—" Oh my God ! I heard a shriek——" ; the assumption is that it is Emma's, but Mr. Corbett had to wait for the next ship before he

---

[1] Cf. also such collections of letters on a slight narrative thread as Croft's *Love and Madness* (1780) and Combe's (?) *Original Love Letters between a Lady of Quality and a Person of Inferior Station* (1784), some of which may have been in part authentic.

[2] v. *History of Miss Pamela Howard* (1773).

knew.[1] The epistolary form in the library novel is either empty of meaning or it is ridiculous. It is either a retrospective narrative, cut into sections and tagged with address and subscription, or it is propped on impossibilities beside which Richardson's are venial. Miss Mariana Melmoth,[2] on leaving her aunt's for a visit to her guardian, promises to devote at least two hours a day to her pen ; but this is nothing, for a young lady in Mrs. Skinn's *Old Maid* (1771) scribbles a vivacious note of eight or nine hundred words while being abducted in a post-chaise. The ability to hold a pen is a mark of convalescence in a heroine, but some letters are punctuated with collapses, which the fair scribbler regards just sufficiently to note : " A glass of hartshorn and water has a little revived me," before she dashes on. Prisoners write when they have no hope that their letters will be conveyed, and tender-hearted gaolers transmit the documents [3] ; characters in the Dark Ages write at length, and the dying Matilda of *The Recess* (1783–5) composes three huge volumes of reminiscences while she awaits her end. Not only are letters written under impossible conditions, but their writers are impossibly communicative. To pass over the cult of detail, which causes idle young men at house-parties to inflict on each other minute character-sketches of their friends, one is continually faced by " moral marvels," like the loyal wife, who details her husband's shortcomings, and the self-revealing villain. Bage, who accepted the epistolary form as he

---

[1] A technique, reminiscent of the cinema, in which we have alternate letters of plotter and victim, and see both approach the crisis, is found in *The Fruitless Repentance* (1769). The immediacy of the letter-form was terribly abused ; cf. the letter of the husband in *The Precipitate Choice* (1772) : " Oh ! my lord, what have I done !—My wife, my adored wife, my Isabella, lies murdered by my side, murdered by me. No, she is not yet dead. She grasps my hand—she strives to speak," etc., etc. This sort of thing is parodied in *Learning at a Loss* (1778) by G. L. Way.

[2] v. *The Modern Fine Gentleman* (1774).

[3] v. *Orlando and Seraphina* (1787) and Miss Knight's *Marcus Flaminius* (1792).

accepted all the conventions of the novel, and handled it with some freshness, yet caused a man to write to his friend a detailed account, worked up in scene and dialogue, of the seduction in her youth of the woman he is about to marry. Then there is the great difficulty of conveying to the reader the data of the story, when the correspondents are supposed to be close friends. " You cannot have forgotten——" begins Bage's James Wallace to his friend, and then goes on to remind him at length, while another sort of improbability is tapped in the long and detailed political arguments which Mrs. Smith's Desmond records in France for his former guardian.

This garrulity was certainly recognized as improbable, and occasionally letter-writers apologize playfully for it, but it was a convention, swallowed with no more difficulty than, for instance, the operatic convention. Like Miss Harriet Byron, the heroines repeat at length the compliments they receive or overhear. Sometimes a long correspondence passes between two people in the same house, who cannot control their emotions sufficiently for conversation. But these things, foolish as they are, are less disturbing than the difficulty of adapting the method for the display of humorous character. Smollett achieves this in *Humphry Clinker* by means of the various humours, active and observant, of the Brambles and Jerry, and Dr. Moore does fairly well in *Mordaunt* (1800) ; but in an age when readers were seldom trusted very far, the tendency was towards an impossibly self-conscious display on the part of the humorist, and Truncheon Stentor, the old actor in Holcroft's *Alwyn* (1780), writes in brogue. Holcroft tackled the difficulty again in the character of Abimelech Henley, in *Anna St. Ives* (1792), and though he overshoots the mark and puts a burden on the reader's patience, he does strike out an appropriate style, " energetic, but half unintelligible," for that shrewd, ignorant and formidable person. Epistolary authors, however, could not on the whole afford to consider probability; it cramped them too much. Melmoth, in the *Tutor of Truth* (1779), made one attempt to construct a novel from letters that are fairly natural in length, occasion and communicativeness; but the result is jejune and dull, and he did not repeat the experiment.

There is little to say about the autobiographical narrative, which was customary among writers of the picaresque. Trusler and Bage varied it by putting the narrative into the mouth of the hero's friend,[1] but the sense of form had to be far more highly developed before the possibilities of such a mirror could be tested. Simple narrative had always been in use for tales of the past, and it grew in popularity as the century waned. We find books in which the epistolary form breaks down into, and is interwoven with, narrative.[2] All these forms perpetuate the inserted narration, which had been a feature of seventeenth-century romance. For the scribbler it was an easy way of padding out three or four volumes, and in the hands of more skilled writers it could be turned to the purposes of contrast. Thus Mrs. Smith inserts the tragedy of the heroine's parents into the last volume of *Celestina* (1791), and makes the discovery the means of ensuring the happiness of their daughter. But already here and there stray voices were raised against this ancient device; it broke the continuity of interest, and, as Cumberland says in *Henry* (1795), a book which eschews narrations, "whatever makes a pause in the main business, and keeps the chief character too long out of sight, must be a defect."

Wearied beyond patience by the monotony of these prattling letters and patchwork adventures, it is with some relief that the reader comes on traces of a similar im-

---

[1] v. John Trusler's *Life; or, the Adventures of William Ramble* (1793) and Bage's *Hermsprong* (1796).
[2] E.g. Lady Mary Walker's *Munster Village* (1778) and Mrs. Bonhote's *Olivia; or Deserted Bride* (1787).

patience in contemporary writers. In 1771 Dodsley published *The Disguise*, a *dramatic novel*, in which the author, finding that " epistolizing, journalizing, and narrating have grown so hackney'd, that Novels grow unprofitable to the writer, and insipid to the reader," tries to introduce a little variety by casting his story into dialogue. He may have taken the hint from *Tom Jones*, where there are chapters essentially dramatic in form. At all events, he carried the method as far as he could, prefixed a list of dramatis personæ, divided his novel into acts and scenes, avoided even stage directions, and managed to produce a readable, though odd book. It would not have met the stage requirements of the day, but its dramatic form favoured a certain liveliness and speed of movement that was eminently desirable in the novel. The example made little impression, for when Mrs. Gibbes threw her novel *The Niece ; or the History of Sukey Thornby* (1788) into the form of conversations with narrative and explanatory links, she described it as " written on a plan *entirely new*." Again the dramatic associations have the effect of tightening up the dialogue.

One trait of fashion which is fairly frequent from the beginning of the period, and received added popularity when stories of the past became common, is the introductory episode, or frame. In its simplest form this recounts how the " editor " obtained the " papers " which form the main body of the book, whether he traced them from the single sheet, wrapped round the butter in a cottage where he sheltered from the rain, or bought them from a disappointed landlord, whose absconding tenant has left them behind ; but it is subject to a good deal of elaboration, and while it serves in the first instance to stimulate the reader's attention and playfully to shift from the author's shoulders the responsibility for the quality of his entertainment, it was often highly finished for its own sake, and for the sake of the contrasts and harmonies to be drawn between the frame and the picture.   Graves was fond of these frames ; *Columella* (1779) is set in a lightly-touched coach-journey from Oxford to London, and *Eugenius* (1785) is introduced by the talk of two old friends in a coffee-house.   Writers of historical novels and Gothic romances made great play with them.   Very often the introductory scene itself was in the past, and the story, thus doubly removed, acquired an added mystery.   The finest example of this type of introduction is the prologue to Mrs. Radcliffe's *Italian* (1797), in which the Church of Santa Maria del Pianto, with the figure of the assassin gliding through it, subdues the reader's mind to the right tone, and, while quite unconnected with the story, may be compared, as Scott suggested, " to the dark and vaulted gateway of an ancient castle."   The most amusing example is certainly the " inner frame " (for the story is doubly enclosed) of James White's *Earl Strongbow* (1789), the conversations of the seventeenth-century gentleman with the lordly and antique ghost on the battlements of Chepstow Castle.

How to begin was a question very present in the minds of authors during the 'eighties and 'nineties, especially of those who had discarded the epistolary form.   The leisurely, low-toned beginnings of the older novelists, though still retained by Mrs. Smith, for instance, were not calculated to catch the eye of the circulating-library subscriber, and no doubt they looked insipid after the performances of Sterne and his school.[1]   Novelists now began to try the effect of plunging instead of wading into their stories.   " Through the rich and beautiful vale of Evesham a hired postchaise was going at a good rate," is the first sentence of *Arpasia ; or, the Wanderer* (1786). Each of Mrs. Radcliffe's three important books begins in

---

[1] Henry Mackenzie evaded the orderly beginning in the *Man of Feeling* by postulating a mutilated MS.   Mrs. Hamilton imitated him in *Memoirs of Modern Philosophers*.

a different way, and in *The Romance of the Forest* (1791) she tried the conversational opening which began to be popular at this time.[1] The author of *Valentine* (1790), however, aims at a far more striking effect. " These are thy trophies, O ambition ! these are thy spoils ! said Valentine, as he rested his right foot on a drum, his body supported by a halbert, both the property of two brave youths, who lay dead at his feet." It is an introductory tableau, with flourish of trumpets.

The dramatic influence, of which we find traces in the scenes, characters and style of the novels, did not extend as far as the structure of the plot. There are exceptions. *The Disguise* has been mentioned, and we may add Mrs. Inchbald's *Simple Story* (1791). The author designed her book on the model of *Winter's Tale*, a story of wrong and reconciliation in two generations, and it is penetrated with her dramatic experience.[2] There is in it an economy of character and incident, a close attention to business, which she probably learnt from the stage, though the lesson was to hand in the French novel ; it is, at any rate, exceedingly rare in contemporary English fiction.

English taste has always inclined towards lavishness of material, and the volumes of the late eighteenth-century novel are crowded with incident. Even in those few comparatively brief and orderly books that suggest French models, such as Mackenzie's *Julia de Roubigné* (1777) and Elizabeth Blower's *Features from Life ; or, a Summer Visit* (1788), the authors have been unable to resist filling in the background, while the epistolary novels suffer from an excess of plot. *Sir Charles Grandison* proved a more practicable part of Richardson's legacy than *Clarissa ;* for the brooding intensity of imagination that made every

---

[1] Cf. *Henry and Isabella* (1788) by Mrs. Rice Hughes, and *Orlando and Lavinia* (1792).

[2] Mackenzie's *Man of the World* (1773) is also a " two-storeyed " book, concerning father, mother and daughter, but it is not influenced in structure by drama.

lumbering sentence and trivial detail of *Clarissa* directly
relevant to the main theme were unique qualities, and
Richardson's imitators could make up for the lack of them
only by a multiplication of situations, for which precedent
was found in the overlapping character-groups and con-
current love-stories of *Sir Charles Grandison*.   In *Anecdotes of a Convent* (1771), for instance, six couples approach
marriage by devious routes, and the arrangement of the
younger characters of Mrs. Skinn's *Old Maid* (1771) is
almost as symmetrical.   This mechanical symmetry,
however, is the only formal quality these books can boast,
for the different love-stories are so loosely tacked together,
the narrations into which some of them are cast are so
inartificially introduced, that there is little more than the
bookbinder's thread to hold them in one book.   The
eighteenth-century novel is disarmingly easy-going.[1]
Even to respectable writers a novel must have presented
itself largely as a certain number of sheets to be filled with
the loosely-concatenated experiences of a group of
characters.   Unity of plot was seldom considered ; the
pillar-to-post movement of the picaresque did not demand
it, while the epistolary form favoured a sort of bisection
of the novel, by which the two chief correspondents
impart to each other two wholly separate sequences of
events.   This is the form that has recently been revived
by Mr. Hugh Walpole and Mr. J. B. Priestley in *Farthing
Hall*, in which, as in some of its predecessors, the two
stories cross at the end ; but the ingenious stroke that
submits the characters of one correspondent to the vision
of the other is unparalleled in the older novels.   Nor was
relevance more strictly interpreted.   Anything was deemed
relevant that might occupy the minds of the characters,

---

[1] So were the critics on points of form ; cf. the mild strictures of
the *Critical* on Harriet Lee's *Errors of Innocence* (1786). The
receiver finds the story obscure, but sets it down to inexperience.
" In the beginning," he suggests kindly, " she seems to have had no
regular plan, and consequently could not provide for the succeeding
events."

whether it had any influence on the story or not. Anecdote, literary criticism and moral disquisition variegate the pages ; minor characters break forth into affecting but superfluous narrations, while, within sight of the end of the book, the heroine may have bequeathed to her, or even accidentally find, the autobiography of a wholly new character, traced painfully in minute detail on her death-bed. Among the better writers the example of Sterne, even where he was not directly imitated, acted as a power-ful solvent on all traditions of coherence and proportion, while to the natural negligence of bad writers were added the hand-to-mouth conditions under which they worked. Thomas Bridges (who is not, however, to be classed as a bad writer) has an odd apology to his readers at the end of the first volume of *Adventures of a Bank-Note* (1770). He is sorry that he cannot now finish the episode of the old genius and his son, but the end of the volume has stolen upon him unawares, and, as the second is already half printed off, he is obliged to pop the old gentleman and his son Jack into the latter part of it. He did so, and in this confused fashion the book was presented to the public.

Gross examples, however, are insufficient proofs of a universal attitude. A finer one can be adduced in the shape of Henry Mackenzie's *Julia de Roubigné* (1777), which Scott admired as " one of the most heart-wringing histories that has ever been written." The story is simple and coherent, framed to exhibit those fine grada-tions of sentiment, those " features of the heart," which were the end and aim of Mackenzie's novel-writing. One is sensible in reading it of that diffused Shakespearian influence which is so common a feature of the time ; for the theme has resemblances to that of *Othello*, though an *Othello* shorn of its deeper harmonies and delicately fingered on Mackenzie's harpsichord. Montauban, middle-aged, Spanish by education, sober and morose by habit, falls in love with Julia de Roubigné, only child

of a ruined nobleman.   Her father's misfortunes, her
mother's death, the obligations under which the whole
family stand to Montauban, force her step by step into
an alliance to which she can bring only respect and
gratitude ; yet she withholds her hand until she learns
that Savillon, to whom her affections are given, has taken
a wife in Martinique.   Then she marries Montauban and
follows him, with vague, unhappy forebodings, over the
dark threshold of her new home.   Up to this point the
story has moved fairly rapidly ; the next step should have
been to bring Savillon to France, to assure Julia of his
constancy, and then with doubled speed, concentration
and pressure to sweep forward to the catastrophe, when
Montauban, convinced by small ambiguous circumstances
of Julia's guilt, in a passion of outraged love and pride
poisons first her and then himself.   Julia and her husband
are the centre of the story, and into that centre he should
have swept the young man from Martinique.   It is,
however, just here that Mackenzie chooses to check the
tragic momentum by inserting an episodical account of
Savillon's experiences, of his humanitarian efforts on
behalf of the negro slaves, and of his friendship with one,
Herbert, who has a story to tell.   It is all extraneous
material, except in so far as it builds up Savillon's
character—which could have been done more economic-
ally in Julia's letters—and Mackenzie was quite aware
of its superfluousness ; but " the picture it exhibited
pleased myself, and I could not resist the desire of laying
it before my readers."   No novelist of the seventeen-
seventies could resist such a desire, and once again
purity of outline is sacrificed to didactic and pathetic
discursiveness.

You hear no word of critical blame for such divagations,
at least until the century is in its last years.   A patch of
information in so light a form as the novel could never
come amiss, while an affecting episode justified itself.

The volumes of periodical essays, which were still favourite reading, had accustomed the public to take their entertainment in disconnected fragments, and the *Spectator*, with its constantly varying interest and its light linkages from paper to paper, served as a model for many novels, and as a quarry for others. A novel could easily be made by adjusting some half-dozen tales and an essay or two in a slight narrative framework, and after this fashion many were constructed.

The point has been sufficiently emphasized, though it is hardly possible to exaggerate it; but it is possible to approach this laxity of structure from another angle. It is abundantly clear that careful articulation of plot and due regard for proportion, even in a simple story, were not among the principles of composition current in the 'seventies and 'eighties. But principles of composition there must have been; and we shall appreciate them more easily if, remembering the *Sentimental Journey* and the *Man of Feeling*, we discard the term structure, with its architectural suggestions, and think of these books rather in terms of colour. What their authors aimed at—at least, the best of them—was delicacy and variety of emotional hue. The novel was to be a sort of artificial rainbow, woven of tears and glinting sunshine, but allowing, at times, of more violent contrasts. The tender hues of sensibility and benevolence lie beside the harsh tones of egoism and brutality, and, though the structural connection between the two may be of the slightest, we are led by their juxtaposition to contemplate the possibilities for good and evil of the human spirit. With this clue to guide us, the excursions of the eighteenth-century novelist appear less wholly irrelevant. Mrs. Brooke, for instance, in her *History of Emily Montague* (1769), having brought two virtuous attachments to fruition and anchored a libertine in matrimony, introduces into her fourth and last volume the episode of an imprudent girl, brought to ruin and death by a villain. The episode is an excrescence on the plot, and only so far connected with the chief characters as to be recounted to Emily, now a happy wife, and to afford her and her husband an opportunity for charity and reflection. It does not in any way affect their actions or their relationship. Yet it is not, as at first blush it seems, a mere bit of padding. It has its place, not in the plot, but in the chiaroscuro of the story. It is the core of shadow as Emily and Rivers are the focus of light. Mrs. Brooke's leisurely and almost plotless book is designed to bring out the quality, the emotional and spiritual colour, of three marriages. There are Emily and Rivers, kindred souls, in whom passion is tempered by that combination of honourable pride and mutual respect which was one of the aspects of " delicacy "; there is Bell Fermor, the honest coquette, who makes a happy marriage with a man who trusts her and delights in her vivacity; and there is Rivers's friend, Temple, settling down after a career of conquest with a wife who, in spite of their reciprocal affection, must often be hurt by his blunted susceptibilities and alarmed for his faith. Lower than this in the scale of sense Mrs. Brooke did not care to go, at least for her principal characters. Yet somehow the errors of passion were to be indicated and the scale completed. She does this by reflection, by allusion and anecdote, and finally and most emphatically by the episode in question. The lovers, safe in harbour, look out at the shoals of greed and ruthlessness which they have avoided, and give thanks.

In this rambling and half-conscious manner, the novelists of the late eighteenth century anticipate at times some of the developments of twentieth-century fiction. Plot, the chain of ordered and interconnected happenings, which became indispensable in the nineteenth century, has not yet established such an ascendancy over their minds, and the gist of their novels is often best expressed

in terms of contrasted sentiment or of mental development. This is notably the case with Mary Wollstonecraft's first book, *Mary, a Fiction* (1788). Compared
with modern work, its handling is sketchy ; one is reading
notes for a novel rather than the novel itself; but it is
designed in accordance with modern values. It was an
attempt to display " in an artless tale, without episodes,
the mind of a woman who has thinking powers," and to
trace her experience to the point when she has learned
self-mastery. During Mary's neglected girlhood, her
sensibilities are exercised by the natural events of an
obscure life, by the wild nature around her, and by a
warm but not wholly reciprocated friendship for a young
woman, Ann. She is married at her mother's death-bed,
for reasons of expediency and property, to a boy who
leaves her at once to go on his travels ; while she, now her
own mistress, accompanies Ann, who is in decline, to
Lisbon. There, in a hotel for invalids, she nurses her,
sees her die, and rallies from her passionate grief to attach
herself with equal intensity to Henry, a sick genius staying
in the house. The situation has to be thought out, and
she comes home alone to England to decide on her course
of action ; Henry follows her and dies. Months of agony
are briefly indicated, during which the ardent soul, under
the discipline of sorrow and loneliness, learns to accept
life ; into these pits the novel had not yet learned to
penetrate, and the book ends abruptly with the information
that Mary joined her husband and devoted her life to the
needs of others. It is a fine theme in inexperienced
hands ; there is a suggestion of richness and depth in the
book that is never wrought out, of impulse, struggle and
attainment which, however poorly conveyed, are felt to
be real. The crises of Mary's spiritual development
come at times in a form so angular and abrupt that the
reader's first reaction is a smile ; but on a second glance
the image of her, standing on deck and singing Handel

into the thunder of the storm, is seen for what it is, the symbol of an ecstasy of pain and nascent fortitude.

In the last ten years of the century, the sustained and elaborately-concatenated plot, which had not made good its footing when put forward by Fielding simply in the interests of beautiful craftsmanship, established itself as a necessary consequence of the cult of suspense, mystery and surprise in the Gothic Romance. The alternating scenes of excitement and explanatory recapitulation, by means of which Mrs. Radcliffe developed her plot, are the most characteristic expression of this new interest, but it was inherent in the Gothic material and is found on a small scale in *The Castle of Otranto* and *The Old English Baron*.[1] Whether or no the public had consciously demanded sustained excitement in the novel, or contrasted it in this respect with the drama, at least they greeted it with enthusiasm when it was supplied. Elaborate plots, propped on suspense, became the fashion, and Joseph Fox in the prefatory epistle to *Santa-Maria ; or, the Mysterious Pregnancy* (1797) explains that his intention is to cause the reader to hasten on, " wishful to ascertain the clue of those complicated paths he has been travelling through," but so to arrange matters that, when he looks back, he shall find " mountains of difficulty . . . levelled at the end, to the plain, smooth surface of probability." [2]

The intricacy of the Gothic plots, based upon the interweaving of a multiplicity of agents and motives, taught novelists to control a complicated story, but left untouched the greatest weakness of the eighteenth-century novel, the disconnection between character and

---

[1] Also the *Duke of Exeter* (1789), a pseudo-historical novel, either translated from the French or based on French models. The whole book is a suspended mystery, and the baffling actions of the hero are not explained until the last few pages, when he reveals on his death-bed that he has acted for months as the villain's confidential secretary, to detect and outwit his plots.

[2] Cf. Courtney Melmoth, who explains and justifies his method in *Family Secrets*, V, p. 379 (1797).

action. There is nowhere an action so directly referable to character as that of Miss Austen's *Emma* ; for Miss Burney's *Cecilia*, deliberate and conscientious as it is, does not escape a suggestion of artifice in the situations based on Mr. Beverly's will. Commonly, plots are kept going by arbitrary devices, while a number of characters, described at full length, are never drawn into the action at all. Miss Burney, however, whose laborious craftsmanship demands recognition if it cannot inspire delight, knew how to make even her minor characters help on the story.

III

In *Cecilia* (1782), which is in many ways an instructive document in the history of the novel, the character-drawing is on two levels. There is the careful, substantial portraiture of individuals,—Monckton, the flighty, generous Belfield and his mother, and Morrice, the young lawyer,—and there are the vigorous sketches of humours and types,—Delvile and Briggs and the male and female fops,—mechanically balanced and hardened by ridicule and exaggeration. The supper-party of " humours " at Vauxhall, broken up by Harrel's tragedy, shows Miss Burney passing from one level to the other. The survival in the novel of the rigid, epigrammatic type of description, formerly associated with the satiric " character," was favoured, though not in Miss Burney's case, by that detachment of character from action of which we have spoken, and is particularly in evidence in those parades of social follies which are marshalled glibly by the heroine's pen, whenever she attends a house-party. The corrective to this excess of satiric analysis, as to the excess of senti-mental analysis which is sometimes though not often apparent, was, to put it roughly, the stage, by which is meant a combination of the influences exerted by plays themselves, by the methods of actors, and by the dramatic character-presentation of Fielding.

A fairly long list can be compiled of novelists who were also dramatists,[1] but not all the names would be relevant, since some of them, far from importing dramatic qualities into the novel, used it for relaxation. Cumberland, however, is worth a glance, and Mrs. Inchbald a somewhat longer study. Cumberland, aware that *Arundel* (1789) moves with greater boldness and rapidity than the usual story of love, though its movement was along conventional lines, prefixed to the third edition (1795) what is rather an excuse than a defence. He refers to his practice on the stage, which " requires a strong cast of characters, and a striking relief of light and shade," and has no time for " that tantalizing and minute precision in developing the passions which the French novelists are so expert in." [2] The most interesting parts of *Arundel* are certainly those which recall the drama; the dialogue has point and pace, and it is with delight that one leaves behind the arduous wit and compliment, the circling, gossiping, unprogressive talk of the school of Richardson. Significant dialogue, which at once reveals character and carries on the action, had languished in the 'seventies; its greater frequency is one of the signs of the improvement of the novel. The influence of *Tom Jones* is felt; Melmoth in *Shenstone-Green* conducts a reconciliation scene between two lovers in eight pages of dialogue without any comment at all, and Bage, who is fond of recording talk and natural at it, writes chapters of *Hermsprong* in which he is plainly trying hard to let character express itself through speech. But the book that is most penetrated with the experience

---

[1] *E.g.* Mrs. Griffith, Mrs. Brooke, Thomas Hull, Thomas Bridges, Henry Brooke, Sophia Lee, Thomas Holcroft, Richard Cumberland.
[2] Cf. Walpole's preface to the *Castle of Otranto*, in which he compares the character-drawing and brief indications of place to those of dramatic art. Here also there was no room for sentimental expansion.

of the stage is the *Simple Story* of Elizabeth Inchbald, actress and dramatist.

The *Simple Story* is too well known for a detailed account of it to be necessary. It was enthusiastically praised by Miss Edgeworth, and is still charming, both in itself and for extraneous reasons, such as its picture of John Philip Kemble in Dorriforth. It was a first novel, written over many years by a woman whose whole training had been dramatic. All the important points are made in dialogue, and the action passes before the eye in a series of small and highly-finished scenes. It is this scenic quality, this power of stirring the visual imagination of the reader, that must arrest our attention.

It is, of course, impossible to point to any age in which fictitious narrative is not illumined by descriptive touches; but there is a difference between these scattered touches and a deliberate policy of visual appeal. During the eighteenth century novelists begin consciously to pay attention to picturesque and dramatic effects of background and gesture. The studied record of movements, which are often in themselves quite trivial, was part of Richardson's circumstantial method of narration. All this unnecessary rising and sitting and bowing and pressing of hands is cumulative in its effect; it convinces by weight of its painstaking exactness; we have to believe a witness who can tell us so much. More lively are the details of satiric portraiture, the movement of Mr. Solmes's splay feet " by pauses," and the stick carried by Mr. Briggs in *Cecilia*, " which he usually held to his forehead when not speaking." Set descriptions of comic characters are frequent, and in these the broad stroke and burlesque comparison of Smollett are much practised [1]; and some-

---

[1] Cf. Dr. Calomel in *Anthony Varnish*, I, p. 52 (1786). He is short, swarthy, blob-nosed, wide-mouthed, with small, piercing black eyes; " his knees formed two angles, which crossed each other alternately as he walked." Also the bishop in *Hugh Trevor*, II, p. 88 (1794): " His legs were the pillars of Hercules, his body a brewer's butt, his

times, when the lines are more flexible, we seem to trace the movements of a comic actor, and wonder if Garrick, or Foote or Shuter so impressed the author that he perpetuated him in a corner of his book. Meanwhile Sterne developed his own variant of the comic description, which, like all his experiments, ran like wildfire through the literary world. It is another aspect of his cult of the trifle,—a minute study of a casual pose or homely gesture, which may have a lifetime of habit behind it, or may be totally void of significance. Part of the effect lies in the mock-heroic suggestion of this elaboration of the unimportant; part in the intensity of interest that so small a splinter of human habit can evoke in the sensible mind. The description, though vivid, is not dramatic. It does not carry the action forward; it checks it; the reader has exactly the impression of turning from the text to glance at an admirable illustration on the opposite page.[1]

With Mrs. Inchbald, however, we come to gesture which is entirely dramatic and which, if not quite new, had the effect of novelty from the lengths to which it was carried. It was remarked by the *Monthly Review* in an enthusiastic notice. " The secret charm, that gives a grace to the whole," wrote the critic, " is the art with which Mrs. Inchbald has made her work completely dramatic. The business is, in a great measure, carried

---

face the sun rising in a red mist. . . . His mighty belly heaved and his cheeks swelled with the spiritual inflation of church power. . . . Clearing his sonorous throat of obstructing phlegm . . . he welcomed me to London."

[1] *E.g.* Jenner's *Placid Man* (1770) : " Why then," said the governor, thrusting one arm into the sleeve of his coat and wrapping his handkerchief round the other as he spoke, " why then—more fool he ! " Also *The Younger Brother* (1770) where the old squire, forced to economize, is advised to sell his horses and hounds. " My father sunk back in his chair, and accidentally broke his pipe; he stared in silent admiration, put the fragment of his pipe softly upon the table, lolled upon his left elbow, and stuck the thumb of his right hand through the third buttonhole of his coat. Thus he sat with his eyes fixed stedfastly on the floor, unable to utter a word."

on in dialogue. In dialogue the characters unfold themselves.[1] Their motions, their looks, their attitudes,
discover the inward temper." To this we may add a
shrewd comment of Miss Edgeworth, in a letter to Mrs.
Inchbald,[2] which brings her art even nearer to the art of
fine acting. " I am of opinion," she wrote, " that it is
by leaving more than most writers to the imagination that
you succeed so eminently in affecting it. By the force
that is necessary to repress feeling we judge of the intensity
of the feeling, and you always contrive to give us by
intelligible but simple signs the measure of this force."
We are worlds away here from Richardson's charted
conversations. Mrs. Inchbald, it is true, sees her whole
scene as a producer must see it ; she knows exactly how
and where all her characters are placed, and, when it is
relevant, imparts her knowledge ; but the movements she
describes are the significant ones, those that would catch
a spectator's eye in a theatre and add to his emotion or his
knowledge. They are more often subtly than obviously
relevant, and frequently they take the place of speech.
Thus Miss Milner, when Lord Frederick has the ill-
breeding to quote Abelard and Eloisa in Dorriforth's
presence, throws open the sash and looks out, and, when
she receives her guardian's command not to attend the
ball, stands with her hand on the handle of the half-open
door, " irresolute whether to open wide in defiance, or to
shut submissive." At moments of retort or tension she
will rapidly sketch the bearing of all the company, flashing
the scene upon us with dexterous strokes, each stroke
leading up to and reinforcing the main conflict. Dorriforth's movements are most carefully studied ; they are
few, and by their restraint help to give the measure of the
force they suppress. His reception of his dead wife's
letter, and his equally silent and characteristic reception

---

[1] Boaden in his *Memoir* mentions the " professional bias " in her
use of dialogue.   [2] Jan. 14th, 1810.

of his daughter on the morning after his rescue of her, were something new in fiction. It was trusting the reader as he had seldom been trusted before. There are suggestions for such a technique in Fielding, but they are flying hints. Holcroft, who does not otherwise carry deep marks of his stage experience, has touches of the same unexpected visualization as Mrs. Inchbald, and with Cumberland we are at times conscious of the boards.[1] But nobody before her saw the possibilities of the dramatic treatment so well, or carried them out so consistently.

Her example did not spread very rapidly. There is a great deal of what may be called stylized gesture in the sentimental parts of eighteenth-century novels and romances,—kneelings and raisings, and liftings up of fine eyes, and pressings of the benefactor's hand to one's heart in silent ecstasy, not to speak of the slapping of villainous brows and other handsome expressions of violent feeling.[2] These may also claim to be dramatic in a bastard sense; that is, they are stagey; for they certainly include some shoddy fragments of the technique which tragic actors

[1] Cf. *Arundel*, Letter XIV (1789)—the entry of the General to his wounded nephew, who rises to greet him : " He led me back by the hand, assisted in arranging my posture, and then with great state and deliberation seated himself at some distance in a chair." N.B. " at some distance." Cf. also *Henry*, Bk. IX, ch. vi. Delapoer hears of the existence of his son : " As she spoke these words, Delapoer's senses seemed lost in astonishment ; he smote his hands together in a transport of joy, gazed upon her eagerly for a while, then cast his eyes to Heaven ; his lips moved, but no voice was heard ; then throwing himself back in his chair, he seemed lost in meditation, till, roused to sudden recollection, he adjured her, in most solemn terms, to confirm the truth of what she had told him by an appeal to Heaven." The influence of the actor is obvious, and in one place Cumberland appeals to his art.

[2] Cf. *The Old English Baron* (1777). Edmund, now reinstated in his patrimony, receives his earlier protectors. " The baron and Sir Philip entered the hall hand in hand ; Edmund threw himself at their feet, and embraced their knees, but could not utter a word. They raised him between them, and strove to encourage him ; but he threw himself into the arms of Sir Philip Harclay, deprived of strength, and almost of life. They supported him to a seat, where he recovered by degrees, but had no power to speak his feelings ; he looked up to his benefactors in the most affecting manner ; he laid his hand upon his bosom, but was silent."

found necessary in the great theatres of the period, or rather of that technique as debased by strollers and barnstormers. They can be accepted by the well-intentioned as a sort of emotional shorthand, but like all artificial tradition they tended to obscure the view of the real, and we find Holcroft in *Hugh Trevor* impatiently discarding the conventions when he makes Hugh say of himself and Wakefield, on their reconciliation : " We did not embrace, for we were no actors." Gradually this old skin was sloughed and spectacular indulgences retrenched, but the spontaneity and freshness of Mrs. Inchbald's dramatic vision remained for a long while unmatched.

Meanwhile the appeal to the visual imagination of the reader had been made upon another ground, and novelists began to pay particular attention to the setting of their stories. We have here to do with two different kinds of material. There is the genre-painting of interiors and there is landscape. The former, of which there is an early example in Smollett's inn-kitchen in *Sir Launcelot Greaves* and a very good specimen in Hutchinson's description of the miser's cottage in *A Week at a Cottage* (1775), finished down to the dangling dishclouts and the blue-and-brown stockings drying on the thorn trees, is a part of manners-painting, and can be paralleled in the satiric and reflective poems of the century, Hutchinson's harsh precision with Pope's " worst inn's worst bed," and Richard Graves's humaner interiors [1] with Goldsmith. There are no new sources of emotion in this work ; poets and essayists had tapped the vein, and it flowed easily and inevitably into the novel, the more so when the failure of strong central ideas caused attention to focus itself on

---

[1] Cf. Parson Pottle's " tolerably neat parlour " in *The Spiritual Quixote*, II, p. 13 (1772): " His elbow-chair stood ready for his reception, and his Tunbridge-ware tobacco-dish, with some scraps of paper folded for the use of his pipe, were placed on the table. There were several old newspapers lying in the window, and a single picture of Cardinal Fleury hung over the chimney-piece."

highly-wrought fragments. Landscape, however, had about it something of a new revelation. That conscious attention to natural scenery and its effect on the mind, which marks the second half of the eighteenth century, together with that discovery of the beauty of barren land-scape, of the mountainous, the abrupt and the picturesque, which was its special excitement, expresses itself in poetry and in landscape-painting, and was soon to over-flow into the novel. The well-known story need not be retraced here. From the lonely house in *Pamela*, with its carp-pond and avenue, to the admired " ruralities " of Charlotte Smith is a simple though slow progression. From lawns and fruitful vales, adapted for picnics, we pass easily to the Welsh mountains and even farther afield, following the travelling chaises of hero and heroine, and drawing on the accumulated stores of the picturesque tourist. A mind delicately sensible to the beauties of nature becomes a *sine qua non* for heroines. Landscape, too, supplements music as the test of the man who is fit for treasons, stratagems and spoils, and we read that " over the gloom of Schedoni no scenery had at any moment power." So lavishly was the new charm applied that critics remonstrated, chid Mrs. Radcliffe for her " exuberance of description "—it was afterwards called, less kindly, the *Radcliffian mania*—and congratu-lated Mrs. Smith, the other great exponent of landscape in fiction, on her growing restraint.

In their endeavour to touch those harmonies that vibrate between the human and non-human creation, the novelists transplant into prose a method which they learned from the great narrative poets, English and Italian, and from Shakespeare. Most of the writers who developed the lyrical mood in fiction were women, such as Charlotte Smith, Ann Radcliffe, Helen Maria Williams and Mary (" Perdita ") Robinson, and they had themselves written poetry before they turned to the novel. If they needed further stimulus, it could be found abroad in *La Nouvelle Héloïse, Paul et Virginie* and *Werter*. The new taste could be modified in favour of a realistic or a romantic temperament. On one hand, we have the sober, veracious sketches of Charlotte Smith, and the less sober but still veracious autumnal woodlands of her admirer, Egerton Brydges; on the other, the glowing, ideal pictures, those sublime baths of colour and radiance, of Mrs. Radcliffe and her imitators. The first were transcripts of English landscapes; the second were recognized attempts to reproduce in words the effect of the great seventeenth-century landscape-painters, Claude, Salvator Rosa and the Poussins. For a generation the connection between descriptive prose and pictorial art was mistakenly close. There had been instances of the same sort of error —for error it is, in that it fixes and flattens the scene into a momentary rigidity, breaking the flow of life in the narrative [1]—in the Renascence; it is easy to trace the influence of pictures on Spenser and Sidney [2]; but the practitioners were too few to set a fashion. In the eighteenth century, however, the spread of the novel and the popular craze for the picturesque combined to form a curious short chapter in the development of technique; for, while the lyrical assumption of scenery into the mood of a narrative was a permanent contribution to prose fiction, the delineation of landscape and figure in the terms of the picturesque was a short-lived aberration. [3]

---

[1] The device can be rightly used to perpetuate a moment of emotional tension. So at the beginning of *Julia de Roubigné*, Julia's father warns her and her mother of misfortune, and their poses as they stand, ready to impart and receive the news, are described. The emotion of the scene is indicated in Julia's comment: " Methought, as I looked on them, I was above the fears of humanity."

[2] *v.* E. Legouis, *Spenser*, Ch. V (1926).

[3] The picturesque description as practised by Scott, who seems to have learned it from Mrs. Radcliffe, provided John Leycester Adolphus with an important clue in laying the Waverley Novels at the door of the author of *Marmion* : v. Letter VI.

An early example of this impingement of pictorial art on the novel is found in *Ferdinand Count Fathom*.[1] It is brief as compared with later developments of the fashion, but its inspiration is unmistakable. The scene is the sick-bed of the rascal count. Elinor, we are told, is on her knees by his bedside, and Don Diego stands at the head, with his right hand on his breast. That is the test sentence. The position of Don Diego's hand has absolutely no psychological or dramatic bearing; it has nothing to do with the story, and it does not express emotion; but it does put the scene before us with picturesque vigour. Later, in *Humphry Clinker*, Smollett with fine comic effect transfers this artist's consciousness to one of his characters, and Sir Thomas Bulford, contriver of the false alarm of fire, watches Lismahago's nocturnal descent by the ladder, with the wind blowing his night-shirt and the links and torches gleaming on his thin shanks, in a rapture of æsthetic enjoyment, calling on the names of Rosa, Rembrandt and Schalken, and ejaculating : " What lights, what shadows, what a group below ! " Smollett's idea was developed in the 'seventies by William Hutchinson and Henry Mackenzie,[2] and most effectively popularized in the 'nineties by Mrs. Radcliffe. The method applied equally to landscape and to figures, and its vogue was perhaps strengthened by the absence of illustrations in English novels ; perhaps also by the belief, occasionally expressed by critics and novelists, that painting is a more expressive art than writing and capable of greater emotional effects. The appeal to the painter to supplement the descriptive prose of the novelist is made openly. " A scene for Salvator, had he then existed," says Mrs. Radcliffe of the Pyrenees, when Emily enters them ; the nun, Olivia, kneeling in the slanting rays of a lamp, is compared to a picture by Guido, and " the dark pencil of a Domenichino " is invoked to strengthen the

[1] *v.* Chap. 67.   [2] *v.* Appendix IV.

description of the burial of Madame Montoni in the vaults of Udolpho. These artists, with Claude, the most popular of all, and Caravaggio, are those most frequently named, though there are occasional allusions to Rembrandt, to Reynolds and, in homely scenes, to Hogarth [1]; and the taste in which these " interesting and affecting pieces " are conceived is moulded on their pictures. There is the same search for the impressive, the same rather superficial emphasis. Figures are revealed in strong but partial illumination, groups composed of strongly-contrasted types; opportunities are sought for the study of chiaroscuro, and the graded lights and shadows traced in detail. The type of female beauty has the purity of outline, the quivering emotionalism, of the saints whose eyes swim heavenward in a luxury of devotion from the walls of the Pitti. In landscape there is an equally close connection with the scenes of Claude and Salvator Rosa. Not that individual pictures are reproduced, but the characteristic themes and compositions of these artists are imitated, and to study Mrs. Radcliffe's descriptions of landscapes in connection with the paintings of Claude is to be aware of a close discipleship. The very closeness of the relation, however, emphasizes the writer's mistake; for whereas in looking at a Claude the mind receives a sense of space, and enters into and expands within the picture, these literary imitations convey the impression of something flat and framed. The reader is too conscious of the process of selection and arrangement, and of his own nicely-adjusted point of view; he beholds, perhaps, but does not move in the scene. The sense of artifice is reinforced by the gratuitous way in which these groups " worthy of the pencil " are sometimes introduced,[2] and by the technical terms in which they are described.

[1] v. Appendix IV.

[2] Cf. the picturesque but wholly irrelevant group of gypsies round the fire in the Pyrenees, in the *Mysteries of Udolpho*, Vol. I, Chap. IV. They do not even speak.

Illusion vanishes as one reads of back-scenes and side-screens, of high-lights and relief, of heightening, finishing, tints and varnishes, and even of the canvas and the brush. To the contemporary novelist, however, the process must have seemed less disturbing, no more, in fact, than the summoning of another spell to strengthen his own ; and, laboured as these designs are, their beauty was salutary to the colour-starved novel.

IV

In the style of the late eighteenth-century novelist there are two points of special interest to the student—the contention of realism and elegance in dialogue, and the experiments in coloured and rhythmical prose. For a period that extends over the last half of the eighteenth century and well into the Victorian age, the dialogue of most moderately good novels is written in two styles. The casual interchanges of conversation, the talk of homely characters and in comic scenes, is recognizably natural and based on the living language. In high-flown or sentimental scenes, on the other hand, in exchanges of compliment between hero and heroine and in monologue no attempt is made to preserve the natural tone of speech ; the author aims here at elegance, a rounded " literary " language, rising at times to impassioned rhetoric, such as never flowed from the lips of human being. The distinction is observed in French fiction. In England it holds good for the books of Miss Burney, Holcroft and Bage, though Charlotte Smith goes near to escape it. In the nineteenth century it survives, to give only two examples, in the novels of Scott and Lever. It is always important to remember that realism of detail was only intermittently interesting to eighteenth-century writers ; they will consult it for a space and then discard it, without any scruples, in favour of other qualities. Bage, who, as has been said, showed a growing consciousness of technique in his later books, took up the question of dialogue in *Man as he is*. He is about to describe an embarrassed meeting between Sir George Paradyne and Miss Colerain, and he stops to explain that he does not give an exact record of their speech. " The real expression I believe was what critics call mutilated," he remarks, and so, as the novel had then no use for the mutilated except as an aid to pathos, he goes on to report the sentiments of the embarrassed pair in perfectly rounded periods. Balance was one great mark of elegance in speech ; another was that odd and stilted use of the third person in speaking of oneself and one's companion. " Will you, madam," asks the penitent Marshall in Mrs. Cox's *Burton Wood*, " permit a wretched youth to ask the fate of those who owe to unhappy Marshall their unprecedented misery ? " The answer is : " Certainly, sir, and I wish my intelligence were such as might encourage your early return to virtue." Miss Burney's special brand of elegance consists in the bandying of sustained metaphors and personifications among the speakers, while her comic scenes are notable for their literal, and sometimes tedious, transcript of the talk of vulgarians. The highest peaks of contorted elegance are scaled by Courtney Melmoth. It is with astonishment that we overhear the Honourable and Reverend Armine Fitz-Orton, in *Family Secrets*, addressing his sons on the choice of a profession. " Your election made," concludes this father, " you will, with general purity of life, connect and improve the general qualifications which are requisite, and it will be my delightful care to give them effect." Melmoth was an educated man, but he dabbled in style, and it is obvious that both he and his readers enjoyed the pastime vulgarly described as cracking one's jaw. Nevertheless, realistic detail does gradually gain ground. It can be seen in the

language of country people and of the poor [1]; it can also
be observed slowly modifying the practice of the inserted
narration. This ancient device, though it does not
necessarily offend probability in its substance, invariably
overrides it in its form. The style, the fullness of detail
and the pace of the narration are the same as those of the
main narrative; the author thinks of what the speaker has
to tell and very little of the circumstances under which he
tells it. Narrator and audience melt from his vision and
do not reappear until the story is over. In Holcroft's
Hugh Trevor (1794–7), however, we have the beginning
of a change, for Miss Wilmot, as she tells her story to
Hugh, is not forgotten, and the movement of her speech
is disconnected and broken with emotion. Still, the
realism does not yet go very deep, and the spectacle of a
woman telling the simple truth about her past to a young
man did not suggest to Holcroft a study of refracting angles
of vision and of the varying transparence and opacity of
speech. Miss Wilmot does tell Hugh the simple truth.

Beside the slow growth of realism, the novel exhibits
the endeavours of that persistent but ill-regulated desire
for colour and sublimity, which everywhere underlies
" classical " form in the eighteenth century, to find
expression. In its most common form this craving is
expressed in high-flown language, often figurative, and
tending strongly towards the blank verse of the theatre.
Long passages run wholly into iambic cadence and the
following passage comes, without any other alteration
than the arrangement in lines, from the letter of the dying
Maria to her brother in Mrs. Griffith's *History of Lady
Barton* (1771).

> Will the most tender and affectionate
> Of brothers, with patience, condescend to read

---

[1] *v.* Holcroft's *Hugh Trevor, passim.* Cumberland, on the other
hand, translates the speech of all his rustics in *Henry* into good literary
English.

The sad confession of a dying wretch,
Who owns herself unworthy of his kindness,
Yet trembling on the verge of life, solicits
To obtain his pardon and his pity.
Alas ! my Edward, they will never reach me.
No friendly voice can ever sooth my ear,
Or speak peace to my perturbed heart !
For soon the motion of this pulse shall cease,
And this poor shattered frame return to dust.
Drop then a fond forgiving tear upon
These passages :—'tis all I now can ask,
Or you, e'er long, can grant.

Mrs. Griffith is taking a leaf out of her husband's book, *The Triumvirate* (1764). Reading his manuscript, she had noticed that in describing a storm he had passed from prose to blank verse ; this was new to her, and she admires it, asking him if it was accidental or calculated. He admits that it began in accident, but he is convinced that blank verse is " the natural Measure of Speech, in strong Passion, or warm Description." [1]   In the published book he arranged the passage in lines.   But it is not necessary to ascribe the fashion to the Griffiths.   English runs easily into the iambic cadence ; heightened feeling tends to rhythm ; there had been examples in much earlier novels, and there was the practice of the stage to confirm the tendency.   " Stand off, grim death !   I will not come so tamely," cries the delirious lover in *The Involuntary Inconstant* (1772) ;   " —give me my sword, if I must come, Francfort shall send me bleeding to your arms, or he shall be my prey."   These rhythmical utterances crop up anywhere, even in the middle of books whose patrons are Fielding and Smollett,[2] but they are most frequent in romances and legendary tales, where the sublimity of the language can be strengthened by all sorts of pseudo-antique inversions and contortions of speech.   There is a good deal of it in Hutchinson's *Hermitage* (1771), while his *Week at a Cottage* (1775) is completely written in

[1] v. *Genuine Letters of Henry and Frances* (1766–1770), III, p. 119.
[2] v. *The Prudential Lovers, or the History of Harry Harper*, II, ch. xxiii (1773), a description of a calm.

iambic measure, and cannot possibly be read in prose. It is less a novel on tiptoe than a relaxed poem. The book, published anonymously, is elegantly printed, with a frontispiece from an antique gem, and has altogether a choice and sequestered air. It is in effect a tragic pastoral in a localized north-country setting, is divided into seven days, and may be supposed contemporary in date. The subject is the love of the young shepherd Alciris for Marianne, who lives in chaste poverty with her mother, and its thwarting by his crooked sister Jennetta ; and it tells how, pleading in vain with his avaricious parents, he bursts a blood-vessel and dies, and how Marianne, discovered too late by a rich uncle, runs mad and joins him in the tomb. The best pages contain the realistic description of Cymon's cottage, and these were quoted by the reviewers ; but they do not tone in with the rest of the book, in which such figures as " Attention . . . reaping Wisdom with the arms of scientific pleasure " and " lean Industry . . . languishing upon her loom " help forward the tragedy. Hutchinson has his moments ; he writes of an old crone with admirable grotesqueness, " in her wither'd carcass, hollow sounds incessantly croaked and wandered " ; but on the whole *A Week at a Cottage* is valuable rather as evidence than art. Similar evidence can be found plentifully scattered in eighteenth-century byways. Thus the movement and the stiff adornment of the nature passages in *Maria, or the Vicarage* (1796) suggests an attempt at a prose equivalent of Thomson's *Seasons*. At moments of crisis, we meet with a great deal of half-obliterated imagery, which conveyed, one imagines, a confused sense of sublimity, even if no clear ideas. " Why will you," cries the noble delinquent in Anne Hilditch's *Rosa de Montmorien* (1787), " relax the braced fibres of a heart formed to be the mark of a malignant destiny ? " Established poets, moreover, when they turned to the novel, carried some vestiges of their singing-robes about them. This had been the case with Henry Brooke,[1] whose tremulous sensibilities flash suddenly and not always suitably into prose poetry; and it became more frequently the case towards the end of the century. Hayley's similes in *Cornelia Sedley* (1789) were admired by his French translator; Mrs. Mary Robinson decorated her *Vancenza* (1792) richly, though later she consented to chasten her style, and Helen Maria Williams's *Julia* (1790) is lit with sparse, bright blazes of metaphor. " When an impassioned mind, wounded by indifference, attempts recrimination," she writes, " it is like a naked, bleeding Indian attacking a man arrayed in complete armour." One feels in such utterances an authentic poetic spirit (though not necessarily a strong or a deep one), boldly carrying its special language into prose fiction, in despite of the resultant incongruity. None of the greater novelists had shown how this was to be done, and it was left to the small ones to experiment. They did so, vigorously if not successfully, for the disposition of purple in a novel is a difficult matter, as Charlotte Brontë, the first major novelist to use much of it, proves.

The critics, anxious to classify and delimit the functions of poetry and prose once for all, did not approve of this overlapping and infiltration of the one into the other. Poetical prose was " *prose run mad.*" [2] One defence of rhythmic prose—(the critic took Griffith's line, called rhythm the language of Nature, and adduced Lord Monboddo's belief that men chanted before they spoke [3])

---

[1] Cf. *Juliet Grenville*, II, p. 81–4. A prose lament in five sections, beginning: " O thou bower of my blessedness, the grave-diggers have come upon thee, and ensconced thee on every side, and they have piled the marbles about thee; and I call, but thou wilt not answer, and my hands are wearied and rent in striving to reach thee, but no part, no relict of thee is to be attained."

[2] Cf. *The Egg; or, the Memoirs of Gregory Giddy, Esq.* (1772): " Let me tell you, sir, that at present our very best prose is written in blank verse, and it is universally allowed, that the blank verse of our modern writers is nothing else but prose."

[2] v. *Monthly Review*, Sept. 1789, on Miss Fuller's *Son of Ethelwolf*.

—is outweighed by a body of condemnation. Measured and poetic prose, we are told, will not do in England ; it is an importation from France, where the fetters of verse are heavier than here, and its great parent is Fénelon, though some responsibility must lie with Ossian. " This sort of writing," says Clara Reeve of the latter, " corrupts and spoils our language, and destroys the barrier, which nature has placed, to distinguish between poetry and prose." This was doubtless the point of view of the industrious versifiers who reshaped Sterne and Rousseau and Beckford into heroic couplets.[1] Prose should be sober ; it was ill-advised to aim at elevated effects or to deal with imaginative material. *Caliph Vathek* is a " subject more adapted to Poetry than to Prose," and should at once be fitted with the regulation dress. The prose epics and idylls of Claris de Florian, of which several translations appeared, extort praise for their detail, but are not approved as wholes. Prose-poetry and poetical prose are mongrel forms, against which critics, anxious to prevent the confusion of the orders, must protest. It is certain, however, that novel-readers, educated or ignorant, enjoyed a raised style. Elizabeth Sophia Tomlins in the *Victim of Fancy* praised Miss Lee's *Recess* for a fire and elegance comparable to that of poetry, and there was an audience, lower down the scale of taste, for the " convulsionary "[2] vehemence of German romance. By many ways, by romantic material, lyrical description and heightened style, the novelist sought to invade the territory held sacred to poetry by academic criticism, and to repossess himself of the liberty which Sidney, Greene and Lodge had enjoyed.

---

[1] v. Jane Timbury's *Story of Le Fevre* (1787); Mrs. Russel's *Julia* (1774) and the versification of *Vathek*, by A. V. in the *Gentleman's Magazine*, 1790.

[2] Cf. *Monthly Review*, Dec. 1796, on Veit Weber : " Every sentence dispatches the imagination to the very boundaries of the universe. This fatigues."

A footnote to this development is the insertion of verse into a prose narrative.[1] Usually it was supposed to be the spontaneous effusion of the hero or heroine, often in moments of great tension, and Beckford's heroine in *Modern Novel Writing, or the Elegant Enthusiast* (1796), who takes up her pen, bends her left knee to the ground, to give herself a greater spring, and breaks into verse, is a parody that hardly overshoots the mark. " As I have before remarked," says a character in Mrs. Robinson's *Walsingham* (1798), " the muse never forsook me, when fortune was most severe : I no sooner entered my prison than, with no light but that which a grated window afforded, I wrote the following little ode, in humble imitation of Pope's juvenile production." Even in more suitable positions these lyrical insertions are, whether consciously or not, a confession of insufficiency. The poet-novelist, unable to elicit from prose the range of tones she requires, seizes her other instrument and plays a brief interlude.[2]

Little remains to be said as to the style of the eighteenth-century novel. The influence of Sterne and his broken pathos is everywhere ; the few who resist it, Clara Reeve and Ann Radcliffe for instance, have recourse in moments of tension to a sententious and balanced dignity, a superb gesture, that solves all difficulties by dint of the sheer sublime. This might be called the superhuman style. The false and now penitent Santmorin in Mrs. Radcliffe's *Castles of Athlin and Dunbayne* thus invites the vengeance of the Earl. " With your sword do justice to yourself and virtue, and spare me the misery of long comparing what I am with what I was." What heroic echoes are

---

[1] Mrs. Radcliffe developed this method but she did not originate it. Setting aside early examples, like Sidney's *Arcadia*, there are sets of verses in Miss Palmer's *Female Stability* (1780) and Mrs. Cox's *Burton Wood* (1783).

[2] Mrs. Jane West, however, who continued to defy critical advice by inserting verse, frankly admits that it is because she cannot otherwise get a market for her poetry : v. *A Tale of the Times.*

these ! But if Mrs. Radcliffe admires a draped nobility, Courtney Melmoth prefers naked candour. *Emma Corbett* opens with a letter, couched in the simple, energetic style, from Emma's father to her lover, Hammond. I give it entire.

> " Hammond, you have hurt me. I can no longer look on you with pleasure. Forbear your visits. My daughter Emma shall not be yours. I have an objection. Will you hear it explained ? Being explained, will you *remove* it ? You can : you ought : you *must ;* or this closes our connection. To be at a word, will you render it *possible* for me to call you my son ? I write in confidence. Reply without delay. I love exactness. Farewell. CHARLES CORBETT."

It is an exercise of the sympathetic imagination to detect in this startling succinctness the force and majesty which Melmoth intended it to suggest.

It is appropriate that this book should end with the name of Courtney Melmoth ; a greater name would be out of place ; for while his exuberance and journalistic facility make him an admirable document in the history of the novel and of public taste, his rare touches of something more individual preserve our sense of the life behind his books. This study has been almost wholly concerned with the ephemeral and the imperfect, with modes of thought and feeling which are now as dry as old river-beds when the current has flowed into fresh channels. To try to see them as they were a hundred and fifty years ago has been a work, if not of piety, at least of curiosity and delight. The living mind of to-day reaches back to touch the living mind of the past ; and there is a special pleasure in drawing to light the inconsiderable author, in blowing upon the still smouldering sparks of his talent, and warming one's hands for a while at his neglected little fire.

APPENDIX I

THERE was a steady trickle of French translations during the last half of the eighteenth century, and French novels were widely known and often reviewed in the original. Rousseau, Voltaire, Baculard d'Arnaud and Madame Riccoboni are the names most frequently referred to in the 'seventies, and to these are added later Marmontel and Madame de Genlis, while the romances of Claris de Florian had a certain vogue. The importations were not confined to the better novels, for inferior ones were often translated to keep up the stock of the circulating libraries. English women of letters frequently practised translation from the French, for which they were supposed to be specially fitted. Mrs. Brooke put into English Madame Riccoboni's *Juliet, Lady Catesby* (1764) and Framéry's *Memoirs of the Marquis of S. Forlaix* (1770); Miss R. Roberts translated among much other work Madame de Grafigny's *Letters of a Peruvian Princess* (1774)—also translated in 1752 by Francis Ashworth, Esq.—and Elizabeth Sophia Tomlins adapted her *Memoirs of a Baroness* (1792) from an unnamed French original. Clara Reeve says of French novels in the *Progress of Romance* (1785) that " the best are the most *excellent*, and the worst the most *execrable* of all others," and this represented the average English point of view. " Our ingenious neighbours " were constantly admired for their grace and deftness, for their painting of manners and analysis of sentiment, which was admitted to be beyond anything the English novel could produce; but their moral tone was constantly deplored. Crébillon's *The Night and the Moment* was noted as an example of " chastity of expression and indecency of sentiment." Sometimes, too, the obvious artifice of French work, especially when the colouring is Arcadian, revolts the English critic, and the *London* dismisses Billardon de Sauvigny's *The Rose ; or, the Feast of Salency* (1771) as " a genuine specimen of the motley, tawdry, modern French romance."

F. C. Green in his *French Novelists, Manners and Ideas*, says that the interaction of the French and English novel was continuous, but that no prevailing influence was exercised by the English on the French. On the whole, this judgment holds good in reverse. The influence of Rousseau's lyrical description, for instance, was considerable, but the English poets and Ossian would have ensured the appearance of lyrical description in the English novel if Rousseau had remained unknown in England. In form and technique the French novelists exemplified a standard which English writers acknowledged, but did not often care to imitate.

Of the other European countries, only Germany is important for the study of the eighteenth-century English novel, though a few stray Italian novels were translated,[1] and Spain, through *Don Quixote*, continued influential.[2] During the 'seventies, the only German novelist at all widely known was Wieland, whose *Reason triumphant over Fancy ; exemplified in the singular adventures of Don Sylvio de Rosalva* was translated in 1773 and followed in 1774 by the *History of Agathon*. At the end of the 'seventies came *Werter* (1779), of which we have spoken. During the 'eighties little attention is paid to German

---

[1] *Rosara ; or the Adventures of an Actress* (1770) and *The Genuine Lover ; or the Adventures of the Marchioness de Brianville* (1771), both from the Italian of the Abbé Pietro Chiari.

[2] One other Spanish novel was translated, Father Isla's *History of the Famous Preacher, Fray Gerundo de Campazas* (transl. 1772).

narrative,[1] and what of it was known came to us through the French. In the 'nineties came the flood of German translation, and the names of Veit Weber, Flammenberg Cramer, Miltenberg, La Fontaine and Kotzebue appear in the book lists. Germany is the land of romance and turbulence; better work gets no hearing until the nineteenth century.

[1] *Faustin, oder das philosophische Jahrhundert* was reviewed in the original by the *Monthly* in 1784; *Henrietta of Gerstenfeld* (1787) and *Heerfort and Clara* (1789) in translation.

APPENDIX II

FOR the full flavour of sensibility, it is necessary to read a continuous passage. The following extract from Courtney Melmoth's *Liberal Opinions*, Vol. V (1777) is characteristic in its parade, its complete lack of logic and its real benevolence. The narrator is a clergyman, confused for years in pedantic commentary, who is walking in his garden one evening, when he hears a voice :—

> " I looked over the hedge, and by the help of a glass, which the commentators obliged me to use, I cast my eye upon two figures very oppositely disposed. The one, a courteous hale-looking man was binding his handkerchief pretty hard round the knee of the other, which was neither more nor less than a *horse*, that had, as I afterwards found, just before thrown his rider—the very man who was now employed in so humane an office.
>
> He no sooner perceived me than he begged earnestly that I would step over the hedge, and hold the bridle. This I did. . . .
>
> The owner of the beast now began to strip, and with the fore-flap of his coat, to rub the blood from the nostrils, and the dirt from the forehead of the creature ; and lastly, in a voice (where tenderness softened rebuke) thus spoke to the brute.
>
> And wert *thou* affrighted ; didst *thou* start aside from thy path, for that thou sawest rags and wretchedness in the way of thy ongoing ? See what thou hast got by it. That fall, and these smarting testimonies of it, are so many judgments upon thy barbarity ! So may every wretch fall ; so may every wretch meet

a fate like thine—O thou unkindly beast—who turneth from that through pride, to which he ought through sensibility to approach. And yet thou wert not wont to be so cruel, and so hard-hearted, neither: from my first putting the bit into thy mouth, even unto this day, I have found no blame in thee, till this hour. On the contrary, whenever I have eased the traveller, or the beggar upon thy back, *thou*, as if sensible of the gentle task in which I had engaged thee, would step as if on a shoe of silk, and tread (even in the most uneven paths) as thou wert treading upon a carpet of velvet.

For this one time, I will heal thy bruises, pity, and pardon thee—but—I charge thee to consider my clemency, and sin no more; for in the day that thou insultest misfortune a *second* time, thou shalt surely die.

It was not till this moment that I discovered a very poor creature of the female sex, sitting in a pensive posture, with a small scrip by her side, and a baby nestled in the softness of slumber within her bosom; a bosom which, in defiance of her circumstances, was white as snow. Pray, said I to the horseman, who is that young woman at the border of the bank? *Who* she is, I really know not, replied the stranger, but *what* she is appeared to me so manifest a little time ago, that I was dismounting to relieve her, when this cruel animal (pointing to his horse) affected to be frightened, flew out of the road, and as you see, got a broken knee and a bloody nose for his pains, for which, though I love him tenderly, I am not sorry: however, if you will continue to hold his bridle— as there is no trusting to man or beast, when the devil has once got possession of him—I will now go and perform my duty.

Saying this, the stranger went to the young woman, gave something from his purse, and immediately returned. I requested to know what she *said*. I know not, my friend, anything about her, replied the horseman, and the only words I ever heard her utter were designed to thank me for not suffering my horse to run over her, as she laid fainting along the road.

But had you, said I to the stranger, so little curiosity as not to inform yourself of her history? I had so little cruelty, so little impertinence, answered he; I offered her as much as my circumstances allowed; I gave her the modicum I could spare, and *that* was too little a recompense for what *she* gave me in return. What did she give you? A tear, said the man: lookee—'tis still upon the back of my hand, verging to the very finger that brought my tribute from the purse; and *there* it shall remain; the heart from whence it rose, consecrated it, ere it fell: I will not wipe it away; it will teach me *sensibility*. How camest thou, my friend, said I, by these peculiar sentiments? By whom wert thou taught them?

By nature, replied the man.
Whose system hast thou studied?
The system of *nature*, said he.

He had now got his foot again within the stirrup, and thanking me for the trouble I had taken, was preparing to go forward. As it was a fine evening, I requested him to go slowly, that I might enjoy the company of so singular a character.

With the most easy and natural complacence imaginable, he dismounted, joined by my side, and led his horse in his hand. Within a few paces we saw a boy with a hat in his hand, and in it a bird's nest, which he had just taken, filled with young: just as we passed him, he took one of the callow creatures from the hat, tossed it into the air, and then let it crush itself against the ground. My companion threw the bridle into my hand, and ran to the boy without speaking; whom, after having held for a considerable while suspended by the leg, he thrashed handsomely with his whip, threw him upon the grass, and left him.

Why did you beat the boy so severely, said I?
For the sake of my *system*, rejoined the stranger.

Presently we took notice of a person, who (though having lost one of his arms) was extricating a lamb from the brambles, partly with his left hand, and partly with the stump of his right : my companion hurried away to the man with inconceivable eagerness —assisted in the business—shook the maimed soldier (for such he was) very cordially by the hand, and gave him money.

And what is all *this*, said I ?

It is my SYSTEM, answered the stranger, it is my SYSTEM : the only rational one in the world : the System of Nature.

It was now almost twilight, and I was about to bid him adieu, not a little struck with the sketch he had exhibited of his temper. At this instant a hare, pursued by a neighbouring dog, crossed our path. The stranger threw his whip at the dog, with the utmost violence, and snapt the leg-bone ; then, rubbing his hands joyously together, skipt about, and seemed infinitely delighted.

And pray what taught thee *this* action ? I exclaimed.

My system, said the man (in a tone elevated at least three full notes above his former articulation).

It began about this time to lighten : the thunder ran along the skies, and the hemisphere was in a blaze. The stranger made a dead pause—folded his arms together—dropt upon his knee—bowed his head even to the earth, and went on. Rain succeeded to the thunder : I was very thinly habited, and had besides a slight cold upon me. The man saw my distress, complained that the night was insufferably hot, and begged I would carry his greatcoat upon my shoulders—There was no resisting him. The coat was on me in a moment, and the owner took shelter under an elm-tree, that offered a luxurious arbourage by the road-side. The storm was soon over, and the moon arose in all her softness, elegance and majesty. The sudden appearance of any glorious object seizes our attention, and the stranger hailed the rising brightness with an unaffected fervour of gratitude.

Pray, sir, said I, have you *read* much? The Bible, sir, he replied, and two *other* books.

What are they?

These, rejoined the man, the volume of Nature, and the volume of Shakespear.

Why Shakespear?

Because *one* is a commentary upon the *other*. Shakespear was born to illustrate Nature. But it grows late, I wish you a very good night, sir. He mounted his horse, and rode on."

APPENDIX III

THE debt of Mrs. Radcliffe to Walpole, Clara Reeve, Ossian and Shakespeare is too obvious to need more than an allusion. The cult of suspense was developed by other writers of the 'eighties, before she began to publish; Miss Lee in *The Recess* (1783–5) gave studies of female sensibility heightened by fear; Elizabeth Blower in *Maria* (1785) and A Lady of Distinction in *Helena* (1788) have Gothic passages in which the heroine wanders at night about an old mansion and is alarmed by apparently supernatural manifestations. The relations of Mrs. Radcliffe and Mrs. Smith are close. Mrs. Smith's first book, *The Romance of Real Life* (1787), provided Mrs. Radcliffe with the starting-point of her plot in *The Romance of the Forest* (1791), according to Miss C. F. McIntyre, and it is impossible not to see in the young beauty of Emmeline, set in its Gothic frame, the prototype of Adeline and Emily, or in the passage in *Ethelinde* (1789), where the heroine invokes her father's spirit and seems to feel it near, a close similarity to the methods which Mrs. Radcliffe was to develop. The influence of Mrs. Smith's travelling heroine and of the Pyrenean scenes of *Celestina* (1791) on the *Mysteries of Udolpho* (1794) has already been noted. On the other hand, the vogue of *The Romance of the Forest* seems to react on Mrs. Smith in the nocturnal wanderings and the momentary supernatural suggestion of the *Old Manor House* (1793), while her device of smugglers is borrowed back in the last part of the *Mysteries of Udolpho*. The suggestive influence of Monk Lewis, Baculard d'Arnaud and Schiller on *The Italian* (1797) has been mooted. Benedicte Naubert's *Herman of Unna* (ascribed in the translation to Cramer) seems certainly to have suggested the kidnapping of the heroine to a mountain convent and her meeting there with her unknown mother. Among many references to *Der Geisterseher* I have found none that mentions the peculiar physiognomy of the Armenian, and its transmission to Grosse's stranger and Schedoni. I therefore append these passages.

> Schiller's *Geisterseher* (transl. 1795). " Never in my life did I see such various features, and so little expression ; so much attractive benevolence, and so much repelling coldness in the same face ; each passion seemed, by turns, to have exercised its ravages on it, and to have left it successively. Nothing remained but the calm piercing look of a person deeply skilled in the science of man ; but it was such a look as abashed everyone on whom it was directed."

> Grosse's *Der Genius*.[1] " Im Gesichte war ein grosses funkelndes Auge, die einzige Schönheit, welche er aus der Flucht der Leidenschaften hatte retten können. Alle Begierden waren sichtbar darinn aufeinander gefolgt, und jede war, wie sie sich genährt hatte, in einer allgemeinen Kälte miterstarrt, welche auf irgend einen entsetzlichen Auftritt hinzeigte, in dem sich die Gesichtsmuskeln ergriffen haben mussten. Allenthalben sah man noch die Trümmer dieser Leidenschaften, und wenn eine von ihnen wieder hervorkam, so schienen alle andern auf einmal aufzuleben."

> Mrs. Radcliffe's *Italian*. " There was something in his physiognomy extremely singular and that

---

[1] The book was twice translated; *v.* p. 281, *n.* 1; as I have not been able to find a translation, I give the passage from the original.

cannot easily be defined.   It bore the traces of many
passions that seemed to have fixed the features they
no   longer   animated.   An   habitual   gloom   and
severity prevailed over the deep lines of his countenance ; and his eyes were so piercing, that they seemed
to penetrate, at a single glance, into the hearts of men,
and to read their most secret thoughts ; few persons
could support their scrutiny or even endure to meet
them twice.   Yet, notwithstanding all this gloom and
austerity, some rare occasions of interest had called
forth a character upon his countenance entirely
different ; and he could adapt himself to the tempers
and passions of persons whom he wished to conciliate
with astounding facility and generally with complete
triumph."   The   convulsive   flashes   of   agitation,
which indicate the past, appear during the course of
the narrative ; the gloom is Gothic.

To Mrs. Piozzi's *Letters*, adduced by Miss McIntyre
as a source for Mrs. Radcliffe's descriptions in the
Mysteries of Udolpho, I would add Ramond de Carbonnière's *Observations faites dans les Pyrenées*, and Grosley's
New Observations of Italy and its Inhabitants ; in the last
book she found, I believe, the hint for the veiled figure
at Udolpho.

APPENDIX IV

THE following four examples suggest the range of this taste :—

Henry Mackenzie's *Man of Feeling* (1771). Chapter XXXIV. " The sun was now in his decline, and the evening remarkably serene, when he entered a hollow part of the road, which winded between the surrounding banks, and seamed the sward in different lines, as the choice of travellers had directed them to tread it. It seemed to be little frequented now, for some of those had partly recovered their former verdure. The scene was such as induced Harley to stand and enjoy it; when, turning round, his notice was attracted by an object, which the fixture of his eye on the spot he walked, had prevented him from observing.

An old man, who from his dress seemed to have been a soldier, lay fast asleep on the ground; a knapsack rested on a stone at his right hand, while his staff and brass-hilted sword were crossed upon his left.

Harley looked on him with the most earnest attention. He was one of those figures which Salvator would have drawn; nor was the surrounding scenery unlike the wildness of that painter's backgrounds. The banks on each side were covered with fantastic shrub-wood, and at a little distance, on the top of one of them, stood a finger-post to mark the direction of two roads, which diverged from the point where it was placed. A rock, with some dangling wild flowers, jutted out above where the soldier lay, on which grew the stump of a large tree, white with age, and a single-twisted branch shadowed his face as he slept. His face had the marks of manly comeliness impaired by time; his forehead was not altogether bald, but its hairs might have been numbered; while a few white locks behind crossed the brown of his neck, with a contrast the most venerable to a mind like Harley's."

Mrs. Radcliffe's *Mysteries of Udolpho* (1794). A landscape. "Behind the spot where they stood, the rock rose perpendicularly in a massy wall to a considerable height, and then branched out into overhanging crags. Their grey tints were well contrasted by the bright hues of the plants and wild flowers that grew in their fractured sides, and were deepened by the gloom of the pines and the cedars that waved above; the steeps below, over which the eye passed abruptly to the valley, were fringed with thickets of Alpine shrubs; and lower still appeared the tufted tops of the chestnut woods that clothed their base, among which peeped forth the shepherd's cottage, just left by the travellers, with its blue smoke curling high in the air. On every side appeared the majestic summits of the Pyrenees; some exhibiting tremendous crags of marble, whose appearance was changing every instant as the varying lights fell on their surface; others, still higher, displaying only snowy points, while their lower slopes were covered almost invariably with forests of pine, larch and oak, that stretched down to the vale. This was one of the narrow valleys that open from the Pyrenees into the country of Roussillon, and whose green pastures and cultivated beauty form a decided and wonderful contrast to the romantic grandeur that environs it. Through a vista of the mountains appeared the lowlands of Roussillon, tinted with the blue haze of distance, as they united with the waters of the Mediterranean, where, on a promontory, which marked the boundary of the shore, stood a lonely beacon, over which were seen circling flights of seafowl. Beyond appeared, now and then, a stealing sail, white with the sunbeam, and whose progress was perceivable by its approach to the light-house. Sometimes, too, was seen a sail so distant, that it served only to mark the line of separation between the sky and the waves."

A figure-group, the midnight burial of Madame Montoni in the vaults of Udolpho. " At the moment in which they let down the body into the earth, the scene was such as only the dark pencil of a Domenchino, perhaps, could have done justice to. The fierce features and wild dress of the Condottieri, bending with their torches over the grave, into which the corpse was descending, were contrasted by the venerable features of the monk, wrapped in long, black garments, his cowl thrown back from his face, on which the light gleaming strongly showed the lines of affliction softened by piety, and the few grey locks which time had spared on his temples ; while, beside him, stood the softer form of Emily, who leaned for support upon Annette ; her face half averted and shaded by a thin veil, that fell over her figure ; and her mild and beautiful countenance fixed in grief so solemn as admitted not of tears, while she thus saw committed untimely to the earth her last relative and friend. The gleams thrown between the arches of the vaults, where, here and there, the broken ground marked the spots in which other bodies had been recently interred, and the general obscurity beyond, were circumstances that alone would have led on the imagination of the spectator to scenes more horrible than even that which was pictured at the grave of the misguided and unfortunate Madame Montoni."

Bage's *Hermsprong* (1796). A scene of distress in the style of Hogarth. " The most conspicuous object was Mrs. Wigley sitting. She certainly was not dead, yet she scarce seemed to live ; nor had she fallen into a swoon, for her eyes were open, and she appeared to see, though not to observe. Her face once so pretty, had lost its colour; her arms hung languidly down; and in a coffin, she would have been taken for a beautiful corpse. Her eldest daughter was on her knees; her head supported by her mother's lap; but her arms thrown round her mother's waist; whilst from her bosom came the bursting sigh, frequent and deep. Not far thence was the younger daughter in hysterics, held by two maid-servants of the family, profuse in tears and loud in lamentation. A little dog, the favourite of the young lady, was at her feet. And now he stood up, looked moaningly at her; turned three or four times, and lay down; then rose again; gave a mournful whine; turned round as before, and again lay down. This circle of movements the poor animal continually repeated. The last of the distressed group was Mr. Wigley himself, leaning against the wall of the apartment, surveying the scene around him with an aspect half expressing grief; and half astonishment bordering on stupidity. Near the door were a bailiff and his attendant, with faces rather of sorrow for their success, than of exultation." It is characteristic of Bage that, though trying his hand at the picturesque, he cannot confine his interest to it, but admits the behaviour of the little dog.

INDEX

A NOTE ABOUT THE AUTHOR

J. M. S. Tompkins was born in London and was educated at Bedford College, University of London, from which she holds the degrees B. A., M. A. (1918, 1921), and D. Lit. (1933). During the '20's and '30's Dr. Tompkins served as Assistant-Lecturer, first in English Language and then in English Literature at Bedford College, and afterward at Royal Holloway College, and became a Lecturer in 1939. She has been a Reader in the University of London since 1948. A member of the Royal Holloway College, Dr. Tompkins has twice held the position of Vice-Principal in the College. She has acted as University Examiner for the University Colleges of Ghana and Ibadan, Nigeria, since the beginning of the Special Relationship between these Colleges and the University of London, and has visited them.

Among Dr. Tompkins' previous publications are *The Polite Marriage* (1938), *The Art of Rudyard Kipling* (1959), and articles in the *Review of English Studies* largely on eighteenth- and nineteenth-century subjects.